S0-BSD-535

CARL A. RUDISILL LIBRARY
LENOIR-RHYNE COLLEGE

*Reproduced by courtesy of* Punch

"DELIVERING THE GOODS"

*By Raven Hill, from* Punch *April 21st, 1915*

# WAR MEMOIRS

*of*

# DAVID LLOYD GEORGE

★

## 1914-1915

WITH ILLUSTRATIONS

LITTLE, BROWN, AND COMPANY

BOSTON  1935

Published October, 1933
Reprinted November, 1933
Reprinted January, 1935

PRINTED IN THE UNITED STATES OF AMERICA

# PREFACE

Most of the leading actors in the Great War, both Statesmen and Warriors, have committed to writing the story of the part they played in it. With one or two exceptions they have written their stories themselves, although the composition of books has been as new a venture to them as it is now to me. With the exception of M. Briand, who never put pen to paper, all the dominant personalities of the War have told their tale of what they did and why they did it; amongst rulers, the Kaiser, the Crown Prince, M. Poincaré, President Wilson (through Mr. Baker); amongst statesmen, M. Clemenceau, Mr. Asquith, Lord Grey, Mr. Churchill, Colonel House, Prince Max of Baden, Von Buelow; amongst the warriors, Foch, Hindenburg, Ludendorff, Hofmann, French, Haig (with the aid of another pen), Henry Wilson, Pershing, and a host of others. My library shelves groan under the burden of war autobiographies. No wonder I hesitated for years to follow the example set me by those who figured so prominently on the stage where I also occupied a not inconspicuous position. I had almost decided to bequeath the undertaking to those with whom I should leave my papers, when two incidents occurred which influenced me to take up my pencil and relate my own story in my own words.

The first was an illness which released me from the irksome and peculiarly thankless duty of leadership in a political party unhappily poisoned and paralysed by internal dissension amongst its better-known members. The other was a visit paid me during my convalescence by an old comrade of the Great War. He entreated me to take advantage of my seclusion from active political warfare to give my account of the events of the War. He reminded me that I was the only official figure who went right through it from the declaration of War to the signing of Peace. He urged that the real history of the War might not — and probably would not — be written for another generation, but that the books written to-day by the men — generals and politicians — who had a share either in the fighting or in the direction would constitute the principal material upon which the historian would draw for his facts and impressions. All these books gave the point of view of the individual writer, biased naturally either by limitation of his opportunities or by a controverted theory of events, or, too frequently, by the exigencies of a personal apologia. It was pointed out to me that I was the only person in authority who was in Mr. Britling's position. I "saw it through" from the outbreak of the quarrel to the settlement of the terms. There are multitudes who were better acquainted with certain aspects of the War; there are, or were, a few who for a limited period were in a better position to view the struggle as a whole; but there is no one (and I often recall the fact with horror) who was as intimately acquainted as myself with the war direction throughout the whole of its rending and tearing course through the vitals of mankind.

To tell the story at all is like repeating what was seen in a nightmare, and I shrank for years from writing my record of the horrifying details. It is not pleasant to remember how men and women devoted energy, intelligence and zeal for four-and-a-half years to the work of destruction and pain. But it must be told if such a calamity is to be averted in the future. It is better that the real facts should be given. I do not pretend to know them all, but some of them I know better than my contemporaries. These I am doing my best to relate accurately in the following pages. I make my contribution, not as one who claims to be an experienced author, but as a witness giving evidence on what he remembers of these tremendous transactions.

Memory is fallible and I may have made a mistake in some details. But I shall welcome correction. I have fortified recollection by a careful perusal of an immense mass of documents which I accumulated at the time. These I have chosen and quoted or used with a full sense of the responsibility resting on every public servant not to reveal or publish anything which may injure the interests of his country. In the exercise of this discretion I owe much to the scrutiny of one of the most efficient and distinguished public servants of his generation — Sir Maurice Hankey. I owe thanks also to a great many kind friends who have assisted me by supplementing and stimulating my memory with their own as to occurrences where I enjoyed their valued coöperation.

D. Lloyd George.

*Bron-y-de,*
*Churt.*
*August, 1933.*

## CONTENTS

# WAR MEMOIRS OF DAVID LLOYD GEORGE

Lloyd George was the only member of the British Cabinet who remained continuously in office throughout the World War. He was Chancellor of the Exchequer at the outbreak of the War, then Minister of Munitions, later Secretary of State for War, and finally in December, 1916, he succeeded Asquith as Prime Minister and held that office until 1922. This fact alone makes his War Memoirs of the highest importance, for no book hitherto published on the War can present a record more consecutive, more sustained and more intimate than his.

The whole work will be published in four volumes. The first two volumes cover the events which led up to the outbreak of the War and the War years 1914–1916. In these two volumes Lloyd George shows conclusively how at every stage the civilian had to be brought in to amend the shortcomings of the military and he is unsparing in his criticism of the early conduct of the War. Instances of obstruction and shortsightedness are fully documented, and the chapter on the strategy of the War is an overwhelming indictment of the military mind.

## ILLUSTRATIONS

# WAR MEMOIRS OF DAVID LLOYD GEORGE

1914–1915

# WAR MEMOIRS OF DAVID LLOYD GEORGE

1914–1915

## CHAPTER I

# THE BREWING OF THE STORM

### 1. First Contact with Foreign Affairs

Lord Rosebery's view of the Entente — My early detachment from foreign affairs — Traditional views of the British political parties — Gladstone at the Châlet — His admiration for France — Whig preference for Germany — Divided views of 1906 Liberal Government — Apprehension roused by the German Navy — Shipbuilding crises in the Cabinet — My four propositions — Defence of Radical view — German challenge to British Fleet — My meetings with Metternich — German diplomatic records of the interviews — The Kaiser's marginal notes — My interview with the Kaiser cancelled — A dinner with Von Bethmann-Hollweg — England's "Iron Ring" — Von Bethmann-Hollweg's view of English decadence — German dismay at Zeppelin wreck.

In the year 1904, on the day when the Anglo-French Entente was announced, I arrived at Dalmeny on a couple of days' visit to the late Lord Rosebery. His first greeting to me was: "Well, I suppose you are just as pleased as the rest of them with this French agreement?" I assured him that I was delighted that our snarling and scratching relations with France had come to an end at last. He replied: "You are all wrong. It means war with Germany in the end!"

About a year after this prophetical utterance I became for the first time a Minister of the Crown. Had anyone then told me that before I ceased to hold office in the British Cabinet I should not only have witnessed a war between Britain and Germany, but have taken an active, and in fact a leading part in its prosecution, I should have treated such a forecast as one of the many wild predictions of good or evil with which every public man is assailed by persons of unbalanced minds.

Before my appointment I took very little part in the discussion of foreign affairs and had no pretence to a greater knowledge of their intricacies than that which is possessed by the average Member of Parliament who has read history, and brings it up to date with such information as is supplied by the leading newspapers and reviews of all Parties. My interests were definitely centred on more domestic matters; on the special concerns of Wales, and on the education controversy, free trade, Home Rule, the land question and social reform. In foreign policy I had always been, as I am to-day, an ardent advocate of the rights of small nationalities, and I had been trained to believe in a peaceable settlement of the differences which arose among the nations of the world. Notwithstanding the sinister growth of armaments and a feverish anxiety to perfect them in all countries, there had been unbroken peace for over forty years between the Great Powers of Western Europe, and this bred a cheerful if illusive hope that the world would ultimately abandon war as a tribunal for adjudicating international disputes. This happy confidence in the gradual and final escape of the world from the perils of war (except against savages) was fostered, as I shall show later, by the extent to which nearly all of us, even Cabinet Ministers, were kept sedulously in the dark about foreign conversations and commitments.

I was, of course, well aware of the secular antagonism between France and Germany and how that antagonism had been kept alive by the tearing from the side of France of two of her best-beloved provinces. The Franco-Prussian War was a memory of my boyhood. After the fall of the Empire, Radical sentiment tended to be pro-French in sympathy with the democratic institutions of our nearest neighbour, whereas Conservative opinion inclined to be more pro-German.

Inside the Liberal Party the tradition of its more advanced elements ever since the days of Charles James Fox had been one of constant friendliness towards the French Republic; English Conservatism had never quite got over the prejudices and apprehensions roused by the French Revolution and the Napoleonic episode, and Liberal Imperialism was inclined to follow in the track of the Anti-Revolution Whigs.

Mr. Gladstone was passionately pro-French in his general attitude. The Bismarckism of blood and iron never appealed to him. He was essentially a Liberal in foreign affairs. When he visited Carnarvonshire in 1892, I was invited by Sir Edward Watkin to meet him at dinner at the Watkin châlet on the slopes of Snowdon. It was a small party. Apart from the members of the family, the late Tom Ellis and I were the only guests. Mr. Gladstone did practically all the talking at the dinner-table and afterwards, and the rest of us, only too thrilled to meet and hear this great figure from a past world, were naturally content to listen in silence.

He was eighty-three years of age but showed none of the usual symptoms of senility. He was vital. His deep, vibrant tones were music to the ear whatever he said. That evening he was at times even gay and merry.

His conversation ranged over a curious variety of topics. He talked for some time on the development of transport in the country and the improvement in the habits of the people who were associated with it; the sodden driver and the drunken ostler of the past against the sober engine driver and railway porter of to-day. To illustrate this theme he told us one or two quite amusing stories of his experiences in the old coaching days. I can recall only one of his tales. When posting from Wales to London he sat on the box seat, and in order to relieve the dreary hours he sought conversation with the driver, who was a fine specimen of what much beef and more beer could produce. Not achieving great success by ordinary conversation, he pulled out a handsome watch of which he was proud, opened it, showed the works to the driver and explained to him the function of the various wheels and levers. The only observation he elicited was: "What puzzles me is how you wind that 'ere watch when you get home drunk."

He then gave us a dissertation on corrugated-iron roofing, and the difficulties which had been encountered in keeping buildings of this kind warm in winter and cool in summer. The last subject was suggested by the fact that the châlet was built of this material. He then diverged to other reminiscences. He recalled with regret the prohibitive price of sugar candy when he was a boy and told us with gusto of his delight when he discovered recently, in walking along the streets of some obscure town in Cheshire, how cheaply you could to-day purchase this joy of his departed youth.

He then launched out into a wonderful panegyric on the people of France. I think it arose out of a reference to the Channel tunnel which Sir Edward Watkin was then promoting. Mr. Gladstone made it quite clear that in his judgment the French were a much more enlightened, broad-minded and civilised people than those over whose destinies he was at the moment privileged to preside. The Radicals of that day might not have accepted his perfervid eulogies on the superiority of French intelligence, but apart from that his outburst more or less represented the Radical attitude towards the French Republic and its citizens at the time when I came into active politics. On the other hand, Germany, with her militarism, her autocracy and her constitutional devices to enhance the voting power of property and to depress and restrict the power of the worker in the State, and her resolve generally to keep democracy in its proper place, evoked a good deal of sympathetic approval amongst the more Conservative elements in the country.

Lord Rosebery and his friends did not share in these Radical sentiments towards French democracy. Their attitude was one of distrust of France and ill-concealed goodwill towards Germany. During Lord Rosebery's occupation of the Foreign Office in 1892–94, he had once or twice engaged the country in grave disputes with France and brought us to the brink of serious conflict. In the House of Commons his Under-Secretary, Sir Edward Grey,[1] in alluding to the menace of some French movement towards the British sphere of influence in the Sudan, had characterised it as "an unfriendly act." The Radical supporters of the Government resented the threat implied in the phrase, and they continued to view with great suspicion Sir Edward Grey's attitude towards France.

When the Campbell-Bannerman Administration was formed, it was sharply divided into two sections: the Radical element, of which the Prime Minister was the chief, and the Liberal Imperialists, relics of that element which deserted Fox and backed Palmerston. Chief among them were Mr. Asquith, Sir Edward Grey and Mr. Haldane. There was a perceptible difference of attitude between the two sections on questions of foreign policy. The old pro-Boers inherited the pacifist doctrines of Mr. Gladstone. The Liberal League members of the Cabinet affected a more Palmerstonian attitude in foreign affairs. The former suspicion of France which characterised them in pre-Entente days had by this time altogether vanished, even from the stubborn mind of Sir Edward Grey, but for it was substituted a worrying distrust of the designs of Germany.

This was by no means confined to the Foreign Secretary. Germany's naval shipbuilding programme was largely re-

[1] Now Viscount Grey of Fallodon.

sponsible for this change in the Tory and Liberal Imperialist attitude towards Germany. The Kaiser frequently boasted that he created the formidable Navy of Germany, and he was always contemplating and reviewing it with the pride of a Creator. He saw and said it was good. What good it brought Germany is not evident, but the story of the evil it wrought will always remain one of the most poignant chapters in the history not only of Germany but of mankind. It was partly responsible for the World War. It undoubtedly helped to range the British Empire amongst the enemies of Germany and later on it brought America into the war. Apart from these facts, it contributed to the spirit of arrogant superiority which dictated the course of German diplomacy, and consequently to the apprehension which drew other powerful nations to military and naval understandings. Its creation undoubtedly helped to stimulate the Kaiser's fatal swagger.

The blustering zeal which he threw into the building of his redoubtable navy was regarded as a threat not only to Britain's supremacy at sea but to her actual security. Foolish speeches delivered by men of no inconsiderable authority and influence in Germany, hinting a challenge to Britain's fleet, were quoted in the British Press and caused uneasiness in minds not readily given to panic. The Radical section of the Cabinet were just as much alive as their Imperialist colleagues to the menace which rival warship programmes offered to the good relations they were anxious to maintain with Germany as well as with all other nations.

I first became directly concerned with this issue when in 1908, on the death of Sir Henry Campbell-Bannerman and Mr. Asquith's accession to the Premiership, I left the Board of Trade to succeed Mr. Asquith as Chancellor of the Exchequer. In this post it became my duty to find the money for naval programmes, and Anglo-German relations thus became a subject in which I was departmentally interested.

I might here say a word as to the two crises which occurred in the Asquith Cabinet over shipbuilding programmes submitted by the Board of Admiralty. The first was in 1908, when Mr. M'Kenna was First Lord of the Admiralty; the second in 1913–1914, when Mr. Winston Churchill held that post.

As Chancellor of the Exchequer, I never resisted any addition to the strength of the Navy which would provide a reasonable margin of security against the increases in the German Navy effected by the shipbuilding programme of the German Admiralty. My opposition to the demands of the Board of Admiralty in 1908 and 1913 might be summed up in the fourfold proposition:

*My four propositions*

1. The Admiralty demand an extravagant margin which is burdensome and provocative;
2. We ought to concentrate more on small craft for the protection of our trade routes and less on mammoth ships;
3. There is a growing reaction in the world against the burden of increasing armaments, and a general desire for a better understanding between the nations. We ought therefore to concentrate more on seeking an arrangement with Germany as to competitive building than on provocative programmes;
4. During the 1913–14 dispute in the Cabinet over the Admiralty estimates I pointed out that Germany was now devoting her attention to strengthening her Army rather than her Navy.

In my first protest against what I conceived to be panic demands from the Admiralty I received the zealous and energetic support of Mr. Winston Churchill. Unfortunately, by 1913 he had become First Lord of the Admiralty, and his inflammable fancy had been caught by the fascination of the monster ship. The fight against "bloated armaments" — to use the old Disraelian phrase — was weakened by so formidable a defection.

I do not propose to discuss at this point the merits of the controversy, but I would like to mention two or three facts in justification of the attitude adopted by the Radical section of the Cabinet. I have consulted the memoranda and counter-memoranda which were put in during the 1913 discussions. The Treasury, which was not without information from expert naval sources, claimed that even if we proceeded with the old accepted programme, rejecting the new proposals, we should still have in 1917 the following margin of superiority:

| | | |
|---|---|---|
| Dreadnoughts | over 84 | per cent. |
| Pre-Dreadnoughts | 127 | " " |
| Armoured Cruisers | 278 | " " |
| Light Cruisers | over 70 | " " |
| Torpedo Craft | 60 | " " |

This estimate was based, not merely upon numbers, but upon a qualitative comparison which included speed, weight of guns and age. These figures were not accepted by the Admiralty. The Treasury computation assumed too great a margin of superiority in Dreadnoughts, but the sifted figures showed a secure margin. There was a further argument advanced by the Treasury and their supporters, *viz.*, that, throughout the whole of the shipbuilding competition between Germany and ourselves for the past ten years, we had always forced the pace by increasing the size of the ships, the weight of guns, and the speed of our vessels, beginning this fatal competition with the laying down of the first Dreadnought in 1904. At that date we had a crushing superiority of strength against any possible combination of foreign fleets. The laying down of the Dreadnought seemed to many of us a piece of wanton and profligate ostentation.

As to the second Treasury proposition, that we ought to concentrate more on small craft and less on big ships, the experience of the War was a complete vindication of the point of view taken by the Treasury in 1913. We suffered severely from the shortage of cruisers and torpedo-boat destroyers for the protection of our vessels, mercantile and naval, against submarine attack; and the Admiralty, under the direction of Sir John Fisher, had to work with feverish energy to make up this serious deficiency. The shortage in itself was created, not so much by the fact that we had not a sufficient number of torpedo-boat destroyers, but because the vulnerability of our great battleships and battle cruisers to torpedo attack was such that we had to detach the best part of our torpedo-boat strength to defend them.

With the third and fourth propositions I shall have to deal in the course of my narrative.

It was of course impossible not to have an uneasy feeling that the German battle fleet was built with the design of challenging British naval supremacy. Grand-Admiral von Tirpitz in his memoirs is quite explicit about this, and so at times was the Kaiser. I do not say that they deliberately set before themselves as their goal a war with Britain that would destroy our fleet. They would have been content if their fleet grew so powerful that it frightened Britain into renouncing her supremacy at sea without a fight. But von Tirpitz, the real creator of the German Navy, avows openly that they would be content with nothing less.

Opposed as I was to inflated armaments, I never hesitated in the view that Britain could not afford and would not allow such a situation to arise. We had no army large enough to defend our country against the enormous conscript armies of the Continent. Our fleet was still just as much the sole guarantee of our liberties and independence as in the days of Napoleon. We should therefore have to go on building ship for ship, and three ships to two, against any effort of the Germans. Our financial resources and shipbuilding equipment were adequate to counter their utmost achievement in naval rivalry. But, this being the position, it was no less obvious that such unrestricted competition would involve quite needless financial exhaustion and growing irritation for both countries, and would only leave them at the end, with empty pockets and burdened backs, in the same position of relative strength as that from which they had started.

As one who had been taught to believe that peace was the only sane and sound basis for human progress, I sought to allay the growing antagonism between the two nations. As Chancellor of the Exchequer, I could not be indifferent to the cost of the useless naval competition. It was an exhausting drain upon resources sadly needed for social amelioration and national development. So I sought some means of reaching an agreement with Germany which would enable us on both sides to slow down the rate and volume of our naval construction.

An opportunity for this seemed to present itself when at the suggestion of Sir Edward Grey in July, 1908, I came into contact with the German Ambassador, Count Metternich. Of our meeting I made some years later a note from memory, which I reproduce here:

"Soon after I became Chancellor of the Exchequer in 1908, Count Metternich, the German Ambassador, invited me to lunch at the Embassy. I had never met the Ambassador and I had a suspicion that the invitation had some political purpose. After lunch he soon made it clear why I had been asked. He knew that I belonged to the more

*Photo. by E. N. A.*

COUNT PAUL WOLFF-METTERNICH

*German Ambassador to Great Britain, 1901–1912*

pacifist group in the Cabinet. He introduced the subject of the growing suspicions between our two countries. I thought it a good opportunity for explaining to him that the real ground for the growing antagonism in this country towards Germany was not jealousy of her rapidly developing commerce but fear of her growing Navy. I pointed out how completely dependent we were on our overseas supplies for our daily bread, and that any country that wrested from us the supremacy of the seas would be in a position to starve our population into abject surrender in a few months. I also urged that if our sea defences were overwhelmed by a superior naval force, our Army could put up no effective resistance against the huge military machines of the Continent. I thought it well to tell him that on the subject of maintaining the invulnerability of our shores by means of an adequately superior Navy there was no difference of opinion in the Cabinet, and that although I was one of those who were opposed to these huge armaments, I should, if our community were in the least imperilled, be the first to propose even a loan of £100,000,000 if that were necessary to inaugurate a programme for building a Navy adequate to our safety. I said to him, 'If this rival shipbuilding goes on to such an extent as to render our people seriously apprehensive of invasion we shall be driven inevitably to adopt conscription and thus raise an army capable of defending our shores against any invader.' He replied quite curtly, 'Do you think we should wait?'

"M. Delcassé had, largely owing to German hostility, just been driven out of the Quai d'Orsay. However, he had been well received in London on his visit to this country immediately after his dismissal. I forget how his name cropped up in our conversation. I only remember one passage. When I said, 'You dismissed M. Delcassé from his position of Foreign Secretary in France,' he cut in tartly,

'But evidently not in England!' I proceeded, 'If Germany had demanded the dismissal of the most unpopular Minister in this country he would by that very demand be translated to the highest altitude of popular favour.'

"The luncheon party was, I fear, not a success."

Since the above note was written, I have, through the courtesy of the German Foreign Office, been able to study the German Diplomatic Correspondence for the period in question. From this I am reminded that there were, in fact, two interviews with Metternich, separated by an interval of about a fortnight.

The first was on July 14th, 1908, when I was invited by Sir Edward Grey to lunch, to meet Count Metternich, and the second was the lunch already referred to at the German Embassy on the 28th. Both of these interviews were reported very fully to Berlin by Metternich, and came before the Kaiser, whose annotations to the reports are highly significant of the German attitude at that time. They are also worth study for the light they throw on the character of the Kaiser—the quick leaps from sense to superciliousness which later on precipitated the world catastrophe. I reproduce the full text of the report on Grey's luncheon party, and extracts from the later interview with myself:

SECRET

London, July 16th, 1908.

*Marginal Comments by the Kaiser.*

The day before yesterday Sir Edward Grey invited me to breakfast[1] at his house with Mr. Lloyd George. The Present Chancellor of the Exchequer has in a short time educated himself from an ultra-radical Welsh lawyer into a leading and esteemed personality in his Party and in the Cabinet.

[1] Lunch.

As he thinks imperially he is also respected by the Unionists. If I remember rightly, he allowed himself some years ago as a representative of the Opposition to have now and then a dig at Germany in jingo fashion. As responsible Minister I found him to be of a conciliatory attitude of mind.

When I touched upon the question raised in Parliament regarding espionage, he agreed with me that unfortunately every bit of nonsense was believed here, as soon as it had to do with Germany.

When I remarked that it was a pity that English politics seemed to wish to exchange French friendship for German hostility, and that the Entente policy had called forth the uneasiness in Europe, Sir Edward Grey stated more or less as follows: During the last ten years England had several times very nearly got into warlike complications with France and Russia. Without an amicable arrangement it would probably have come to a war already. There was only an Entente with France. None "yet" with Russia. Against this, Germany had the Triple Alliance. It was incomprehensible how one could speak in this connection of a policy to isolate Germany.

Mr. Lloyd George joined in by saying that it probably was the diplomatic support of France by England which had upset Germany (1). Sir Edward Grey replied that as far as Morocco was concerned, England was pledged to give that support.

(1) *Yes.*

I remarked that France was in an absolutely safe position as long as she recognised the *status quo* in Europe (2). Alone she could not attack this. However, supported by England the idea of revenge might one day come to life again (3). *Avis au lecteur:* The article in the "Temps," which recommended England to have a strong army in order to become qualified for an alliance.

(2) *German Territory!*

(3) *Well said!*

When Mr. Lloyd George expressed the opinion that he did not believe France had intentions of war, although the French had not been able to make up their minds to recognise the past, I replied that I also did not believe in any such intentions of the French. Also, that I had not the slightest objection to England settling its disputes with other nations. On the other hand, in political journalism the friends and defenders of English foreign policy took care to spread the conviction that here one was not dealing merely with a settling of disputes, but simultaneously with the producing of a bulwark against the German Power. This procedure did not comply with a friendly tendency, and could not be taken as such in Germany, but was bound to call forth uneasiness there, and specially in Europe (4). Sir Edward Grey then remarked that the unpleasant part of the situation was caused by the fact that we mutually blamed each other for having hostile intentions. The belief in an eventual English attack existed in Germany; here, however, one believed

(4) *Quite right.*

(5) *Wrong! A result of England's ambitions for world empire and*

that the German Fleet was built to threaten England's position.

Both Ministers were of the opinion that the situation between England and Germany turned round the naval question. The expenditure for the English fleet would as a result of the German naval programme (5) and the speeding up (6) in naval construction increase to such an extent, and at the same time apprehensions of the German danger would increase so in intensity, that relations between the countries could not improve as long as they were getting up against each other in naval rivalry (7). Every Englishman would spend his last penny to preserve their superiority at sea (8), on which depends not only England's position in the world, but also its existence as an independent State. The ruinous expenditure to which the naval rivalry led (9) could not make the relations between the two nations prosper. Anybody who only knew England a little, knew that there was no intention here to threaten (10) Germany with the English fleet or attack Germany at all. Taking into consideration the proportions of the English Army, a landing would be clearly out of the question. Mr. Lloyd George remarked jokingly that Prince Bismarck had said, when on some occasion or other the question of an English landing was discussed, that in a case like that he would leave it to the police to arrest the English corps on landing. The conditions to-day were

*tendency to see phantoms.*

(6) *Has not been speeded up!*

(7) *Does not exist! Ours is limited by law!*

(8) *See Nauticus, they have it 3 times over already!!!*

(9) *Such insolent talk has never been heard from England, not even in the days of acutest tension with Russia about Afghanistan! It has never ventured to require Russia to withdraw its troops from the border, or to stop the reinforcements of its garrisons.*

(10) *? ! They have done so permanently already.*

(11) *Will never be powerful compared with England! and still less of a*

*danger than the already superior English fleet is to us.*

(12) *That after my speech at the Guildhall is first-class cheek!*

(13) *Quite right.*

(14) *Very good.*

(15) *Wrong! We will not discuss that! We shall never be dictated to as to how our armament should be constituted.*

(16) *We have no*

still exactly the same when it was a question of England threatening Germany. To England, on the contrary, a powerful German Fleet (11) with a still more powerful Army in the background, was a real danger (12).

I replied that a German invasion existed only in the imagination of the English. No sensible person was thinking of it in Germany (13). Unfortunately fleet building had become more expensive through the invention of the "Dreadnought" (13) through which England had lost its immense advantage and other seafaring nations had been compelled to adopt the same large types of ships and consequently to high expenditure in connection herewith. But, *à qui la faute?* During the last few days there had been a discussion in the House of Commons about the introduction of a still larger type of ship, a floating fortress. As long as the English defence policy tended to create uneasiness in Germany, I considered a curtailment in the armaments at sea as being out of the question (13). Sir Edward Grey would first have to introduce a political *détente* between both countries and through his policy in Central Europe reëstablish the belief that his Ententes would not be one day misused against us (14) before the ground would be cleared for a possible discussion about the curtailment of sea armaments (15), not before. Mr. Lloyd George, who took a lively part in the discussion about the naval construction, answered that a slowing down of the tempo in our fleet building (16) would contribute more quickly to reassure public opinion than any political action could. We should find them on this side most ready to meet us halfway in establishing a joint basis for curtailment of the fleet building on both sides (17). The introduction of the Dreadnought type had been a great mistake from the English side. The Government here would give every possible guarantee (18) that no new type should be introduced (19) if we could come to an understanding. He had very much regretted that the correspondence between His Majesty the Kaiser and Lord Tweedmouth had not been published at the time. From that correspondence the friendly feeling of His Majesty the Kaiser for England would have become clear to the public and he would also have seen in His Majesty's letter a justification for entering into confidential discussion with us about naval expenditure (20). If he had at the time had the responsibility for the State Finances he would indeed have insisted in the Cabinet on the publication of the correspondence (21). A conference at The Hague was not the proper way (22) to reach curtailment in naval expenditure. If, as he fervently hoped, it should ever come to this, it must not be tried in an official manner, such as with an exchange of notes (23). Unofficial confidential discussions which must not be made public at

*fast tempo. Neither are we building SECRET "Dreadnoughts" for other nations — which are then bought by England — or camouflaged as an armoured cruiser, suddenly turn up as battleships.*

(17) *This unheard-of demand the English Minister should put first to Roosevelt, Clemenceau, Mirabello*[1] *or Japan! The replies would be cheerful! Why* only *to* us? *Because they believe that my diplomacy is fed up, and is being impressed by their shoutting for war.*

(18) *We don't need it.*

(19) *Is the same to us.*

(20) *He would have received* a *nice reply from*

[1] Italian Naval Minister.

*me. Would have no result!*

(21) *Aha.*

(22) *Right.*

(23) *I should answer them with bombs.*

(24) Out of the question! *So that the German people don't rise and smash the windows of the Minister in with bricks!*

(25) *No.*

(26) *That would be a declaration of war!*

(27) *Right.*

(28) *We should look upon that as a declaration of war.*

(29) *Definitely war.*

(30) *No! There will be no talk about that at all!*

(31) *Out of the question! They will first have*

all (24), would, if an understanding between England and ourselves in this matter were at all possible, be more likely to conduce to the desired end (25).

Sir Edward Grey agreed with his colleague except on the point where the latter had recommended the timeliness of the publication of the correspondence.

I told Mr. Lloyd George he was right: that neither a conference at The Hague nor even less an official proposal by way of a note (26) from the English to the German Government, would solve the question of decreasing the fleet expenditure (27); that I even considered an official movement (28) in this direction under the circumstances very dubious (29) and grave and dangerous, but for the rest I would not be moved from the safe ground which I had taken up with my demand: First a policy of reassurance, then we can talk about the fleet (30).

In reporting this discussion I have left out a good deal and have, in order to be brief, only mentioned the most important parts. The incidental things, however, contribute to the right colouring of the whole picture. I allow myself, in order not to be misunderstood, to add the following supplementary final remarks.

Your Highness knows that for a long time the English Government has entertained the wish to come to an agreement with us about naval expenditure (31). Before and during the second Conference at *to achieve this with other great Powers!*

The Hague an abortive attempt was made in this direction. If I have been rightly informed, the fear has already arisen on our side that the English Government might, alone or with others, put an official proposal to us for limitation of our naval programme and that from this an immediate danger of war would result (32). It is my firm belief that the present Government is far (33) from setting before us, through any sort of ultimatum, the issue of either giving in or going to war. She has no sort of intention of putting a threatening question to us (34). She desires much more to prevent later possibilities of war through timely agreement. If I decline somebody's wish, I need not for that reason fight with him at once. This comes only then into consideration when I see that the other one puts on the air of forcing (35) his wish (36) upon me.

(32) *Yes.*

(33) *? ?*

(34) *In the conversation of the Ministers lies already a hidden threat! Let them compare themselves first with America! The latter is much stronger than we are!*

(35) *In our position it is better that such a wish should not be expressed!*

(36) *He does that.*

To both Ministers I have made the fulfilment of their wish dependent on one condition, the explanation of which lies in our hands. I would have needlessly constricted future possibilities, and made the position more acute, if I had given them to understand that we never and under no circumstances would be prepared to come to an arrangement with them about naval expenditure. The price which I mentioned for this will certainly not soon be paid to us by Sir Edward Grey.

*(Signed)* P. Metternich.

*Final Remarks of the Kaiser:*

Bravo! Metternich! Has done his business very well, except in one point, which is the most important. The Ambassador has overlooked entirely that he was not permitted, even if entirely non-committally and only as a private opinion, to [? agree] [1] to the insolent demands of the English Ministers to make their peacefulness dependent on the diminution of our sea force. Through that he has put himself on a very dangerous slope. I am sorry for him because of that. It must be pointed out to him that I do *not* wish a good understanding with England at the expense of the extension of the German fleet. If England only intends graciously to hold out her hand to us with the indication that we should curtail our fleet, then this is an excessive impudence, which contains a great insult for the German people and its Kaiser, and which should be refused *a limine* by the Ambassador! By the same rights France and Russia could then demand a curtailment of our land force. As soon as one allows any foreign Power under any pretext whatsoever to have something to say about our own armaments, then one may retire, like Portugal and Spain! The German fleet is not built *against* anybody and not *against* England either! But according to *our* needs! This has been said quite clearly in the Navy Law and has remained unchanged for eleven years! This law is being carried out to the very last tittle: whether the British like it or not does not worry us. If they want a war, *they* may *start* it, we are not afraid of it!

*(Signed)* Wilhelm R.I.

Here are the most important passages in the report Count Metternich sent to Berlin of our second conversation — with the Kaiser's marginal notes:

[1] Word missing in original.

*Kaiser's Marginal Notes.*

". . . On the same day I had a long discussion with the Chancellor of the Exchequer, Mr. Lloyd George. . . . I explained to him why the political course followed by England during the last six years was bound to lead to the present uncomfortable situation: formerly on the side of the Triple Alliance, now on the side of Germany's opponents; Morocco thrown as an apple of discord between Germany and France; France encouraged in the idea of *revanche* through hope of help from England; Entente politics as a bulwark against alleged German expansion and aggressiveness; spy scares and fears of invasion; a twisting of German intentions in political journalism, a slandering of the motives of German politics, and nothing done to stop it (1). Through the unchecked poisoning of public opinion, I said, we are being pushed unwillingly into the perilous position of seeing the spectre of war rising on the horizon — a spectre which Mr. Lloyd George and I are alike convinced that both our Governments as well as both our countries wish to expel (2).

(1) *A very good summary!*

(2) *That's not my idea at all! If England wants to have war, just let her start it, we'll give her what for!*

The Minister showed an understanding of all this, but, like every one of his countrymen, he sees in the naval question the central point of German-English relations, around which everything turns and of which all other happenings are a result. . . . England, he said, had the money and would strain every nerve to retain supremacy at sea (3). With a race in fleet building (4)

(3) *Nobody wants to dispute that!*

the tension would unavoidably be increased, and therewith at the same time the danger of a collision would grow. At the end of the crushing armaments (5) the distance between the two fleets would still be great, and we should not be any nearer to our object (6). We should be playing into the hands of two tendencies here which he was fighting against, and which were not in our interest. With the growth of expenditure for the Navy in the race between Germany and England, new financial sources would have to be found and all thoughts would be turned to the Tariff Party, which promised new receipts at the expense of foreign countries and without further burdening the Englishman. . . . Further: the more the German fleet approached the English in strength (7) the stronger the thought would become that English safety no longer depended on its fleet alone, but that England must also develop an Army. In order to have a really strong Army there was only one means: Conscription. With the quick growth of the German Navy the possibility of an invasion increased—although he did not at all believe in such (8) an intention — and then England would be pushed into the introduction of Conscription (9). The military party and a great number of Conservatives were already anxiously wishing for this. With the approach of the German menace, the great mass of the people, which as yet would not have anything to do with Conscription, would

(4) *Does not exist at all; only in the English brain!*

(5) *? Not for us!*

(6) *But that is not our object.*

(7) *Absolutely out of the question and has never been attempted.*

(8) *! !*

(9) *It would do them good.*

(10) Tant mieux.

soon be won for it (10). . . . I replied that Germany had sufficient means at its disposal to produce a very respectable fleet, apart from its army. . . . Even if the burden were heavy, it would be necessary in view of the international situation. At least ten (11) years' hard work would be necessary to produce an armed country, and an army equal to the Continental pattern. If we saw that England was going over to Conscription, with its eyes on Germany, in order to reach an alliance with France, I did not believe that we should wait patiently for this process to be carried to completion (12). . . . Mr. Lloyd George then returned to his pet idea, the slackening down in the speed of naval construction (13) and exhorted me to make use of the time during which the peace-loving Liberal Government was at the helm. . . . Considering how much greater importance the fleet has for England than it has for Germany, the English fleet must always be a good bit stronger than ours, in order to be able to furnish that feeling of security which England requires from it, and at the same time sufficiently powerful to keep any wanton idea of attack on her from arising on our side (14) The German fleet, however, should be strong enough to give adequate protection for our overseas interests, and at the same time to give the English fleet, despite the latter's necessary superiority, the feeling that it would be risky to pick a quarrel with us (15). The relative

(11) Sancta Simplicitas! 50!

(12) *We should be totally indifferent.*

(13) *This is unheard of! and is a result of Metternich going into the idea at all.*

(14) *This is talk which until now has been only used against fellows like China or Italy! It is unheard of!*

(15) *We have not got that far yet!*

(16) *! !*

(17) *Bluff!*

(18) *No! Three times no. After the above words NEVER!*

(19) *Bosh!*

strength of 2 : 3, it seemed to him, would establish the right balance (16) at sea between us. He could not cite the authority of the English Government for this, but only uttered his own personal view; he knew, however, that we should find the greatest friendly response from the Liberal Cabinet (17) if we should be inclined to discuss the slackening down of the speed of naval construction (18). If even we only agreed to build one Dreadnought less every year, this would result in a complete change of the feeling in England towards us (19). . . ."

The above extracts give a fairly good picture of the course of my discussion with Metternich. How the whole report, and in particular my unspeakable impertinence in daring to suggest, on any grounds and for any consideration, that there should be an agreed limit to the German Navy, affected the Kaiser is best seen in his footnote to the report, which I transcribe in full:

"This sort of conversation as it has been carried on between Lloyd George and Metternich is utterly unworthy and provoking for Germany! I must beg him in future to have nothing to do with that sort of expectoration. Here he has accepted very patiently as a listener the opinions and orders of English statesmen, and has only ventured protests which had no effect at all. He should give these gentlemen, *who do not wish to see 'our wanton ideas of an attack,' realised*, an answer like 'Go to H——,' etc. That would bring these fellows to their senses again. That Lloyd George even dared to come out with an order for defining the speed of OUR building is beyond the limit, but is a result of Metternich putting himself during the first discussions on the dangerous path of *'a possibility not being out of the question.'* The clever British are trying to hook him, and sooner or later they will pull the string and drag him out; despite this 'private talk,' 'non-committal character of expression of opinion,' etc.! He should *ab ovo* refuse everything with such remarks as, 'No country allows itself to be dictated to or admonished by another country about the size and kind of its armaments.' 'I refuse to discuss such a matter.' For the rest, let them read the Navy Law — known for eleven years — and Nauticus!

"Metternich should give that sort of fanatic a kick in the —— ; he is too soft!"

The luncheon party had a further sequel, of which I was not made aware at the time, and have only recently learned through a perusal of the German Diplomatic papers.

At the time of my interview with Metternich, I was planning to visit Germany in the following month of August, 1908, in order to study on the spot the German systems of industrial insurance, with a view to preparing my own scheme of health- and unemployment insurance for this country. Metternich, reporting this to Berlin, had urged that the British Chancellor of the Exchequer, whom he described as "one of the most outstanding personalities in England, and one who most probably would be called upon one day to stand at the head of a Liberal Government", should be treated with the utmost consideration. The Kaiser accordingly arranged that I should be invited to pay him a visit. But in the meantime Metternich came over hurriedly to talk to the German Imperial Chancellor, Von Buelow, who had reprimanded him for his incautious conversation with me. I understand that Von Buelow was warned that I should certainly discuss the Navy with His Imperial Majesty, and that if Wilhelm used to my face the sort of remark he had noted on Metternich's report, a grave instance of *lèse majesté* would be liable to ensue. A hasty warning was sent to Court and I never received the Kaiser's suggested invitation.

I was, however, successful in securing an interview with the Vice-Chancellor, Von Bethmann-Hollweg, who was in Berlin at the time. He was then in charge of Health Insurance and had a very thorough acquaintance with its working. He was very helpful to me in my investigations on that subject. He was good enough to invite me and my party to be his guests at a big dinner which he gave at the Zoologischer Garten.

Von Bethmann-Hollweg was an attractive but not an arresting personality. He gave me the idea of an intelligent, industrious and eminently sensible bureaucrat, but he did not leave in my mind an impression of having met a man of power who might one day shake destiny. He gave us a good dinner, and at its close great tankards of lager beer were brought round, and Von Bethmann-Hollweg grew talkative and combative.

He embarked upon a discussion of the European situation, and was very bitter about what he called "the encirclement of Germany with an iron ring by France, Russia and England." I did my best to assure him that, so far as England was concerned, there was not the slightest desire to enter into any hostile combinations against Germany, and that we were most anxious to live in peace and neighbourliness with his great country. I told him, however, that England was very uneasy about the growth of the German Navy, and felt that it was aimed straight at her heart; and I repeated all that I had said to Count Metternich about our being an island and completely dependent upon the sea for our very existence. He was not very enthusiastic about the German Navy, and I perceived that he was no advocate of a shipbuilding programme that would be regarded as a menace by Great Britain; but he did his best to convince me that German people had no desire to attack England. The impression he left on my mind was that official Germany was genuinely apprehensive of the *rapprochement* between France and England, and England and Russia. They were quite convinced that King Edward was organising a Confederacy with a hostile purport against Germany. The King was regarded as an inveterate enemy of German might.

This led to one extraordinary outburst in the course of his conversation, when he reverted to the theme of the growing hostility of England, France and Russia against Germany, and the "iron ring" they were pressing round her. "An iron ring!" he repeated violently, shouting out the statement, and waving his arm to the whole assembled company. "England is embracing France. She is making friends with Russia. But it is not that you love each other; it is that you hate Germany!" And he repeated and literally shouted the word "hate" thrice. He became very excited, and his discretion was certainly not under control, for he went on to show a distinct antipathy even to Bavaria, when he contrasted the attachment of the Eastern provinces of Prussia, and of Berlin, to the Kaiser, and their readiness to die at a word from him, with the more lukewarm attitude of Bavaria.

Incidentally, he let in a flood of light upon the view of the ordinary German as to the decadence of England. He was clearly of the opinion that we were no longer a hard-working people; he thought that we loved our ease too much, and that we were a nation of week-enders. He gave a description of his own day: how he rose at seven o'clock, and worked until eight; then went for a ride until nine, then had his breakfast; afterwards resumed his daily tasks; worked practically till dinner, and kept going right through the week. He said, "In England, you go to your office at eleven; you have a long luncheon hour; you leave at four; on Thursday you go to the country; you remain there until Tuesday morning, and you call it a week-end!"

It is fair to say that this was after dinner! But I am not at all sure that this revelation of the Continental pre-war idea of English degeneracy had not something to do with the contempt with which military Germany contemplated the possibility of our intervention later on. It was very generally assumed that English fibre had been softened and disintegrated by prosperity. The poor show we had made in the Boer War had confirmed this idea.

What made it more significant was that his personal attitude towards England and Englishmen was extremely friendly, and this was not a mere matter of words, for he had sent his son to Oxford. His view was that the German worker was a better man than the English worker; that the German scientists were easily superior in quality and numbers to the insignificant band of British scientists. On the other hand, he seemed to have a better opinion of the English than of the German upper and middle classes. He attributed the superiority of the German worker to the fact that in his early years he received a stern military training in obedience which taught him habits of discipline and continuity.

I left Berlin gravely disturbed by the expressions of distrust and suspicion I had encountered in so high and friendly a quarter. It seemed to me to be ominously significant of what must be the general opinion at the time in leading German circles.

At the other end of the scale, I was also deeply impressed by a scene I witnessed at Stuttgart during the same tour. On our arrival there we learnt that a "Zeppelin" was about to make an exhibition flight. We went along to the field where the giant airship was moored, to find that by a last-minute accident it had crashed and been wrecked. Of course we were deeply disappointed, but disappointment was a totally inadequate word for the agony of grief and dismay which swept over the massed Germans who witnessed the catastrophe. There was no loss of life to account for it. Hopes and ambitions far wider than those concerned with a scientific and mechanical success appeared to have shared the wreck of the dirigible. Then the crowd swung into the chanting of "Deutschland über Alles" with a fanatic fervour of patriotism. What spearpoint of Imperial advance did this airship portend? These incidents were cracks in the cold surface, through which the hot, seething lava of unrest could be seen stirring uneasily underneath.

After these few glimpses of our foreign problem, I was drawn back during the succeeding years into the anxious preoccupations of domestic affairs. I understood, nevertheless, that there was a growing menace to peace abroad, and social order at home, which we must strive to avert if possible by peaceable methods, though I realised that we could not altogether rule out of account the possibility of a failure of such methods.

### 2. Plan for a Party Truce

Anxiety as to adequacy of our naval defences — Need for national training — My proposals for a party truce — Mr. Asquith approves the suggestion — Approval of Conservative leaders — My retirement demanded — Akers-Douglas kills the project — What national training might have done for us — Limitations of Party system.

My observation to Metternich, in the conversation already reported, about the possibility of our being driven to adopt Conscription, was by no means a casual sentence thrown out by me as a debating point in the course of an argument. Still less was it a piece of bald bluff, used in the hope of convincing or impressing the German Ambassador.

I had for some time past been growingly concerned with

the precariousness of our position in the event of our naval defence being broken through. We had depended upon it for centuries to protect us against invasion from the Continent. Hitherto it had not failed us, and this immunity had given us a sense of complete security. This feeling was expressed by Sir John Fisher in his famous remark that "We could sleep soundly in our beds because of the invincibility of our Navy." But the rapid march of scientific discovery, constantly revealing the existence of hitherto unsuspected forces, which were capable of the most formidable utilisation for service and disservice to mankind, made me feel that it was quite within the realm of possibility that one day there might be an invention which would neutralise our superiority, and reduce us to equality with, if not inferiority to, our neighbours. Inventions which portended such a menace had already appeared. Whether the peril would come from the air or from under the waters, I knew not; but no one could feel assured that such possibilities were altogether out of the reckoning. In such an event our position would be one of complete helplessness in the face of an invader with a powerful army.

We had two fundamental weaknesses in such a contingency. The first was that our army was too insignificant to stand up against the gigantic forces of the Continent. The second was that we were so overwhelmingly dependent upon overseas supplies for our food, that if these were cut off we should, within a few months, be brought to the very verge of starvation. It was this consideration amongst others that always led me to urge that we ought to devote more thought to the development of the resources of British soil.

I did not agree with Lord Roberts' case that a large force could at that time be landed from the Continent to capture London. In the absence of some invention which had not yet been found, or at least had not yet been developed, our Navy was powerful enough to prevent any emergency of that kind arising. My apprehension was entirely as to what the unknown future had in store for us if science neutralised the efficiency of our warships.

There were ominous clouds gathering over the Continent of Europe and perceptibly thickening and darkening. The submarine and the Zeppelin indicated a possible challenge to the invincibility of our defence. I felt we should be safer if we had in this country a system of training for our young manhood which would fit it for the defence of the Realm in the possible event of an invasion of our shores. I was opposed to conscript armies of the Continental type, and thought them designed rather for aggression than for defence. For the latter purpose it seemed to me that something resembling the Swiss militia system would suffice and might be adopted here.

It was with these thoughts in my mind that I ventured in 1910 to submit to the leaders of both political parties in this country a series of proposals for national coöperation over a period of years, to deal with special matters of urgent importance.

In the year 1910 we were beset by an accumulation of grave issues — rapidly becoming graver. The gravest have not yet been solved. It was becoming evident to discerning eyes that the Party and Parliamentary system was unequal to coping with them. There was a jam at the legislative dock gates and there was no prospect of the growing traffic being able to get through. The shadow of unemployment was rising ominously above the horizon. Our international rivals were forging ahead at a great rate and jeopardising our hold on the markets of the world. There was an arrest in that expansion of our foreign trade which had contributed to the phenomenal prosperity of the previous half-century, and of which we had made such a muddled and selfish use. Our working population, crushed into dingy and mean streets, with no assurance that they would not be deprived of their daily bread by ill-health or trade fluctuations, were becoming sullen with discontent. Whilst we were growing more dependent on overseas supplies for our food, our soil was gradually going out of cultivation. The life of the countryside was wilting away and we were becoming dangerously over-industrialised. Excessive indulgence in alcoholic drinks was undermining the health and efficiency of a considerable section of the population. The Irish controversy was poisoning our relations with the United States of America. A great Constitutional struggle over the House of Lords threatened revolution at home, another threatened civil war at our doors in Ireland. Great nations were arming feverishly for an apprehended struggle into which we might be drawn by some visible or invisible ties, interests, or sympathies. Were we prepared for all the terrifying contingencies?

Moved by this prospect I submitted to Mr. Asquith a Memorandum urging that a truce should be declared between the Parties for the purpose of securing the coöperation of the leading party statesmen in a settlement of our national problems — Second Chamber, Home Rule, the development of our agricultural resources, National Training for Defence, the remedying of social evils, and a fair and judicial enquiry into the working of our fiscal system.

Mr. Asquith regarded the proposal with considerable favour, and it was decided to submit it to four or five members of the Cabinet for their observations. So far as I can recollect, the only Cabinet Ministers who were called into consultation were Lord Crewe, Sir Edward Grey, Lord Haldane, and Mr. Winston Churchill. I cannot recall any criticism in detail from any of them. They all approved

*Photo. by Keystone View Co.*

THE RT. HONOURABLE HERBERT HENRY ASQUITH

*(subsequently created Earl of Oxford and Asquith)*
*Prime Minister of Great Britain from 1908–1916*

of the idea in principle, and it was agreed that the proposal should be submitted to Mr. Balfour, who was still the Leader of the Conservative Party. The only outsiders to whom I showed the document were Mr. F. E. Smith (subsequently Lord Birkenhead) and Mr. Garvin. They were much pleased with the whole conception.

Mr. Balfour was by no means hostile; in fact, he went a long way towards indicating that personally he regarded the proposal with a considerable measure of approval. He was not, however, certain of the reception which would be accorded to it by his party. Unfortunately, at that time he was not very firmly seated in the saddle. The Die-Hard cry against his leadership was getting audibly shriller each day. However, he consulted some of his leading colleagues, and he received from them replies which were by no means discouraging. I understand that Lord Lansdowne, Lord Cawdor, Lord Curzon, Mr. Walter Long, and Mr. Austen Chamberlain favoured the plan. When he came to summon a more formal and general meeting of his colleagues, he again found that the ablest members of the Conservative Party were by no means antipathetic to the idea. So far as I can recollect, the only opposition came from the late Lord Londonderry. But when Mr. Balfour proceeded later on to sound the opinion of the less capable and therefore more narrowly partisan members of his party, he encountered difficulties which proved insurmountable. He called upon me one evening at 11 Downing Street to discuss the matter, and I found him then much more hesitant and reluctant. I gathered from him that the chief objection entertained by his colleagues was to my presence in such a combination. I was so completely associated in their minds with extreme radical proposals, I was so much in the front of the offence at that time, and I had said so many wounding things in the scrimmage, that they were more than doubtful whether they could secure the adhesion of their supporters to any Coalition of which I was a member.

I instantly assured him that, as far as I was concerned, I would not make my inclusion in the Ministry a condition of my support. On the contrary, I was quite prepared to keep out of it and give it my whole-hearted and zealous backing as an independent member of the House of Commons, so long as it tackled its job with courage and conviction. He then told me that there was one other man he felt he would have to consult. He said: "You will be surprised when I give you his name." When I heard it, I think I was rather surprised that this individual should still hold such an important and influential position in the councils of the Party, for he had retired from active political life for a good many years: it was Mr. Akers-Douglas, who had formerly been Chief Whip of the Conservative Party, and was then Lord Chilston. I remember one of the last things Mr. Balfour said to me on that occasion. Putting his hand on his forehead, looking down and more or less soliloquising, he said: "I cannot become another Robert Peel in my party!" After a short interval he added: "Although I cannot see where the Disraeli is to come from, unless it be my cousin Hugh, and I cannot quite see him fulfilling that rôle!"

Mr. Akers-Douglas turned down the project for coöperation in settling these momentous national issues, and there was an end to it. It very nearly came off. It was not rejected by the real leaders of the Party, but by men who, for some obscure reason best known to political organisations, have great influence inside the councils of a party without possessing any of the capabilities that excite general admiration and confidence outside. I am not concerned, in these War reminiscences, to examine the possibilities of this project, had it been adopted and carried out, except insofar as it might have altered or modified the international situation. Had it materialised then, there would by 1914 have been a body of trained young men aggregating between a million and one-and-a-half million, fit for incorporation in our armies, shortly after the declaration of war. What is still more important, there would have been rifles and other equipment for them, which it took us over eighteen months to manufacture in the Great War, and the requisite machinery for manufacturing still more for ourselves and our Allies. There would also have been a staff of trained and competent officers fit to lead such an army into the field. Had such a force been in existence when the crisis arose in 1914, and had Germany been conscious of the fact that the British contribution would not be limited to her "contemptible little army" of six divisions, but that there was a large body of trained and equipped men behind that small Expeditionary Force which could soon be made fit to take an effective part in the fighting line, Germany would have hesitated before plunging the world into the disaster of the Great War. The young men who were sent to the trenches during the last two years of the War had received much less training than an application of the Swiss Militia System would have given to those who would have been called to the Colours in 1911, 1912, 1913, and 1914.

Even if the existence of such a formidable force had not influenced the course of events in the direction of peace, the contribution made by it in the earlier stages of the War might well have been decisive and have shortened the term of this devastating struggle.

I have heard it said that, at the battle of Ypres, the troops on both sides were so tired out by the end that the irruption of one fresh division on either side would have achieved victory for the army lucky enough to secure so timely a reinforcement. A number of Territorial battalions, not one of which had received anything like the Swiss training, were thrown into the battle line before the end of the fight, and, according to the testimony of Sir John French, rendered invaluable aid to our exhausted troops. If, instead of nineteen battalions of Territorials with able but amateur officers, there had been three or four hundred battalions of more fully trained men, led by thoroughly equipped officers, the battle of Ypres would not have been a stalemate, but a victory which might have liberated Flanders and ended the War.

The same observation applies to the Dardanelles, where the fatal delays in landing troops which enabled the Turks to bring reinforcements, were due to the fact that we could not spare the one extra division necessary to make up an Expeditionary Force — not even a spare division — until it was too late to achieve any results. Even from the point of view of filling up the serious gaps in the ranks of our Regular Army, due to the disastrous retreat from Mons, the heavy fighting on the Marne and at Ypres, the possession of a trained Militia would have been invaluable. Young men with an aggregate training of about a year, mixed up with the Regulars, would have been more useful than the Reservists, a large number of whom had been softened and debilitated by years of civilian occupation. All these considerations constantly leapt to my mind during the progress of the campaign, and always brought with them a regret for the "Great Refusal" of 1910.

There is much to be said in favour of the Party system. The open conflict of Parties is better for a country than the squalid intrigues of personal ambitions or of rival interests conducted in the dark. But there are times when it stands seriously in the way of the highest national interests. On these occasions it hinders, delays and thwarts real progress, and in the event the nation suffers heavily. I shall always regard the rejection of the proposals for coöperation in 1910 as a supreme instance of this kind of damage. On the other hand, the ground for coöperation must be one of genuine national well-being. A suspension of Party hostilities merely in order to ensure a distribution of patronage and power amongst the leading contestants, degrades and enervates politics.

### 3. The Agadir Crisis, 1911

British commitments in regard to Morocco — History of the crisis — War talk in Germany — Germany ignores the British protests — My statement approved and authorised — My responsibility for the statement — Effect of the speech: Germany climbs down.

As to the part I took in the Agadir incident, it is hardly necessary for me to write at any length. The story has been so fully and fairly told by both Mr. Winston Churchill and Sir Edward Grey that there is little which I need add.

My intervention was due largely to the fear that if things were allowed to drift, we might find ourselves drawn into a great European War on a question in which we were inextricably involved. For the French position in Morocco was part of the Lansdowne Treaty, and Sir Edward Grey in his book, "Twenty-Five Years," makes it clear that he regarded a dispute on anything which constituted a challenge to that settlement as something which we were bound to put in a different category from any dispute which might arise between France and Germany outside the four corners of that arrangement. I still think there is very great force in his contention in that respect.

The situation can be outlined in a few words. France, who had been accorded a zone of influence in Morocco by the Treaty of Algeciras, found it necessary to send an expedition to Fez. Germany, conceiving with some reason that France had annexationist designs, thought she would be entitled to corresponding compensations elsewhere, and promptly took steps to indicate her claim, and opened the negotiations by sending a gunboat to the Moroccan harbour of Agadir. This was a blundering and blustering kind of diplomacy, and when Britain, naturally concerned at its meaning and possible outcome, sent a communication to Berlin on the subject, our letter was left unanswered for weeks, while we learnt from France that the German Government was pressing quite impossible demands upon her as the price of withdrawal from Agadir.

It is hard to say whether there was real danger of war. There is an ominous passage in a dispatch from Von Bethmann-Hollweg to the Kaiser, dated July 15th, 1911, when the German silence *vis-à-vis* Britain had already continued for eleven days. The Imperial Chancellor reported that Herr von Kiderlen, the German Foreign Secretary, had gathered from his discussion with the French Ambassador the impression "that in order to reach a favourable result, we shall certainly have to take a very strong line!" To this the Kaiser makes a marginal note:

> Then I must return home at once. For I can't let my Government take that sort of action without being right on the spot so as to keep a careful watch on the consequences and have them well in hand! Anything else would be unpardonable, and too parliamentary! *Le Roi s'amuse!* And meantime we are steering straight for mobilisation! That must not happen WITHOUT ME!
>
> Besides, our Allies must first be informed about this! For it may draw them in, in sympathy!

There can be no doubt as to the meaning of those words. The Kaiser clearly contemplated the mobilisation of his armies as a not unlikely result of the diplomatic situation. In 1914 mobilisation made for war — it meant war.

When the rude indifference of the German Government to our communication had lasted for seventeen days — from the 4th to the 21st of July — I felt that matters were growing tensely critical and that we were drifting clumsily towards war. It was not merely that by failing even to send a formal acknowledgment of the Foreign Secretary's letter the Germans were treating us with intolerable insolence, but that their silence might well mean that they were blindly ignorant of the sense in which we treated our obligations under the Treaty, and might not realise until too late that we felt bound to stand by France. These reasons prompted me to make the Mansion House speech which has already been so fully dealt with by Sir Edward Grey and Mr Churchill.

On the 21st of July I was due to speak to the Bankers at their annual banquet to the Chancellor of the Exchequer and I decided to take advantage of the occasion to make a statement which would warn Germany of the peril into which her Ministers were rushing her so heedlessly.

I felt that I had no right to intervene in a matter which was in the sphere of the Foreign Office, and to make a declaration which might involve our relations with Germany without obtaining the consent of both the Prime Minister and Grey. Before delivering it, therefore, I submitted its terms to the Prime Minister. He fully approved, and sent immediately to the Foreign Office to ask Sir Edward Grey to come to the Cabinet Room in order to obtain his views and procure his sanction. My recollection is that when he arrived, he cordially assented to every word of my draft, and I delivered the speech later on to the Bankers at the Mansion House.[1]

[1] The passage of my speech in question was as follows:

"But I am also bound to say this—that I believe it is essential in the highest interests, not merely of this country, but of the world, that Britain should at all hazards maintain her place and her prestige amongst the Great Powers of the world. Her potent influence has many a time been in the past, and may yet be in the future, invaluable to the cause of human liberty. It has more than once in the past redeemed continental nations, who are sometimes too apt to forget that service, from overwhelming disaster, and even from national extinction. I would make great sacrifices to preserve peace. I conceive that nothing would

The genesis of that speech is, as I have said, quite correctly recorded by both Grey and Churchill, but I have here given my own confirmation of their narrative, because my public intervention at that time in the sphere of foreign affairs was so unusual that a rumour gained currency, and even finds place in German and Austrian official diplomatic correspondence, that I was merely acting as a mouthpiece to read out a statement prepared by the Cabinet, and was at most but vaguely aware of its implications. Even E. T. Raymond avers that what I read was a passage carefully prepared for me by Sir Edward Grey. But I have not the least desire to shuffle off my true responsibility in this connection. The initiative in this matter was my own, as was the wording of the statement. Certainly I secured authoritative approval before I made it, but it was not actually submitted to the whole Cabinet in advance.

The effect of the speech was unquestionably to clear the air, and avert any danger of Europe drifting unawares into war. The German Government, naturally, was furious, for its gunboat diplomacy had received a severe and well-merited rebuff. Metternich was instructed to make representations about my speech to the British Foreign Office. He did so in a very stern manner, but found little to cheer him in his reception. He reported to von Kiderlen-Waechter that "With reference to the speech of the Chancellor of the Exchequer, Grey was thoroughly uncompromising, defended it as moderate, and stated that it had been entirely right for this speech to be made." The truth was, of course, that the

justify a disturbance of international good will except questions of the gravest national moment. But if a situation were to be forced upon us in which peace could only be preserved by the surrender of the great and beneficent position Britain has won by centuries of heroism and achievement, by allowing Britain to be treated, where her interests were vitally affected, as if she were of no account in the Cabinet of Nations, then I say emphatically that peace at that price would be a humiliation intolerable for a great country like ours to endure. National honour is no party question. The security of our great international trade is no party question. The peace of the world is much more likely to be secured if all nations realise fairly what the conditions of peace must be . . ."

Wilhelmstrasse had over-reached itself, and taken a course which it was difficult either to explain or to explain away. The Austrian diplomatic correspondence shows that the Kaiser and his Minister thought the Government then in office in France was a weak one and lacked backbone. The German Foreign Office doubtless conceived that a sudden and dramatic rattling of the sabre would terrify this feeble Ministry and that by this means Germany would win substantial concessions in Morocco. But they were not prepared to go to war with both France and England, to make good this gamble.

Von Kiderlen-Waechter described my speech to the Austrian Ambassador at Berlin as "an unfair and colossal bluff." However, it was a bluff he was not prepared to call. It was in truth by no means bluff, and if an equally clear statement of our attitude had been made in July only three years later, it is conceivable that once again the peril of a recklessly incurred war might have been averted.

### 4. No Cabinet Consideration of Foreign Policy

Preoccupation with domestic affairs — Secrecy of the Foreign Office — Foreign affairs known only to a select few — Lord Northcliffe's view of ministerial ignorance — The method of private correspondence with Ambassadors — Cabinet ignorance of our strategic arrangements — Our consternation on hearing of our commitments — Our liabilities contingent on violation of Belgium.

During the eight years that preceded the war, the Cabinet devoted a ridiculously small percentage of its time to a consideration of foreign affairs. This was partly, but not altogether, due to the political conditions under which we worked. The 1906–1914 Governments and Parliaments were engaged in a series of controversies on home affairs, each of which raised more passion than any dispute between the rival political parties within living memory. Education, Temperance, Land Taxation — culminating in the most serious constitutional crisis since the days of the Reform

Bill — the Parliament Act, Home Rule, and the Disestablishment of the Church in Wales: these subjects challenged an infinite variety of human interests, sentiment, and emotion, and the partisan warfare that raged round these topics was so fierce that by 1913 this country was brought to the verge of civil war.

Of course, certain aspects of foreign policy were familiar to those Ministers who attended the Committee of Imperial Defence, but apart from that the Cabinet as a whole were never called into genuine consultation upon the fundamental aspects of the foreign situation. There was a reticence and a secrecy which practically ruled out three-fourths of the Cabinet from the chance of making any genuine contribution to the momentous questions then fermenting on the Continent of Europe, which ultimately ended in an explosion that almost shattered the civilisation of the world. During the whole of those eight years when I was a member of the Cabinet, I can recall no such review of the European situation being given to us as that which Sir Edward Grey delivered to the Colonial Conference in 1907, or to the Prime Ministers of the Dominions at the Committee of Imperial Defence in 1911. Even there the information that was withheld was more important than that which was imparted. For instance, nothing was said about our military commitments. There was in the Cabinet an air of "hush hush" about every allusion to our relations with France, Russia and Germany. Direct questions were always answered with civility, but were not encouraged. We were made to feel that, in these matters, we were reaching our hands towards the mysteries, and that we were too young in the priesthood to presume to enter into the sanctuary reserved for the elect. So we confined our inquisitiveness and our counsel to the more mundane affairs in which we had taken part in Opposition during the whole of our political careers. Discussions, if they could be called discussions, on foreign affairs, were confined to the elder statesmen who had seen service in some previous ministerial existence. Apart from the Prime Minister and the Foreign Secretary there were only two or three men such as Lord Loreburn, the Lord Chancellor, Lord Morley, Lord Crewe, and, for a short time, Lord Ripon, who were expected to make any contribution on the infrequent occasions when the Continental situation was brought to our awed attention. As a matter of fact, we were hardly qualified to express any opinion on so important a matter, for we were not privileged to know any more of the essential facts than those which the ordinary newspaper reader could gather from the perusal of his morning journal. I recollect the late Lord Northcliffe, at a dinner at Lord Birkenhead's house, where he was invited to meet a number of Cabinet Ministers in the Liberal Administration, telling us all quite bluntly that the Editor of a great London journal was better informed about what was happening in the capitals of the world than any Cabinet Minister. He maintained that all the information we got was carefully filtered. He might have gone further and said that much of the information essential for forming a sound opinion was deliberately withheld. When a Cabinet Minister first takes office, nothing gives him a greater sense of his personal importance than the stout little leather bag with a specially constructed key which is sent after him every night to any address which he may give. It is supposed to contain communications of the most deadly import and secrecy as to what is happening in Courts and Chancelleries throughout the world. As a matter of fact it is just a series of harmless dispatches from our representatives in every foreign country, great and small. There is not a dispatch which contains anything that the Foreign Office clerks who copied it, and the Foreign Office printers who set the type, and the numerous Private Secretaries who have access to these printed copies, could not read without the danger of any indiscreet revelation by any of them disturbing our relations with the most insignificant kingdom or republic in the world. All the things that mattered were conveyed in private and confidential letters from our Diplomatic Representatives abroad to the Foreign Secretary personally, in his private and unpublished replies, and in the interviews which he held with the Ambassadors at the Foreign Office in Downing Street. What mattered just as much, perhaps even more, were the secret arrangements arrived at between the military and naval staffs of Britain, France, and Russia as to the part their respective forces were expected to play in the event of war with Germany. None of these vital communications were placed at the disposal of the Cabinet. They were passed on to the Prime Minister, and perhaps to one or two other Ministers. The rest of us were left in the dark and were therefore not in a position to assess the realities of the foreign situation. When Lord Ripon[1] was made leader of the House of Lords, having been in Cabinets since the days of Palmerston he knew from previous experience of the existence of secret interchanges of this character, and he asked Sir Edward Grey for an opportunity of perusing them, as he was leading the House of Lords and could hardly do so with judgment unless he were really informed.

There is no more conspicuous example of this kind of suppression of vital information than the way in which the military arrangements we entered into with France were kept from the Cabinet for six years. They came to my knowledge, first of all, in 1911, during the Agadir crisis, but the Cabinet as a whole were not acquainted with them before

[1] When I first entered the Cabinet, Lord Ripon was the oldest member and I was the youngest.

the following year. There is abundant evidence that both the French and the Russians regarded these military arrangements as practically tantamount to a commitment on our part to come to the aid of France in the event of her being attacked by Germany. When the British Government was hesitating at the end of July, 1914, as to whether it would support France in the event of a German attack, French statesmen almost reverted to the "Perfidious Albion" mood, and even the meek M. Paul Cambon said that the only question was whether the word "honour" was to be expunged from the British dictionary. On the whole, the view summarised in that pungent comment is the one I heard expressed by most supporters and opponents of our intervention in the Great War; and yet the Cabinet was never informed of these vital arrangements until we were so deeply involved in the details of military and naval plans that it was too late to repudiate the inference. To attempt then to set right the impression produced in the minds of our Allies would have created a new situation involving a return, in an aggravated form, of the unpleasant relations with France which the Lansdowne Agreement of 1904 had, for the time being, brought to an end. In 1906 both Sir Henry Campbell-Bannerman and Mr. Asquith expressed grave doubts as to the wisdom of proceeding with these discussions. They ultimately assented to that course being pursued under pressure from Sir Edward Grey and Lord Haldane. When in 1912 (six years after they had been entered into) Sir Edward Grey communicated these negotiations and arrangements to the Cabinet the majority of its Members were aghast. Hostility barely represents the strength of the sentiment which the revelation aroused: it was more akin to consternation. Sir Edward Grey allayed the apprehensions of his colleagues to some extent by emphatic assurances that these military arrangements left us quite free, in the event of war, to decide whether we should or should not participate in the conflict. The Prime Minister also exercised his great authority with the Cabinet in the same direction. In spite of these assurances a number of Cabinet Ministers were not reconciled to the action taken by the Foreign Office, the War Office and the Admiralty, and these commitments undoubtedly added a good deal to the suspicions which made the task of Sir Edward Grey in securing unanimity in 1914 very much more difficult.

Personally, I was prepared to accept the Foreign Secretary's assurances that we were not committed. I was strengthened in my conviction that there was no definite commitment to give military support to France in her quarrels with Germany by the meetings of the Committee of Imperial Defence during the Agadir crisis. There Sir Henry Wilson, with the aid of a pointer and a big map, explained to us the whole of the arrangements which had been entered into with the French Foreign Office: they were contingent upon a German attack upon Belgium, and the march of German divisions through that country to attack France. In that contingency our Expeditionary Force was to be taken to the Belgian frontier along the French railways, for the purpose of giving every support to the army which was resisting the invader in that quarter. I never doubted that, if the Germans interfered with the integrity and independence of Belgium, we were in honour bound to discharge our treaty obligations to that country.

## CHAPTER II

# THE CRASH

### 1. Unexpected Plunge into War

War not foreseen by people in general — Responsible statesmen unprepared — Cabinet unaware of a crisis — Sir Edward Grey's first announcement — Russia anticipates war.

How was it that the world was so unexpectedly plunged into this terrible conflict? Who was responsible? Not even the astutest and most far-seeing statesman foresaw in the early summer of 1914 that the autumn would find the nations of the world interlocked in the most terrible conflict that had ever been witnessed in the history of mankind; and if you come to the ordinary men and women who were engaged in their daily avocations in all countries, there was not one of them who suspected the imminence of such a catastrophe. Of those who, in the first weeks of July, were employed in garnering their hay or corn harvests, either in this country or on the Continent of Europe, it is safe to say that not one ever contemplated the possibility that another month would find them called to the Colours and organised in battle array for a struggle that would end in the violent death of millions of them, and in the mutilation of many more millions. The nations slithered over the brink into the boiling cauldron of war without any trace of apprehension or dismay.

When I first heard the news of the assassination of the Archduke Ferdinand, I felt that it was a grave matter, and that it might provoke serious consequences which only the firmest and most skilful handling could prevent from developing into an emergency that would involve nations. But my fears were soon assuaged by the complete calm with which the rulers and diplomats of the world seemed to regard the event. The Kaiser departed for his usual yachting holiday in the Norwegian fiords. His Chief Minister left for his usual shooting party on his estate in Silesia. The acting Head of the German Foreign Office went off on a honeymoon trip. A still more reassuring fact — the military head of the German Army, Von Moltke, left for his cure in a foreign spa. The President of the French Republic and his Prime Minister were on a ceremonial visit to Russia and only arrived back in Paris on July 29th. Our Foreign Office preserved its ordinary tranquillity of demeanour and thought it unnecessary to sound an alarm even in the Cabinet Chamber. I remember that some time in July, an influential Hungarian lady, whose name I have forgotten, called upon me at 11 Downing Street, and told me that we were taking the assassination of the Archduke much too quietly; that it had provoked such a storm throughout the Austrian Empire as she had never witnessed, and that unless something were done immediately to satisfy and appease resentment, it would certainly result in war with Serbia, with the incalculable consequences which such an operation might precipitate in Europe. However, such official reports as came to hand did not seem to justify the alarmist view she took of the situation.

I cannot recall any discussion on the subject in the Cabinet until the Friday evening before the final declaration of war by Germany. We were much more concerned with the threat of imminent civil war in the North of Ireland. The situation there absorbed our thoughts, and constituted the subject-matter for the major part of our deliberations. Mr. Churchill recalls the fact that on that Friday, the 24th of

July, we met in the Prime Minister's room in the House of Commons to discuss once more the Irish crisis, which was daily becoming more menacing. When that discussion was over the Cabinet rose, but the Foreign Secretary asked us to remain behind for a few more minutes as he had something to impart to us about the situation in Europe. When we resumed our seats he told us, for the first time, that he thought the position was very grave, but he was hopeful that the conversations which were proceeding between Austria and Russia might lead to a pacific settlement. So we separated upon that assurance. On Saturday Sir Edward Grey left for his fishing lodge in Hampshire, and all other Ministers followed his example and left town. On Sunday came the news of the landing of arms by Nationalists at Howth, near Dublin, and of a conflict with the military which arose out of that incident. The excitement over this event overshadowed, for the time being, the Continental situation. At that very hour Isvolzky, the Russian Ambassador in Paris, who was then at St. Petersburg, and M. Paleologue, the French Ambassador in Russia, both said: "It is war this time"; and later on the same Sunday afternoon, Monsieur Sazonow, the Russian Foreign Minister, made a similar statement to Monsieur Paleologue, and added: "It is too terrible to contemplate." Mr. Harold Nicolson, in his Life of his father, the late Lord Carnock, who was then permanent Head of the Foreign Office, states that Sir Arthur Nicolson, as he then was, became so alarmed about the situation on this Sunday, that he took immediate steps to bring Sir Edward Grey back to London. War was declared by Austria on Serbia two days later and by Germany on Russia five days later.

Even then I met no responsible Minister who was not convinced that, in one way or another, the calamity of a great European war would somehow be averted.

## 2. Nobody Wanted War

The man who was willing for World War — Drive for a Serbian campaign — Lack of great statesmen — Manslaughter: not murder — Grey's diplomatic proposals for a conference.

In looking back upon the incidents of those few eventful days one feels like recalling a nightmare, and after reading most of the literature explaining why the nations went to war, and who was responsible, the impression left on my mind is one of utter chaos, confusion, feebleness and futility, especially of a stubborn refusal to look at the rapidly approaching cataclysm. The nations backed their machinery over the precipice. Amongst the rulers and statesmen who alone could give the final word which caused great armies to spring from the ground and march to and across frontiers, one can see now clearly that not one of them wanted war; certainly not on this scale. The possible exception is the foolish Berchtold, the Austrian Premier, upon whom must be fixed the chief personal responsibility for most of what happened.[1] As to the rest, they all shrank from the prospect. Least of all could it be said that the aged Franz Josef wanted war. The last thing the vainglorious Kaiser wanted was a European war. The feeble and simple-minded but sincere Czar of the Russias certainly did not desire war. During his reign the occasional outbursts of truculence against strikers, Jews, and revolutionaries, for which he was held responsible, were not any expression of natural ferocity on his part. They always occurred as a result of official

[1] That Berchtold was prepared if necessary to launch a European war in furtherance of his projects is evidenced by a dispatch from him on July 25th, 1914, to the Austrian Ambassador at St. Petersburg, where he gives him the following instructions:

". . . When your Excellency reaches this point in your conversation with Herr Sazonow, it will be a suitable opportunity for stating in connection with your account of our motives and intentions, that we — as your Excellency would be already in a position to make clear — are seeking for no territorial gain, and have no intention of impairing the sovereignty of the Kingdom (of Serbia) but that on the other hand we shall go to the utmost limit in carrying through our demands, *and shall not even recoil from the possibility of European complications.*" (My italics.)

incitement, usually as a means of countering some domestic crisis. But on this occasion his principal official adviser, Sazonow, displayed a real horror at the prospect of a great war, and in the Czar's more intimate circles, even Rasputin warned the Court of the danger to the Dynasty which would be involved in plunging Russia into a great conflict with her powerful neighbours.

Austrian and German rulers and statesmen had a hankering desire for a small war against a tiny neighbour who, standing alone, would easily and speedily be overwhelmed. It would soon be over, the prestige of Austria would be restored by this exhibition of her irresistible might, and Germany would once more prove herself the undoubted master of Europe and the unchallengeable arbiter of its destinies. But the last thing any of these rulers and statesmen wanted was a prairie fire that would scorch up a whole continent. Those who directed affairs amongst the Central Powers only felt that they must burn out that "wasps' nest," as they called Serbia, and they never seemed to take cognizance of the fact that the grass on the plains of Europe at that time was all tinder. There was no arresting voice anywhere to call a halt: no dominant personality to enforce attention or offer acceptable guidance amidst the chaos. The world was exceptionally unfortunate in the quality of its counsellors in this terrible emergency. Had there been a Bismarck in Germany, or a Palmerston or a Disraeli in Britain, a Roosevelt in America, or a Clemenceau in authority in Paris, the catastrophe might, and I believe would, have been averted; but there was no one of that quality visible on the bridge in any great State. Von Bethmann-Hollweg, Poincaré, Viviani, Berchtold, Sazonow and Grey were all able, experienced, conscientious and respectable mariners, but distinctly lacking in the force, vision, imagination and resource which alone could have saved the situation. They were all handy men in a well-behaved sea, but helpless in a typhoon. In Germany, which counted most in this crisis, navigation was complicated by the august presence on the bridge, of a weak, fussy and egotistical personage, who, at critical moments, overawed and overrode all his subordinates. He never contemplated a great war as a possibility when in the early days of July he issued his first directions as to the course of German diplomacy, and then sailed away to the Norwegian fiords, where he depended for his information as to the course of a crisis whose issue was in his hands, upon some local newspaper.[1] When he came back and realised that he might be involved in a great European struggle, he visibly shrank from the prospect, but he had not the strength to countermand his orders. He was afraid of being taunted with cowardice in the face of danger. So he allowed himself to be dragged into a conflict, for leadership in which he was utterly unfitted by training, talent or temperament.

The picture which the events of the last fateful days present to me is that which you see in an estuary, when a river, which has been gliding steadily along towards the sea for a long distance without any consciousness of the final destiny which awaits it in the direction in which it flows, suddenly finds itself confronted with the immensity of the ocean and the terror of its waves. The confusion and tumult of waters which ensue mean that its reluctance has come too late. If I were on a jury trying any of the men who

[1] ". . . My fleet was cruising as usual in the Norwegian fiords, while I was on my summer vacation trip. During my stay at Balholm I received but meagre news from the Foreign Office and was obliged to rely principally on the Norwegian newspapers, from which I received the impression that the situation was growing worse. I telegraphed repeatedly to the Chancellor and the Foreign Office that I considered it advisable to return home, but was asked each time not to interrupt my journey. . . .

". . . When, after that, however, I learned from the Norwegian newspapers — *not from Berlin* — of the Austrian ultimatum to Serbia, and immediately after, of the Serbian Note to Austria, I started upon my return journey without further ado. . . ." ("My Memoirs," 1878–1918, ex-Kaiser Wilhelm II, pp. 241–2.)

were in control of affairs at that date, I should bring against most of them a verdict of manslaughter rather than of murder. A brief summary of what happened will give an idea of the aimlessness and muddle that prevailed.

Grey wanted Russia and Austria to talk it out amongst themselves. He then suggested the mediation of Germany with Austria, of France with Russia, and of Russia with Serbia. On the other hand, Germany preferred to leave Austria to talk it out alone with Serbia without any intermediary or intervener. Sazonow leaned towards conversations between Russia and Austria; Germany, later on, but much too late, inclined in the same direction. Grey then cut athwart this idea with his proposal for a conference of Ambassadors in London, but he wished to leave both Austria and Serbia out of this gathering — a fatal omission which undoubtedly led Germany to reject the proposal. In Von Bethmann-Hollweg's opinion a Conference so constituted looked too much like a tribunal to try Austria's case, when the country which was arraigned would not even be present to state her defence, and, in any event, all the judges being biased and the majority definitely hostile, would have but one friend on the bench. Germany still preferred a continuation of the Austro-Russian talks. And, besides, it was quite clear that the Germans did not care for the idea of a meeting in London. England, France, and Russia would be represented there by skilled and experienced diplomatists, rootedly opposed to the Austrian objectives in the Balkans; on the other hand, the German Ambassador had not the full confidence of the German Foreign Office, for many reasons. Amongst others, he was suspected of hesitancy and lukewarmness in his attitude towards the Austrian pretensions. Even Russia was not enthusiastic about the notion of a Conference, preferring to continue direct negotiations with Austria. Sazonow only accepted the proposal of a Conference in the event of these direct negotiations breaking down. The Four Power Conference was, therefore, turned down. The suggestion had only served to waste invaluable time. It was not wisely framed, and it was not put forward with conviction; it was not pressed home and it was finally dropped; in fact, it was dropped at the first objection. It was a timid and half-hearted approach, and at the first difficulty it encountered it was abandoned by its distracted author. Then came the muddle about mobilisation and semi-mobilisation of the Austrian, Russian, and Serbian Armies. The Willy-Nicky letters followed, with the Czar's suggestion of a reference to the Hague, and the Kaiser's counter-suggestion of a cancellation by the Czar of his Decree for mobilising the Russian Army. The letters were written to the tramp of battalions and the rumble of cannon pressing on towards frontiers, and the inevitable clash that was to come. A multitude of moidered Counsellors, by their conflicting advice, now hustled Wisdom into the arms of the bravos who had for years waited eagerly for this hour, and were standing impatiently outside the Council Chambers ready to strangle their victim.

### 3. Attitude — Military, Political and Civilian — to War

Military wish for war — A decisive factor in Germany — Kaiser Wilhelm's indecision — Austria's "Little War" — Reputed invincibility of German Army — French military confidence — Popular war fever — Demonstrations in Whitehall — Sympathy with Belgium — Evidence of *Daily News*.

Whilst diplomacy desired peace and worked for it by confused and bewildered methods, there were powerful elements in every community that thirsted for war. The Military Chiefs, high and low, in at least three of the countries principally concerned were not averse from putting their theories, plans, and hopes to the test. All of them believed in the machine they had helped to perfect, and they were confident that if tried it would prove triumphant. In this country this desire did not count in the estimation of a hair! Our overwhelming confidence in the power of our Navy may perhaps have influenced opinion in certain quarters, but that influence was not decisive. In Germany, on the other hand, military sentiment counted a good deal. I am inclined to believe, after a careful perusal of the evidence, that it was a decisive factor. The Kaiser had, owing to certain incidents and indiscretions, lost much of his popularity. His popularity with his Army was definitely on the wane. They realised that he had not the heart of a soldier, and that he was not the man who would lead them into battle — if he could avoid a fight. The Crown Prince was their favourite. The Kaiser was becoming sensitive to this rather contemptuous opinion formed of his courage by the Army he idolised. He knew that any symptom of shrinking or shuddering at the prospect of a great fight would finally forfeit the last remnant of respect for him in the breasts of the soldiers he adored. This he could not face. So the last fatal days before the War present the pitiable spectacle of a man torn between fear, common sense and vanity, the two former pulling him back from the chasm — the latter pushing him relentlessly over the brink. His letter of the 28th of July to Von Jagow is a perfect specimen of the distracted state of mind which was produced by this inward struggle. In it he said: 'that the requests of the Danube Monarchy had been broadly met; the Serbs' few reservations could probably be cleared up by negotiation; the reply amounted to a capitulation in the humblest style, and with it there disappeared *all reason for war.*' (The italics were the Kaiser's.) [1]

This part of the letter is often quoted. What is not so often quoted is the following sentence in the same note in which he stated that he considered that a guarantee was needed for the execution of the demands upon Serbia, and

[1] Lutz: "Lord Grey and the World War" (pp. 257–8).

also that as "a visible *satisfaction d'honneur* for Austria the Austrian Army should temporarily occupy Belgrade as a pledge." The letter is a proof of the fatal hesitancy in the Kaiser's will, prompted by conflicting appeals. His subordination of judgment to the will of the Army is further illustrated by his attitude towards the invasion of Belgium. When he realised that a march across Belgium without the consent of its Government would bring Britain into the War, he sent for Von Moltke and asked him whether it would not be possible to change the war plan and concentrate on Russia. Von Moltke replied that it was too late, as all the preparations had been made on the assumption that the German Army would immediately march through Belgium and capture Paris in a given time. The Kaiser is stated to have replied: "Your uncle would have given me a different answer." Nevertheless he surrendered.

The "little war" to occupy Belgrade was the bait of the General Staff to land the Great War. Once its hook was in the gills of the Kaiser he was dragged along. The "little war" involved the mobilisation and declaration of war by Austria. That brought on the partial mobilisation of Russia. That drove Germany into the declaration of war against Russia. Then we were already in the World War.

In Austria and Russia the High Command were finally responsible for the War. They insisted on mobilisation whilst not unhopeful negotiations were still going on. Austrian mobilisation led to Russia mobilising her army so as to prevent any surprise movement across the frontier. Austria mobilised to strike at Serbia. Russia mobilised for a counter-blow. When the Kaiser, frightened by the thunder clouds, intervened personally with the Czar to avert war, he begged "Nicky" to cancel his Decree which had already gone forth, for the mobilisation of the Russian army. The Czar was willing to accede to this not unreasonable request, but the army leaders assured him that the "technical" difficulties of cancellation and even of partial demobilisation were insuperable. It was thus that the military chiefs in the leading countries of the Continent thrust the nations into war, whilst their impotent statesmen were still fumbling for peace. Each army believed in its own invincibility and was anxious to demonstrate it.

The belief in the superiority of the German Army was by no means confined to the Germans. I remember two or three years before the War, Lord Kitchener, who was then Sirdar of Egypt, calling upon me at the Treasury in connection with a loan for the development of the Sudan. As it was shortly after the Agadir crisis, we got on to the subject of the Franco-German position. He had a poor opinion of the French Army, and thought the Germans would "walk through them like partridges." Shortly afterwards, there was a banquet at Buckingham Palace to entertain some foreign potentate, and I sat next to a foreign Prince, who was not German. He also entertained the same opinion of the invincibility of the German Army, and used exactly the same metaphor as Lord Kitchener about the way it would scatter all other armies like partridges.

The French Army, on the other hand, were equally confident of their powers. They believed they had the best gun in the field — the famous *soixante-quinze* — and they were not far wrong. It is not the first time that rapture over the possession of a new military invention has made a nation less averse to war. The French had also great confidence in the training given to their officers and in the fine quality of their troops. They knew their organisation was excellent and they had the inevitable "plan." There never was a time since 1870 when the French Army had less fear of its great rival. The Russians had improved their Army in equipment and organisation since their defeat in

Manchuria. They felt infinitely superior to the Austrian Army, and deemed themselves quite a match for what was left of the German Army, after the better half of it had marched to the West. Generals in this frame of mind hungered for war and had no difficulty in manœuvring statesmen who did not know their own minds into positions where war became inevitable. Thus great armaments made war.

But the Army was not the only element that desired war. The populace caught the war fever. In every capital they clamoured for war. The theory which is propagated to-day by pacifist orators of the more cantankerous and less convincing type that the Great War was engineered by elder and middle-aged statesmen who sent younger men to face its horrors, is an invention. The elder statesmen did their feckless best to prevent war, whilst the youth of the rival countries were howling impatiently at their doors for immediate war. I saw it myself during the first four days of August, 1914. I shall never forget the warlike crowds that thronged Whitehall and poured into Downing Street, whilst the Cabinet was deliberating on the alternative of peace or war.

On Sunday there was a great crowd. Monday was Bank Holiday, and multitudes of young people concentrated in Westminster demonstrating for war against Germany. We could hear the hum of this surging mass from the Cabinet Chamber. On Monday afternoon I walked with Mr. Asquith to the House of Commons to hear Grey's famous speech. The crowd was so dense that no car could drive through it, and had it not been for police assistance we could not have walked a yard on our way. It was distinctly a pro-war demonstration. I remember observing at the time: "These people are very anxious to send our poor soldiers to face death; how many of them will ever go into battle themselves?" It was an unworthy doubt of the courage and patriotism of the demonstrators. A few days later recruiting stands were set up in the Horse Guards Parade, and that great open space beheld a crowd of young men surging around these stands and pushing their way through to give their names for enlistment in the Kitchener Armies. For days I heard, from the windows at Downing Street and the Treasury, the movement of a myriad feet towards the stands and the shouting of names of eager volunteers by the recruiting sergeants. The War had leapt into popularity between Saturday and Monday. On Saturday the Governor of the Bank of England called on me, as Chancellor of the Exchequer, to inform me on behalf of the City that the financial and trading interests in the City of London were totally opposed to our intervening in the War. By Monday there was a complete change. The threatened invasion of Belgium had set the nation on fire from sea to sea. By then Sir Edward Grey had ample evidence that his stipulation to Monsieur Cambon that we could only come to the aid of France if public opinion demanded it, was completely fulfilled. But Belgium was responsible for the change. Before then the Cabinet was hopelessly divided — fully one third, if not one half, being opposed to our entry into the War. After the German ultimatum to Belgium the Cabinet was almost unanimous. Had Germany without any provocation attacked France, I have no doubt that public sentiment in this country would have demanded that the Government should go to the aid of the victim of such wanton aggression. But it was thoroughly understood that on this occasion France was drawn into the quarrel by her Treaty obligations with Russia, and that if France had stood out of the dispute, Germany would have been only too pleased to leave her alone. The Franco-Russian Alliance was offensive and defensive. France was therefore bound to support Russia, whether she was interested in the *casus belli* or not. But Britain was not in that position. We had given no undertaking to come to the aid of Russia in any dispute, whether in the East or in the West. Russian autocracy was almost as unpopular with the people of these islands as Bolshevism is to-day. It was identified with Siberian prisons for political offenders, and with wholesale pogroms of harmless Jews, and with the massacre of workers whose only crime was the presentation of a petition for the redress of their undoubted wrongs. So long therefore as the war was likely to take the form of a contest between the autocracies of Germany and Austria on the one hand, and of Russia and her Allies on the other, British opinion was definitely opposed to intervention. It is a misfortune that Sir Edward Grey did not play sooner and more boldly this card of our treaty pledges to Belgium. It might have averted war altogether.

The London demonstrations had their counterparts in St. Petersburg, Berlin, Vienna and Paris. Blood was up and blood must flow. The populace and the military were at last of one mind. This combination took decision out of the hands of quivering and hesitant statesmanship, which desired peace but had not the resolution and boldness to do the simple things that could alone ensure it. Mr. Emil Ludwig's description of huge assemblies in the London squares demanding peace, whilst a small mob of French residents in London gathered together to clamour for war, is nonsense — and mischievous nonsense, because such a false picture deludes and misleads the statesmanship of the future as to the real perils against which it has to guard.

There is no better evidence of the change which came over public opinion than the following extracts from the *Daily News*. The great Liberal journal came tardily to the conclusion that war was justifiable. It represented the reluctance with which Liberals throughout the country contemplated the prospect of Britain entering into the War. Its testimony as to the state of public opinion during these eventful days is therefore not biased by any bellicosity. Here is a paragraph which appeared in that paper on the 3rd of August, which gives a very faithful account of the temper of the nation up to and including Sunday:

"There is no war party in this country. On the contrary, the horrors of war have already seized on the popular imagination, and in the highways and public vehicles in London yesterday, the populace were heard to express their indignation at the swift and tragic movements on the Continent."

Here is an account of the crowds on the following day, after it came to be known that Germany was threatening Belgium:

"The crowd continued to grow and grow. It extended from Trafalgar Square where it formed a dense mass, right along to the House of Commons, where its greatest number gathered about Downing Street, opposite the War Office. Groups of young men passed along in taxi-cabs singing the 'Marseillaise.' During the earlier part of the day there had been little disposition to demonstrate by the wearing of colours, but the tendency spread, and hundreds were buying Union Jacks. At seven o'clock in the evening, when Mr. Asquith left the subsequent Council Meeting to go to the House of Lords, the crowds cheered him with extraordinary fervour. It was a scene of enthusiasm unprecedented in recent times."

Here follows an extract from the account of the temper of the crowd of the 4th of August, after it had been known that we had delivered our ultimatum to Germany:

"In anticipation of the receipt of Germany's reply, huge crowds gathered in Whitehall and outside Buckingham Palace, and extraordinary scenes of enthusiasm were witnessed. . . . Ministers entering 10 Downing Street were loudly cheered.

"Not for years — since Mafeking night — have such crowds been seen in London, and Whitehall, the Mall, and Trafalgar Square, were all packed with excited throngs."

Then follows an account of the frenzy with which the Declaration of War was received:

"The enthusiasm culminated outside Buckingham Palace when it became known that war had been declared. The word was passed round by the police that silence was necessary, inasmuch as the King was holding a Council for the signing of the necessary proclamations. . . . The news that war had been declared was received with tremendous cheering which grew into a deafening roar when King George, Queen Mary and the Prince of Wales appeared on the balcony. . . .

"Westminster, Charing Cross, and the main thoroughfares round Westminster were thronged all last night with excited throngs, who displayed marked tendencies towards mafficking. Both in numbers and in noisiness it far exceeded the crowds of Monday. Union Jacks were everywhere to be seen, and the air was filled with the sound of patriotic songs; Trafalgar Square was almost impassable.

"A hostile crowd assembled outside the German Embassy, and smashed the windows. A special message was sent to Cannon Row, and a force of mounted and unmounted police was quickly on the scene, but had considerable difficulty in restoring order."

In face of these reports, given by a witness whose leaning was definitely against war, what becomes of the suggestion that we entered into the War against the vocal opposition of the people of this country? All wars are popular on the day of their declaration. To quote Walpole's famous observation upon a war into which he had been reluctantly forced: "They are ringing the bells now: soon they will be wringing their hands." But never was there a war so universally acclaimed as that into which Britain entered on the 4th of August, 1914.

### 4. 4TH OF AUGUST, 1914

Belgium the crucial issue — My proposals for preparedness — Belgium defies Germany — False charges against financiers — The Cabinet waits for news — Warning the Navy — The hour strikes — Emergency powers granted by Parliament: work of the Committee of Imperial Defence — Omissions from C.I.D. Survey: finance and munitions.

The 4th of August, 1914, is one of the world's fateful dates. The decision taken on that day in the name and on behalf of the British Empire altered the destiny of Europe. It is not too much to say that it gave a different turn or direction to the advance of the human race. The trumpets of war had already sounded in the East and in the West, and colossal armies were hurrying to the slaughter. Millions of men were either on the march or strapping on their armour for the conflict, and roads and railway tracks trembled with the weight of guns and munitions and all the sinister devices and mechanisms of human destruction!

Was there any hope that the great catastrophe could be averted? There were continuous meetings of the Cabinet on Friday, Saturday and Sunday. I experienced much difficulty in attending throughout because of the Conference at the Treasury to deal with the grave financial situation into which we had been plunged by war. But I heard and took part in most of the discussion. It revealed serious differences of opinion on the subject of British intervention in a Russo-German war even although France were forced by her Russian alliance to join in. Grey never definitely put before the Cabinet the proposition that Britain should in that event, declare war. He never expressed a clear and unequivocal opinion either way and no decision was therefore taken on that point. But it was quite clear from the course of the debate inside the Cabinet and the informal conversations which took place outside during our short adjournments that we were hopelessly divided on the subject of Britain entering the War on the issue as it had developed at that date.

Had the question of defending the neutrality and integrity of Belgium been raised there would not have been a dissentient voice on that issue. Lord Morley and John Burns might conceivably have stood out. Of that I am not convinced had a decision on that point alone been reached in time as a means of circumscribing the area of war and possibly of persuading Germany of the futility of waging it at all under conditions which would have been unfavourable to her preconcerted military schemes. But such a proposal was never submitted to our judgment.

The one faint glimmer still visible in the lowering sky was in the direction of Belgium. The dark clouds were rapidly closing up, but there was still one visible corner of blue. The Germans had signed a treaty not merely to respect, but to protect the neutrality of Belgium. Would they honour their bond? Great Britain was a party to that compact. If any one broke its terms, Britain was bound to throw in her might against the invader. Would the faith of Prussia, strengthened by the fear of Britain, prevail? If the treaty stood, the situation might yet be saved.

The policy I urged upon my colleagues was not one merely of passive non-intervention in the struggle between Germany and Austria on the one hand and Russia and France on the other. We were not in the position of France. She was bound by Treaty to support Russia in her quarrels with Germany. We were under no such obligation. I proposed, therefore, that we should take immediate steps to increase and strengthen our Army in numbers and equipment, so that when we judged the time had come for intervention, none of the belligerents could afford to disregard our appeal. Had Germany respected the integrity of Belgium, that policy would have been the wisest course to pursue. There would have been plenty of time for passions to exhaust their force and for the sanguine expectations of military enthusiasm to evaporate. The problem of France would have been a different one; the march of events would have been slower. France, instead of having to defend a frontier of over five hundred miles, without fortresses or artificial barriers, could have concentrated all her strength on defending a frontier of two hundred and fifty miles protected by formidable fortresses. An army (including reserves) of 3,000,000 men, holding entrenched positions on this narrow frontier, would have been invincible, and Germany might well have been content merely to defend her frontiers in the West, and throw her armies into Poland. There, difficulties of transport, bad roads, inadequate railways, immense distances, would have postponed decision for weeks if not for months. It took Germany over twelve months' hard fighting to conquer Poland. Even then the Russian Army was still in being and ready to resume the conflict in 1916. British intervention in the cause of peace might then have induced saner counsels. Britain was the one Power in Europe that had never yet been beaten in a European war. With her immunity from attack, with her immense fleet manned by the most skilful seamen in the world, with her enormous resources, she could be reckoned upon to wear down any Power. Had Britain been able to throw into the scale a well-equipped army of a million men to support her fleet, Germany would have hesitated before she rejected terms of peace and thus brought the British Empire into the conflict on the side of her enemies. These were the arguments I advanced in favour of non-intervention in the struggle if the neutrality of Belgium were respected.

The invasion of Belgium put an end to all these possibilities. Then our Treaty obligations were involved. On Sunday, the 2nd of August, the omens were not propitious. There were clear indications that the German forces were massing on the Belgian frontier. Germany had appealed to Belgium for permission to march through her territories to attack France. Belgian Ministers hesitated, but the answer given by Belgium's heroic King constitutes one of the most thrilling pages of history. The British Government, on hearing the news, issued an ultimatum to Germany warning her that unless by twelve o'clock on August 4th assurances were received from Germany that the neutrality of Belgium would be treated as inviolate, Britain would have no alternative but to take steps to enforce that treaty. Would Germany realise what war with Britain meant, arrest the progress of her armies, change her strategy, and perhaps consent to a parley? How much depended upon the answer to these questions! We could suspect then what it meant: we know now. There were many of us who could hardly believe that those responsible for guiding the destiny of Germany would be so fatuous as deliberately to provoke the hostility of the British Empire, with its inexhaustible reserves and with its grim tenacity of purpose once it engaged in a struggle.

Amongst those who criticised the intervention of Britain there are two sections. There are those who pretend to believe that this was a war intrigued and organised and dictated by financiers for their own purpose. In Germany and amongst the friends of Germany in other lands there are those who ascribe our action to the irritation produced by a growing jealousy of Germany's strength and prosperity, and British politicians are pictured as eagerly on the pounce for an opportunity to destroy this redoubtable rival. As to both, the tale of these days is a complete answer. I was Chancellor of the Exchequer and, as such, I saw Money before the war; I saw it immediately after the outbreak of war; I lived with it for days, and did my best to steady its nerve, for I knew how much depended on restoring its confidence; and I say that Money was a frightened and trembling thing: Money shivered at the prospect. It is a foolish and ignorant libel to call this a financiers' war. As to the second form of attack on British action, big businesses everywhere wanted to keep out of it, and as to the rest this narrative will be a reply. Here were no eager men praying for the hour to arrive when they could strike down a great commercial rival.

It was a day full of rumours and reports, throbbing with anxiety. Hour after hour passed, and no sign came from Germany. There were only disturbing rumours of further German movements towards the Belgian line. The evening came. Still no answer. Shortly after nine o'clock I was summoned to the Cabinet Room for an important consultation. There I found Mr. Asquith, Sir Edward Grey, and Mr. Haldane, all looking very grave. Mr. M'Kenna arrived soon afterwards. A message from the German Foreign Office to the German Embassy in London had been intercepted. It was not in cipher. It informed the German Ambassador that the British Ambassador in Berlin had asked for his passports at 7 P.M. and declared war. A copy of this message was passed on to me, and I have it still in my possession. A facsimile of this fateful document as it was submitted to us at this solemn conference is reproduced on the next page.

"Time: 9.5 P.M.
Date: Aug. 4th, 1914.

"The following message has been intercepted by W.O. Censor:

'To German Ambassador from Berlin.

English Ambassador has just demanded his passport shortly after seven o'clock declaring war.

(*Signed*) JAGOW.'"

No news had been received from Sir Edward Goschen.[1] We were therefore at a loss to know what it meant. It

[1] We learnt subsequently that his telegram to us announcing his action had been held up by the German authorities. It never reached us, and not until Sir Edward Goschen arrived back in Britain some nine days later did we hear of its despatch and obtain a copy of its text.

looked like an attempt on the part of the Germans to anticipate the hour of the declaration of war in order to effect some *coup* either against British ships or British coasts. Should this intercept be treated as the commencement of hostilities, or should we wait until we either heard officially from Germany that our conditions had been rejected, or until the hour of the ultimatum had expired? We sat at the green table in the famous room where so many historic decisions had been taken in the past. It was not then a very well-lighted room, and my recollection is that the lights had not all been turned on, and in the dimness you might imagine the shades of the great British statesmen of the past taking part in a conference which meant so much to the Empire, to the building up of which they had devoted their lives — Chatham, Pitt, Fox, Castlereagh, Canning, Peel, Palmerston, Disraeli, Gladstone. In that simple, unadorned, almost dingy room they also had pondered over the problems which had perplexed their day. But never had they been confronted with so tremendous a decision as that with which British Ministers were faced in these early days of August, 1914.

And now came the terrible decision: should we unleash the savage dogs of war at once, or wait until the time limit of the ultimatum had expired, and give peace the benefit of even such a doubt as existed for at least another two hours? We had no difficulty in deciding that the Admiralty was to prepare the fleet against any sudden attack from the German flotillas and to warn our coasts against any possible designs from the same quarter. But should we declare war now, or at midnight? The ultimatum expired at midnight in Berlin. That was midnight according to Central Europe time: it meant eleven o'clock according to Greenwich time. We resolved to wait until eleven. Would any message arrive from Berlin before eleven informing us of the intention of Ger-

TELEPHOHE MESSAGES RECEIVED BY CHIEF CENSOR

FROM CHIEF CENSOR. WAR OFFICE.

---

Time: 9.5 p.m.

Date: August 4th 1914.

The following message has been intercepted by W.O.Censor:-

To:.German.Ambassador........................ .

From.......Berlin................................

English Ambassadår has just demanded his passport shortly after seven o'clock declaring war

/Signed/ Jagow

Asst Chief Censor
[signature]

THE BRITISH CABINET'S FIRST INTIMATION OF THE OUTBREAK OF WAR CONVEYED IN AN INTERCEPTED TELEGRAM FROM THE GERMAN GOVERNMENT TO THE GERMAN AMBASSADOR IN LONDON, PRINCE LICHNOWSKI

many to respect Belgian neutrality? If it came there was still a faint hope that something might be arranged before the marching armies crashed into each other.

As the hour approached a deep and tense solemnity fell on the room. No one spoke. It was like awaiting the signal for the pulling of a lever which would hurl millions to their doom — with just a chance that reprieve might arrive on time. Our eyes wandered anxiously from the clock to the door, and from the door to the clock, and little was said.

"Boom!" The deep notes of Big Ben rang out into the night the first strokes in Britain's most fateful hour since she arose out of the deep. A shuddering silence fell upon the room. Every face was suddenly contracted in a painful intensity. "Doom!" "Doom!" "Doom!" to the last stroke. The big clock echoed in our ears like the hammer of destiny. What destiny? Who could tell? We had challenged the most powerful military empire the world has yet brought forth. France was too weak alone to challenge its might and Russia was ill-organised, ill-equipped, corrupt. We knew what brunt Britain would have to bear. Could she stand it? There was no doubt or hesitation in any breast. But let it be admitted without shame that a thrill of horror quickened every pulse. Did we know that before peace would be restored to Europe we should have to wade through four years of the most concentrated slaughter, mutilation, suffering, devastation, and savagery which mankind has ever witnessed? That twelve millions of the gallant youth of the nations would be slain, that another twenty millions would be mutilated? That Europe would be crushed under the weight of a colossal war debt? That only one empire would stand the shock? That the three other glittering empires of the world would have been flung to the dust, and shattered beyond repair? That revolution, famine, and anarchy would sweep over half of Europe, and that their menace would scorch the rest of this hapless continent?

Has the full tale yet been told? Who can tell? But had we foreseen it all on the 4th of August we could have done no other.

Twenty minutes after the hour Mr. Winston Churchill came in and informed us that the wires had already been sent to the British ships of war in every sea announcing the fact that war had been declared and that they were to act accordingly. Soon afterward we dispersed. There was nothing more to say that night. To-morrow would bring us novel tasks and new bearings. As I left I felt like a man standing on a planet that had been suddenly wrenched from its orbit by a demoniacal hand and that was spinning wildly into the unknown.

On the morrow Ministers woke up to a new and unaccustomed outlook. Hitherto we had been dealing with Britain and the world at peace. Now we were confronted with the problems of Europe, including Britain, plunged into the vortex of war.

Measures which conferred unheard-of powers on the Executive were passed through both Houses of Parliament after a few hours' discussion. Most of them had been carefully thought out during the tranquil years of peace by the numerous sub-committees of the Committee of Imperial Defence. Of what was accomplished by that remarkable body in the years before the War, and of its foresight, nothing has yet been written. Its founder — Earl Balfour — when he set up the Committee of Imperial Defence as an essential part of the organisation of defence, rendered a service to his country which deserves immortality. Under Mr. Asquith it carried on its task and traditions with undiminished vigour and persistence. It therefore came to pass that when war was thrust upon us, plans which played a vital part in our achievement of victory lay at hand in the pigeonholes of the Committee of Imperial Defence, prepared down to the last detail and ready to be put into execution. Credit must be given to Lord Balfour for the creation and direction of this body and to Mr. Asquith for making the fullest use of its powers and for further developing its area and scope, but above all it is due to three indefatigable secretaries, Sir George Clarke, later Lord Sydenham, Admiral Sir Charles Ottley, and the ablest and most resourceful of them all, Lieutenant-Colonel Sir Maurice Hankey. The War Book, perfected under Mr. Asquith's chairmanship, and the work of Lord Haldane at the War Office — his organisation of the Territorials, creation of a General Staff as a thinking brain for the Army, and the foundation of the Officers' Training Corps — constitute a powerful answer to those who taunt the Liberal Government with being quite unprepared for the contingency of war.

To these instances may be added the preparedness of the Navy, more especially in the matter of capital ships, under the guidance of Lord Tweedmouth, Mr. M'Kenna, and Mr. Winston Churchill.

But the C.I.D. had by no means completed its exhaustive survey of the possibilities and demands of war, when the storm broke upon us. That probably accounts for the fact that two contingencies which turned out to be of vital consequence had not yet been explored. The first was the financial chaos which would inevitably ensue, especially in a country which transacted most of the intricate business of financing international trade.

The second was the enormous expenditure of munitions which would be involved in war under modern conditions. No one had contemplated the construction of earthen fortifications on so gigantic a scale as that which developed in the Great War upon which Europe had now entered. The

Torres Vedras lines were a matter of a few miles. So were Todleben's earthen ramparts at Sebastopol. The colossal earthworks of 1914–18 extended over hundreds of miles. The myriads of heavy guns, trench mortars, and machine guns, the millions of projectiles which became an essential part of the equipment of armies engaged in such vast operations, were beyond the contemplation of any student of the exigencies of war. With these two unforeseen emergencies it was my destiny to be called upon to deal.

### 5. Cabinet Ignorance of French's Strategical Advice

Sir John French's proposals — Lord Kitchener and the Cabinet — Joffre's ideas of German strategy — News of the retreat from Mons — Cabinet without news of military situation — Two vital facts not fully and promptly appreciated by Allied Generals — Marshal Foch on lessons of 1914 fighting.

To weave the events of the War into a consecutive narrative is no part of my undertaking. That task has already been discharged by other and more expert pens than mine. I simply set myself to contribute to the story of the War more or less detached incidents with which I was especially concerned. The Cabinet were told very little about military or naval movements. Insofar as there was any civilian consultation it was confined to the Prime Minister, Mr. Winston Churchill, and occasionally Lord Haldane and Sir Edward Grey.

The Cabinet was ignorant of the fact that in the Councils of War held immediately after the declaration, Sir John French was opposed to the Expeditionary Force being taken to the Belgian frontier. The first War Council held after the entry of this country into the War was on August 5th. Ministers were represented by the Prime Minister, Lord Haldane, Sir Edward Grey and Mr. Winston Churchill; the Navy by Prince Louis of Battenberg, and the Army by Lord Kitchener, Lord Roberts, Sir John French, Sir Ian Hamilton, Sir Charles Douglas, Sir H. C. Sclater, Sir John Cowans,

Sir Stanley von Donop, Sir Douglas Haig, Sir J. M. Grierson, Sir A. J. Murray and Sir Henry Wilson. At this Council Sir John French said: 'that the prearranged plan to meet this situation had been that the Expeditionary Force should mobilise simultaneously with the French and concentrate behind the French Army at Maubeuge by the fifteenth day of mobilisation. The intention then had been for it to move eastward towards the Meuse and act on the left of the French Army against the right German flank. It had, however, always been felt that, if we were late in commencing our mobilisation, as had actually happened, we should have to change our plan. Maubeuge, in his opinion, was no longer a safe place at which to concentrate. He suggested that Amiens would now be the safer place at which to concentrate. The general tenor of his opinion was that the Expeditionary Force should be sent to France; a safe place for concentration should be selected, and events should be awaited. He added that, as an alternative, and owing to the existing conditions, he was inclined to consider a landing at Antwerp with a view to coöperation with the Belgians and Dutch. The three forces would form a considerable army, and would necessarily contain a large German force, and they might be able to advance southward. The feasibility of this plan, however, was largely a naval question. As an alternative to a landing at Antwerp, he proposed a landing in France and a movement to Antwerp by the coast route.'

He does not seem to have received any support from any quarter for his suggestions and he appears not to have pressed them any further. The general effect of the consultations which took place on that and the following day was that we should conform our strategy with that of the French army.

Had either of the two courses been adopted, it is clear now that the whole course of events would have been different, and particularly could this have been the case if five

British Divisions had occupied Antwerp. There would have been then on the German flank five excellent Divisions of picked troops. This would have provided the necessary stiffening for the Belgian militia. The Germans would not have considered it safe to penetrate as deeply into France as they subsequently did without clearing their flank from this redoubtable menace. They would thus have lost valuable time, and time was the essence of their plan.

This advice given by the Commander-in-Chief of the Expeditionary Forces was withheld from the Cabinet and was therefore never discussed by Ministers. During the three or four weeks that followed the declaration of War the attention of the Cabinet was concentrated upon questions of recruiting, the escape of the *Goeben,* the conjecture as to what Turkey was likely to do, messages from Greece, and occasional obscure reports from the Front, which were delivered to us at the beginning of each sitting by Lord Kitchener in his loud staccato voice, and with that remote look in his eyes, directed at no one in particular, which was a sure indication of his unease amid surroundings with which he was not familiar. He was sitting in council with men belonging to the profession with which he had wrestled all his life, and for which, in his heart, he had the usual mixture of military contempt and apprehension. His main idea at the Council table was to tell the politicians as little as possible of what was going on and get back to his desk at the War Office as quickly as he could decently escape. Now and again he flashed out an illuminating sentence of information. Just before the first German blow was delivered, I recollect that Lord Kitchener departed from his usual secretiveness so far as to reveal to us what General Joffre's intentions were. The French Commander-in-Chief, according to him, did not believe that the Germans would march through the Central and Western Provinces of Belgium, because it was an industrial area where the roads were not good and not in the least suited to the movement of large bodies of men with transport and artillery. His idea was that the German Army would swing towards the southeastern corner of Belgium, and attempt to pierce the Allied defences in the direction of Namur. Lord Kitchener said that Joffre's idea of the French strategy was that of a boxer who covered himself from his antagonist's blows with his left arm whilst he came round with the right and hit an unexpected blow at his antagonist's weakest point. Lord Kitchener informed us that he thought General Joffre's conception of the German plan of operation was all wrong. He was firmly convinced the Germans would march along all the eleven roads that made for the frontier, and would endeavour to outflank the Allied forces at a point much higher up than that indicated by General Joffre. However, he said, Joffre held stubbornly to his view. We were soon to know the result of this fatal miscalculation.

One morning I was engaged in the Treasury, disposing of a few urgent financial problems before the meeting of the Cabinet, when Mr. Winston Churchill walked into my room with an unusually gloomy mien. He had clearly some grave news to communicate, and as I was surrounded by officials he beckoned me to come outside. We went into another room, and he then told me what he had just heard from Kitchener: that the Germans had advanced with enormous forces along the upper Belgian roads; had driven our troops from Mons, and that the whole British force was now in full retreat pursued by a German force of overwhelmingly superior strength. Mr. Churchill records that he was "relieved and overjoyed at my response," but I certainly felt, more than ever, that we were up against it, and that nothing but a mobilisation of the whole of our strength could save Europe and the world from an incalculable disaster.

For several days we had no reports as to what was happening. We heard nothing of the great struggle in Lorraine where the French invading army was hurled back across the frontier after a pitched battle in which the Germans won a decisive victory more by a superiority in artillery than in numbers. We heard nothing of the defeat of the French on the Meuse and the advance of the German Army from that direction towards Paris. We were in a complete fog as to the movements and plans of our own little army. All we knew was that they quitted their positions on the Belgian frontier and were pressed — if not pursued — southwards by overwhelming German forces. We were assured, however, day-by-day, that the retreating army had at last taken up a position in which they were prepared to make a stand with every hope of successfully repelling their assailants. And then on the following morning we were informed that they had abandoned this position and resumed their retreat, but were prepared to fight on a more defensible line, which we observed, was many leagues nearer Paris.

We heard nothing of the hurried crossing of the Somme, the Aisne, the Marne, the Oise, and we were not told for days of the retirement behind the Seine, miles to the south of Paris. The Cabinet was bewildered by the scrappy and incoherent reports given to it each morning by Lord Kitchener. He was pressed to give us a more satisfactory account of what was really happening. But he protested that he had imparted to his colleagues all the information which had been vouchsafed to him from our Headquarters in France. The first intimation we received of the seriousness and the magnitude of the defeat inflicted upon the Allied Armies was a report in the *Times* — published in defiance of the Censor — giving a graphic account of the march of the German troops through Amiens singing the "Wacht Am Rhein" along the deserted streets. The Cabinet ultimately decided to send Lord Kitchener to France to find out. Conflicting accounts of what passed between our great Generals on this occasion have already appeared, and I feel it is no part of my task to reconcile them. It was my first experience of the fallibility of the Military Leaders — the stubborn miscalculation, muddle and lack of coördination, which resulted in mowing down the flower of the finest armies ever put in the field by France and England. I need hardly say that we were surprised and disappointed by a collapse that had not in the least been anticipated by us or our military advisors. But there was no panic. Reinforcements were hastened to France. Soon afterwards the victory of the Marne — one of the great historical battles of the world — checked the German advance. For the moment utter disaster was averted, and we had time to make fresh plans for the future.

From the fighting of the first two months of the War there emerged two facts of supreme importance in their relation to the strategy of the War. Had these facts been fully appreciated by the Allied generals at the time and had they conformed their plans to this understanding the War would have taken a different course. The first fact was the enormous superiority of the Germans in artillery — not so much in numbers as in weight and the definite advantage accruing to them in this respect. For the first time the heavy gun was treated as a mobile weapon and its superiority in range and destructive effect to the ordinary field gun broke up the French offensive and crumpled up the French plan of campaign.

The second was the difficulty — even with superior gun power — of dislodging a brave and tenacious enemy from prepared positions where the defender operated under cover. The French failed completely in open warfare in Belgium and Lorraine. The longer range and more shattering power of the German artillery broke up their attack, demoralised their troops and forced them to a speedy retreat to save their armies from utter destruction. On the other hand the defeated troops successfully repelled all attacks by the victorious foe on the Grand Couronné of Nancy, although made with the same overwhelming gun superiority. The French dug themselves in on these hills and the Germans were beaten off with great loss in spite of their more powerful artillery.

Marshal Foch in his Memoirs, writing of the lessons taught (but not learnt) by the fighting of August and September, 1914, says:

"Generally speaking, it seemed proved that the new means of action furnished by automatic weapons and long-range guns enabled the defence to hold up any attempt at breaking through long enough for a counter-attack to be launched with saving effect. The 'pockets', which resulted from partial attacks which were successful and seemingly even decisive, could not be maintained, in spite of very costly losses, long enough to ensure a definite rupture of the adversary's line. They could be too quickly rendered uninhabitable and useless for the assailant.

"When a defensive front has been forced by superior numbers to fall back, it has not thereby been broken. Counter-attacks on the assailant's flank have often consumed the latter's reserves and threatened his communications, to the extent of eventually stopping his partial advance and causing him to retire.

"Many new subjects for reflection are offered when we examine the limitations and the weaknesses of an offensive which, while tactically successful at first, is continued in violation of the principles which modern weapons have now imposed. . . ."

When did the Allied generals come to these wise conclusions? Not before the bloody assaults of Artois and Champagne in 1915 — not even with the still more sanguinary battles of the Somme in 1916.

## CHAPTER III

# SIR EDWARD GREY: FOREIGN SECRETARY

Influence of the personal factor on historical events — Importance of Sir Edward Grey's character for understanding of war story — Appearance and reality — Aloofness from Party conflicts — His hesitations in the fateful days — His belated appeals not heeded — His diplomatic failures — High office by heredity and tradition — Ignorance of foreigners.

I CANNOT give a fair presentation of the events that led to the war, prolonged its duration, and aggravated and extended its desolation, without a candid picture of the personalities who controlled and directed these events. Their characteristics were responsible for much that happened for better or for worse. It is a mistaken view of history to assume that its episodes were entirely due to fundamental causes which could not be averted, and that they were not precipitated or postponed by the intervention of personality. The appearance of one dominating individual in a critical position at a decisive moment has often altered the course of events for years and even generations. A gifted and resolute person has often postponed for centuries a catastrophe which appeared imminent and which but for him would have befallen. On the other hand a weak or hesitant person has invited or expedited calamity which but for him might never have happened or which at least could have been long deferred. I cannot therefore tell my tale of the Great War without giving some idea of the men whose qualities either hastened or failed to avert it, or had the effect of prolonging its devastating course once it had started.

I have found it an exceedingly difficult and occasionally

disagreeable task to give an accurate account of the prominent figures in the War when so many of them were colleagues with whom I always enjoyed the most pleasant personal relations: some of them men with whom I worked in perfect amity for over a decade — some to whom I owed many personal courtesies and kindnesses — some who accorded help in the kind of attacks which now and again threaten to overwhelm any man who in politics chooses the more controversial rôle.

These considerations more especially apply to my examination of the attributes of Mr. Asquith, Sir Edward Grey, Mr. Bonar Law, Mr. Churchill and the other distinguished political leaders with whom I was privileged to work for so many years in cordiality and good fellowship.

As Lord Grey (or as he then was, Sir Edward Grey) was among those who played a decisive part in the movements and occurrences that led to the war, it is necessary to an understanding of my narrative that I should give a frank estimate of his qualities. His tenure of the crucial office of Foreign Secretary constituted an essential part of what happened, and his personality was distinctly one of the elements that contributed to the great catastrophe. I cannot therefore leave out my impressions of his character in my tale of events. It would not be worth while doing so — it would not be fair to my readers — unless I gave a frank analysis of the man who strove honestly to avert war but failed, and said something of the characteristics and shortcomings that were largely responsible for that failure. I appreciate the imperative duty of not allowing any irrelevant considerations to influence judgment. For that reason in my character sketches of political personages I have sternly repressed every tendency to partisan bias.

The public know less of Sir Edward Grey than of any conspicuous statesman of his time. His reputation is therefore

*Photo. by Dudley Glanfield, London*

VISCOUNT GREY OF FALLODON, K.G.

*Secretary of State for Foreign Affairs, 1905–1916*

on a purely conjectural foundation. Sir Edward Grey's position in public life was always entirely different from that which Mr. Asquith established for himself. The latter had neither rank nor wealth to help him along. He won his way to the Premiership entirely by superb talent and parliamentary achievement. No Prime Minister in history — with the notable exceptions of Gladstone and Disraeli — possessed a better mental equipment for a political career. Sir Edward Grey has high intelligence but of a more commonplace texture. It is reflected in his speeches, which are clear, correct and orderly, but are characterised by no distinction of phrase or thought. His handling of foreign affairs was of the same conventional type. His influence is derived from other sources. He had qualities, largely of appearance, manner and restraint, which gave the impression of the "strong, silent man" whom the generation brought up on Carlyle earnestly sought, and, when they thought they had discovered him, fervently adored. In the war and post-war days of Clemenceau, Foch, Lenin, Mussolini, Roosevelt and Hitler — all talkers — that legend has become a little mildewed. The strongest men of history have never been silent. One of the strongest — Napoleon — could on occasion even be garrulous. Just before 1914 the vogue of the taciturn was still prevalent and no man profited as much by it as Grey. His striking physiognomy with the thin lips, the firmly closed mouth, and the chiselled features give the impression of cold, hammered steel. Add to this exterior the reticence of speech and the calm, level utterance on the rare occasions when he spoke, and you were led to expect imperturbable strength in an emergency. He did not command the flaming phrase that illumines but sometimes also scorches and leaves behind an irritating burn. On the other hand he possessed to perfection that correctitude of phrase and demeanour which passes for — and sometimes is — diplomacy, and that serene flow of unexceptionable diction which is apt to be reckoned as statesmanship until a crisis comes to put these urbanities to the test.

Apart from these attributes, Grey's unique position was due to the care with which he kept almost entirely out of the clash of party conflicts, and never measured his prowess against the formidable gladiators who held the arena in his time. It is not that he was less contentious than Mr. Asquith: for Mr. Asquith was the least contentious of politicians. He shrank from the combat until duty forced him into it. But he never failed then to play a redoubtable part in the front of the fight whatever the hazard. He was therefore subjected to every kind of assault, fair and foul, to which all active politicians are liable from exasperated adversaries. On the other hand, although Sir Edward Grey's uneasy attitude towards all his various leaders in turn proves him to be temperamentally fractious, he was fortunate throughout his political career in avoiding any trial of dialectical strength or skill with the deadly swordsmen who held the arena during his political life. Even when he was busily negotiating faction inside his party he preferred to remain behind the lines, leaving the actual fighting to Lord Rosebery, Mr. Asquith, and Mr. Haldane. He thus succeeded in attaining high position in Party Governments without incurring any of the risks of active engagement in Party struggles. The only office he ever held was by tradition deemed to be immune from the slings and arrows of partisan warfare. In opposition he substantially confined his sparring activities to impartial comments on foreign affairs. His administration in office and his allotted function out of office alike were therefore not subjected to the fierce onslaughts that test the quality of political leaders. His face was never disfigured by any blows received in action, for he consistently shunned the political battlefield. He was specially fitted to discharge the duties of an office administered under such tranquil conditions with a dignity and grace which appealed to all parties alike. Hence the unique position of immunity from severe criticism which he has always enjoyed.

In the policy which led up to our participation in the war, Sir Edward Grey, amongst British statesmen, played the leading part. His navigation of foreign waters was not seriously challenged. Whether he could have steered Europe clear of the rocks must always be a matter of conjecture and inference from the facts. Men who are at all interested in that aspect of the problem will for some time draw differing conclusions. I am inclined to believe that the verdict of posterity will be adverse to his handling of the situation.

Of one thing there can be no doubt: he failed calamitously in his endeavours to avert the Great War. As to Sir Edward Grey's hesitations during the fateful days when the thunderclouds were deepening and rapidly darkening the sky, I have endeavoured to give an accurate summary of the facts. They tell their own tale of a pilot whose hand trembled in the palsy of apprehension, unable to grip the levers and manipulate them with a firm and clear purpose. He was pursuing his avowed policy of waiting for public opinion to decide his direction for him. He reminded me of a Chairman of Committees whom I knew in the tumultuous days of the 1892–95 Parliament. It was peculiarly a Parliament that demanded firmness as well as fairness in the occupant of the Chair. Mr. Mellor was an able, cultured and upright man of gentlemanly exterior and demeanour, who would have been acclaimed by all parties as an ideal Chairman in quiet times. But the Home Rule Parliament of 1892–95 was the most tempestuous I have seen, and there Mr. Mellor's suavity and judicial courtesy were a pitiable sight. I can hear him now, rising in his place and looking at neither side lest it be suggested that he was accusing one or the other of being responsible, and calling out in an appealing but not compelling voice: "Order, Order!" Sir Edward Grey's impartial but weak and uncompelling appeals to the raging nations of Europe to keep the peace always recall this parliamentary incident to my memory. In the din he was barely heard — he certainly was not heeded. Had he warned Germany in time of the point at which Britain would declare war — and wage it with her whole strength — the issue would have been different. I know it is said that he was hampered by the divisions in the Cabinet. On one question, however, there was no difference of opinion — the invasion of Belgium. He could at any stage of the negotiations have secured substantial unanimity amongst his colleagues on that point. At the very worst there would have been only two resignations, and those would have followed our entry into war, whatever the issue upon which it was fought. The assent of all the Opposition leaders was assured, and thus in the name of a united people he could have intimated to the German Government that if they put into operation their plan of marching through Belgium they would encounter the active hostility of the British Empire. And he could have uttered this warning in sufficient time to leave the German military authorities without any excuse for not changing their dust-laden plans. When the ultimatum was actually delivered, war had already broken out between Germany and her neighbours, and the German staff were able with some show of reason to inform the Kaiser that it was then too late to alter their arrangements without jeopardising the German chance of victory. As a matter of fact, the Kaiser was even then anxious, in order to avoid a conflict with us, to divert his forces from the Belgian frontier, and turn their faces towards the East. Von Moltke gave him the answer which I have already indicated.

It was a temperamental failure. Grey's mind was not

made for prompt action. It is reported of the late Sir Hugh Bell, the great Northern industrial magnate, who was a colleague of Sir Edward Grey for years on the N. E. Railway, that he once said of him: "Grey is a good colleague because he never takes any risks: and he is a thoroughly bad colleague for the same reason." That saying explains why he did not take his stand on Belgium in time to give those who dreaded war in Germany a chance of reconsidering their plans in time. He would not take the risk involved in making such a bold declaration. He was still hoping that war could be averted by quieter and more conventional methods. He altogether lacked that quality of audacity which makes a great minister.

His Arbitration Treaty with America was a notable event. The rest of his big efforts came to naught. His Balkan Settlement in 1913 fell to pieces as soon as it left our shores. His London Convention was luckily rejected, for had it been in operation during the war, it would have deprived us of our most effective weapon against Germany. He failed to keep Turkey, and afterwards Bulgaria, out of the war. His stiff and formal beckonings to them to cross over to our side could only provoke ridicule. There were many obvious expedients — including the sending of a special envoy to Turkey and Bulgaria who would be empowered to promise financial support — that he might have employed to keep both or either out of the war. He resorted to none of them. These last two failures, which a more strenuous or resourceful Foreign Minister would have converted into success, prolonged the war by years, and very nearly caused the defeat of the Allies. His advice to Greece in 1914 not to join forces with the Allies was a calamity which cost us the Gallipoli Peninsula, and conduced to the overthrow of Serbia. He hesitated and fumbled in his negotiations to bring Italy into the war. As Luigi Villari says in his interesting and illuminating book, "The War on the Italian Front": "The negotiations had been shilly-shallying for months." Had it not been that Grey had taken a few weeks' holiday and left Mr. Asquith — who was quite capable of coming to bold decisions — in charge of the Foreign Office in his absence, Italy might have sulked at the cold, critical treatment accorded her advances. In a few days Mr. Asquith brushed aside trivialities and brought the negotiations to a stage that led to a speedy decision. Had he not done so, what would have happened to the Allies? The Austrian armies could have concentrated their whole strength on Russia, and that great country would have succumbed in 1915 to the joint attack of Germany and Austria. Throughout, Grey mistook correctitude for rectitude.

Sir Edward Grey belongs to the class which, through heredity and tradition, expects to find a place on the magisterial bench to sit in judgment upon and above their fellowmen, before they ever have any opportunity to make themselves acquainted with the tasks and trials of mankind — and some of them preserve those magisterial airs through life. They are remote from the hard work of the community. They take it for granted. The men drawn from that class who attained preëminence, like Palmerston, Randolph Churchill, Salisbury and Balfour, threw themselves into the arduous conflicts of politics and fought their way to the top, giving and taking on the way the blows that hammer character. Sir Edward Grey stepped into generalship without ever doing any soldiering — not a good training for facing real danger. It was all right when things went smoothly, and all you had to do was to put forward a soldierly appearance on parade. It is a different thing when you are suddenly confronted with the greatest and most deadly diplomatic struggle ever seen between great nations. The conflicts of politics are as good a discipline and hardening for the troubles of an official career as war is for the military leader. The veteran who never fought a battle may escape the perils of shot and shell through which his comrades have passed, but he also misses the experience which would be useful to him when at last he finds himself thrown into action.

He was the most insular of our statesmen, and knew less of foreigners through contact with them than any other Minister in the Government. He rarely, if ever, crossed the seas. Northumberland was good enough for him, and if he could not get there and needed a change, there was his fishing lodge in Hampshire. This was a weakness — and it was a definite weakness in a Foreign Secretary, and especially in a Foreign Secretary with no imagination — which accounted for some of his most conspicuous failures. He had no real understanding of foreigners — I am not at all sure that for this purpose he would not include Scotland, Ireland and Wales as foreign parts. Moreover, when a Conference in some foreign capital might have saved the situation, his dislike of leaving England stood in the way. When he suggested a Conference of Ambassadors of the Four Powers a few days before the War, he proposed that it should be held in London. I shall point out later on how this egotistic insularity prevented the summoning of a Conference which might, and I think would, at that stage have brought Bulgaria on to the Allied side. The ideal Foreign Secretary would be a cross between a recluse and a tramp, *e.g.* between Sir Edward Grey and Mr. Ramsay MacDonald.

A Cabinet which was compelled by political and economic exigencies to concentrate its energies on domestic problems left the whole field of foreign affairs to Sir Edward Grey. Anyone reading with care and impartiality the record of the way in which he missed his opportunities must come to the conclusion that he lacked the knowledge of foreign countries and the vision, imagination, breadth of mind and that high courage, bordering on audacity, which his immense task demanded.

CHAPTER IV

# THE FINANCIAL CRISIS

## 1. How We Saved The City

Breakdown of foreign exchanges — Effect on London Accepting Houses — Effects on Banks and Stock Markets — Stock Exchange closed — Increasing the fiduciary issue — Conferences at the Treasury — Prolonging the Bank Holiday — Mr. Chamberlain brought into the Financial Conference — My statement to the House of Commons on August 5th — Currency and Bank Notes Act — Releasing credit: Bank of England rediscounts bills — Loans to Accepting Houses — Ending the moratorium — Act of Indemnity — Absence of general panic — Character sketch of Lord Cunliffe — Lord Cunliffe in France — Government losses trivial — Lord Rothschild's help.

The political situation naturally did not develop without immediate and violent reaction on the inherently unstable financial equilibrium of the whole world, which is maintained by perhaps the most sensitive organisation devised by man; and the financial crisis which marked the outbreak of the War began some days before hostilities actually commenced. This was inevitable, because finance, or indeed the conduct of business operations of every nature, is based on successful anticipation and the ability to foresee and to discount or prepare for coming conditions. It was in July, 1914, before the Austrian ultimatum was presented, that uneasiness showed itself on the bourses of the world, when Vienna, Berlin, and Paris commenced to sell securities to an unusual extent. These transactions were for the most part effected in New York, where the stream of orders to sell quickly grew into a torrent. On the 27th, after diplomatic relations between Austria-Hungary and Serbia had been broken off, the volume of selling became such that the foreign exchange market in New York gave way under the unprecedented pressure to remit to Europe the proceeds of sales. From New York this breakdown spread to other foreign exchanges generally and was, in fact, the immediate cause of the world financial crisis. It affected England to a special degree, since London was the financial centre of the world, and more sensitive than any other capital to disturbances in the complex credit system through which international economic relations function. The business of London as a financial centre depends for its smooth working upon the punctual payments by foreign debtors of the money owing to British creditors. This is particularly the case where liability of the debtors arises out of bills of exchange "accepted" on their behalf by the creditors, so much so that mercantile tradition, embodied everywhere in law, insists on the prompt payment of a bill of exchange on maturity. This special obligation, indeed, is considered paramount; and default is looked upon as a deadly sin. And every accepting house which accepts a bill and assumes the obligation implied by it on behalf of a foreign trader does so on the understanding that the latter will provide the necessary funds in good time.

London was not the only but easily the first of all the "accepting" cities of the world. The crackle of a bill on London with the signature of one of the great accepting houses was as good as the ring of gold in any port throughout the civilised world. A long experience maturing into a sure instinct taught these commercial financiers what to endorse and what to reject. When I asked the Governor of the Bank, Sir Walter Cunliffe, how he knew which bills were safe to approve, he replied, "I smell them." When the delicate financial cobweb was likely to be torn into shreds by the rude hand of war, London was inevitably thrown into a panic. The sudden paralysis of the foreign exchanges and of the London money market made it impossible for the very numerous foreign traders whose bills had been accepted in London to acquire money in London — wherewith to meet their obligations of this nature — in exchange for the money which they possessed in their own countries. In the aggregate the liabilities of this type amounted to hundreds of millions of sterling. If there were a general default it followed that the accepting houses would fail to pay bills upon which the whole business of the discount market depended, and which were among the most important assets of the London banks. In the last week of July, therefore, there was every prospect of such a crash in London as had never before been known. The position of the banks, upon whose continued operation depends the supply of the means of payment in all business transactions, was also menaced from another direction. So soon as it became possible for the proceeds of the sales of securities to New York to be remitted to Europe, the pressure of sales was diverted to the London Stock Exchange, and there naturally followed a great depreciation in prices of stock all round. Though it was possible for the banks to withstand the depreciation of the investments they themselves owned, it was another matter when the solvency of the very large number of borrowers on the security of stocks was endangered. Thus, during the week, everything contributing, prices continued to move in a vicious circle of depreciation. So far there had been no real panic, the difficult situation which had arisen being due almost entirely to the inability of other nations to meet their liabilities. Though in this particular I do not think the actual course of events had been generally anticipated, something of the kind had been foreseen by the Sub-Committee of the Committee of Imperial Defence which considered the question of Trading with the Enemy in 1911 and 1912, and was referred to in its report.[1] The declaration of war by Austria

[1] Report of Proceedings of the Standing Sub-Committee of the C.I.D. on Trading with the Enemy, Sept. 1912, pp. 8 and 9.

precipitated matters. The outlook on that day was so serious that Mr. Montagu, the Financial Secretary to the Treasury, collected together a number of financial and business men to meet me at luncheon to discuss the situation.

On Friday, the 31st, the London Stock Exchange was closed, all the other stock exchanges except that of New York and the official market in Paris having closed the previous day.

Up to this point the Government, though keeping in close touch with developments in the City and watching events, had refrained from any action. But on Friday the Bank of England, which had this time felt the pressure for several days, found its reserve position seriously weakened and raised the bank rate (which had already been raised from 3 per cent. to 4 per cent.) to 8 per cent. Next day the Governor of the Bank applied to me as Chancellor of the Exchequer for permission to exceed the fiduciary issue of the notes prescribed by the Bank Charter Act, 1844. This request was granted in a letter signed by the Prime Minister and myself, modelled on the precedents of 1847, 1857, and 1866, when a similar course was forced on the Government. As permission had, on those occasions, been made conditional upon no discounts or advances being granted at less than 10 per cent., the bank rate was raised to that figure. On this day, though no panic was shown by the public, there were unusual demands for gold on the Bank of England on the part of people seeking to cash the notes supplied to them by their own banks.

It was fully realised, of course, that increasing the issue of notes was a first step to ease the immediate situation in one direction only, and that it did nothing really to relieve the accepting houses or the Stock Exchange. But the two days, Sunday, the 2nd, and Monday, the 3rd of August, which happened to be a Bank Holiday, gave a breathing space, and nearly the whole of the Sunday was taken up in conferences at the Treasury, at which the situation was reviewed and a policy formulated. During these discussions, in addition to the help of Sir John Bradbury, the able permanent head of the Treasury, and of other permanent officials, I had the advantage of the advice of Lord Reading and Sir George Paish.

The outcome of our deliberations was a decision that the next step to be taken should be one calculated to relieve the accepting houses; and a proclamation was issued that evening granting a moratorium of one month to the acceptors of bills. This emergency measure obviously afforded no help to the banks or the discount houses. In fact, it ratified and consolidated a position which was detrimental, especially to the latter, in so much as it definitely froze up their chief liquid assets.

Partly in consequence of this, many of the leading representatives of these two financial interests and of trade generally met together to consider the situation from their point of view. After sitting till 2 A.M. on Monday, this conference formulated certain resolutions which were forwarded to the Government. To one of their recommendations effect was given on the 3rd, when it was announced that the 4th, 5th, and 6th of August would be additional Bank Holidays. This was done in order to obtain a further respite and to gain time to devise measures appropriate to the situation; but there was some doubt as to its advisability, owing to the fear that the cash circulated during the holidays might be accumulated by the trading community, and not be passed to the banks, where it would be put into circulation again. On the same day an Act was passed through all its stages in both Houses regularising the proclamation in regard to a moratorium and giving the Government power to declare a general moratorium.

These three holidays were some of the busiest and most anxious days I ever spent. I had summoned a conference composed of Ministers and other officials and some of the leading bankers and traders, which sat morning and afternoon under my chairmanship. Ultimate decisions had to be taken by me subject to consent and, if necessary, revision by the Cabinet in so unprecedented a situation, where a mistake might injure the credit and confidence so essential to full strength and use of "the sinews of war." I resolved to consult every person whose ability, knowledge and experience would assist me in coming to the right conclusion. Mr. (now Sir) Austen Chamberlain, the Chancellor of the Exchequer in the preceding Unionist Government, was, amongst others, invited by me to the Allied War Conferences and assisted in the deliberations. This was an unusual, if not an unprecedented step to take; but the situation warranted any measures that might help, however novel. I well remember Mr. Chamberlain's surprise when I asked him in the House of Commons if he could give us the benefit of his experience and knowledge, and the prompt manner in which he placed himself entirely at our disposal. During the morning of the 5th, indeed, when I was obliged to leave the conference to attend the Cabinet, Mr. Chamberlain took my place as chairman; and so was brought about the unique situation of a member of the Opposition presiding at a Government Conference, a foretaste of the Coalition. I gladly acknowledge the value of the service he rendered in helping to unravel the complexities of the financial crisis and to succour those who had been caught in the tangle. He had that admixture of experience, authority, common sense and courage which is so essential in an emergency. A point which impressed me specially at the beginning of our discussions was the difficulty of reconciling the interests of the different sections of the banking community. Nevertheless, during the whole of our deliberations I was most ably backed up and advised in my position as chairman by all my colleagues, of whom four notable members have since died, *i.e.*, Lord Cunliffe, Governor of the Bank of England, Sir Edward Holden, Chairman of the London City and Midland Bank, Mr. Huth Jackson, and Lord St. Aldwyn. It was the first time I had been brought into direct contact with the latter since 1891, when as Sir Michael Hicks-Beach he piloted the Tithe Bill through the House of Commons. The late Sir Samuel Evans and I fought it for several nights. Sir Michael was a consummate Parliamentarian. He had a reputation for explosive irascibility in his private dealings, but in the House of Commons he was a model of suavity and address. He was chosen by the distracted and specially vocal financiers as their chief spokesman at these Treasury Conferences, where he handled his duties with all his old tact and mastery.

Our labours were not completed till the 6th of August, the last day of the holidays, but we had advanced far enough by the 5th for me, on that day, to give the House of Commons an interim account of our activities and recommendations, and after announcing that steps had already been taken to suspend the Bank Act, to state definitely that it had been decided not to suspend specie payments. The latter decision, which marked the main difference between our treatment of the situation and that adopted by other countries, was one which in fact did greatly help us to recover financial normality, because it tended towards a restoration of confidence which was so vitally necessary at the moment. In accordance with this view, I made an appeal to the public to refrain on patriotic grounds from attempting to hoard gold, and accentuated the great part that finance was going to play in the struggle upon which we were entering. In order to deal with the need for currency, I explained

*Photo. by Reginald Haines, London*

THE RT. HONOURABLE DAVID LLOYD GEORGE, M.P.

*In his robes of Chancellor of the Exchequer, 1914*

that the Government was about to issue Government notes of the value of £1 and 10s., and that though the preparation and printing of these notes in the short time available entailed an immense effort, the Treasury officials and others concerned had made such progress that three million pounds would be ready at the end of the holidays, after which notes would be available at the rate of five million pounds a day. Postal orders were temporarily to be legal tender. Another announcement I was able to make, which was a sign of the strength of the Bank of England and would tend to reassure the business community, was that after the holidays the bank rate would be reduced from 10 per cent. to 6 per cent. I explained the reasons for the limited moratorium which had already been announced and that a more general moratorium extending for a month would be proclaimed, during which period bankers would pass cheques through the clearing houses as usual, and would supply cash to their customers for the payment of wages and the normal requirements of daily life. Mr. Chamberlain also spoke with a view to allaying alarm. As a matter of fact, the 10 per cent. bank rate was in actual operation on one day only, Saturday the 1st of August, before the holidays intervened.

In the House next day I introduced the Currency and Bank Notes Bill legalising the issue of the new currency notes and the suspension of the Bank Act, and it passed through all its stages in both Houses during the day. As the conference had by then completed its deliberations, I was also able to give further details of the extended moratorium, which was announced that day in what was known as the First General Proclamation. Not the least of the numerous anxieties weighing on the Government at this time of general upheaval and stress was this problem of establishing the financial stability of the nation itself, and as the responsible Minister I awaited with great anxiety the moment when business should again start, to learn the outcome of our experiments. It was with great relief, therefore, that on Friday, the 7th, I was able, after the banks had reopened, to communicate to the Commons the favourable nature of the reports on the banking situation which had come in from all parts of the country, to the effect that there was no panic and that cash was being freely paid in.

Nevertheless, though much had been done, we had by no means reached the end of our difficulties. As I have said, the moratorium had originally been instituted to save the accepting houses from bankruptcy, but it was no more than a temporary expedient and it did not settle what was going to happen after the month had elapsed — still a real and very urgent question. So long as the accepting houses were threatened with bankruptcy the position of the banks and discount houses which held bills drawn upon them was precarious; and credit remained paralysed. The first remedial measure taken was in the form of an arrangement announced on the 12th of August, by which the Bank of England undertook to discount pre-moratorium bills and to relieve the holders of the bills of all liability in respect of them. The bills so discounted amounted during the next few weeks to over a hundred million pounds, and the Bank, of course, could only take them subject to a guarantee against loss, being in reality merely the agent of the Government in the matter. This was a bold and important step, for by it the Government, in order to reëstablish the foreign trade situation through the speedy rehabilitation of the discount market, temporarily assumed immense liabilities; and its action was generally approved. But sweeping though the measure was and valuable as was the relief it afforded, it did not accomplish all that was required, since the accepting houses still remained liable for the bills at maturity, and being still uncertain of their own solvency hesitated to enter upon fresh business, the very course which was essential to the reëstablishment of the situation. In other words, the normal machinery for financing international trade, which was so vital a factor in our economic existence, was not working. To help the accepting houses, therefore, the Government took a further step. By an arrangement which was made public on the 5th of September, the Bank of England, still with the indispensable guarantee, undertook to advance funds to acceptors to pay off the bills at maturity, and to postpone until a year after the end of the War any claim against them for repayment. By this means time was given to the accepting houses to recover the sums due from their clients, and they were enabled to proceed and carry on business free from embarrassment.

Thus at last was the problem of the pre-moratorium bills solved, and the position of the accepting houses consolidated. But we were not yet out of the wood. There were several other sources of danger to be dealt with before the moratorium could be removed. The Courts (Emergency Powers) Acts, passed on the 31st of August, relieved the hardships of debtors who could not pay owing to war conditions. Schemes, into details of which I need not here enter, were also devised to meet the difficulties arising out of advances to the Stock Exchange and of debts due from foreign countries to British traders. The next important point was both a grave and a difficult one to settle and occasioned long and anxious discussion, for there was room for great difference of opinion. The moratorium had undoubtedly saved the situation during the height of the crisis, but, once it should have served its purpose and helped to restore the normal flow of international business, its continuation could only be detrimental in many ways. The trend of events during August and September, however, had furnished considerable experience upon which to form a judgment, and at the end of the latter month it was decided that the moratorium should come to an end on the 4th of November. The adoption of this course, which proved to be the correct one, was very largely due to the advice of Lord Reading and Sir George Paish, by both of whom it was urgently pressed. There was another matter which was of no slight moment to us as Ministers. In the various schemes which had been improvised against time and carried out during the crisis, the guarantee of the Government, it must be remembered, had been given on our sole responsibility. It was imperative, therefore, that Parliamentary authority should at the earliest opportunity be given to our actions. This was done by the Government (War Obligations) Act, which received the Royal Assent on the 27th of November, and was in essence an act of indemnity for the Ministers.

Thus were matters tided over. During the worst part of it, whether it be regarded as a week or ten days, which covered the period whilst Europe changed from a state of unstable peace definitely to war, the City of London could not guess how near to ruin it was. But it suspected the worst, and many of its leaders were too overwhelmed by the great dangers to which they saw themselves exposed to be able to think with their accustomed composure and to preserve unshaken their wonted touch. Financiers in a fright do not make an heroic picture. One must make allowances, however, for men who were millionaires with an assured credit which seemed as firm as the globe it girdled, and who suddenly found their fortunes scattered by a bomb hurled at random from a reckless hand. The strongest and sturdiest figure amongst them was Sir Edward Holden, with the brogue and stout heart of Lancashire in all his utterances. He stood out amongst all these money barons. Not unnaturally the Ministers and officials, who could afford to take a more detached and impersonal view of the affairs of the country, were better able to perceive what was required from the larger point of view and to act immediately. One great difference between our policy and that of other nations was that we definitely endeavoured as soon as possible to reëstablish our economic system on a normal basis, a task which was frankly abandoned by most of the other governments. And this we succeeded to a very great extent in effecting immediately. In fact so successful was our recovery that the pendulum perhaps swung too much in the opposite direction and led on the part of some to the attitude expressed by the catchword "business as usual." This, though valuable at the moment of doubt to help reëstablish confidence, later on led to an entire misconception in many quarters of the effort demanded by what proved to be a struggle for our very existence.

Throughout these conferences I found Lord Reading's aid invaluable. His knowledge of finance, his mastery of figures, his dexterity and his calm and sure judgment helped at many turns.

The nation passed through the great financial crisis in a marvellous way. There was no sign of panic on the part of the public in a situation that for us as a nation was unprecedented. In this emergency the main duties of the Government were to keep things going and to restore normality as quickly as possible by prompt and wise and, if necessary, drastic action, and meanwhile to maintain the community as a whole in that state of composure which is barren soil for the breeding of panic. In doing the former the Government and the Treasury were greatly assisted by the steadfast attitude of the Governor of the Bank of England, whose wise, far-sighted and broad point of view on the national aspect of affairs, and whose massive strength were a source of comfort and good counsel. His sense of humour, which he concealed under a dour and almost surly countenance, was an encouragement in those trying days. He was fond of little practical jokes to lighten the dismal anxieties of our common burden. He affected a deep resentment at our issuing the £1 notes as Treasury and not Bank of England Notes. He scoffed at the inferiority of our issue in the quality of its paper and its artistry as compared with the crisp £5 note of the great Bank over which he presided. (The first issue of Treasury Notes was a temporary one and very rough.) I can see his impressive figure with its rolling gait, coming one morning through the door of the Treasury Board Room. He had a scornful look on his face. He came up to my desk with a mumbled greeting, solemnly opened the portfolio he always carried, and pulled out a bedraggled £1 Treasury Note, dirty and barely legible. He said: "Look at that. It came into the bank yesterday in that condition. I told you the paper was no good — far better have left it to us." He had scrubbed the note in order to reduce it to this condition of effacement for the pleasure of ragging me. I told him so and he laughed. His manner was not propitiatory to strangers, but when you got to know him he was a genial, kindly man, and I liked him. I relied on his shrewdness, his common sense and instinct.

He was a man of very few words. I cannot recall a single sentence he uttered at any of these numerous conferences. What he said was half whispered in my ear. He accompanied me later on to Paris to meet M. Bark, the Russian Finance Minister, and M. Ribot, the French Finance Minister, at a conference to discuss the subject of financing Russian contracts in America. When a question arose as to a transshipment of gold the Governor of the Bank of France expressed himself with great fluency. I then said: "The Governor of the Bank of England will state the British view on the subject." He rose slowly, and after a few preliminary puffs he

*Photo. by Press Portrait Bureau*

THE LATE LORD CUNLIFFE

*Governor of the Bank of England, 1895–1920*

said: "We do not mean to part with our gold," and then subsided into his seat.

During his visit we drove to Boulogne to catch the boat. On our way I was anxious to make a detour through Bethune, which I was eager to see. It was occasionally bombarded, but the risk was trifling. However, the Governor would not consent to my proposal. I was surprised, for he was a man of undoubted courage. He said: "A predecessor of mine was killed visiting the trenches at Namur. But he was there on business with the King, and the city said, 'Poor fellow!' But if I were hit in the stomach at Bethune they would all say, 'D——d fool — what business had he to go there?' " That was conclusive, and I never saw Bethune.

To revert to our financial arrangements in the first few weeks of the war: The risks of every course were undoubtedly great. But decisions had of necessity to be prompt. Panic had to be anticipated at every turn. It was no time for sitting indefinitely in Council in order to evolve the perfect course of action which would reduce to a minimum the eventual cost to the National Exchequer. The possible consequences of delay or of the adoption of inadequate measures, which did not at once restore public confidence, were so appalling that immediate action was imperatively demanded. In the result the Government loss was negligible. We guaranteed about £500,000,000 of securities in respect of debts incurred across the seas — some of these on enemy security. In due course it was all gathered in except a few millions. In this aspect the problem before us was akin to that presented at the same time by the State Insurance of Shipping, though in the latter case it was only necessary to put into operation a scheme, worked out under the auspices of the Committee of Imperial Defence, and all ready to be applied. I had gratifying proof, indeed, that the share I had taken in the policy of the Government met with the approval and gained the confidence of a section of the business and financial world which had not previously regarded my efforts as Chancellor of the Exchequer with any favour.

Amongst those whose advice I sought was Lord Rothschild. My previous contact with him was not of a propitiatory character. He had led the opposition in the City to my scheme for Old Age Pensions and to my Budget proposals in 1909, and I had assailed him in phrases which were not of the kind to which the head of the great house of Rothschild had hitherto been subjected. My attack was strongly resented by all his friends. However, this was no time to allow political quarrels to intrude into counsel. The nation was in peril. I invited him to the Treasury for a talk. He came promptly. We shook hands. I said, "Lord Rothschild, we have had some political unpleasantness." He interrupted me: "Mr. Lloyd George, this is no time to recall those things. What can I do to help?" I told him. He undertook to do it at once. It was done.

When he died, shortly afterwards, I attended his funeral. On a grey, damp morning the streets to the cemetery were lined with poor Jews who were there to pay their humble tribute of reverence to the great Prince in Israel, who never forgot the poor and the wretched amongst his people.

In the long run not only did the measures undertaken achieve their object, but the liabilities incurred by the Government at that time did not result in appreciable loss. Having, after an interval of eighteen years, carefully considered all the circumstances, I am of opinion that it was the bold policy of the Government, relying on the strength of the national character, which enabled the City of London to recover quickly from the stunning blow at the outbreak of war, and to continue to pulsate and fulfil one of its functions as the economic heart of the whole Empire of which it was the centre.

### 2. Supplementary Budget and First War Loan

**Need for more revenue in 1914–1915 — Terms of the Supplementary Budget — Mr. A. Chamberlain decides not to share responsibility for beer taxes — The first War Loan — Criticism of Mr. M'Kenna's War Loan.**

On November 17th, 1914, I introduced my first War Budget. Virtually it was my only War Budget, for although on May 4th, 1915, I made the customary Budget statement, shortly before vacating the Exchequer to undertake the office of Minister of Munitions, I did not on that date introduce any new features or modifications of taxation. My reasons were twofold: In the first place, the additional taxes I had already imposed in November, 1914, were only beginning to fructify, and I pointed out that while additions to taxations would be necessary, we should have to wait till the autumn to decide what they should be; and in the second place, the only extra charges I had in mind in May for immediate application, were on alcoholic liquors; and the storm of opposition which these encountered made it impossible to introduce them at that time without raising most violent and undesirable political controversy. This is a story which I deal with more fully in a subsequent section when discussing the drink problem in the War.

The real 1915 Budget was that introduced in September by my successor, Mr. M'Kenna, and it was memorable for the imposition of the M'Kenna Duties, which in subsequent years were to play so important a part in political controversy, and were the prelude to a revolutionary change in our fiscal system.

By November, 1914, it was obvious that the additional expenditure caused by the War would far outrun anything provided for by the peace-time Budget I had introduced in the spring. Already, on August 8th, the House of Commons had voted the Government a credit of £100,000,000 for War purposes, and it was now necessary to ask it for a further credit of more than twice that amount. If the war were to continue far into 1915, much greater sums still would be required.

The issue before the country, and particularly before myself as Chancellor of the Exchequer, was whether these huge sums should be raised entirely by loans, and added in full to the National Debt, or whether we should aim at paying our way as far as possible by current taxation, and thus reduce the debt burden to be handed on to the next generation.

I took the view that the immense spending of the Government was bound to cause a very considerable inflation of our currency. War-time demands would stimulate our industries to unprecedented activity; and in addition, the closing down of the international commerce of Central Europe and the crippling of the industrial capacities of France and Belgium, would, for the time being, mean that a heavy extra demand for goods by other countries would fall on us. The result would be a much bigger circulation of money here, and it would be far easier to pay for the War while this state of things lasted, than later on, when trade depression supervened and deflation removed our spare cash.

Accordingly, when Parliament reassembled in November, 1914, for an unexpected Autumn Session, and I laid before the House of Commons a proposal for a second vote of credit for £225,000,000, I introduced at the same time a supplementary Budget, with the object of raising a portion of this sum by additional taxation.

The additions were as follows: I doubled the income tax — raising it from 1s. 4d. to 2s. 8d. in the pound. I also doubled the super-tax. Already I had in the spring introduced the graduation of this tax, making it range up from 5d. in the pound on income exceeding £3000, to a maximum of 1s. 4d. on income in excess of £11,000. These charges I now doubled. The beer duty I raised from 7s. 9d. per barrel to 25s., and the tea duty from 5d. to 8d. per lb. On the other hand, as a compensation to publicans for the sharp restrictions on facilities for drinking which were being introduced, I cut down their licence duty — a concession involving about half a million.

The beer and tea duties went on, of course, at once. But the higher income and super-taxes only took effect for the final quarter of the current financial year. Had there been no additional taxation, the revenue realised in 1914–15 would have been below the estimate, through reduced yield of certain taxes and duties. As a result even of the short currency of these added levies, the 1914–15 revenue exceeded my estimate of May, 1914, by about 19½ millions. In a full year these extra taxes would produce upwards of £60,000,000 of additional revenue.

When I decided to frame a supplementary budget, I asked Mr. Austen Chamberlain, who had been Chancellor under the last Conservative administration, to coöperate with me in working out its details, in order that the party truce might be fully preserved in the matter. He accepted my invitation, and we entered on consultations; but before long he resigned his connection with the Government. This was not the outcome of any personal disagreement. Indeed, when making a statement on this matter in the House on November 24th, he declared:

"During the confidential conversations I have had with the Chancellor of the Exchequer and his colleagues since he invited me to discuss the details of his Budget with him, I could make no complaint whatever of the spirit with which the Right Honourable gentleman approached the questions with which we dealt, and I desire to state that he has looked on the questions which came before him as revenue questions pure and simple, and that he has not allowed his mind to be diverted by any ulterior object."

But Mr. Austen Chamberlain was in a difficult position when it came to the additional duties I proposed to levy on beer. The links between the Conservative Party and the "Trade" were very strong. As a representative of that party he could not possibly associate it in advance with proposals to more-than-treble the tax on beer. "Even as a compromise," he declared, he could not assume personal responsibility for such a measure.

The House of Commons, however, did not shrink from the beer taxes, and the Budget with its drastic additions to our fiscal imposts was passed speedily into law. Such complaisance may not strike us to-day as very wonderful, faced as we are by annual budgets which in a time of peace are four times as large. But the Britain of 1914 had no experience of such burdens, and would have been aghast at my suggestions had it not been for the moment too elevated by the enthusiasms of its war task.

In the course of my Budget speech of November, 1914, I made a statement which is not without interest to-day. Urging the importance of raising as much as possible of our war expenditure by immediate taxation, in place of leaving it all for repayment in future years, I predicted that immediately after the War there would be a short spell of booming industry, while here and abroad the deficits of goods which had been held up by the War were being made good. "But," I continued, "when that period is over we shall be face to face with one of the most serious industrial situations with which we have ever been confronted. We shall have exhausted an enormous amount of the capital of the world which would otherwise have been available for industries. Our purchasers, both here and abroad, will be crippled. Their purchasing power will have been depressed. Let us make no mistake. Great Britain will be confronted with some of the gravest problems with which it has ever been faced."

Unhappily, the last dozen years have conspired to verify this prophecy all too thoroughly.

In bringing forward this supplementary Budget, I also announced the issue of the first War Loan. The vote of credit granted in August for the War had been for £100 million, and I was now asking for a fresh credit of £225 million. It was clear that further votes would before long be required. For the present, however, I contented myself with the proposal of a War Loan of a face value of £350,000,000. It was to be a 3½ per cent. security, issued at 95, and thus yielding the Government £332½ million of actual cash. Of this total, £45 million were required for loans to our Allies and Dominions. The remainder would be used, along with the yield of the additional taxes imposed, for financing our own immediate war expenditure.

The loan was made redeemable at par in 1925-28. In view of its issue price of 95, its interest yield was approximately 3⅔ per cent. The whole loan was very quickly over-subscribed.

This was the only War Loan for which I was immediately responsible. The second War Loan was that issued on June 21st, 1915, by Mr. M'Kenna. It was for an unspecified amount (with an upper limit of £910 million), and consisted of stock issued at par, bearing interest at 4½ per cent. It brought in about £570 million of new money by the time the list was closed on July 10th, as well as Consols and other Government securities for conversion, to an amount equalling about £276,500,000 of the new War Loan stock.

Looking back, I cannot help regretting that Mr. M'Kenna should have thought it necessary to raise the interest rate of a Government loan to 4½ per cent. Maybe this corresponded to the price that was being offered in the money market for other gilt-edged securities. But in view of the increase in our nominal capital resources due to war inflation and to the restriction of an overseas market for investment money which was also one of the effects of the War, there can be little doubt that the Government could have continued to obtain as much money as it required by voluntary investment, without raising its interest rate beyond the level of 3⅔ per cent. at which my first loan had been negotiated. Investors would have had to take this, for lack of an alternative. And if they had been unwilling to do so, there would have been a clear and popular ground for the conscription of capital for war purposes—a step which would have been an appropriate corollary to the conscription of man-power which we were soon to introduce.

As it was, the adoption of the principle that the British Government had to pay the commercial rate for money needed to defend the country had a costly sequel. This principle governed the plans for the Third War Loan, for which arrangements were begun toward the end of 1916, and carried through in January, 1917, by Mr. Bonar Law, who had just replaced Mr. M'Kenna at the Exchequer. That loan was issued at 95, bearing interest at 5 per cent., and over £2000 million was raised at this penal figure. The same rate governed subsequent borrowings, which by the end of the War had added a further £4,000,000,000 to our National Debt. It cost the country a dozen years of remorseless deflation and concomitant depression to bring interest rates down again to a level that would enable this vast sum to be reconverted to 3½ per cent. Throughout the interval, not only was the country taxing itself to pay a sum ranging at one time as high as £100,000,000 a year more than it would otherwise have done, but the high yield of a gilt-edged Government security kept up rates all round, and made money dearer for all enterprises, industrial, commercial and national. It would be hard to estimate the sum total of the price paid by the nation in every department of affairs for the decision of Mr. M'Kenna in 1915 to increase the rate of interest paid by the Government on its war-time borrowings. His action had, no doubt, the fullest authorisation from the leading circles of banking and finance. But the country has since then had ample evidence that these circles are by no means to be reckoned as infallible advisers.

CHAPTER V

# THE FIGHT FOR MUNITIONS

## 1. Introductory

Exclusive reliance on the Navy — Reactionary outlook of the War Office — Man-power supply ample — Failure to equip recruits — Neglect of high explosive — Lack of heavy artillery — Machine guns and shells — Where the War Office was to blame — A war of science and engineering.

The outbreak of war found this country totally unprepared for land hostilities on a Continental scale. Our traditional defence force has always been our Navy, and this weapon has been kept efficient and ready at all times. But our Army, mainly used for policing our widely scattered Empire, was a small, highly trained force of professional soldiers, excellent for their normal tasks, but lacking both the numbers and the equipment for large-scale fighting against European armies.

Unhappily, too, the War Office was hampered by a traditional reactionism. Its policy seemed ever to be that of preparing, not for the next war, but for the last one or the last but one. The Boer War found us still in the mentality of the Crimea, and the Great War caught our military thinkers planning for the next war under the conditions of the Alma in so far as these were modified by the irrelevant experiences of the African veldt. Unfortunately, they only remembered the lessons that were better forgotten because they were inapplicable, and forgot all the experiences by which they ought to have profited because they were a foretaste of the methods of future warfare. Todleben's famous earthworks at Sebastopol had no meaning for them, nor had the trenches of Magersfontein and the Tugela, where our massed troops were slaughtered by riflemen they never saw. But the thin red line of Inkerman and the glorious charge which sabred the gunners at Balaclava, and the Boer horsemanship which rushed Methuen's camp at Klip's Drift dominated the military mind. Military imagination makes up in retentiveness what it misses in agility.

The man-power needed for our new armies was fortunately not dependent for its production on the unsympathetic organisation of the War Office. Lord Kitchener's outstanding name and fame constituted a great appeal, which was organised with expert efficiency and understanding by the agents of the two great political parties. From farm and village and city street young men thronged into the recruiting offices at the sound of Lord Kitchener's call to arms. The first half-million managed within the first month to press its way through the recruiting stations, and it speedily grew to a million, then to two, then three. The immortal story has been told and retold, and it is not my business to tell it again. In the magnitude and grandeur of the response it has no parallel in history. Considering the fact that there were neither rifles, machine-guns, cannon nor mortars available for training, the dugout officers and non-commissioned officers achieved wonders in the turning of their material into armies.

The equipment of these armies, however, is another story; and insofar as that equipment included the provision of munitions, that duty was eventually placed upon me. The story is therefore mine to tell.

The whole business was at the outset jealously retained by the War Office in its own hands, even to the tailoring contracts. The result was shortage, delays, misfits and muddles.

Happily for the world, the weapons of modern slaughter do not grow naturally. They have to be designed and manufactured; and although Britain was the leading manufacturing country in the world, its industries were almost entirely concerned with the arts of peace. It was deficient in machinery for the production of rifles, machine-guns and artillery, especially of the heavier calibres. Armament firms were few, and the methods of the national arsenals were obsolescent and primitive to a degree. The Army Chiefs were mostly horsemen—Lord French and Sir Douglas Haig were both cavalrymen, and won their reputations as cavalry generals. Lord Kitchener was a sapper. His only experiences of war, however, would have left him with the impression that mobility counted more than weight and quantity of shell.

High-explosive shell, which the German forces were using against us with such shattering effect, was regarded up to the outbreak of war by our own Ordnance Department as being merely in the experimental stage, and the problem of a satisfactory filling and fuse for it had not been solved. It had not been seriously and systematically investigated. The War Office was obsessed with the importance of shrapnel. It was the only artillery lesson of the Boer War which they remembered, and in September, 1914, our War Office generals were still preparing to slug African kopjes with Boers hiding behind bushes or boulders. It was the most useful shell in Africa. Why not in Europe? They had been criticised in 1900 because the supply was inadequate, they were not going to be caught and castigated this time. Their mental arsenals had no room for anything but shrapnel.

As to heavy artillery, the regular establishment of the Army at the outbreak of war did not provide for anything beyond the 60-pounder. The 4.7 was considered almost too cumbrous a weapon for the field. There were a few specimens of six-inch howitzers in existence, of obsolescent pattern and some six-inch guns, which could be gleaned here and there, partly from coastal forts. There was only one 9.2-inch howitzer just completed. There was very little ammunition for any of these heavy guns. Our old siege train guns were muzzle-loaders! It had been the official view of the General Staff that the tendency of field operations to approximate towards siege warfare, displayed in the Russo-Japanese fighting in Manchuria — the most recent example of modern war — should not be accepted as a general tendency, and they had made no plans or preparations for dealing with such a situation. The Japanese armies walked round the field defences of the Russians without attempting to destroy them or storm them, just as French did with his cavalry at Magersfontein. Why not in France? A trench hundreds of miles long from Switzerland to the sea, which you could not outflank, either on the right or the left, was beyond their limited vision.

Some of our old-fashioned six-inch howitzers arrived in France in time to be used in the battle of the Aisne, but even by the end of January, 1915, the British had only 24 of these weapons in the field, or one battery per corps — one-sixteenth the number that were being used against us by the Germans. And the Germans had shells for their howitzers; we had a very scanty ration for ours. The official allowance of machine-guns to our troops was two per battalion, and even this meagre dole was not available for our new armies during the first months of their service, although they were sent to fight against German forces equipped with sixteen machine-guns per battalion. As to shells, the production of shell cases was absurdly inadequate, but such as it was it greatly exceeded the provision for filling the empty cases with explosives or for manufacturing fuses to detonate them. When I paid a visit to Woolwich Arsenal some months after the outbreak of the War, I found stacks of empty shells which were being slowly and tediously filled, one at a time, with ladles by hand from cauldrons of seething fluid. The production of the fuses for detonating the shells was governed by the same lack of imagination, and consequently there was a similar deficiency in output.

It was not so much a question of unpreparedness at the outbreak of war. No one before the War contemplated our raising armies aggregating hundreds of thousands of men for any war in which we were ever likely to be engaged. Our military arrangements with France never went beyond the dispatch of an Expeditionary Force of six divisions to support the French armies on their left flank. When the Cabinet decided to appeal for volunteers they only asked for a recruitment of 100,000. What followed that appeal exceeded the most sanguine anticipation. When the German armies overran Belgium and broke the French front, marching up to the gates of Paris, the youth of Britain rolled up in such numbers that the whole idea of our contribution to the War was changed by this uprising of indignant valour. The Cabinet, excited by the spectacle to a fit of audacity, raised the limit of enlistment to 500,000. The flood did not take long to overflow even that limit.

No blame can, therefore, be attached to the War Office or its responsible heads for failing to have in store, at the outbreak of the War, a reserve of equipment and munitions for the hitherto undreamed-of forces we were compelled to raise and put into the field. But they cannot be held guiltless of mental obtuseness in their neglect to keep abreast of modern development in pattern of munitions and machinery for munition production, and still more of a most pitiable breakdown of initiative in facing the new task which confronted them, of bringing munition production up to the standard demanded by the actual conditions of warfare as they soon manifested themselves in the campaign of 1914.

Modern warfare, we discovered, was to a far greater extent than ever before a conflict of chemists and manufacturers. Man-power, it is true, was indispensable, and generalship will always, whatever the conditions, have a vital part to play. But troops, however brave and well led, were powerless under modern conditions unless equipped with adequate and up-to-date artillery and mortars (with masses of explosive shell), machine-guns, aircraft and other supplies. Against enemy machine-gun posts and wire entanglements the most gallant and best-led men could only throw away their precious lives in successive waves of heroic martyrdom. Their costly sacrifice could avail nothing for the winning of victory.

This question of munitions supply, thus, emerged as the crucial issue of the War. Before long it became clear that unless we could solve it, and solve it promptly, we were doomed to certain futility in this War.

### 2. Finance of Production

**The mock battle of Hungerford — Financial provision for munitions — Cutting out Treasury red tape.**

At the outbreak of the War my only connection with the problem of munitions supply was the responsibility, as Chancellor of the Exchequer, for finding money to pay the bills.

My instructions as to what the actualities of war were likely to be was confined to a visit which the Secretary of State for War (Mr. Haldane) invited me to pay with him to Army manœuvres in the vicinity of Hungerford in the summer of 1908. I was thrilled with the anticipation of viewing a battle, even although it was only a stage fight. I felt that, under such auspices, one would see something of what the terrible reality would be like. There were real soldiers, real rifles, bayonets, swords, cavalry, cannon, commanded by real generals who had fought more than once in real wars. Mr. Haldane and I were perched, with the staff of one of the opposing armies, on a hill which was defended by infantry supported by field guns. When some years later I saw the Messines Ridge and Kemmel I realised with what prevision the General Staff had chosen the terrain for the military manœuvres of 1908. It was explained to us that the hill was to be attacked by a force not visible at the moment but which was expected soon to deploy from a valley about a mile off. It was an exciting moment when we saw the skirmishers of the enemy emerge from the defile, whence they were followed by masses of infantry spreading and swarming over the plain. The volleys fired by attackers and defenders and the roar of the cannon on both sides were deafening. This must be something like real war! The issue did not tremble long in the balance, for a regiment of cavalry hitherto hidden in the woods dashed out of cover, and, half-concealed by a heavy shower of rain which then fell providentially, galloped along to the foot of the hill, gallantly scrambled up the slopes in the face of shot and shell, reached the parapet, swept over our poor guns and captured the position. I felt then that I knew something of what our Generals expected the next war would be like. When Mr. Haldane asked me afterwards to find out of the Exchequer an additional sum for the provision of light guns I felt they were quite necessary to avert the possibility of such a catastrophe happening in a Continental war when the mounted hordes of the Continental armies attacked our Expeditionary Forces on the hills of Flanders. Machine-guns were too trivial a toy to be included in the schedule of fresh demands on the Exchequer. This interesting military experience came to my mind when eight years later I saw masses of cavalry ride up to the lines to storm the trenched and wired plateau of the Somme above Guinchy. I remembered the Hungerford manœuvres and I understood better than ever that a military obsession, however fantastic it may be, is stronger than death — than many deaths.

Let me state at the outset that neither at the outbreak of war nor at any subsequent period in its course was the provision of munitions hampered by failure to furnish the money for their purchase or production. On the contrary, I repeatedly made it clear that as far as the Treasury was concerned no obstacle would come from that quarter in providing every supply that could possibly aid us to victory. If the choice were between spending gold or British lives, I was ready to take the responsibility of calling on the nation to yield its last coin, provided it were wisely and effectively spent. Nor did the country itself ever hesitate to support this attitude.

On the 5th of August, 1914, the day after the declaration of War, the House of Commons was invited by me to vote an initial sum of £100 million towards the cost. I let the War Office know that it could have whatever funds it needed to expedite supplies, and in September I took the further step of definitely setting aside a sum of £20 million and earmarking it as a fund to be drawn on to finance extensions of factories and works for the production of munitions. I must add that the Master-General of Ordnance decided in his wisdom not to inform the trade at first of this provision, as is proved by the following extract from a minute by him, dated October 2nd, 1914:

"The Secretary of State told me on September 30th that the Cabinet had decided that day that the various firms supplying munitions of war were to be called upon to increase their plant so as to allow of large orders over and above those already placed to be executed in order that we should be able to obtain additional supplies of guns, rifles, ammunition, etc., in the same time if possible as those already ordered and promised, and that in addition our Allies should also be able to procure the same.

"He informed me that the Chancellor of the Exchequer had agreed to place twenty millions sterling at the disposal of the trade for the purpose of increasing their plant. . . .

*"It has been considered by me inadvisable at this stage to inform the trade that grants of money will be made,* as hitherto I have received no hint or notice of difficulties of that sort. . . ."

That last sentence illuminates the War Office horror at the thought of adopting to meet this unprecedented emergency any method not sanctioned by "pigeon-holed" tradition wrapped in red tape.

I soon realised that the ordinary methods of Treasury approval for expenditure were inapplicable to the exigencies of war and that to make orders for essential supplies dependent on discussions of every detail between the War Department and Treasury officials would delay and hamper action.

Pointing out that in the present emergency it was not possible to insist on the normal routine and Treasury control in regard to departmental commitments for contracts which now often had to include abnormal financial conditions, I suggested that throughout the War such contracts should be concluded without reference to the Treasury. The departmental heads in the War Office were thus given freedom to take full and immediate responsibility for whatever contracts they held necessary. I assented to this procedure all the more readily because there was installed at the War Office as its financial adviser an able Treasury official — Sir Charles Harris. Not in the whole public service could be found a more faithful and vigilant watchdog for the public money.

### 3. Red Tape at the War Office

Reliance on traditional sources of supply — The official routine — Departmental dread of responsibility — Refusal of help offered by industrialists — Reckless contracting by armament firms — Military distrust of the business man.

But although a financial *carte blanche* had thus been offered to the responsible authorities for all measures necessary to supply munitions, and although the needs of our troops at the front were urgent and terrible, the shortage of munitions continued and increased. The War Office neglected to utilise to the full its powers to remedy the lamentable shortage from which our armies were suffering so severely.

Admittedly the authorities were faced with an unprecedented situation. To cope with it, measures equally unprecedented were necessary. The gravamen of the charge against them is that they completely failed to show the resource and flexibility of mind requisite to grapple with that situation and to improvise those exceptional measures. The only defence they have been able to produce is the plea that the demands on them were out of all proportion to previous experience; that they strove to meet them through their traditional channels of supply; and that those channels became choked in the effort. But that was obvious from the outset. Their task should have been to increase those sources of supply in ways available to us as one of the three greatest and most resourceful and adaptable manufacturing countries in the world. Any powers they sought for the purpose would instantly have been accorded to them by Parliament. They not only failed to do this; they put all kinds of obstacles, both at the outset and later on, in the way of everyone who tried to help them, or relieve them of some part of their burden.

Up to the beginning of the War the normal routine was for the Minister of War as the instrument of Government to decide what operations he would sanction. The Commander-in-Chief would notify him of his requirements for carrying out those operations. On the basis of this information the Master-General of Ordnance would decide what stores must be obtained, and would in turn inform the Director of Army Contracts, who would approach the recognised armament firms, and refer their quotations for consideration to the Financial Secretary of the War Office. After due discussion, a contract would eventually be placed.

As soon as the War started, however, the Financial Department, on the suggestion of the Treasury, informed the Director of Army Contracts that he need not refer quotations to them before closing contracts, so long as he let them know of all liabilities incurred. This should have considerably expedited procedure. I am inclined to believe that in practice this relaxation had the effect of increasing the delays. It turned out to be a psychological blunder. The explanation casts an interesting light on the limitations of Departmentalism. As long as the officer ordering the supplies had the check of scrutiny and sanction by the officer of another department, he put forward his requisitions boldly. His responsibility in the event of any accusation of extravagance was by this means shared if not altogether transferred. But now the whole undivided burden of decision was cast upon him. Responsibility to the strong is a stimulus — to the weak it is a palsy. There were many unpleasant memories lingering in the military mind of select committees and commissions appointed in past wars to investigate extravagant orders inefficiently executed. The Master-General of Ordnance hints that he felt most uneasy without the support of his customary financial strait-waistcoat, and complains that it "threw increased responsibility for the expenditure on the shoulders of the Master-General of Ordnance, who, feeling that he had not every item checked as usual before commitment, had to look still closer into each proposal involving expenditure, whether for contracts placed with the Trade for finished war material or for buildings, machinery and staff required for his own department." The Ordnance Department therefore felt constrained by the sense of an unaccustomed responsibility to find good and sufficient excuses for going slowly, and halting and hesitating in front of the munitions problem.

The War Office had always dealt direct with the Government Arsenals and a certain small circle of contractors only, and could not bring itself to launch out into dealings with a wider circle. The taking in hand of an array of new and untried firms and the organisation of them for munitions production would beyond question have been a serious and unprecedented responsibility. The Ordnance Department recoiled from that risk.

When, therefore, prominent industrialists all over the country clamoured to be of assistance, and made offers to supply military stores and munitions, the War Office did all it could to keep them at bay. Complaints reached me that they were treated as if they were greedy suppliants for profitable war contracts. The general policy of the War Office was to give these would-be helpers a list of the traditional contracting munition firms, and invite them to approach these firms with offers to sub-contract for supplies. It must be borne in mind that these firms were already working at full pressure, choked with orders from the War Office for not only their maximum output, but for whatever extended output they could hold out any hope of developing. It was obvious that their overworked staffs would neither have the time to organise a large system of subsidiary firms, nor the inclination to spare some of their best skilled men to train workers in other concerns in the processes of munition manufacture; and furthermore, they would naturally be none too eager to teach other firms which might thereafter develop into awkward rivals and competitors with themselves in days to come. In peace-time there had been between Admiralty, War Office and foreign orders only barely sufficient orders for armaments to go round, and few guessed how long it would be before peace returned.

It was subsequently discovered that not only had some of the armament firms accepted contracts from the British War Office which were far beyond their capacity to execute, but that some of them had undertaken orders on a gigantic scale from the Russian Government. When they accepted these Russian contracts they must have known that they had not the faintest chance of executing them in time if they were to deal fairly with their British orders. Their failure to execute these orders was largely responsible for the disasters which befell the Russian armies in the campaign of 1914–15. War is the harvest of the armament firms. But in all countries they were inclined to over-estimate the capacity of their own fields and barns.

The policy of the War Office relieved it of the dreaded responsibility for the control of work from these outside firms, but at the cost of interposing between the crying needs of our front line on the one hand, and the vast manufacturing capacity of Great Britain on the other, the narrow bottle-neck of a handful of overworked firms, far too busy with their own tasks to undertake the gigantic duty which the War Office sought to thrust upon them, of organising the whole potential productive capacity of the country for munitions manufacture.

The military organisers appear to have been handicapped by that ingrained distrust, misunderstanding and contempt of all business men (not on the War Office register) which was traditionally prevalent in the Services; and doubtless the business men on their side were — to say the least — puzzled by their contact with the military mind and army manners. The Master-General of Ordnance has explained that the method adopted with some of these would-be helpers was to send them down to one of the arsenals to see the work being carried out and form an opinion as to their firm's capabilities of undertaking it; and he adds that while many went, comparatively few returned to say that they could do it. In the light of the subsequent achievements of such men under the direction of the Ministry of Munitions, one has an idea of the sort of encouragement these men must have received at official hands. And it shows that there was a genuine, though mistaken, under-estimation of the capacity, skill and adaptable engineering ability of the nation at large. Doubtless there were many incompetents and exploiters among those eager applicants for orders. But a filter of red tape was ill adapted to sift them out and still retain the really efficient business men, who are often the first to recoil, perplexed and disgruntled, at such treatment. The good men and the rubbish alike failed to squeeze through the fine and resistant mesh. Meantime the War Office, aware that it was not in sight of obtaining the gigantic supplies required by the front line, spent much time begging the soldiers not to use up shells so quickly.

### 4. First Signs of Shell Shortage

**Startling effect of German big guns — British shrapnel not effective for smashing trenches — Army asks for high-explosive shells — Stocks of all shells inadequate — Sir John French's appeals: War Office replies — The first Battle of Ypres — Further appeals from Sir John French.**

After the first rapid fluctuations of the War in the retreat from Mons and the advance from the Marne to the Aisne, the battle-front began to settle down, in September and October, 1914, into that long line of deep entrenchments which were to characterise the Western Front up to the end of the War.

The utilisation of the 5.9 howitzer by the Germans as a field gun was a surprise to the French and British alike. Its effect on the nerve of the troops was shattering, and it contributed largely to the break-up of Allied resistance in the early stages of the War.

Already the Allied forces had experienced the immense weight of the German artillery, and the crashing moral effect of the high-explosive shells which they freely employed. The ability of the Germans to use, even when it was a war of movement, heavy guns of a calibre far greater than we had begun to think of as practicable in the field of battle, and the devastation wrought by their "coal-boxes" and "Jack Johnsons," as their giant shells were irreverently nicknamed, had been a revelation to our military chiefs, British and French alike. Such defences as were hastily improvised proved quite inadequate to protect the retreating armies against the attacks of this deadly gun. No trenches had been prepared, and such shallow trenches as were here and there hurriedly scratched in the soil during the retreat offered no shelter from the explosives rained upon them by Germany's heavy artillery. On the other hand, when it came to the German turn to retreat, their engineers dug deep into the earth, and the bombardment by light guns was quite ineffective against such defences. As the War thus passed to the stage of trench warfare, we found that the shrapnel of our field guns was powerless not only to level parapets, to destroy trenches and to obliterate machine-gun emplacements, but even to tear down barbed-wire entanglements, and that the only way to save British lives was to churn up enemy defences with a crashing barrage of high-explosive shells that would smash the machine guns, level trenches and break lanes through the wire before an attack was attempted.[1]

By the first week in September, 1914, General Headquarters in France were writing to the Master-General of Ordnance, asking for supplies of H.E. (high explosives). The request was emphatically reiterated on the 15th, and by the 21st a definite request for 15 per cent. of H.E. shells for the field guns was made — a proportion raised presently to 25 per cent. and by the 6th of November to 50 per cent. A week later this request was modified to 25 per cent. but raised on December 31st again to 50 per cent. The War Office refused to supply this proportion, on the plea that "the nature of the operations may again alter as they have done in the past." Thus persistent was the refusal of the War Office to recognise the fact, demonstrated ten years earlier by the Russo-Japanese conflict in Manchuria, that modern warfare tended to become a war of entrenchments and siege operations. I may add that on the 22nd of October, 1914, the French General Deville had informed the War Office that the French were giving up shrapnel altogether and concentrating on H.E.

But even more serious than the failure of a supply of H.E. was the general shortage of shells of any kind whatever. By September 17th, Sir John French was wiring for increased supplies of shells for his howitzers, pointing out that the reserves in stock on the lines of communication had fallen dangerously low, and that "in view of the large expenditure of this ammunition now taking place and to be expected, this is a serious matter. No effort should be spared to send out further supplies at once."

[1] Note. — H.E. was first used by 18-pounders on 31/10/14.
At that time the War Office was supplying only shrapnel for the field guns, and of the shell even for field howitzers and 60-pounders, 70 per cent. was shrapnel. The few six-inch howitzers and the lonely 9.2-inch howitzer which was sent out in October, fired high explosive, but had only a limited amount of ammunition.

The War Office replied that they were sending out what they could — it would increase Sir John French's stock to about ten days' supply at his then rate of expenditure — and warned him that "this will run our stock very low, and we cannot supply at this rate until manufacturers reach their maximum output."

The shortage of ammunition for the larger guns became the theme of almost daily telegrams of Sir John French. By September 28th he was writing to draw attention also to a pending shortage of field-gun ammunition. He said: "For 18-pounders the proposal is to dispatch 15,000 rounds a week, or less than 7 rounds per gun a day. This is by far too small an amount. During the last fortnight there has been an average daily expenditure of 14 rounds per gun, notwithstanding the fact that these guns, as a whole, have been, comparatively speaking, but lightly engaged during the action on the Aisne. I need hardly say that a shortage of ammunition for Field Artillery might be attended with the gravest results. It may be thought that the nature of the recent operations has been abnormal, but in my opinion future operations in this campaign will to a great extent be of a similar kind, and in order to maintain the Army in an efficient fighting condition I am compelled to represent that the proposed rate of ammunition supply cannot possibly suffice to meet demands."

In its reply, dated to this letter, October 7th, the War Office excused itself in the following terms: "With reference to your letter of September 28th, I am commanded by the Army Council to point out that they have provided in the first instance, and have also sent out, replenishments in almost every case fully up to *the quantities of gun ammunition which were laid down before the War*." (My italics.) This letter went on to promise increased amounts, and Sir John French, answering it on the 10th of October, retorted that even this larger rate of supply would provide the army with only 9 rounds per gun per day for the 60-pounders, 11 rounds per day for the 4.5-inch howitzers, and if all the divisions were counted, only 6 rounds per day for the 18-pounder field artillery. Thereafter a series of urgent telegrams came from France for more shells. The tremendous attempts made by the Germans to throw the British Army into the Channel and to capture the ports had just started. The first battle of Ypres, the last fought in the open field on this front, had developed, and in the middle of that terrible struggle the Field-Marshal wired Lord Kitchener: "If the reserve on the lines of communication is not at once made up to at least the authorised scale and maintained on that scale, it is possible that the troops may soon be required to fight without the support of artillery. The great battle which has now lasted for several days still proceeds, and the gravest result will be entailed by a shortage of artillery ammunition." In reply he was told by the Secretary of State for War: "As soon as I can work out the rate you are expending ammunition I will answer the last paragraph. . . . You will of course see that economy is practised. . . ." Three days later, the Master-General of Ordnance wrote to G.H.Q. declaring: "I cannot say what our future supplies will be, as it entirely depends on the promises of the firms to whom we have given large orders being kept up to date." He added that he could not increase supplies of 4.7-inch shell without depleting the equipment of the fresh divisions now being made up. French replied that he had been compelled to reduce supplies for the howitzers to 10 rounds per gun a day, and would shortly have to bring down the 18-pounder field guns to the same ration. He begged for the ammunition which the Master-General of Ordnance was holding up as equipment of batteries not yet sent overseas — "I submit that it is of greater importance to keep the batteries which are already here adequately supplied with ammunition, than it is to retain ammunition in England for the batteries which are to come out later" — and in an urgent postscript added:

"I *must press* this point: *The offensive is of the last importance during the next two weeks or so!* I wish to emphasise third paragraph of my letter. — J.F." (His own italics.)

Two days later, on the 31st of October, French wired repeating this plea, to which the War Office acceded. Kitchener also suggested to him that Joffre ought to send more French guns with a plentiful supply of ammunition. But, as a consequence, when two days later Sir John French asked for another infantry division, he was offered a choice of Stuart Wortley's Territorial Division "without artillery, for which we have not got ammunition," or the incompletely trained 8th Division,[1] with its artillery depleted by the supplies sent out already.

Throughout November and December the shortage of ammunition was growing. On the 12th of November G.H.Q. wired for more shells for the 4.7-inch guns, and the War Office stated in reply what they had sent in the last week, and added: "We cannot continue to supply at this rate." On the 12th of December, Sir John French wired Lord Kitchener: "I am very anxious about our supply of ammunition." Kitchener replied that the output was insufficient for the guns already in the field, and that he doubted the wisdom of sending more batteries to France, as "it is obviously uneconomical to keep batteries in France that cannot be used because of the want of ammunition." On the 31st of December French wrote to the War Office: "The present supply of artillery ammunition has been found to be so inadequate

[1] "The Official History of the War: Military Operations, France and Belgium," Vol. II, page 450, notes that the 8th Division "was 'untrained' according to home standards. . . . The Division assembled at Hursley Park, near Winchester, between the 19th September and 2nd November; it began embarking on the 4th November. There was, therefore, no opportunity for training in brigade and division."

as to make offensive operations, even on a small scale, quite out of the question. Recent experience has shown that the ammunition available suffices for scarcely one hour's bombardment of a small portion of the enemy's line, and that even this operation leaves no ammunition to repel a counter-attack or to give the assaulting columns sufficient support. Owing to the nature of the operations in which we are, and shall continue to be, engaged, *the supply of artillery ammunition is the governing factor. . . . It is on the supply of ammunition for artillery that the future operations of the British Army will depend.*" (My italics.)

The members of the Cabinet saw none of these letters from Sir John French at the time, and knew nothing of their existence.

### 5. The First Cabinet Committee

Early indifference to problem of munitions — I secure appointment of a Committee — Summary of its work — Negotiations with ordnance factories — Their capacity exhausted — My visit to France — Arrival in Paris — French methods of munition production — General St. Clair Deville — A meeting with Lord Robert Cecil — General Gallieni — Visit to General Castelnau's H.Q. — Improved spirit of the *poilus* — Meeting with General Balfourier and General Foch — A German prisoner — French peasants in the war zone.

It was not perhaps obvious at first to everyone how vital this question of munitions was, or how urgent and grave it was to become. The eyes of the nation during those early months were set more upon the spectacular massing of our man-power, and the enrolment of the first million of the new Army. Indeed, this public attitude caused an accentuation of the difficulty, for vast numbers of highly skilled workers, whose technical ability was of the first importance for increasing the output of munitions, were swept by the torrent of public enthusiasm or driven by the undiscriminating taunts of their neighbours into the ranks of these recruits. But it was clear to some of us that the arming and equipment of our forces would be no less essential than their numbers, and far harder to attain. And when the first warning echoes of the shortage in France began to be heard, and rumours of the congestion in our munition firms at home came to our ears, we felt that special action must be taken to deal with the matter.

In September I urged the appointment of a special Committee of the Cabinet to look into the question of guns, shells and rifles. At first, Lord Kitchener resisted so strongly that the Cabinet turned down the proposal. He was held in such awe at this date that his colleagues did not dare challenge his authority. Eventually, however, early in October, I prevailed upon the Cabinet to appoint a Committee to examine the question of our munition supplies, and to advise as to means of increasing production and expediting deliveries. The Committee consisted of the following seven persons:

The Secretary of State for War (Lord Kitchener).
The Lord Chancellor (Lord Haldane).
The Chancellor of the Exchequer (Mr. Lloyd George).
The First Lord of the Admiralty (Mr. Churchill).
The Home Secretary (Mr. M'Kenna).
The President of the Board of Trade (Mr. Runciman).
The President of the Board of Agriculture (Lord Lucas).[1]

This Committee met altogether six times between the 12th of October, 1914, and the 1st of January, 1915, and took the initiative in some of the more important questions of policy and procedure which arose. As the work done by this short-lived Committee formed the basis of later developments for the supply of munitions, I give some brief account of it. At the first meeting on the 12th of October, it reviewed the question of the provision of guns for the new armies and recommended that orders should be given for the manufacture of artillery on a much larger scale than had

[1] Subsequently killed in action.

hitherto been contemplated by the War Office. Instructions were given for the ordering of 3000 18-pounder field guns, to be delivered by May 1915, instead of the 892 already ordered for delivery in June. I pressed hard that the capacity of the existing armament firms should be extended, that the great engineering capacity of this country outside the armament works should be immediately mobilised for the production of munitions and that the works of large engineering firms should be taken over and converted to that purpose. The Master-General of Ordnance objected on the grounds that the manufacture of guns, rifles and shells was a very delicate operation and needed long experience and trained skill of a high order; that the few firms who possessed the necessary experience and training subcontracted in respect of all work which outside firms were capable of doing; and that by this means all the engineering capacity which could safely be trusted was fully engaged. To go beyond that process and leave the whole production of any munitions of war to inexperienced establishments would be too risky. He dwelt on the dangers arising from faulty shells. The whole of our guns might burst. Such was his case for the existing procedure. There can be no doubt that any great expansion under the pressure of necessity was bound to lead to some defective work, but the sequel proved that the risk was far greater from badly designed fuses — for which the Ordnance Department was responsible — than from the carelessness of British manufacturers. The rifle shortage was also considered. There was no prospect of supplying our recruits with rifles for many months to come unless special efforts were made to quicken supply. A message was sent to the representative of the War Office in the U.S.A., instructing him to ascertain the maximum output which could be secured from firms capable of manufacturing field guns or rifles to a total of 1500 18-pounder guns and half a million rifles. I may say that the reply to this inquiry showed that there appeared to be little hope of securing additional output from that source before September, 1915.

On the next day, October 13th, representatives of the Ordnance Factories, and of Messrs. Armstrong, Vickers, the Coventry Ordnance Works, and Beardmore, met our Committee. In regard to finance, I promised the representatives of the armament firms who were called in that the Government could find the capital required to extend the works of the armament firms or those of their sub-contractors, and would compensate them for any resulting loss. Thus encouraged, the contractors engaged to increase their output by every possible means, and as a result of this meeting the commitments of the works represented were raised from 878 guns to 1608 — deliveries in all cases to be completed not later than August, 1915.

It was after this second meeting that I decided to pay a visit to France to inspect methods employed there to expand and quicken production.

At successive meetings on the 20th and 21st of October we took up the question of propellant and explosives, which was left to the Secretary of State for War to investigate further, and that of the supply of rifles — it being decided to increase largely the number already ordered for delivery in July, 1915. As a result, big orders were placed in the United States, and grants of money made to firms in this country for the increase of their plant. Then, in regard to the organisation of trade resources, it was decided that a Committee of the armament firms should be formed to distribute the orders to individual firms.

This summary gives some of the main points dealt with during the first four meetings of the Committee in October; but it was not long before I discovered that grants of money, though essential, were not all that was necessary to meet the situation.

The difficulty at this time of increasing the orders for munitions, or of accelerating delivery of existing orders under the War Office procedure, was becoming every week more apparent, for the existing armament workshops were already working to their full capacity, and the War Office seemed unable to organise any effective increase in their capacity or their number. The country was richer than any other in a wide variety of manufacturing plant, a vast amount of which we subsequently found ways and means of adapting to the production of munitions. Labour difficulties were systematically pleaded by the munition firms as an excuse for failure to carry out their contracts; yet there was still in the country an ampler supply of labour than we enjoyed at any subsequent period of the struggle. The numbers of skilled workmen were dwindling day by day owing to indiscriminate recruiting. The head officials at the War Office, who were responsible for the whole field of munition design and production, made no effort to retain pivotal men in our engineering works, and they clung most tenaciously to their methods of assigning contracts. They refused stubbornly to adopt the only effectual measures for utilising and organising the manufacturing and labour resources of this country in order to secure an adequate output.

In order to obtain a further insight into the possibilities I paid a visit to France. On this visit I was accompanied by Lord Reading, then Lord Chief Justice, and by Sir John Simon, then Attorney-General.

Our party — Lord Reading, Sir John Simon and myself — left Newhaven at midnight on October 16th and crossed on a destroyer to Dieppe. It was my first experience of the physical proximity of war. As soon as we left Newhaven the lights were put out, as a German submarine had been seen off Cherbourg that morning. We had to steam out of the ordinary route and hang about a good deal, so that the crossing took twice as long as the ordinary packet boat would have taken.

At Dieppe we were met on behalf of the French Government and were taken to visit some of the battlefields north of Paris. One of the cars which met us was driven by the dramatist, Henri Bernstein, who had recently taken a prominent part in denouncing M. Caillaux during his wife's trial. We were taken to Senlis and Beauvais among other places. The lower part of Senlis was a complete ruin after its bombardment by the Germans. That was our first view of the ruin caused by war. At Creil the bridge over the river had been blown up by the French to cover their retreat from the Germans, and we passed over a pontoon bridge. Motoring through a country which seemed in some districts to have been almost abandoned by its inhabitants, for we were on the track of the German march, we reached Paris in the evening. Paris itself looked like a deserted city. All the gaiety, bustle and vivacity had gone. The Government was still at Bordeaux, whither it had fled during the panic of August. The Élysée, the Chamber of Deputies, the Luxembourg and all the Government offices were locked up and left in charge of a few heroic caretakers. The President, the Ministers, the Deputies — almost all except Clemenceau and Briand — had gone. It will be recalled that M. Clemenceau, when asked whether he thought the Government ought to leave Paris, as the Germans were almost at the gates, replied: "Yes, Paris is too far from the front!" The young men of Paris were away at the front: older men were outside on guard armed with obsolete rifles with long bayonets. A considerable number of the remaining population, especially in the richer quarters, had sought safety farther south when the Germans were approaching with great strides towards the *banlieue*. The hotels were closed, and shops which did not dispense the necessaries of life had neither purchasers nor window-gazers. The sparse population of the streets looked grave and preoccupied. Before the war the dress of the ordinary Parisian women always seemed to me to be sombre, just as the apparel of the average British women gave one the impression of being drab; but on this occasion garments, both male and female, were blacker than ever, for the French army during the terrible battles of September had suffered casualties more appalling than had ever been inflicted on any armies within so short a space of time. It was, indeed, a grim city.

On Sunday morning, at ten o'clock, we achieved the object of our journey, which was to ascertain how far the French Government had organised private industry for the purpose of producing munitions of war, and how far, in view of French experience, similar organisation could be undertaken in the United Kingdom. General St. Clair Deville, the inventor of the famous 75-millimetre gun, had been authorised by the French Government to give us all the information he possessed, and he and Captain Cambefort placed their knowledge and experience at our disposal. General Deville struck us as a splendid type of the quiet, thoughtful, and efficient Frenchman. Cambefort spoke English excellently (he was a big merchant and manufacturer at Lyons in times of peace), and knew England well. They explained to us what arrangements the French were making to increase their supplies of guns, shells, etc., and what provision they were making for future development. They explained how the Government, as soon as war broke out, called engineers and manufacturers together in order to make the best available use of all factories and workshops capable of assisting in Government work. The great difficulty was shortage of skilled workmen, because at the mobilisation no thought had been given to this necessity, and all of military service age, not then actually engaged in munition work, had gone to the front. The Government was now doing its utmost to get them back, though this was very difficult, as they were scattered over different regiments and in different parts of the battle front. Still, a number of these skilled men had now been recovered. Munitions were being manufactured by private firms, and private production would rapidly increase.

The return of essential and pivotal skilled men who had been drafted either into the Territorials or the Kitchener Armies was not seriously taken in hand in Britain until after the formation of the Ministry of Munitions in May, 1915. By that time many of these workers had already fallen in futile battles, owing largely to lack of guns and ammunition they could have helped to provide. Production suffered seriously from this mistake.

General Deville said that England had such an immense number of splendidly equipped engineering works, with every variety of machines, plant and tools, that our situation was, for the purposes of increasing supplies, better than that of France. He offered to be at the disposition of our Government for advising us on the method of munition production they had evolved. We reported this offer to the War Office, but I never heard that it came to anything. If he repeated to the Ordnance Authorities at home the advice he gave to me it certainly did not fructify.

While in Paris I received a visit from Lord Robert Cecil, who had been on a search for his sister's son, reported missing. He learned as a result of his inquiries that the boy had been badly wounded, and taken with others in the same condition to a French country house. Here their wounds were being attended to when the Germans took possession of the mansion. The men's wounds were only partially dressed, the hæmorrhage in many cases being only temporarily stopped. The doctor who was attending them warned the German officer that to move these men meant their death, but in spite of this the officer insisted on their being bundled into carts and taken away as prisoners. As a result of this they all died. Had they been left behind and recovered, they might have returned to the front and helped to kill German soldiers. Such are the ruthless alternatives of war.

Lord Robert was also arranging for a burial service for the dead British soldiers, who were to be exhumed where that was possible, and buried again with religious rites — a rather gloomy and gruesome task. He was anxious that the British Government should arrange a mission for this purpose. I promised to see to it.

We were privileged to have an interview with General Gallieni, who was Military Governor of Paris. He was certainly a very remarkable person. He was evidently a very ill man; he looked sallow, shrunken, and haunted. Death seemed to be chasing the particles of life out of his veins. Afterwards we learnt that he was suffering from a serious internal disease. He died from this disease in 1916. Still, he was fearless, resolute and confident. He had just made a notable contribution to the victory of the Marne. We discussed with him very fully the whole military position.

Early on Monday morning we left Paris and motored to Amiens, the General Headquarters of the Northern Army of France. On the way we passed through Mondidier. German aëroplanes had just bombed the town and the fragments of their bombs were hardly cold when we arrived. Here I heard, for the first time in my life, the crack of shells fired with murderous intent against human beings, and my first experience of it gave me a shudder. At Amiens we came to the headquarters of General Castelnau, one of the ablest military leaders in the War. He had already won a great reputation in the fierce battles of the Grand Couronné in front of Nancy, where under his leadership the French repulsed the German efforts to break through on that critical front. His personality created a deep impression on our minds. He was a short man with a high forehead and intelligent dark eyes — quiet and grave in demeanour. I drove with him up to the French lines beyond Doullens. On the road the General explained how the War was progressing and how differently things had turned out from what military staffs on both sides had anticipated and planned. It was clear that neither German nor French generals had foreseen that the War would develop into a siege operation on a colossal scale.

"I imagined," he said, "that we should have had great pitched battles, with a fortnight or so in between for rest and preparation. But here am I — I have marched with my men from Lorraine to Normandy, and they have been fighting incessantly for seventy-nine days and nights — and are still fighting."

He had a habit of giving answers to my questions which were curiously irrelevant, but always striking. On the way up to the front we met an ambulance, and I asked him whether that was carrying the wounded to the hospital behind the lines. His answer was: "The man who is responsible for this war has the soul of a devil!" He discussed the losses, which had been enormous on both sides. The Prussian Guards, he said, had been wiped out, and the French had lost too many brave men. He deplored their loss, and said: "I look at the lists of these dead heroes, and learn how they died, and I weep, and say: 'There is not one of these men who is not a greater man than I'."

Two of his own sons had been on these lists of the killed. He was in the habit of reading out to his staff every morning the names of fallen officers. One morning the list contained the name of his own son. When the name was reached his only sign of emotion was a gulp, a catch in the throat, before the name "Charles Castelnau" passed his lips, and he then proceeded calmly to the end of the list. In commenting on the military position he grew grave when talking of the clutch in which the two armies were locked, and the apparent impossibility of breaking it. I asked how many men were under his command, and he said there were nine army corps. "Well," I remarked, "that is a greater army than Napoleon ever commanded in any single battle."

His answer was a kind of soliloquy. "Ah, Napoleon, Napoleon! If he were here now, he'd have thought of the 'something else'." Asked what he thought of the chances of the War, and whether the French would succeed in driving the enemy out of France, Castelnau's answer was: *"Il le faut!"*

The answers which both General Castelnau and subsequently Generals Foch and Balfourier gave to my questions on the military situation left on me the impression that even the ablest of the French military leaders were, for the time being, completely baffled by the military dilemma presented to them by the unexpected change in the tactics of the German Army. A war of movement had been anticipated and provided for in the equipment and organisation of the Army. A great siege operation where the *soixante-quinze* and the Chasseurs played a subordinate part had clearly not been thought of. They had attempted here and there to penetrate this earthen fortress and had everywhere failed with heavy losses. They were now looking for the "something else." Unfortunately for the Allies they looked for possibilities straight in front of them only and failed to look around and far beyond.

General Castelnau seemed very popular with his men, visiting them in the trenches and cheering them, calling them *"mes enfants"* and enquiring whether they had enough to eat. *"Trop!"* said one soldier, who was marching to take his place in the trenches with a yard of the delicious French bread under his arm.

I was told that the men were entirely different in spirit from what they were at the beginning of the War. Then they were terrified by the big shells of the enemy and recoiled in horror from the hideous explosives. It needed a very firm hand to put a stop to the effect of this terror. We heard that General Maud'huy, who had by that time joined our party, and who had the record of being one of the most daring of French Generals, had dealt with his men in a very drastic way. A section of them had broken under the fire of the German artillery. The next day, therefore, the General marched them out again until they were under shell fire, when he ordered them to halt and face about. He then began to put them through their ordinary drills, on the understanding that any man who attempted to run away would be shot immediately. When he thought that they were used to shell fire, he marched them back again. I asked Maud'huy if this story I had heard about him were true. He smiled, and said, "Ah, but I gave them their reward afterwards!" "And what was that?" I asked. *"Monsieur,"* was the answer, "when we were attacking I permitted them the next time to advance two hundred metres in front of the rest." "Was there any further trouble with their *morale?" "Jamais!"* was the reply. The complaint about *morale* arose mainly concerning soldiers drawn from certain French departments remote from the German frontiers and with no memories of any Teutonic invasion in the past; peasants drawn from these areas were inclined to treat the fight as something which more particularly affected the northerners. The spirit of the men from these districts had now been completely established. They all knew that it was a struggle to the death for France to which their devotion was beyond challenge or fear. I observed the countenance of men who had passed through the fiery furnace. Though they were resigned and calm, yet the horror of it all was stamped on some of their faces — a horror that habitude and resignation had not yet been able to smooth out.

We proceeded to General Balfourier's headquarters, and there for the first time saw something of the bombardment of villages by the German artillery. It was continuous but leisurely. There was no serious fighting going on, and I have no doubt that the report on both sides would be: "All quiet on this front!"

I did my best during this visit to inform myself by question directed to General Castelnau and General Balfourier, and everyone I met, as to the real character of the problem with which the Allies were confronted owing to the digging in of the German Army.

This was the first occasion on which I met General Foch. He was a totally different type from General Castelnau. The part he had taken in the recent victory on the Marne added to my eagerness to meet him. He was more of the British idea of what a typical Frenchman is like — vivacious, demonstrative, emphatic and gesticulatory. He talked just as much with his hands and arms as he did with his tongue. But whether he expressed himself with hand or voice he always talked well and to the point. His high, broad forehead and his penetrating eye proved him a man of exceptional gifts. I asked him if he had any message for the British Cabinet and he said, "Tell them there will be no more retreats." I asked him whether I could also tell them there would be any more advances. He hesitated and was evidently perplexed by the question. After a perceptible halt he replied: "That depends on the men and material you will be able to throw into the battle line." He said that the

Belgians had been obliged to retreat before the German advance, but his advice to them had been, "If you want to keep your country, dig yourselves into it, and hang on to it!"

At the Headquarters of Balfourier's Division we saw a German prisoner who had just been brought in — a Prussian Guard. He was wounded in the arm, and evidently in pain. The Lord Chief Justice spoke to him, and ascertained that he came from Berlin. The prisoner behaved with great dignity, being neither surly nor communicative, but evidently feeling his position keenly. He had every appearance of an educated man. "Well," said the French General, "you need not worry. You will be taken to the hospital, and looked after just as well as our own men." "Your men are well treated by us, too," replied the German. The General shrugged his shoulders. "At any rate," he said, "for you it is now only a question of time. When the war is over you will be free to return to your home." "Ah!" said the prisoner, with weary longing, "home is the only thing that matters in life!"

I inquired of a young French officer who was helping to guide us round the front whether the stories of German cruelty to women were true. "No," he answered. "They leave them alone as a rule." And he added with a cynical shrug, "They do not appreciate women."

At this stage of the War there was not much outward visible sign of its devastation. The hundreds of long-range guns which later on smashed towns and villages and churned up fields had not yet begun their ruinous activities. The country as a whole showed no signs of pillage or destruction. The peasants were in the fields, often working stolidly within range of the German shells. I heard of one old woman who was working in a potato field when a shell burst dangerously near. She stopped for a moment, looked at it and then went on with her work. Everywhere there was a sense of everyone having calmly settled down to an established condition of things which threatened to last for some time. The inhabitants of villages which were being bombarded were leaving the villages during the day and returning at night to sleep. It was early in the morning when we met an old man and woman who had left their home in a bombarded village just for the day. The old woman was carrying under her arm a duck, probably destined for their mid-day meal. They were engaged in deep conversation, but to all appearances were taking the situation very philosophically.

When we reached the British Headquarters at St. Omer, Sir John French had left for the Menin road where "some fighting" was reported to be going on. It was the beginning of the terrible battle of Ypres.

## CHAPTER VI

# THE FIGHT FOR MUNITIONS—*Continued*

### 1. A Policy of Short Views

Rifles from America: War Office delays — Excuses for shell shortage — Transfer of labour: Board of Trade efforts — Canvass of employers — Approaches to outside firms.

In spite of the recommendation of the Cabinet Committee that it was advisable to mobilise the engineering resources of this country more fully for the production of munitions, the War Office adhered to its dependence on the established armaments firms. Had the War been "over by Christmas," then the official policy might have carried us through. Although Lord Kitchener, on December 4th, 1914, in one of the very few interviews he granted to the Press, spoke of the possibility that the War would last three years, the authorities at the War Office responsible for the supply of munitions were slow to envisage the character and the probable duration of the struggle. This came to light in the course of negotiations for the purchase of rifles from America.

The War Office decided that no more rifles than those already on order should be arranged for unless delivery was promised by May 1st, 1915. In this connection I transcribe a letter I wrote to the Master-General of Ordnance on November 23rd, 1914, relative to the War Office action:

"Dear General von Donop, — Lord Reading has shown me your letters to him on the subject of further American orders for rifles. I understand that you are of opinion that unless delivery by the 1st of May is promised the Army will not stand in need of additional rifles beyond those which have already been promised to you after that date. I must say this rather surprises me in the face of the figures supplied to the Committee of which I was a member. Unless you have arranged for an enormous addition to the supplies which you then foresaw, we shall certainly be very seriously short even in the month of September. We were then working on the assumption that the Kitchener Armies were limited to the figures which Parliament had then sanctioned. Since then Parliament has ordered the enlistment of another million men. Do the promises received by you from various sources for the delivery of rifles provide for the equipment of this additional million?

"I should have thought that as long as you had a responsible firm in America who were prepared to undertake the delivery to you of additional rifles—even although they were only received in substantial numbers late next year—it would have been worth while accepting their services.

"Kindly let me know, as I promised to inform Mr. Grenfell definitely what the decision of the War Office is on the point.—

Yours sincerely,
D. LL. GEORGE.

"P.S. Further supplies of rifles will be required for the Central Association of Volunteer Corps, which has been quite recently sanctioned by the War Office, in which there are already some 200,000 men and which, according to War Office anticipation, will amount eventually to a million."

I have no record of any reply to this letter, but the Master-General of Ordnance probably spoke to me on the matter when he saw me.

This failure to realise the scale of warfare to which we were committed, and the corresponding scale of armament and munition output that would be required, was characteristic of the War Office during those early months. When it was discovered in December that the deliveries of gun ammunition promised by the main contractors were not coming forward, it was not inferred that the scheme of production was at fault. The contractors' estimates had been too sanguine; the sub-contractors had broken down over unforeseen difficulties. These failures were, indeed, taken by the War Office to be proof of the fundamental soundness of their contention that the technical difficulties of armament work were likely to defeat the inexpert manufacturer, and could only be tackled by the established firms.

Accordingly the War Office enlisted the aid of the Board of Trade for a scheme to transfer skilled workers from other engineering firms in the country to the established munition works. Though in regard to its intended object this scheme was a fiasco, it had the effect, not foreseen by its originators, of helping to break down the War Office policy of dealing exclusively with the traditional sources of supply. For when these independent firms were approached as to transfer of their men, many of them protested that they were already doing a certain amount of Government work as sub-contractors, or were supplying materials to firms engaged in sub-contracts; and even those which as yet were doing nothing of this kind raised the strongest objection to handing over their best skilled men to private armament firms, and offered instead to undertake munition production themselves.

The canvass of employers was carried out during the first fortnight of January, 1915, and Sir H. Llewellyn Smith, of the Board of Trade, reviewing its meagre results in a note dated January 23rd, said:

"I have therefore been led to the conclusion that, if a large amount of labour in addition to what can be obtained from among the unemployed British and Belgian workpeople is required for armament purposes, it is necessary in the first place to ascertain precisely how much additional work can be devolved on other engineering firms by the armament firms, or given to them direct, and to distribute this work judiciously so as to take advantage to the fullest extent of the plant and labour available. . . ."

One useful outcome of the action of the Board of Trade was that the Master-General of Ordnance was persuaded to sanction a proposal that firms should be informed through the Labour Exchanges that they might make requests for contracts for Army supplies, subject to having been inspected and found to be capable of undertaking the task in question. In the course of the first eighteen months of the War about 11,000 firms were thus inspected through the Labour Exchanges. This led to a scheme by the Board of Trade for a survey of engineering firms, a project which, however, broke down when the Engineering Employers' Federation, which was to have taken an active part in carrying through the survey, took objection to the absence of any specific information as to the types of contract which the War Office might be prepared to offer. The Home Office also arranged to carry out a census of machinery, which was conducted in March by the factory inspectors, and its results communicated to the War Office. No substantial progress, however, was made with the utilisation of the full engineering resources of the nation.

### 2. The Shell Shortage Grows

Lord Kitchener's memorandum — Continued appeals from G.H.Q. — My memorandum of 22/2/15 — Need to mobilise all manufacturing resources — Death of the Cabinet Committee — Conference of 5/3/15.

A memorandum issued by Lord Kitchener to the G.H.Q. of the Expeditionary Force on January 9th, 1915, states the ammunition position at that date with a frankness which must have had a discouraging effect upon the Commander-in-Chief and his army in France:

"It is impossible at the present time to maintain a sufficient supply of gun ammunition on the scale which you consider necessary for offensive operations. Every effort is being made in all parts of the world to obtain an unlimited supply of ammunition, but, as you are well aware, the result is still far from being sufficient to maintain the large number of guns which you now have under your command adequately supplied with ammunition for offensive operations. You have pointed out that offensive operations under the new conditions created by this war require a vast expenditure of artillery ammunition, which may for even ten or twenty days necessitate the supply of 50 or 100 rounds per gun per day being available, and unless a reserve can be accumulated to meet an expenditure of this sort it is unwise in embarking on extensive offensive operations against the enemy's trenches. It is, of course, almost impossible to calculate with any accuracy how long offensive operations once undertaken may last before the object is attained, but it is evident that the breaking-off of such operations before accomplishment owing to the want of artillery ammunition, and not on account of a successful termination or a convenient pause in the operations being reached might lead to a serious reverse being sustained by our forces."

Neither this memorandum nor the purport of it was communicated to the Cabinet.[1] It was not merely a question at that time of supplying a sufficiency of shells for an offensive, but enough to reply to the German bombardment of our trenches. There were no offensive operations undertaken until the following March and then only on a limited scale. The evidence pouring in from the front proved that the shell supply was pitifully unequal to making even a show of defence by artillery. Throughout January and February the burden of telegrams from G.H.Q. to the Master-General of Ordnance is continually: "Stock of shell very low"; "Amount received much below proportion"; "Request that further

[1] The first week of the battle of the Somme we had 3½ times as many guns in France as on January 1st, 1915, and the expenditure of shells during that week by the artillery taking part in the battle was 237 per gun per day.

supplies may be expedited as much as possible." On January 21st, General von Donop wrote to the Chief of the General Staff in France: "It seems quite hopeless for me to give you any dates for delivery of guns or ammunition."

Such information as I was able to obtain, despite the reticence of the military authorities, about the situation increased my already acute uneasiness. I therefore, circulated a memorandum to the Cabinet, four days later, on February 22nd, 1915, submitting some Considerations on the Conduct of the War, from which I quote the following:

"The first and the greatest difficulty is equipment. The number of men we could put in the field is seriously limited by the output of guns and rifles. In this respect we have a great advantage. We are at a disadvantage as compared with the Germans in one material respect, but we are at a great advantage in other respects. As to the disadvantage, the Germans and Austrians between them had, even at the commencement of the War, much larger supplies of war material and more extensive factories for the turning out of supplies than the Allied countries possessed, and they have undoubtedly since made much better use of their manufacturing resources for the purpose of increasing that output. Germany is the best organised country in the world, and her organisation has told.

"Those are the disadvantages. What about the advantages? The manufacturing resources at the disposal of the Allies are enormously greater than those which Germany and Austria can command. In this computation Russia barely counts, but the manufacturing resources of France and Great Britain between them are at least equal to those of Germany and Austria, and the seas being free to them they can more easily obtain material. But apart from that they have practically the whole of America, which is the greatest manufacturing country in the world, and Japan to draw upon.

"I believe that France has strained her resources to the utmost, and she can hardly do much more. She has now abolished the sale of absinthe, and that will have an appreciable effect upon the productivity of her workmen. She is, therefore, doing all she can to contribute. I do not believe Great Britain has ever yet done anything like what she could do in the matter of increasing her war equipment. Great things have been accomplished in the last few months, but I sincerely believe that we could double our effective energies if we organised our factories thoroughly. All the engineering works of the country ought to be turned on to the production of war material. The population ought to be prepared to suffer all sorts of deprivations and even hardships whilst this process is going on. As to America, I feel confident from what I have heard that we have tapped only a small percentage of this great available reserve of supply.

"Special attention should be given to the laying down of machinery which is essential to the turning out of rifles and cannon. I hear it takes months to complete these machines, but even if they are only ready in September we shall need them all.[1] My first suggestion, therefore, would be that full powers should be taken, if we do not already possess them, as I think we do, to mobilise the whole of our manufacturing strength for the purpose of turning out, at the earliest possible moment, war material. I have always thought that our complete command over the railways equips us with the necessary powers without resorting to legislation. But legislation which would enable us to commandeer all the works in the United Kingdom, and, if necessary, to deal with labour difficulties and shortcomings, would undoubtedly strengthen our hands. We might even take full powers to close public-houses altogether in areas where armaments were being manufactured. As to our railway powers, I made the suggestion some time ago to the War Office that they should be used. I am not sure of the extent to which that has been done."

At this time the Ordnance Department had manœuvred the political meddlers with munitions out of action. The

[1] Without the necessary machines and gauges manufacture could not start. These additional machines were not ordered by the War Office and by the armament firms in any appreciable quantities for another six months. It was done then after the big gun programme which had followed the Boulogne Gun Conference. It was one of the first steps taken by the Ministry of Munitions.

Cabinet Committee on Munitions had ceased to exist. Its last meeting was held on January 1st, 1915. The Board of Trade was supposed by the rest of the Cabinet to be functioning entirely in the direction of organising our engineering skill. As a matter of fact it was then conforming to the War Office policy and trying vainly to carry out its scheme for transferring skilled workers from factories and workshops not engaged in war work to the traditional armament firms. The War Office seemed to be carefully shutting its eyes to the magnitude of the task confronting it, and our army in the field was watching with dismay the approach of the summer campaign, conscious that its supplies were quite inadequate, and that the outlook for any increase was of the blackest.

At a Conference held at 10 Downing Street on Friday, March 5th, 1915, at which the Prime Minister, Lord Kitchener, myself, General von Donop, Mr. M'Kenna, Lord Crewe, Sir George Gibb and Sir George Askwith were present — a conference of which some account appears in a letter to Mr. Balfour, which I reproduce a little farther on — I urged again that there should be a fuller utilisation of existing engineering firms, and in particular I drew attention to the need for expediting the supply of rifles, which was still so inadequate that many of our troops in training had no rifles to drill with. Both Lord Kitchener and General von Donop seemed quite satisfied with the prospects about rifles, of which they hoped we should have about two million by the beginning of 1916. When I pointed out that the House of Commons had already voted 3,000,000 men, Kitchener was taken aback, and declared that they had not yet begun to calculate the military equipment — guns, ammunition, etc. — for such a force.

The conference decided that an investigation should be set on foot to find out what machinery was lying idle which could produce war material, and that Lord Kitchener should be asked to calculate what munitions would be required for an army of 3,000,000.

### 3. Correspondence with Mr. Balfour

**Balfour's interest in munitions — His letter of 5/3/15 — Views on War Office limitations — Suggestions about strategy — My letter of 6/3/15 — Problem of rifles — Industrial organisation.**

With the disappearance in January of the Cabinet Committee on Munitions there had ceased to be any effective instrument either for prodding along the War Office officials in regard to this vital issue, or for carrying out the tasks they were leaving undone.

Some time before the conference on March 5th, I had established contact with Mr. Balfour, who was a member of the War Council and of the Committee of Imperial Defence. Mr. Asquith had retained him on these bodies in order to secure his experience and advice in the national interest. From time to time I had poured into his ears my misgivings as to the whole position, and I had especially impressed upon him the delays in providing our troops with adequate support owing to the refusal of the War Office to make full use of our manufacturing resources. I had an implicit belief in his patriotism and a great admiration for his high intellectual gifts. Moreover, he had some war experience. He knew his generals well. He had not forgotten the incompetent complacencies of the Boer War. He had suffered from them at that time. Their blunders had helped to discredit his administration. On returning from the Conference I received the following letter from him:

"4, Carlton Gardens,
Pall Mall, S.W.1.
March 5th, 1915.

"My dear Chancellor of the Exchequer,

"I know you won't take it amiss my dictating this letter, for my own handwriting is rather a trial to my correspondents. I most earnestly trust that you are not letting slide the matter about which we talked the day before yesterday. Putting labour troubles altogether on one side, the position seems to me to be most unsatisfactory, and unless you will take in hand the organisation of the engineering resources of the country in the interests of military equipment, I do not see how any improvement is to be expected. I am afraid it really *is* the fact that the Contracts Department of the War Office deliberately rejected the opportunity of getting the rifle-making plant which was offered to them some time ago. They supposed, poor things, that they had already had enough!!

"I find it very difficult to understand how we have enough even for our own needs, putting aside the needs of our Allies. Apart from what we can purchase abroad, I gather that our output at the present moment is quite insufficient for our own needs. We make about 45,000 *new* rifles a month, and we enlist 60,000 a month; and large numbers of our existing levies are unarmed.

"Lord K. seems, however, more preoccupied about the shell question than about the rifle question.

"Everybody seems to admit that there would be no difficulty in making the *metallic* framework of the shell to any extent we may desire. It is the *fuses* which present all the difficulty. Now will anybody tell me that with proper organisation it is materially impossible greatly to increase the output of fuses? It may be so, but I do not feel at all inclined to accept it on the authority of the Ordnance people at the War Office. They are admirable people, and are doing splendid work, but their training cannot have been of the kind which would enable them successfully to exploit the manufacturing resources of the country.

"In this connection I cannot help feeling surprised at the attitude which the Russian Foreign Office are now taking up. They are not only indifferent to the augmentation of the Allied Forces by the adhesion of fresh States to the Entente; they appear positively to dislike it. This would be perfectly intelligible if they themselves possessed an overwhelming strength in well-equipped armies. But if they are as ill-provided as in our moments of pessimism we suppose, their confidence is truly amazing.

"Personally, I should rather like to see the Greeks sent off to occupy Smyrna and the adjacent country. This might bring in the Italians, and it would be an additional reason for not employing the Greeks in Gallipoli. I do not quite understand why the Admiralty ever expressed a strong desire for their assistance; and their plan of landing a large force on the Peninsula and fighting the Turks inch by inch seems to me altogether absurd. With the only road over which supplies can reach the Turks partly destroyed and effectively enfiladed by ships of war, we can well afford (it seems to me) to leave the garrison at Gallipoli to stew in its own juice — provided always the ships of war are able unassisted successively to reduce the forts, which the Admiralty assures us is the case.[1]

"I did not mean, however, to trouble you with all this; my object in writing was merely to beg you to do what is possible to bring in outside manufacturers to the assistance of the War Office.

Yours sincerely,

ARTHUR JAMES BALFOUR."

Before I received the letter I had written Mr. Balfour as follows:

"March 6th, 1915.

"Dear Mr. Balfour,

"Yesterday we had an informal meeting to discuss the labour difficulties on the Clyde and on the Tyne. The Prime Minister and Lord Kitchener were there; M'Kenna, Sir George Gibb and Sir George Askwith were also present, but the Admiralty were not represented. After disposing of the issue raised by the Clyde strike we proceeded to discuss the important question of munitions of war.

"Von Donop assured us as far as rifles were concerned that the position was satisfactory. He is confident that he will be able to supply the men now in course of training with rifles of sorts by the end of September. This equipment will include resighted

[1] I did not accept Mr. Balfour's views as to the possibility of forcing the Straits for navigation without occupying Gallipoli. Had we deputed this task to the Greek army early on in the war, all our subsequent difficulties would have been averted.

rifles; it also includes 130,000 to 140,000 rifles which von Donop said were not worth resighting but were good enough to kill Germans with in this country.

"If recruiting goes on at the rate at which it is proceeding now we shall be able to equip the whole of our new forces with rifles by about the beginning of February next year. All this is accepting von Donop's optimistic estimate of the output. Now they are being turned out at the rate of 30,000 or 40,000 a month, and von Donop is entitled to say that they are well ahead of contract time. Gradually he hopes to expedite the rate of output until in September it becomes 100,000 a month, and in December 155,000 a month. *He cannot quicken the pace now because it takes nine months to construct the necessary plant and machinery for the purpose of turning out a rifle.* Had this been done in August of last year we should have had our rifles ready for the new armies by June instead of September — the difference being a vital one, for the present figures mean that we cannot send all our new forces into the field until the summer is past. They are much better than I hoped, but there is no provision made in them for supplying a single rifle to our Allies, and that is the most serious feature in the outlook. The Russians, as you know, are deplorably short of rifles; they are better off for shells.[1]

"Once more we decided yesterday to take the step in industrial organisation which we resolved upon in October and which until recently we were all under the impression had actually been taken. The War Office admit that they were deplorably short of shells, of rifle ammunition and of fuses; they also admit that they can do nothing this year in this country to supply the deficiencies of our Allies. That is almost a disastrous admission as far as the prospects of the War for the next twelve months are concerned. Nothing can remedy this state of things except the placing at the head of this new Executive of an energetic, fearless man who will not be cajoled and bamboozled by von Donop nor bullied by anyone else.

"I sincerely wish you had been present. These views have to

[1] The War Office had withheld from the Cabinet all information as to the serious shell shortage on the Eastern Front.

be pressed on the War Office, and as the mere fact that it should be necessary to do so at the end of eight months' war is in itself a reflection upon War Office organisation, it is quite an unpleasant function to undertake, and I am sorry to say I had very little support. It is essential that your influence and position should be behind this pressure. There will be an adjourned meeting for Kitchener to produce further figures. I hope it will be held early in the week and that it will be possible for you to attend. *The fate of the War depends upon strong action being taken immediately to organise our engineering reserves for the purpose of increasing the output not merely for ourselves but for our Allies.* During yesterday's discussion it was assumed that we could do nothing in this country to aid Russia, and that it was quite as much as we could do between now and the end of the year to equip our new forces.

Yours sincerely,
D. Ll. G."

### 4. D.O.R.A. and Munitions

Provisions of D.O.R.A. III — Problem of profiteering — Comments of Mr. Bonar Law — A man of "push and go" wanted — Munitions of War Committee appointed: Prime Minister's letter — Kitchener's objections — Montagu's memorandum — Armaments Output Committee — Hindrances to efficiency of Munitions Committee — Work of the Committee.

Four days after the conference above described I laid before the House of Commons, on March 9th, 1915, a Bill to amend and extend the provisions of the Defence of the Realm Act.

This was the third edition of D.O.R.A., and was designed to give very greatly increased powers to the Authorities to secure munition production.

The first "Defence of the Realm Act" had been carried on August 8th, 1914, and gave general powers to His Majesty's Government to make regulations for the conduct of affairs under war conditions; the second, passed on August 28th, 1914, extended these powers and included powers of control over armament factories and their workers.

This third D.O.R.A. extended the power of control so as to enable the Government to take over and use any factory or workshop whatever, to control its processes and output, to remove its plant elsewhere if necessary, to commandeer empty premises for the housing of workmen engaged on war work, and to annul any contracts which stood in the way of firms carrying out the production of war material.

The possession of the powers conferred on the Government by this new measure undoubtedly strengthened its hands in subsequent negotiations with firms and workers. Had those powers been resolutely and intelligently applied, without loss of time, they might have gone far to solve some of the most serious difficulties with which we were at the time confronted. An attempt was indeed made by the Board of Trade to apply the power of taking over armament works as a means of checking the excessive profits these were making — profits which had led to grave discontent among the workers, who felt with some reason that the appeals made to them to put forth their utmost efforts were in fact appeals to increase the wealth of war profiteers. But the negotiations over this proposal broke down, and later on this matter was dealt with by me by means of provisions with regard to Excess Profits incorporated in the Munitions Act.

In the course of the discussions on the Bill, Mr. Bonar Law made some very helpful observations which are relevant to the story. He began by saying:

". . . I wish to say at once that the powers which are now demanded are probably the most drastic that have ever been put to any House of Commons. They enable the Government to go to any factory and tell them what they are to make and what they are not to make, or to go to any factory and tell them that their machinery is not being employed to the best advantage, and that we are going to take it away and use it for another purpose."

The Chancellor of the Exchequer: "For war material."

Mr. Bonar Law proceeded to say that the mere fact that the Government were asking for such drastic powers and rushing the Bill through gave him ground for anxiety, and he continued:

". . . I have said, speaking in this House last Monday, that I had some doubt whether in one respect the Government were doing everything they could to end this war. I expressed that doubt. I had no knowledge, and I have none now; but I did express the doubt whether we had shortness of ammunition or of other munitions of war, and I said I believed that if that was so after seven months of war, in a country like this, which is the greatest manufacturing country in the world, and where there is immense power of adapting one form of manufacture to another — that if there is that shortage, I do not think the industrial resources of the country have been used to the greatest advantage. I cannot understand why, if this Bill is necessary to-day, the necessity of it could not have been foreseen in August or September, and why it should not have been introduced then."

This quotation shows that the uneasiness as to the failure of the War Office to make the best use of our manufacturing capacity was spreading. It was in the course of this discussion that I said that "the Government was on the look-out for a good, strong business man with some 'push and go' in him who would be able to put the thing through." The phrase caught on and the public anxiously awaited the advent of the "man of push and go." There were several experiments made by Lord Kitchener in the way of satisfying the demand.

The Bill was passed without any division or challenge. The Ordnance Department could not complain that they were not equipped with the fullest powers to make the best use of the manufacturing capacity of this country. There were no symptoms, however, of any eagerness on their part to exploit these new powers by setting works outside the Armament ring to the manufacture of war material. I therefore urged the Prime Minister to summon another Council meeting to discuss the position once more. At this meeting it was decided to appoint a special Committee to deal with the questions I raised. On March 22nd the Committee met and drew up the outlines of a plan, as the result of which the Prime Minister wrote me the following letter:

"10, Downing Street,
Whitehall, S.W.
22nd March, 1915.

"My dear Chancellor of the Exchequer,

"In reference to the discussions of this afternoon, and the conclusions to which we came, I wish to submit to you one or two supplementary observations.

"(1) I think, on reflection, that the scheme as a whole is on right lines.

"(2) It is essential to its working that Kitchener should be brought in.

"(3) As regards the composition of the proposed committee, I am disposed to think that (on the political side) in addition to yourself and A.J.B. you should have a working financier, such as Montagu.

"(4) That given your two (more or less capable) business men, say Grant and Arthur Pease (as to both of whom I hope you will make further enquiries), you ought to have — in what Balfour calls a session — *two* representatives of the Admiralty and War Office. The Admiralty men might be Black and perhaps Hopwood. The War Office, von Donop and Sir Charles Harris (the latter a man of really high quality). You might tell me what you think of these suggestions at or after the Cabinet.

Yours always,
*(Signed)* H. H. A."

But on March 25th, Lord Kitchener wrote to him, requiring that the Committee should be subject to a variety of strict limitations; it must not interfere in any way with any of the regular armament firms, nor must it place any contracts with any firms who were already doing any contracting or sub-contracting for the War Office; nor make any use of labour from any firms which might in future be registered at the War Office as possible sources of supply of war material. It was, in short, to be a quite powerless body, which would act as an adviser to the War Office — all pertinent and serviceable advice being rejected in advance, as a condition precedent to the acceptance of the Committee.

Mr. Balfour, to whom this letter was shown, wrote me:

". . . I cannot help suspecting that K. has only an imperfect grasp of the problem with which he has been faced for seven months.

"I do not believe you will get 'forrader' by correspondence. The only thing is to talk it over with K. directly, although I know how difficult it is to make this operation a success. . . ."

But no discussion was successful in inducing the Secretary of State for War to agree that this Committee should have really effective executive powers. Its constitution was in the main that of an advisory body. The conversations which led to this lame conclusion occupied three weeks. In the course of these discussions a very trenchant memorandum was put in by the late Mr. Edwin Montagu, a man of exceptional insight and grasp of realities. This memorandum is worth reading as a contemporaneous statement of the difficulties experienced in dealing with the War Office:

"The Prime Minister.

"The Chancellor of the Exchequer, Mr. Balfour and I are going to see von Donop and Booth this afternoon, but I want to put once again, in a nutshell, the position as I see it.

"You can have alternatively in contemplation two Committees or kinds of Committee. On the one hand you may leave Lord Kitchener directly responsible for the supply of munitions of war, working through the agency of the various men he collects for the purpose. You can have all the contracts, all the opportunities for resource, initiative energy and large view concentrated through von Donop and an overworked Secretary of State who admits again and again that he is incompetent by reason of his lack of knowledge of English conditions. If you do this, Lord Kitchener will welcome a Committee to tell him when he is wrong. Neither he nor his subordinates will be under any necessity to accept the advice of the Committee, the Committee will have no responsibility and will, I do not hesitate to say, suffer the same fate as your Cabinet Committee of last September. You can appoint such a Committee but I am quite certain it will not lead to the production of any new munitions of war and you will not find the Chancellor of the Exchequer or Mr. Balfour or anybody who does not wish to waste his time, serving on such a Committee.

"It is not for me to suggest any explanation of the War Office's . . . continued, bigoted, prejudiced reluctance to buy rifles or to increase the munitions of war, but that the solution of the suggestion above is most unsatisfactory can be supported by the evidence that:

"(1) Lord Kitchener, as he says, knows nothing about the problem.

"(2) Lord Kitchener is overworked.

"(3) Lord Kitchener admits that it would have been better to take the advice (and he did not take it) of the Committee in September.

"(4) Lord Kitchener views with complete complacency figures which *mean nothing* unless labour is obtained, looks with complete satisfaction at machinery provided at Government expense which is idle because there is no labour, and works quite happily to a maximum of 350,000 shells a month, a maximum not yet by any means in sight. If you assume that an Army Corps wants 100 guns and each gun wants 17 shells per day, that shows a requirement of 1700 shells per day per Army Corps, or 51,000 shells per Army Corps per month, which means that 350,000 will supply shell for seven Army Corps and we are talking of an Army of one million men.

"On the other hand you can have a Committee which will be responsible and take the blame for any shortage of munitions of war from this time forward, which will try to infuse new life into von Donop, Lord Kitchener having failed, which will be responsible directly, under whatever scheme of devolution it may work, for all Army contracts for munitions of war in the future. There need be no necessity for strict terms of reference, for Lord Kitchener can rest secure that the members of the Committee have no motive but to increase the supply of munitions of war. All that it requires is an assurance that the War Office will not continue to bonnet it, to hoodwink it and to neglect its advice and to conduct its own business independently of the Committee. The Committee wants not only existence but power. It wants the surrender by Kitchener of this part of his activities and he will be represented on it by Baker, von Donop and Booth. This Committee Kitchener will not have. That he will not have it is evidenced by his continued objections and his repeated attempts to forestall its appointment. In a private letter to you I am sure you will forgive me in describing as impertinent to you his treatment of the suggestions you made for the working of the Committee, for he accepted them when you sent them across after they had been approved by the Chancellor of the Exchequer and then inserted words in putting them into his own document which made them quite useless for the purpose you and the Chancellor of the Exchequer had in mind. You stipulated that the Committee should concur in all new contracts; he made you stipulate that the Committee should concur in all new contracts which the Committee placed. This is making a meaningless farce out of a practical suggestion.

"Therefore it really seems to me that there is a difference of principle which cannot be bridged except by you. The responsibility is now yours. George's view or Kitchener's must prevail. If you take the first alternative above, very well then, the project fails and Kitchener stews the British Army in his own juice. If you take the second alternative, Kitchener is relieved of responsibility, which falls on George and Balfour (and as an accidental result George negotiates in his own way with the men working on munitions of war). I submit most respectfully that the situation is serious, that delay does not improve it, that if you think the situation is as satisfactory as it can be, if Kitchener has his way, then I say no more. If you think that the situation demands that George's suggestion should be carried out, then you must impose your will on Kitchener, for I am certain that there can be no accommodation of this vital difference of principle except by the surrender of one or the other to your wishes."

In the event the Prime Minister seems to have decided on a compromise which turned out to be quite unworkable. The first meeting of the Committee was held on April 12th, 1915, three weeks after the War Council had decided to appoint it as a matter of extreme urgency. There were in all five further meetings between that date and May 13th. With the reconstruction of the Government and the formation of the Ministry of Munitions at the end of May, its functions were taken over by that new Department.

Five days before its first meeting Lord Kitchener had constituted at the War Office an "Armaments Output Committee" with the help of Mr. George M. Booth, of the Booth firm of engineers. It was he who became known as the "man of push and go," with the ostensible function of securing labour for the established armament firms, which had been subsidised considerably to extend their works, and were finding difficulty in staffing the extensions.

This Armaments Output Committee became informally, though not technically, subordinate to the Munitions of War Committee, and from the outset Mr. Booth consulted with me as to the steps he was proposing to take to organise labour in different areas for munition production.

With the work of the Munitions of War Committee it is hardly necessary to deal here in much detail. It was given, by the Prime Minister, terms of reference that nominally empowered it to take all steps necessary for the purpose of ensuring the promptest and most efficient application of all the available productive resources of the country to the manufacture and supply of munitions of war for the Navy and Army. Actually it was doomed to futility, first by the extreme reluctance of the War Office to supply it with information which was essential to the proper discharge of its duties, and ultimately by the blank refusal of the War Office to relinquish to it the task of organising munition production. The first difficulty is referred to by Mr. Balfour in a note he sent to the Committee.

"The War Office have a natural objection to stating the number of men they propose to put in the field on any particular date, and probably the Committee would be reluctant to press them upon such points of policy. This reticence, however, makes it extremely difficult to draw up trustworthy statistical estimates of the amount of munitions of war that will be required at different dates."

But it was historically of importance because its setting-up marked the clear recognition by the Government that the War Office and Admiralty could not be expected to carry out in addition to their other duties a task so vast as the supply of munitions in war-time had become; and thus it proved a stepping-stone to the creation of a Ministry of Munitions.

The original members of the Committee were myself, as its chairman, supported by Mr. Balfour, Mr. Edwin Montagu, Mr. George Booth, and Mr. Arthur Henderson, together with General von Donop and Mr. Harold Baker from the War Office, and Sir Frederick Black and Admiral

Tudor from the Admiralty. Sir H. Llewellyn Smith from the Board of Trade was coöpted at the first meeting, and Sir Percy Girouard on April 26th.

Among the tasks which this Committee undertook was the carrying out by means of a deputation to France of a further and more detailed survey of the way in which the French were organising their munition production, and the adoption of a scheme prepared for its consideration by Sir Percy Girouard, for the regional organisation of munition firms.

It is significant that at the last meeting held by the Munitions of War Committee, on May 13th, the first business considered was a memorandum prepared by Mr. Balfour in which he pointed out that there were not enough field-guns to supply the divisions then being sent out, and that even for the guns they had, there would be only half the necessary ammunition in June and less than half in July.

### 5. The Great Shell Scandal

Sir John French's requirements — Actual supplies sent by War Office — Neuve-Chapelle — Sir John French's bitter complaint — War Office reply — Explanation of Kitchener's frugality — His horror at amount of ammunition expended — Kitchener sounds a warning note — False impressions of improved situation — Mr. Asquith's Newcastle speech — My speech in the House — Gas at Ypres — Festubert: Sir John French's account — A deputation from G.H.Q. — The *Times* exposes the shell shortage — Public consternation — My letter to Mr. Asquith of 19/5/15 — Need for high explosive — Munitions of War Committee kept in ignorance — Northcliffe attacks Kitchener — Bishop Furse's letter — Letter from Capt. FitzHerbert Wright, M.P. — Censored letters: Tom Clarke's account — Extracts from the letters — Effect on public opinion.

But although the munition shortage with which we were faced in the spring of 1915 covered all or most branches of war material, the most pressing need in the field was for shells for our artillery.

On December 31st, 1914, Sir John French had informed the War Office, on the basis of his experience during the first five months of war, what his requirements in the way of shells would be in order to maintain the regular defence of the front and the exceptional expenditure necessitated by special attacks. For the principal artillery of his forces — the 18-pounders, the 4.5-inch howitzers and the 4.7-inch field-guns — he laid down his requirements as:

50 rounds per gun per day for the 18-pdrs.
40 " " " " " " " 4.5-in.
25 " " " " " " " 4.7-in.

The number of rounds per gun per day actually supplied to him for these weapons, month by month, were:

| | Month | 18-pdr. | 4.5-in. | 4.7-in. |
|---|---|---|---|---|
| 1914 | Nov. | 9.9 | 6.8 | 10.8 |
| | Dec. | 6.0 | 4.6 | 7.6 |
| 1915 | Jan. | 4.9 | 4.2 | 7.6 |
| | Feb. | 5.3 | 6.5 | 5.3 |
| | Mar. | 8.6 | 6.5 | 5.3 |
| | Apr. | 10.6 | 8.2 | 4.2 |
| | May | 11.0 | 6.1 | 4.3 |

These figures require no comment from me. They speak for themselves. The consequences of this deficiency were tragic for the troops who had to hold the line during these months. Throughout those months our men were being battered by the Germans without any effective means of retaliation. Retaliation meant protection. The Germans would have hesitated to open fire on our trenches had they known we could return shell for shell. But they knew too well that they could rain explosives on our poor fellows with practical impunity. And when we attacked, our advance was not supported by adequate artillery preparation or counter-battery work, and our men were held up by unbroken wire and there slaughtered by machine-guns. This calamity was due to the utter inadequacy of the preliminary bombardment. It was not the fault of our artillery; their guns were not heavy enough and their shell supply for heavy and light guns was not only painfully inadequate but inappropriate to the task, for it was mostly shrapnel.

On December 21st, 1914, I stated in the House of Commons: "What we stint in material, we squander in life; that is the one great lesson of munitions." The truth of that statement was brought home to us in the following months, when our men were left without any means of replying effectively to the German fire.

I have already shown how Sir John French constantly called for more munitions at the end of 1914. He continued to send urgent messages for greater support. When the battle of Neuve-Chapelle had been in progress three days, Sir John French had to wire to Lord Kitchener on the 13th of March, 1915:

"Cessation of the forward movement is necessitated to-day by the fatigue of the troops, and above all by the want of ammunition. If we are to obtain results of value, we must have all possible support in men and ammunition from home."

On the 16th of March he wired:

"The supply has fallen short, especially in 18-pounder and 4.5-inch, of what I was led to expect and I am, therefore, compelled to abandon further offensive operations until sufficient reserves are accumulated."

And in a reinforcing telegram of the same date he added:

"The delay is really most deplorable. Now is the time to strike. Can nothing be done to expedite action operations now?"

Sir John French followed up these telegrams by a letter to the War Secretary, dated March 18th, in which he declared that the results of the Army Council's efforts to supply him with ammunition had been "consistently disappointing."

"If the supply of ammunition cannot be maintained on a considerably increased scale it follows that the offensive efforts of the Army must be spasmodic and separated by considerable intervals of time. They cannot therefore lead to decisive results. . . .

"Up to the present time the mud and the shortage of artillery munition have been the most potent factors in restricting us to the defensive. But the weather and the state of the ground have no longer to be reckoned with as limiting the scope of our operations. . . .

". . . I desire to state with all the weight of my authority as Commander-in-Chief of the British Army in France, that the object of His Majesty's Government cannot be attained unless the supply of artillery ammunition can be increased sufficiently to enable the Army to engage in sustained offensive operations, and I further desire to impress on them the very serious nature of the effort that it is necessary to make to achieve this end."

The War Office reply to this letter complained that the artillery had used, in the first sixteen days of March, 200 to 220 rounds per gun — about 13 rounds per gun per day! This included the shells fired at the battle of Neuve-Chapelle. For this operation shells had been saved up for weeks. The War Office asked that *"in view of the effects achieved, which appear to have been to reduce the defence to a dazed and demoralised condition* [my italics] the utmost economy will be made in the expenditure of ammunition," and begged that less ammunition of the heavier natures should be expended.

There was an explanation for Lord Kitchener's abnormal frugality in the matter of shells, apart from the natural bent of his mind. The one campaign that had brought him renown and rank — in fact made him "Lord K. of K." — was waged on the basis of a tender for the total cost of the operation, which he submitted to that most austere of all Chancellors,

Sir Michael Hicks Beach. The latter refused to give his sanction to operations against the Mahdi without having a most careful estimate of the cost, and the expenses were consequently cut down to the lowest figure. Lord Kitchener undertook to keep within this estimate and succeeded in doing so. The formidable Chancellor had won for himself a reputation by fighting every proposal, from whatever quarter it came, which would involve any additional expenditure. He looked at every project entirely from that angle. Sometimes this provoked a combination of all the spending Departments against the Treasury. There is a story told of those days which illustrates the internal conflicts in the Cabinet which were aroused by this attitude of mind. A Conservative Minister was asked after a Cabinet meeting whether anything important had been decided that day. He replied: "Nothing, except that we gave Hicks Beach the usual 19 to 1." Lord Kitchener, knowing the Chancellor's reputation, very astutely played upon it by contracting with him to run the expedition on the cheap.

It is a curious illustration of the way in which Lord Kitchener's mind worked about these matters, that just after this battle of Neuve-Chapelle, Kitchener stalked into the Cabinet with his most military stride, and with that ominous cast in his eye exaggerated and emphasised — a sure sign of surging anger — and as soon as he sat down he exclaimed in husky tones charged with suppressed emotion: "Oh, it is terrible — terrible!"

"Were the casualties very heavy?" we inquired, anxiously. "I'm not thinking for the moment about the casualties," replied Kitchener, "but of all the shells that were wasted!" He had just been given the actual figures of the artillery ammunition fired in the course of the battle.

Sir John French's retort to the War Office complaint (quoted above) about his rate of ammunition expenditure, was that he had said nothing about the German defence being "dazed and demoralised" and that such impression as had been made on them was due to the high-explosive shells from our heavier artillery. He added: "There is no evidence in my possession to show that the preliminary bombardment of Neuve-Chapelle was unnecessarily severe. In fact, at two places it was inadequate, and very heavy losses resulted. . . . Our losses and the amount of ground gained are the best indication as to whether the expenditure of artillery ammunition was on an unnecessarily extravagant scale."

(The total ground gained by us was equal to about one square mile in area; and our casualties were 12,892 — *i.e.*, 583 officers and 12,309 other ranks.)

Speaking in the House of Lords on March 15th, 1915, on the Second Reading of the Defence of the Realm (Amendment) Bill, to which I have already referred, Lord Kitchener so far departed from his habitual reticence as to state:

> "The work of supplying and equipping new Armies depends largely on our ability to obtain the war material required. . . . Notwithstanding these efforts to meet our requirements, we have unfortunately found that the output is not only not equal to our necessities but does not fulfil our expectations, for a very large number of our orders have not been completed by the dates on which they were promised.
>
> "The progress in equipping our new Armies and also in supplying the necessary war material for our forces in the field has been seriously hampered by the failure to obtain sufficient labour and by delays in the production of the necessary plant. . . ."

This open admission by Lord Kitchener of the serious nature of the munitions situation created some uneasiness in the public mind, and considerably helped the negotiations in which I was engaged during the next few days with the representatives of the Trade Unions, to arrange for the prevention of strikes and lock-outs in establishments engaged on war work, and for the dilution of labour by the introduction of unskilled workers — negotiations which resulted in the "Treasury Agreement" on this matter, of which I give an account later on.

For the next few weeks there was a comparative lull in the reports about munition shortage. No very big operations were undertaken on the British front in France, and possibly the fact that we were at the time engaged in negotiations with Italy, with a view to her intervention in the War on our side, made the military authorities chary of allowing any fresh details of our munition difficulties to leak out.

The illusion that things were going well in this respect was heightened by a letter which Lord Kitchener wrote to Mr. Asquith on April 14th, in the following terms:

"War Office,
April 14, 1915.

"My dear Prime Minister,

"I have had a talk with French. He told me I could let you know that with the present supply of ammunition he will have as much as his troops will be able to use on the next forward movement."

On the strength of this assurance, the Prime Minister delivered on April 20th, his famous Newcastle speech, in which he declared that there was no truth in the statement that our Army or that of our Allies were being crippled or hampered by our failure to supply the necessary ammunition; and that it was neither true nor fair to suggest that there had been anything in the nature of a general slackness in the armaments industry on the part of either employers or employed.

On the following day I had to take part in a debate on munitions in the House of Commons, and in the course of my speech I gave full credit to the War Office for their actual achievements, and stressed the magnitude of the task with which they had been confronted. The telegrams from the front complaining of the shell shortage were not communicated to the Cabinet. I have no knowledge as to whether the Prime Minister saw them. Lord Kitchener had given me his assurances as to the present adequacy of the Army's equipment, and on the strength of such information as was given me by the War Office I put up the best defence I could for the shortage. I was anxious to conciliate the War Office and carry it along with us in the efforts we were making to increase the munitions supply. I knew this could not be done without persuading those who were in supreme control to depart from traditional ideas and practices, and I was at that time doing my best to convince them. I therefore dwelt in my speech in the House rather on their achievements than on their shortcomings. I pointed to the fact that whereas we had only promised the French six divisions we had already put six times as many in the field. "That was the problem which confronted the War Office, and which they had to face. I do not say that they could not have done more, but I want the House of Commons to know what has actually been done by the War Office."

I passed on to make a brief reference to some of the difficulties we were experiencing: drink, short time, trade union restrictions and to the efforts which were being made by the Munitions of War Committee and the Armaments Output Committee to cope with these matters.

I ended on a note of optimism, based on my confidence that there was nothing in the problem confronting us which our nation was incapable of meeting and overcoming. But I was in fact far from optimistic about the progress we were making at the time, though to have given public expression to my views would at that moment probably have done more harm than good, in view of the diplomatic situation in reference to Italy.

The Opposition drew attention to the discrepancy between what Mr. Asquith had said at Newcastle on the previous day and Lord Kitchener's statement five weeks previously in the House of Lords, about the output of ammunition being equal neither to our expectations nor to our necessities. They put in a plea for more information as to the situation and for better coördination of effort in the production of ammunition, with which latter recommendation I expressed myself in my speech as in full agreement.

It must, I think, be accepted that Lord Kitchener had somehow misunderstood what French said to him about the adequacy of the shell supply in France. Certainly the statement, expanded emphatically as it was by Mr. Asquith at Newcastle, received a prompt and dramatic refutation only two days later, when the Germans opened a fresh offensive at Ypres, with the new and added horror of the first gas attack; for our army found itself deplorably deficient in artillery ammunition with which to extricate the doomed infantry from the death-cloud that was annihilating them.

The introduction of gas gave fresh emphasis to the lesson that the technical side of this war was supremely important. It was a method of fighting which we were not ready to employ; we were, therefore, not prepared to meet such an attack. A feeling of anger and horror ran through the whole nation. The main criticism we had to face was the fact that no preparations whatever had been made to protect our men against this deadly weapon, although we had received through French sources more than one warning — on the 30th of March and 15th of April — that the Germans were reported to be preparing this new method of attack, and on April 17th, five days before they themselves used it, the Germans published the false charge that the British had been using shells and bombs with asphyxiating gas. That was obviously designed as a defence in advance for the use they were proposing to make of this cruel weapon of war. I may add that the French, though warned before ourselves, were equally unprepared.

Rough-and-ready methods of protecting troops against the chlorine fumes were improvised by the officers at the front, and at home Lord Kitchener took a deep personal interest in the providing of appliances for anti-gas defence, which were promptly put in hand by the War Office; but the episode added to the growing public anxiety as to our unpreparedness to cope with a foe that had at his disposal the resources of science directed by a skilled and highly organised industrialism, and who was resolved to make the most ruthless use of all his advantages.

The serious breach which had been made by this weapon in our front induced the Army Commanders to attempt a counter-attack at Festubert on May 9th, in an effort to relieve the pressure on the troops at Ypres. In his book, "1914," Sir John French wrote of this battle:

> "After all our demands, less than 8 per cent. of our shells were high explosive, and we had only sufficient supply for about 40 minutes of artillery preparation for this attack. On the tower of a ruined church I spent several hours in close observation of the operations. Nothing since the battle of the Aisne had ever impressed me so deeply with the terrible shortage of artillery and ammunition as did the events of that day. As I watched the Aubers Ridge, I clearly saw the great inequality of the artillery duels, and, as attack after attack failed, I could see that the absence of sufficient artillery support was doubling and trebling our losses in men."

Our losses at this battle were very heavy — gains there were none.

Three days after this battle started I received an unexpected visit from two gentlemen — one being Sir John French's secretary, Brinsley Fitzgerald, and the other one of his A.D.C.'s, Captain F. Guest. They had been sent over by the Commander-in-Chief to lay before Mr. Balfour, Mr. Bonar Law, and myself certain facts and documents referring to the shortage of ammunition. They had with them copies of correspondence and a memorandum by Sir John French, emphasising the need for high-explosive shell and containing a demand for a monthly supply of gun ammunition to be furnished within the next three months. The Commander-in-Chief was tired of remonstrances to the War Office which produced nothing but counter-remonstrances, so he decided to appeal over their heads to leading politicians and Press men. This was the first communication on the shell question that I had received from the Commander-in-Chief.

Sir John has since stated that the reason why he selected me to be a recipient of his complaint was because I had always shown a special interest in the subject. As part of his campaign to expose what he considered a dangerous situation, he also furnished information and gave his views to the Military Correspondent of the *Times*, and on May 14th there appeared a report from him in that paper, under the headlines: "NEED FOR SHELLS: BRITISH ATTACKS CHECKED: LIMITED SUPPLY THE CAUSE."

As this report is practically an epitome of the information communicated to me by Sir John French's emissaries, I quote the following passages:

"The results of our attacks on Sunday last in the districts of Fromelles and Richeburg were disappointing. We found the enemy much more strongly posted than we expected. We had not sufficient high explosive to level his parapets to the ground after the French practice, and when our infantry gallantly stormed the trenches, as they did in both attacks, they found a garrison undismayed, many entanglements still intact, and Maxims on all sides ready to pour in streams of bullets. We could not maintain ourselves in the trenches won, and our reserves were not thrown in because the conditions for success in an assault were not present.

"The attacks were well planned and valiantly conducted. The infantry did splendidly, but the conditions were too hard. *The want of an unlimited supply of high explosive was a fatal bar to our success. . . .*

"The value of the German troops in the attack has greatly deteriorated, and we can deal easily with them in the open. But until we are thoroughly equipped for this trench warfare, we attack under grave disadvantages. . . .

"To break this hard crust we need more high explosives, more heavy howitzers, and more men. This special form of warfare has no precedent in history.

"It is certain that we can smash the German crust if we have the means. So the means we must have, and as quickly as possible."

This article created very considerable public anxiety and consternation. It was the first time the public had ever been so plainly told from the army front how serious was the munition shortage; and I may add that the visit of Sir John French's representatives similarly gave me my first clear and authoritative information as to the full gravity of the position. As I have said, the Cabinet had not been shown the Commander-in-Chief's frequent telegrams on the subject, and we had been compelled to form our opinions on the basis of general statements, rumours, and a common-sense interpretation of the facts known to us. Although I had taken an active interest in increasing the output of munitions and had assisted the War Office by every means at my disposal to achieve this aim, all vital telegrams from the front on the subject of the shell shortage had been withheld from me, even when I was Chairman of the Committee appointed by the Prime Minister to consider the munition question.

Now, however, it was clear that after eight months we were still fatally short of munitions for the kind of war in which we were entangled. An even graver trouble was that as far as I could see, there was no prospect of our getting an adequate supply with the present methods of organisation. The unavailing sacrifice of the lives of our men would continue, the War would be prolonged, and ultimate victory would be jeopardised, unless someone took the matter in hand.

So strongly did I feel on the subject that I addressed the following letter to Mr. Asquith:

"May 19th, 1915.

"My dear Prime Minister,

"Certain facts have been brought to my notice on the question of munitions which I have felt bound to call your attention to. I write to you inasmuch as my appointment as Chairman of the Munitions Committee came direct from you.

"In order properly to discharge our functions as a Committee it was essential that all information as to the character of the explosive most urgently needed and the present supply available should be afforded to us. I am now informed, on what appears to be reliable information:

"(1) That in order to attack highly developed trenches protected by barbed-wire entanglements, shrapnel is useless, and high-explosive shells indispensable;

"(2) That those who are responsible for conducting operations at the front have for months impressed this fact upon the War Office, and asked in the first instance that 25 per cent. of the shells sent to France should be high explosive, and that afterwards this percentage was increased to 50 per cent.;

"(3) That notwithstanding these urgent representations, the percentage of high-explosive shell provided for the 18-pounders has never exceeded 8 per cent.; that when the great combined attack to break through the German lines was made by the French and British armies last Sunday week, the French prepared the attack with an overwhelming bombardment of high explosive which utterly demolished the German trenches and barbed-wire entanglements, thus enabling the French to penetrate the German lines for four miles without any excessive loss of life. In spite of the fact that the French spent their high-explosive munitions lavishly, they have still in reserve hundreds of thousands of shells of the same kind for the purpose of continuing their operations. On the other hand, our armies had less than 45,000 high-explosive shells in all. Of these about 18,000 were 18-pounders. They therefore had to rely on shrapnel, so that when our troops advanced to the attack the German fortifications were barely pockmarked. The Germans rose in their trenches and mocked at our advancing troops, and then calmly mowed them down in thousands. The Germans themselves have barely lost 200 men.

"I am also told that the attack on Saturday last had to be made by night — a risky operation — because of the deficiencies in high-explosive shell, and that after the battle there were not more than 2000 high-explosive shells left for all our guns.

"(4) That a full report on ammunition was sent to the War Office weeks ago from Headquarters in France, and that later on another report on guns was sent. Neither of these reports has ever been shown to the Munitions Committee, and I gather they have not been seen by you.

"If these facts are approximately correct, I hesitate to think what action the public would insist on if they were known. But it is quite clear that the proceedings of a Munition Committee from which vital information of this character is withheld must be a farce. I cannot, therefore, continue to preside over it under such conditions. *It is now eight months since I ventured to call the attention of the Cabinet to the importance of mobilising all our engineering resources for the production of munitions and equipments of war*. In October of last year I brought a full report from France showing how the French Ministry for War had coped with the difficulty. The Cabinet at that date decided that the same course should be pursued here, and a Cabinet Committee was set up for that purpose. We met at the War Office, and it was there agreed, with the Secretary of State in the chair, that steps of that kind should be taken in this country. *I regret to say after some inquiry that action on those lines has not been taken even to this hour except at Leeds.*

"A Cabinet Committee cannot have executive power; it can only advise and recommend. It is for the department to act. They have not done so, and all the horrible loss of life which has occurred in consequence of the lack of high-explosive shell is the result.

"Private firms cannot turn out shrapnel because of the complicated character of the shell; but the testimony is unanimous that the high explosive is a simple shell and that any engineering concern could easily produce it. That has been the experience of France.

Ever sincerely,
D. Lloyd George."

This letter played its part — an important one — in the course of events which led to the reconstruction of the Government by the formation of the first Coalition — a matter with which I deal in more detail elsewhere in this narrative.

Lord Northcliffe (who at that time owned the *Times* as well as the *Daily Mail*) was personally responsible for the publication by the *Times* of the dispatch from its Military Correspondent, Colonel Repington. Lord Northcliffe had for some time been receiving an unending stream of letters and statements from men at the front about the shell shortage, but all efforts to give publicity to these complaints had been diligently blacked out of his proofs by the Censor. He was not content with the news that the Ministry was to be reconstructed. He attributed the blame for the shell shortage to Lord Kitchener, and he resolved to drive him out of office if he possibly could. On hearing that he would be retained in the reconstructed Ministry, he came out on May 21st with an article in the *Daily Mail* with a headline that ran: "THE SHELLS SCANDAL: LORD KITCHENER'S TRAGIC BLUNDER."

The *Daily Mail* and the *Times* were solemnly burned on the Stock Exchange that afternoon. But the campaign for more shells went on. On May 25th the *Times* published a letter from Bishop Furse, at that time Bishop of Pretoria, now Bishop of St. Albans, who had just returned from a visit to the front. The following extracts from his letter give some picture of the situation which the Bishop had found:

". . . When battalion after battalion of infantry — and, as was recently the case in the Ypres salient, regiment after regiment of cavalry, too — have to sit in trenches day after day, night after night, being pounded by high explosives from enemy guns, with no guns behind them capable of keeping down the enemy's fire, then the conclusion they draw is obvious — namely, that the nation has failed to provide sufficient guns or ammunition to meet those of the enemy.

"When, night after night and day after day, the men in the trenches know that for every one hand grenade or rifle grenade or trench mortar bomb which they throw at the enemy they will get back in answer anything from five to ten, then the conclusion they draw is also obvious — namely, that the nation does not somehow realise the situation, or, if it does, has not made it its business to supply what is necessary. . . . They know that it is little short of murder for a nation to ask men, however full of the right spirit, to face an enemy amply equipped with big guns and the right kind of ammunition, unless they are at least equipped with equally effective munitions of war.

"There can only be one impression left on the minds of men in such a case, and that is that somehow or other the nation does not know the truth, does not understand, and is not backing them, for, knowing the old country as they do, they have no doubt that if Germany can produce these things we can, if we will. . . ."

An officer home from the front stated in the *Northwich Chronicle* of May 22nd, 1915:

". . . People at home do not appear to realise how critical the position is out here. . . . The Germans have still unlimited supplies of munitions. . . . You can rub it in about our need for men and munitions of war. I am sorry to say that in the ten days' battle about Ypres our men suffered heavily owing to lack of ammunition. The Germans poured shells into our lines. . . . For our men it was a terrible time, while the Germans shelled us heavily and we, owing to shortage of ammunition, could not reply effectively. It is up to everybody at home to realise what such a situation means, and for people to understand that successful war cannot be waged without enormous supplies being available on the spot."

The two foregoing extracts represent the point of view of an onlooker and of a man in the trenches. I will quote, as the view of the man behind the guns an extract from a striking letter written to me at the time by Captain H. Fitz-Herbert Wright, M.P. for Leominster, who was serving as an artillery officer on the Western Front. The address on his letter was "Belgium, 29/5/15." He said:

". . . I rejoined the 4th North Midland Brigade (Howitzer) on the outbreak of the War and have been serving out here for nearly 13 weeks as a Captain and Officer Commanding the Ammunition Column. . . . As O.C. Amm. Col., all the shells fired by my brigade pass through my hands. We have been attached to two divisions — the 4th and the 46th, both in the 2nd Army. When we first got into the firing line in the first week of March we were allowed 20 rounds per gun per day: *80 rounds per day per battery*. We have been in action throughout. Our allowance is now two rounds per gun per day, *or eight rounds per battery per day*. It isn't that our fellows have made bad practice, or that there are not any targets suitable for our 50-pound lyddite shells. General Smith-Dorrien has publicly and privately given us the highest praise for the accuracy and effectiveness of our fire, and our fellows are made much of by all the infantry over whom they have fired; and, as to targets, we daily see the German trenches, and works growing and growing, simply asking to be pounded. I have to-day returned from having a week with our 1st Battery, spent mainly in an observation station, and I speak of what I have seen. The battery commanders in our Brigade, the Q.F. brigades, the R.H.A. and the Heavy are now not allowed to fire except by order of the General even one round.

"The R.H.A. adjutant told me he had to send 1500 rounds down to the 1st Army for the recent fighting down South, and he had now an empty park and column; one of the officers of the Heavies told me his park and column are at this moment empty (4.7-inch shells) and he may not fire even in the event of an attack without express orders. My batteries in 12 weeks have averaged a little over 60 rounds per battery a week. Naturally, I don't know the reason, but I suspect, and we all suspect, that there are no shells for us. Anyhow, here we are inviting attack, seeing the enemy firing daily 20 or 30 rounds into our lines to our one into theirs. We don't know or care who is to blame; we only know that we are being starved to death for want of shells, and our infantry fated daily to a more and more terrible task if an attack either by the Germans or ourselves takes place in our zone. I know nothing of other zones except by hearsay. We want to be fed; soldiers do not live by bread alone. . . .

"Nor is that all; we are outclassed in guns, number and quality; we are outranged; I am not now speaking of our Brigade, but generally. So far as our Brigade is concerned, our guns were pretty old in South Africa, and are, therefore, getting into years now. The 5-inch Howitzer never should have come out here. I raised this matter last September through Talbot and tried to get the 4.5-inch Howitzer, the Regular gun, but got the answer direct from W.O. that it was impossible as there were none, and the output of guns hadn't yet overtaken the wastage. However, we are doing our best and, having had good positions well concealed, at short ranges have, as I already quoted, done well. If we got into the open or had to shoot at anything over

3500 yards we should be off the map in five minutes. We fire one round a minute, and the shell takes 20 seconds to go the distance. A q.f. at from 10 to 15 rounds a minute would find us easy victims.

"Nor is that all: outclassed in guns; little or no ammunition; that sums up the Artillery part of the show, except to say that much of the shells we have are shrapnel — that does not apply to my Brigade, which has only lyddite — which is less useful than rain, not being wet, against the German trenches.

"Now for the infantry — and more magnificent infantry will never be seen. In our division there are two machine-guns per battalion. The Germans have 16; our Regulars have six or eight; in our Division we have two trench mortars on a front of not less than three miles; the Germans have them at frequent intervals all along; our hand grenades are in many cases "hand"-made and truly "hand" grenades; a few are thrown and the Germans promptly answer with 50-pound bombs. We call that showing our superiority. I suppose of courage — certainly not of equipment. Our lights are ridiculous beside the German lights . . . we do not use gas. Personally, I hope we shan't have to, though if it is true that our air reconnaissance reports that what were supposed to be light railways coming up their lines are in reality 18-inch pipes conjectured to be used for gas on a large scale, it is probable we shall never have the chance, even if we want to.

"Now are these facts anything for England, the richest country in the world or nearly, anything to be proud of? Are they not a matter rather for sackcloth and ashes?

"If we get ammunition we can hold on, though the poor infantry will go on getting cut to pieces. If we get plenty of ammunition we can go ahead. I suppose you know that the Artists, now a training corps for officers, rejoices in the name of the Suicides Club — magnificent, cheery fellows? Where is the responsibility for that name being more than justified by the casualty lists?

"Never mind where is the responsibility; get the mess cleared up. You have the pluck and go of ten. More power to you!

"I hope I haven't by any fault of diction or over-emphasis

led you to think I am exaggerating, I am but dotting the 'i's' and crossing the 't's' of the Bishop's letter. He and I are old friends since the Eton days. . . ."

I have in my possession a bundle of letters, blue-pencilled by the Censor or stamped by him "NOT TO BE PUBLISHED" which were sent to me by Northcliffe about this time to show me the sort of reports he was receiving from France, but was not allowed to print. The circumstances in which these came to me from him are described as follows by Tom Clarke in his interesting book, "My Northcliffe Diary":

"May 25, 1915: Several stories from officers at the front supporting Northcliffe's allegation *re* shell shortage having been refused publication by the censors at the Press Bureau, the Chief has given instructions that we must not submit them to the Censor. When it was pointed out that we might be trapped on a technical point, he said, 'I have been threatened so much in the past few weeks that I do not mind now. Send all these censored proofs to Lloyd George and Curzon. They know the truth, and it will let them see how the Press Bureau is keeping it back.' "

Here are a few specimens culled from this collection of appeals and complaints:

"We had some artillery officers to mess the other evening, and they were very worried. They had had orders from General Headquarters to fire only a certain number of shells a day and their requests for supplies were always avoided by some excuse. . . ."

". . . We have just to sit tight in the trenches while the German high explosives batter them to bits, and the main part of our casualties in the 16-hour bombardment which I described in the last letter were from this cause. . . . Out of our company of from 150 to 200 men only 13 came out of the trenches after the last attack."

". . . It makes your heart break to see those men going forward and then held up — one after another, fighting and struggling, until, wearied out, they collapse like a wet cloth. And why? Because there is not an adequate supply of high explosives to blow the wire to bits, and let our men go at the enemy."

". . . I have often heard the wish expressed that a representative of the manufacturing population at home might be present in one of our front trenches to witness the eagerness and anxiety of officers and men as they watch the enemy's trench being bombarded preparatory to an assault. There is not one who does not realise that on the intensity and volume of that fire his life and all his chances of success depend. On these occasions shrapnel gives no confidence to those who have had a little experience; they know that it has as much effect as one would expect from a handful of gravel on a German machine-gun emplacement, and they know that over some 200 yards it is only machine-guns that can stop them. When the first line has been destroyed by them (*i.e.* by German machine guns) many of us have seen the second immediately throw themselves over our parapet to certain and conscious destruction.

"Actually to witness this heroic perseverance and self-sacrifice of a fighting body which in quality and war experience cannot soon — if ever — be replaced, and to know that it is all due to the tardy organisation of the war machinery at home raises thoughts that cannot be expressed 'in print.' "

Although statements of this nature were banned by the Censor from the columns of the Press, the facts they set out were becoming common knowledge in every newspaper office, and in countless homes throughout the land. That knowledge doubtless played an important part in making the country ripe for the change of Government which was announced on May 19th, when Mr. Asquith, having invited his fellow-ministers of the Liberal Government to resign their offices, reconstructed his Ministry as a Coalition Government, including the leaders of the Conservative Party.

## CHAPTER VII

# THE POLITICS OF THE WAR

British preoccupation with Ireland in July, 1914 — Unity created by advent of World War — Effect in the Commons — Unionist support for the Government — Popularity of war with Germany — Influence of Lord Kitchener — The Parties in Parliament — Politics disappear in the Army — Advantage of Liberal Government initiating the War — Growing criticism of the Government: Mr. M'Kenna challenged — Uneasiness over munition shortage.

No nation engaged in a struggle with a redoubtable foe can afford to dissipate its energies and distract its executive by party controversy. The last days of July, 1914, found the traditional British parties confronting each other in the fiercest political conflict waged since the suppression of the last Jacobite rebellion. We were faced with the prospect of an internecine struggle which would have rent the nation into warring factions such as these islands have not witnessed since the great Civil Wars. The threatened uprising of Ulster against the dominion of an Irish Parliament was not a bluff. The Orange North would have fought before it submitted. The Curragh incident, the gun-running in Ulster, followed by the arming of the South (which was the beginning of the bloodshed of the six years that followed) all pointed towards the possibilities of bloody strife once more on a political battlefield. Political and religious issues had not so long ago been referred in these islands to the arbitrament of the sword. It is never safe to say that such things will not happen again. "The thing that hath been, it is that which shall be, and that which is done, is that which shall be done, and there is no new thing under the sun." This saying, uttered over 2000 years ago, is being verified in every generation, and it is never quite wise to assume that it has exhausted its application to any branch of human thought or activity. The thinker and the striker have always worked in a close partnership — more or less willing, and less rather than more understanding. Unionists who attended Ulster meetings in England tell me that they never saw such depths of fierce indignation as that aroused by the threat of force to subject the Protestants of the North to the rule of the Catholic South. On the other hand, I myself never witnessed such an outburst of ferocious anger as that which was aroused in the House of Commons when the late Mr. John Ward and Mr. J. H. Thomas denounced the attempt of certain Army officials to override the Constitution by threatening to disobey orders and refusing to carry out laws of which they disapproved. The North had armed, the South was arming. What would have happened?

There was no surety that if bloodshed ensued its flow could have been confined to Ireland. There are towns on this side of the Channel where it would have been difficult to keep the peace amongst the votaries of warring creeds if their fellow-religionists in Ireland on either side were being slain. Wisdom might have intervened. But it might not. Mankind was only too ready for the shedding of blood, as we were to discover in a few days.

Then there came real war, like a mighty rushing wind, the struggle not of sects and factions, but of nations and continents, and the incipient fires of civil war were swept into the great conflagration. All the same the spreading flame of national dissension in Britain encouraged the war-mongers of Germany and Austria to plunge. England was supposed to be temporarily out of the reckoning. Without her tenacious aid, France and Russia would soon collapse. The Ulster trouble was an undoubted factor in precipitating the

Great War. How little the German rulers knew the temper of the British people! At the sound of the trumpet they all fell into line and wheeled against the common danger. There was not a perceptible break or gap in their ranks. This coming together of all creeds and sections to face a national peril was immediately reflected in the House of Commons. Its mood quickly changed. A few days before the outbreak of war the Prime Minister had been howled down by Unionist members excited beyond the bounds of Parliamentary decorum. A little later and the same members were cheering to the rafters the moving eloquence with which he called the nation to wage war with all its strength against the invaders of Belgium. In the course of a single day angry political passions were silenced and were followed by the just wrath which is too deep to be easily lashed into the frothing fury that so often churns the shallow waters of party recrimination. During the autumn and winter of 1914 and the early spring of 1915 this temper continued in the political world. Party politics and party bitterness disappeared. In fact, the Liberal Government received more unanimous and cordial support from Unionists confronting them than from the Liberal and Labour benches behind.

The reasons for this attitude are interesting and significant, and account to a large extent, if closely examined, for the political developments of the next six years. Previous wars in which this country had been engaged by no means closed down the hostilities of parties. They rather stoked political and personal antagonisms into fiercer enmity. Some of these wars actually became the dividing line of parties. The change which took place in 1914 cannot be explained by the supposition that we are more patriotic than our ancestors. The Conservative Party had in recent years become increasingly Germanophobe. Rivalry between the two Empires for supremacy on the seas and in the marts of the world accounted largely for the remarkable swing round in the Conservative attitude towards Germany. The Conservatives were far from desiring war anywhere. But when war with Germany came, there could be no doubt as to its popularity with Conservative-Tory leaders, Press and rank and file. It was something many of their most ardent spirits had hoped for. Others feared it was inevitable that we should be forced, sooner or later, to try conclusions with a Power that seemed to be preparing to destroy us. So when it came with a Liberal Government in power it was an auspicious combination of events of which they had not dreamed. There was a note of exhilaration in their support of the War. On the other hand, the Liberals felt the obligation of honour involved in the Belgian Treaty, and they promptly if unhappily followed a course prescribed by the greatest of their leaders in 1870 when he protected Belgium from invasion during the Franco-Prussian War. So the Conservatives entered the War with enthusiasm and the Liberals with reluctant conviction. Conservatives in particular were well pleased by Mr. Asquith's choice of Lord Kitchener as War Director inside his Cabinet. Lord Kitchener had no Party associations; but if he had any leanings they were towards Conservatism. Even those leanings were inherited prejudices rather than convictions. The latter he had neither the time nor the inclination to acquire during his busy life on duties for his country in environments far removed from our Party conflicts. At any rate his appointment to the War Office was a guarantee of the Government's intention to prosecute the War vigorously, and that Party considerations should not enter into its conduct. His selection for what was practically a War Dictatorship gave satisfaction and confidence to the nation generally and to the Conservative Party in particular. It undoubtedly had the effect of restraining criticism, for doubts cast on the

War direction implied censure of Lord Kitchener. For the first few months of the War his influence was paramount. His very picture on the walls counted more than all the appeals of all the political leaders of all parties.

The Liberal Government commanded a working majority in the House of Commons. It is true it was dependent for that majority on a Coalition of groups — the Liberal, Nationalist, and Labour groups. The country has been governed by Coalitions for the greater part of the last half-century. In the 1914 Parliament the Conservatives, in fact, constituted the largest party in the House, but they could not attract the support of any other section. It followed that the Liberal Government could not be dismissed except by dissolution, and that was unthinkable in the agony of the Great War. It would have been an unspeakable crime to divide the nation when even united it could barely be saved from defeat, so formidable was the foe we had challenged. The Conservatives were led by men of high character and capacity whose patriotism was above suspicion — Mr. Bonar Law, Mr. Balfour, Lord Lansdowne, Sir Edward Carson, and Lord Curzon. Such men were much too high-minded to desire electoral victory bought at such a cost to their country. Liberals will admit that Conservative actions throughout the War were dictated by the highest motives of patriotism and that during that period they were willing to sink all Party dealing and rivalries and maintain their opponents in full possession of power so long as that power was wielded in the achievement of victory for their country's banner.

The men of the Army and Navy who at the bidding of their country were undergoing hardships and facing death on the seas from Scapa Flow to Coromandel, and in strange lands from Nieuport to Nineveh, were of many different political faiths, and there were multitudes whose faith had not yet been cast in any party mould. Men of political parties and unions left their badges at home and joined the new fraternity of sacrifice, and others whose opinions were unformed and who were still unattached entered the same comradeship. They expected — and they had a right to expect — that their jeopardy should not be increased by the irrelevant bickerings at home of those men who could afford to indulge in untimely animosities with complete immunity to themselves. Diversion and dissipation of thought and energy in attack or defence in time-honoured Party quarrels which had no bearing on the issues of the War (and which could not be dealt with during the War) would have weakened a front which had no superfluous strength to spare and intensified dangers already almost too appalling for human nature to bear. That is why France with her face all wrinkled with Party lines, displayed the *union sacrée* to the eyes of the world, and Britain, also riven with Party schisms, presented the spectacle of a united front.

There was an undoubted advantage from the point of view of national unity in having a Liberal rather than a Tory Government in power when war was declared. There was a further advantage in having a Government at the head of affairs which had the support of Labour. This secured the adhesion of the great Labour organisations whose action and sympathetic aid was essential to its vigorous prosecution. Had Labour been hostile the War could not have been carried on effectively. Had Labour been lukewarm victory would have been secured with increased and increasing difficulty. The most prominent and influential leaders of Trade Unionism worked for victory throughout the War. Without their help it could not have been achieved. But beyond and above all these considerations, as a factor in the attainment of national unity, was the circumstance that the War had been declared by a party which by tradition and training regarded war with the deepest aversion, and has more especially since the days of Gladstone, Cobden and Bright, regarded itself as specially charged with the promotion of the cause of peace.

The spring of 1915 witnessed a growing change in the attitude of Parliament. Questions multiplied, debates became more prolonged, the atmosphere became more critical, the note more challenging. Mr. M'Kenna's administration of the Home Office provoked much dissatisfaction, and not merely on the Unionist benches. His policy towards residents of enemy extraction in this country was thought to be too protective, too indifferent to the dangers which might arise from espionage. The country was all camp and arsenal, and valuable information for the enemy was visible everywhere without speering or spying. Mr. M'Kenna's rigid and fretful answers, though always technically complete, were provocative. Whilst administering the letter of his trust, he showed too clearly that he had no sympathy with its spirit. And the nation was uneasy. Its sons were falling, and information was undoubtedly getting through from the shores of Britain which helped the enemy in the slaughter. Subsequent events proved that intelligence of great value to the enemy percolated to Germany through the agency of persons living unmolested in England under Mr. M'Kenna's indulgent régime. War is a ruthless business and those who wage it cannot afford to be too discriminating. The nation was right in thinking that this was not the time to risk the national security on glib pedantries. The anxiety of the people found expression in both Houses of Parliament, and the challenge, at first friendly, quickly became more insistent and ended on a note of undisguised anger.

Then came the rumour that our gallant troops were being inadequately provided with ammunition. Men were falling fast under the continuous bombardment of an enemy well equipped with the most formidable guns lavishly provided with an overwhelming supply of high explosives. Casualties were multiplying at an alarming rate. Though the figures were withheld from the public by a prudent War Office there was, as I have already shown, a growing feeling that our losses were great. With that in the mind of the nation, information leaked through as to the helplessness of our troops under the hammering of the Teutonic Thor. The facts were too poignant not to provoke a cry from those who knew them. The article in the *Times* would have forced Parliament to take sharp cognisance of the lamentable deficiency had not Mr. Asquith anticipated its intervention by a dramatic move.

CHAPTER VIII

# THE POLITICAL CRISIS IN MAY, 1915

The gathering storm: Munitions; Dardanelles — Government lacks energy — Opposition grows restive — Lord Fisher's resignation — How I heard the news — Mr. Asquith fails to turn him — Mr. Bonar Law roused to action — Mr. Asquith agrees to a coalition — Letters from Mr. Bonar Law — Controversy over M'Kenna and Haldane — Haldane's work for the Army — M'Kenna forgiven and Haldane sacrificed — Shell debate in the Commons — Coalition announced — My munitions tour postponed — Unjust treatment of Mr. Winston Churchill — Decision to form Ministry of Munitions — My appointment announced.

POLITICAL crises never come out of the blue. Clouds gather in the sky, sometimes from one quarter, sometimes from many. Suddenly one of those clouds is black with menace, approaches with surprising speed, hangs right overhead, and breaks into angry flashes.

The political crisis of May, 1915, was no exception to this meteorological rule. It was due to a combination of factors which had been at work for some time. The final addition of one extra cause for discontent at the existing conditions provoked the storm which swept away the Liberal Government, which had weathered many tempests. It is not correct to ascribe the change in government solely, or mainly, to the shortage of shell for our armies. The general dissatisfaction with the conduct of the War, of which there were many symptoms, and of which the culmination was reached in the second half of May, was not only due to the realisation of the munitions situation. Other contributing factors were the failure of the offensive in France, as to which expectations had been unduly raised; and disappointment over the result of the Dardanelles, with a growing feeling that the expedition was either misconceived or muddled. The disagreement between the First Lord of the Admiralty and the First Sea Lord deepened this feeling.

Underlying the various specific grounds for anxiety in different directions was a sense of revolt against the attitude of the Government and what was regarded as its leisurely and take-for-granted attitude in dealing with vitally serious matters, matters of life and death to the whole of the Allies and the British Empire, and to hundreds of thousands of gallant young men who had offered their lives to their country. The War was not being treated either with sufficient seriousness or adequate energy. So far back as the beginning of this year I had urged that more constant attention should be paid to the higher conduct of the War. *And for five and a half weeks, from the 6th of April to the 14th of May, the War Council had not been convened,* and the machinery set up by the Government for exercising a general supervision over the conduct of the War had not been afforded an opportunity to exercise the functions for which it had been created and for which it was responsible.

There was a genuine conviction on the part of many who had no desire to provoke a Ministerial crisis that if an improvement were not soon effected we should lose the War. This opinion was held very strongly by many members of the Opposition, who had so far loyally supported the Government, but were becoming increasingly restive. In fact, it was obvious that unless prompt action were taken to convince the country that a fresh urge was being put into the direction of affairs there would be a most dangerous division in the nation, and that this division might develop on party lines. Nothing could have been more fatal to that national unity which was essential to victory in so deadly a struggle.

On the 14th of May the War Council sat again for the first time after a long period of coma. Its meeting was purely formal, and only one or two members were summoned. On that day there appeared in the Press the violent outburst on the shell situation to which I have already referred in a previous section, and next day occurred the incident which actually brought matters to a head. This was the resignation from the Admiralty of Lord Fisher over our Dardanelles policy. In view of the controversy which arose later on as to the interference of the political with the naval chiefs in the matter of strategy, it is interesting to note that this particular crisis arose partly from the complete subservience of Ministers to our chief military adviser in the conduct of the War on land, and partly from the overriding of our principal naval adviser by a combination of generals and statesmen in the conduct of the War at sea. It had long been known that Lord Fisher was opposed to the attempt to force the Dardanelles by the Navy alone, but his resignation, which deprived the country of the services of its most distinguished naval expert, was the match which, applied to the discontent generated everywhere, blew up the complacency of statesmen. With it went the Government under which the War began.

I heard of Lord Fisher's contemplated resignation quite accidentally. On the morning of Saturday, May 15th, as I was passing through the entrance lobby of No. 10 Downing Street, I met Lord Fisher, and was struck by a dour change in his attitude. A combative grimness had taken the place of his usually genial greeting; the lower lip of his set mouth was thrust forward, and the droop at the corner was more marked than usual. His curiously Oriental features were more than ever those of a graven image in an Eastern temple, with a sinister frown.

"I have resigned!" was his greeting, and on my inquiring the reason he replied, "I can stand it no longer." He then informed me that he was on his way to see the Prime Minister, having made up his mind to take no further part in the Dardanelles "foolishness," and was off to Scotland that night.

I tried to persuade him to postpone his departure until the Monday, which would give him an opportunity of placing his case before a War Council, but he declined to wait another hour. I told him that so far as the Council was concerned he had never expressed any dissent from the policy or the plans for the expedition; that though I was a member of the War Council and had been opposed to that venture from the start I had not heard one word of protest from him; and that it was only right that we should be given an opportunity of hearing his objections, weighing his advice, and taking the appropriate action. His answer was that Mr. Churchill was his Chief, and that by the traditions of the service he was not entitled to differ from him in public. On being reminded by me that the Council was a Council of War, and that he was bound as a member of that Council to speak his mind freely to all his colleagues around the table, he continued that he had at the outset made an emphatic protest against the whole expedition to the Prime Minister privately, and had left to him the responsibility of communicating or withholding that knowledge. Here he was referring to a conversation he and Mr. Churchill had with Mr. Asquith before the War Council meeting on the 28th of January. This protest had never been passed on to the Council.

Failing to shake him in his purpose, I sent a message to Mr. Asquith. He was at Mr. Geoffrey Howard's wedding. (He had a queer liking for weddings and funerals and rarely missed one which he might be expected to attend.) I conveyed to him that I thought it was important he should see

Lord Fisher at once. But the Prime Minister's powers of persuasion and authority were equally unavailing with the First Sea Lord, who subsequently visited Mr. M'Kenna, his former Chief at the Admiralty. Mr. M'Kenna was also an opponent of the Dardanelles expedition. At this period Mr. Winston Churchill was Mr. M'Kenna's pet aversion, for Mr. Churchill had supplanted him at the Admiralty. He was, therefore, not in a mood to extricate his supplanter from his troubles. Whatever happened at this interview, the impulsive old sailor left for Scotland that night, his departure producing an inevitable crisis, for political circles in London were seething with disquieting rumours, and there was a general feeling that things were being muddled badly and that the War was therefore not going well for us. The next I heard of the matter was when I saw Mr. M'Kenna that afternoon. Lord Fisher had reported to him the conversation he had with me. Mr. M'Kenna said that the "old boy" was quite obdurate and was not open to persuasion.

The following Monday morning Mr. Bonar Law, who had for years been a personal friend of mine and on terms of greater cordiality with me than is usual between political adversaries who are taking a strenuous part in party conflicts, came to see me at the Treasury.

Informing me that he had received a communication which seemed to him authentic indicating that Lord Fisher had resigned, he asked me point-blank if that were the case. He alluded to an unsigned letter received by him which had obviously been written by the First Sea Lord. Lord Fisher's characters and style were so dashing and on so bold a scale that no one could fail to know at a glance who had written a letter of his. The signature was superfluous.

On being told by me that his information was correct Mr. Bonar Law emphasised the grave nature of the political question raised, especially as he was convinced that the Government were misinformed about the shell situation. His party had supported the Government consistently throughout the months of the War, without seeking party advantage, but there was a growing discontent amongst Conservatives at this attitude of unqualified support, especially over the treatment of alien enemies, the deficiency of shells, and the failure of the Dardanelles expedition. Matters, indeed, had come to such a pitch that it would be impossible for him to restrain his followers, and yet it was essential to avoid any division in the nation in face of the enemy. He was specially emphatic as to the impossibility of allowing Mr. Churchill to remain at the Admiralty if Lord Fisher persisted in his resignation. On this point he made it clear that the Opposition meant at all hazards to force a Parliamentary challenge. After some discussion we agreed that the only certain way to preserve a united front was to arrange for more complete coöperation between parties in the direction of the War. I asked him if he would wait a few minutes while I went to No. 10 to see the Prime Minister. I went alone to see Mr. Asquith and put the circumstances quite plainly before him. The Prime Minister at once recognised that in order to avert a serious Parliamentary conflict, which would certainly lower the prestige of the Government, if it did not actually bring about its defeat, it was necessary to reconstruct the Cabinet and admit into it some of the leaders of the Unionist Party.

This decision took an incredibly short time. I left Mr. Asquith and returned to Mr. Bonar Law and invited him to accompany me to the Cabinet Room to talk things over with the Prime Minister. In less than a quarter of an hour we realised that the Liberal Government was at an end and that for it would be substituted a Coalition Government. It was decided that Mr. Bonar Law should write a letter to the Prime Minister explaining the position in order to enable the latter to sound his leading colleagues.

Later in the day I received the following letter from Mr. Bonar Law. The enclosure fairly represented the attitude he adopted in the morning conversations, first with me and then with the Prime Minister.

"Lansdowne House,
Berkeley Square, W.
17th May, 1915.

"Dear Lloyd George,

"I enclose copy of the letter.

"You will see we have altered it to the extent that we do not definitely offer Coalition but the substance is the same.

Yours sincerely,
A. BONAR LAW."

"Lansdowne House,
17th May, 1915.

"Dear Mr. Asquith,

"Lord Lansdowne and I have learnt with dismay that Lord Fisher has resigned, and we have come to the conclusion that we cannot allow the House to adjourn until this fact has been made known and discussed.

"We think that the time has come when we ought to have a clear statement from you as to the policy which the Government intend to pursue. In our opinion things cannot go on as they are, and some change in the constitution of the Government seems to us inevitable if it is to retain a sufficient measure of public confidence to conduct the War to a successful conclusion.

"The situation in Italy makes it particularly undesirable to have anything in the nature of a controversial discussion in the House of Commons at present, and if you are prepared to take the necessary steps to secure the object which I have indicated, and if Lord Fisher's resignation is in the meantime postponed, we shall be ready to keep silence now. Otherwise I must to-day ask you whether Lord Fisher has resigned, and press for a day to discuss the situation arising out of his resignation.

Yours, etc.,

A. BONAR LAW."

The story of the formation of the new Ministry has been told from different angles by many writers great and petty. The actual appointments were a subject of something which in business might be termed haggling between the Parties. The worst controversy came over Lord Haldane and Mr. M'Kenna. The Conservatives had taken a fierce dislike to both on quite unreasonable grounds, and were bent on leaving them out. They were both personal friends of the Prime Minister — his friendship with Lord Haldane being of very long standing. What was the offence of these special objects of Conservative animosity? Lord Haldane was the originator and organiser of the Expeditionary Force, which had served the Allies so promptly and so effectively. It was a fine piece of organisation. He was the creator of the General Staff, which might have saved us many a tragic error had it not been practically dismantled by Lord Kitchener. The Officers' Training Corps, which equipped the new armies with a splendid team of young lieutenants, was also his idea. But in one of those philosophic dissertations which gave him and his friends equal pleasure he had referred to Germany as his "spiritual home." That was an *ex post facto* crime for which he must be banished from the sight of all patriotic men. There was also a rooted conviction in the Unionist mind that Lord Haldane, after his visit to Berlin, had failed to warn the Cabinet as to the German preparations for war which he must have observed. All these criticisms were in my judgment fundamentally unjust, and inflicted a deep wrong on a man whose patriotic energy had rendered greater service to the nation in the reorganisation of the

Army than any War Secretary since the days of Cardwell. However, temper was bitter and unconscionable on this subject, and Mr. Asquith and Sir Edward Grey sacrificed friendship to expediency.

Mr. M'Kenna's crime, as I have already explained, was that in his administration at the Home Office he had been too tender to aliens. And in days when a rush-light at a farm building on the coast became a signal to the enemy the Home Office indulgence to alien enemies dwelling within our gates was considered to be treason. So he also must go. Mr. Asquith saved him and sacrificed Haldane. Lord Haldane was not qualified to fight a personal battle for himself. Mr. M'Kenna was. So Lord Haldane was driven in disgrace into the wilderness and Mr. M'Kenna was promoted to the second place in the Government.

Meanwhile, on the same day the subject of munitions was debated in the House of Commons, where, as a member put it, the one word impressed on the hearts of most members would be "Shells." Arguments were put forward for the formation of a Coalition Cabinet, and the Government were pressed to have a debate on the whole subject of munitions. This was refused by Mr. Asquith. The next day, in the House of Lords, Lord Kitchener admitted the delay in producing the material which it had been foreseen would be required, and attributed it to the unprecedented and almost unlimited calls on the manufacturing resources of the country. On the 19th, the Prime Minister announced to the House that steps were in contemplation which would involve the "reconstruction of the Government on a broader personal and political basis." In other words, he had been persuaded by the general discontent with the conduct of the War shown on all sides to form the first Coalition Government. On the same day I again wrote to Mr. Asquith, who had been responsible for my appointment as Chairman of the Cabinet Munitions Committee, a letter on the subject of munitions, which has already been recorded in an earlier section of this narrative. I was anxious that the munitions situation should be recognised as an essential part of the problems which the new Coalition would have to face at the outset of its existence. I did not think it was in the national interest that it should be submerged in controversies about the Dardanelles or the treatment of aliens.

As the whole political situation was in the melting pot, I decided to postpone for a few days a tour I had contemplated making round some of the centres of munition production in order to address the workers. On the 21st some of the Ministers and the leaders of the Opposition met in conclave at Downing Street in what was really the first joint meeting of the new combination. The main subject of our deliberations for that meeting and for almost all the rest of the week was the composition of the new Government. It was only settled at a late hour on the 25th. The task was a difficult one, for it entailed much consideration of the balancing of parties, as well as of personal claims inside the parties.

Mr. Asquith honoured me with his particular confidence during these discussions. The appointments took up valuable time, but at last they were concluded. The most notable change was the taking of Mr. Winston Churchill out of the Admiralty and placing him in charge of the Duchy of Lancaster, a post generally reserved either for beginners in the Cabinet or for distinguished politicians who had reached the first stages of unmistakable decrepitude. It was a cruel and unjust degradation. The Dardanelles failure was due not so much to Mr. Churchill's precipitancy as to Lord Kitchener's and Mr. Asquith's procrastination. Mr. Churchill's part in that unfortunate enterprise had been worked out by him with the most meticulous care to the last particular, and nothing had been overlooked or neglected as far as the naval operations were concerned. The fatal delays and mishandlings had all been in the other branch of the Service. It is true that the conception of a one-sided Naval operation without simultaneous military action was due to Mr. Churchill's impetuosity, but both the Prime Minister and Lord Kitchener were equally convinced that it was the right course to pursue. When I learned the office finally offered to Mr. Churchill, it came to me as an unpleasant surprise. I reckoned it would have been impossible to keep him at the Admiralty, in view of the dispute which had precipitated the crisis. The Unionists would not, and could not in the circumstances, have assented to his retention in that office. But it was quite unnecessary in order to propitiate them to fling him from the masthead, whence he had been directing the fire, down to the lower deck to polish the brass. In the first sorting out and allotment of offices in which I had taken part, it had been arranged that he should be placed in the Colonial Office, where his energies would have been helpfully employed in organising our resources in the Empire beyond the seas; and I cannot to this hour explain the change of plans which suddenly occurred. The brutality of the fall stunned Mr. Churchill, and for a year or two of the War his fine brain was of no avail in helping in its prosecution.

Apart from the appointment of individuals, one of the most important decisions reached, and one which concerned me most particularly was that taken to form a separate department under a Minister of Cabinet rank, to undertake the difficult and complicated work of mobilising the national resources for the production of munitions, and so to relieve the executive military authorities from a duty which had grown far too heavy to be carried out by them. Since I had consistently taken a great interest in the subject, had shown by every means in my power the importance I attached to it, and had been the head of the Cabinet Committee dealing with it, the Prime Minister invited me to take charge of the new Ministry of Munitions.

On May 26th, 1915, the names of the first Coalition Cabinet were published, and the following announcement appeared in the Press:

> "The Prime Minister has decided that a new department shall be created, to be called the Ministry of Munitions, charged with organising the supply of munitions of war. Mr. Lloyd George has undertaken the formation and temporary direction of this department, and during his tenure of office as Minister of Munitions will vacate the office of Chancellor of the Exchequer."

The change in the Government had taken place; the Coalition was formed, and the War Council reorganised under the title of the Dardanelles Committee, which more accurately described its scope. Owing to the general upheaval occasioned by the political change, the newly formed Committee did not actually meet until the 7th of June, or three weeks after the last session of the body it superseded. In fact, at this stage, when both in the east and west there were urgent questions awaiting decision, those especially charged with the control of our war policy met only once during a period of nearly nine weeks. So fully occupied was I in organising the new Ministry of Munitions, that for a time I was personally unable to pay as much attention as I had done to the general conduct of the War, and did not, during June, attend any of the sittings of the new Committee.

## CHAPTER IX

# THE MINISTRY OF MUNITIONS:

## Establishment and Labour Problems

### 1. My Appointment

Reluctance to become Minister of Munitions — Departmental jealousies — Problems confronting the new Ministry — Mr. Asquith's letter of appreciation — Letter from Theodore Roosevelt — Roosevelt and Asquith — First quarters of the Ministry — The problem of furniture — Colonel House's Account — A victory over red tape — Too many mirrors — Surveying the field — Creation of a staff — Choosing the right type of men — The "three-ton" man — Personalities in the new Ministry — Character of Sir Percy Girouard — My statement in the Commons on the new appointments — Analysis of the munitions situation — Tour of the engineering centres — Speech at Manchester — Defence of compulsory measures — Appeal for relaxation of trade union restrictions — Reception of speech — The Liverpool meeting — Ministry of Munitions Act — Definition of the Ministry's powers — Verdict of "Official History" — Defence of the Ministry's achievements — War Office orders ineffective — Defects of the War Office policy — M. Albert Thomas on Woolwich — War Office failure to work out programmes — Unwillingness to adopt new methods — Contracts taken over by the Ministry — Wide range of Ministry's task — Ministry's direct concern with every stage in production.

It was on Whit-Monday, 1915, that I finally left the Treasury to take up my duty as Minister of Munitions. It was a serious decision for me to make. As Chancellor of the Exchequer I had been holding the highest and most responsible office under the Prime Minister — the post which ranked next to his in Parliamentary importance, and in that position had been initiating and carrying through schemes of social amelioration which were very congenial to my disposition and upbringing. I was exchanging all that for the terrible task of manufacturing engines for human mutilation and slaughter.

Whatever I had done directly or indirectly to hasten or assist in the creation of this department, which I regarded as most urgently necessary, the last thing I desired was to have to assume control of it. I had no wish to give up the Chancellorship of the Exchequer for something of an unknown nature. I cannot say that I undertook the functions of my new office with any feelings of exhilarate confidence. I was taking in hand the organisation of a business that was quite new to me. The only insight given me into its workings had revealed a state of utter confusion and chaos. I was leaving a well-established and well-organised department, staffed by some of the picked men of the Civil Service, and directed in all its ramifications by well-defined rules and traditions which worked with perfect smoothness. I was taking in hand a department with no staff, no regulations, no traditions. All new departments are viewed with a certain measure of suspicion by the older establishments. But the department which mattered most to the success of the new Ministry regarded it not only with distrust but with profound dislike, veiled behind a mask of contempt. Its very existence was a statutory expression of a national verdict of failure delivered by the High Court of Parliament against the War Office. It was cut out of the living body of the War Office, and that hurt. There is no historical testimony as to Adam's sensations after the rib had been torn out of his side. But he must have felt sore and resentful. In his case, however, the knowledge that by the operation he had secured a helpmate more than reconciled him to the excision. The War Office was surly, suspicious, and hostile, and no help the new Ministry tendered or gave softened the animosity of the War Lords towards it. Although Lord Kitchener personally treated me with every courtesy, his entourage was unsympathetic to the new venture, and later on he was stimulated by the hostility of his own and other departments to acquiesce in the erection of barriers in my way. This antagonism was one of the difficulties I foresaw and certainly endured.

Politically it was for me a wilderness of risks with no oasis in sight. There were numerous possibilities of serious conflict with organised labour over trade union regulations, hours of labour, wages, restrictions on mobility, and, most serious of all, over what I called dilution, *i.e.,* the mixing of the skilled labour with unskilled. Here you touched one of the most sensitive nerves of Trade Unionism. The question of drink had to be tackled, foreboding quarrels with a powerful trade in England and Wales, Scotland and Ireland. No wonder my old uncle and foster-father, Richard Lloyd, whose advice I was wont to listen to above all others, wrote to me and counselled me not to leave the Treasury. Yet in spite of all this, I felt as I reviewed all the circumstances of the national situation, and realised beyond a shadow of doubt the supreme and vital importance of a proper supply of munitions for our success in the war, and remembered the insistence with which I had urged this upon the Government, that I was in honour bound to accept if the Prime Minister thought I was the man best fitted for this post. I made my decision; and I never had cause to regret it. As I look back to-day upon the problems which were then presented to me, the extraordinary difficulties that surrounded the work which I took in hand, my own inexperience in that kind of work, the chaos and tangle with which I was confronted, I feel that in many ways the creation of the Ministry of Munitions was the most formidable task I ever undertook.

I was heartened to face the overwhelming responsibility of this step by a letter which I received at the time from Mr. Asquith. It ran as follows:

"10, Downing Street, S.W.
25th May, 1915.

"My dear Lloyd George,

"I cannot let this troubled and tumultous chapter in our history pass without letting you know what incalculable help and

10, Downing Street,
Whitehall. S.W.

Tu. 25 May 1915

My dear Lloyd George,

I cannot let this troubled & tumultuous chapter in our history close without trying to let you know what an incalculable help & support I have found in you all through. I shall never forget your devotion, your unselfishness, your powers of resource, what

FACSIMILE OF A LETTER WRITTEN BY MR. ASQUITH, WHEN PRIME MINISTER, TO MR. LLOYD GEORGE ON MAY 25TH, 1915 is (after all) the best of all things your self-forgetfulness.

These are the rare things that make the drudgery and squalor of politics, with its constant revelation of the large part played by petty & personal motives, endurable, and give to its dullness a lightning streak of nobility.

I thank you with all my heart.

Always your affecte

H H Asquith

support I have found in you all through. I shall never forget your devotion, your unselfishness, your powers of resource, and what is (after all) the best of things, your self-forgetfulness.

"These are the rare things which make the squalor and drudgery of politics, with its constant revelations of the large part played by petty and personal motives, endurable, and give to this drabness the lightning streak of nobility.

"I thank you with all my heart,

Always yours affectionately,

H. H. ASQUITH."

This letter from the man who had been my colleague for ten years, and to whom I had been principal Parliamentary lieutenant for seven years, gave me great delight. The black squad of envy had not yet succeeded in poisoning the wells of confidence between captain and second officer.

I received further encouragement from many quarters from friends near and far who wished me well and realised the terrific responsibility of my new venture. Amongst the letters which came to me was one which I specially prized for its understanding and sincerity from a great American statesman whose vision and superb courage I had always admired — Theodore Roosevelt.

"Oyster Bay,
Long Island, N. Y.
1st June, 1915.

"My dear Lloyd George,

"In a sense it is not my affair, but as one of your admirers and sympathisers I wish to congratulate you upon the action that has been taken in getting a Coalition Cabinet, and especially upon your part therein. More than all I wish to congratulate you upon what you have done in connection with this war. When the War is over, you will again take up the work of dealing with the Labour question, with Irish Home Rule, with many other matters. But the prime business at present for you to do is to save your country; and I admire the single-hearted manner with which you have devoted yourself to this great duty. I am sorry Redmond could not see his way to take office also, but, of course, there may have been reasons of which I know nothing that made it inadvisable for him to do so.

"Give my regards to Edward Grey,

Faithfully yours,

THEODORE ROOSEVELT."

The contiguity of these three famous names — Roosevelt, Asquith and Grey — reminds me how, shortly before the War, I met the former at a luncheon party given by Sir Edward Grey to Mr. Roosevelt when Mr. Asquith and I were the only other guests. Mr. Roosevelt was not the type of man who would attract Mr. Asquith. His vehemence repelled the unexcitable Englishman. Asquith was a man of refractory prejudices which he never concealed. This gave a certain arrogance to his manner when dealing with men he did not care for. It was obvious during the table talk that Mr. Asquith had an instinctive dislike, which was not far removed from contempt, for the dynamic American. The Prime Minister made no allowance for the real greatness of the man. He was irritated by his mannerisms. Roosevelt flung out commonplaces with the same forceful and portentous emphasis as he uttered truths which showed penetration and breadth of judgment. The more stale the platitude the greater the emphasis. This kind of conversation always annoyed the British Premier and gave a note of supercilious derision to his mien and voice. Roosevelt felt it and gradually his torrential flow of sense and sentiment dried up. The meal was hardly a success.

The Royal Warrant formally appointing me Minister of Munitions was not actually issued until June 9th, the day on which the Ministry of Munitions Act became law.

But without waiting for this I had begun immediately to set about the organisation of the new department.

The quarters allotted to the Ministry were at No. 6 Whitehall Gardens — a pleasant, old-fashioned house, just off Whitehall, not at all designed for office purposes. It had been vacated a short time before by that well-known art dealer, Mr. Lockett Agnew. It was more suitable for the residence of a man of artistic proclivities than for the head office of a manufacturer.

I went there with my two secretaries, and found that before I could even start to build up a new Ministry it was necessary to provide at least the bare requirements of an office. My first encounter with red tape was characteristic of the action of this departmental bindweed.

The sole articles of furniture in the office of the new department were two tables and a chair. My secretaries gave urgent orders for an adequate supply of furniture, but before this had been delivered, a squad from the Office of Works appeared on the scene to take away the little we had, on the ground that it did not belong to the new department and therefore must be removed. They were ultimately prevailed upon to be merciful, and until the new equipment arrived, I was allowed one table to write upon and one chair to sit at the said table.

This is Colonel House's description of his visit to me at this time:

"This was, I believe, George's first day as Minister of Munitions in his new Whitehall quarters. There was no furniture in the room except a table and one chair. He insisted upon me taking the chair, which I declined to do, declaring that a seat on the table was more suitable for me than for a Cabinet official.

"He spoke again and again of 'military red tape,' which he declared he would cut out as speedily as possible. He was full of energy and enthusiasm, and I feel certain something will soon happen in his department. He reminds me more of the virile, aggressive type of American politician than any member of the Cabinet. . . . He has something dynamic within him which his colleagues have not and which is badly needed in this great hour. . . ."

Red tape, then, was worsted in its first round — the only casualties being a temporary general inconvenience. I retained my table and chair against all rules and orders until a reasonable consignment of suitable furniture was allocated to me. I was soon to find that this was not a serious attack but a reconnaissance to investigate and to rattle. Later on red tape resorted to all the devices in its well-stocked armoury to delay, impede and thwart. A more formidable and unexpected antagonist next appeared in the person of human vanity. My room was an old Adam drawing-room, where every panel glittered with long pier-glasses. They no doubt would be an essential accessory to a hairdresser's or haberdasher's trade, but I found them fatal to the transaction of business in armaments. When callers came in I noticed that their eyes wandered from my direction, and that their minds soon followed the rambling gaze. I realised the cause of this distraction. The glistening mirrors reflected the face and figure of my interviewers from every angle. This was too much for the most hard-faced business man. I do not pretend to be above the ordinary human weakness in this respect, but a day's contemplation of a countenance full of anxiety and dubiety more than satisfied my own appetite. I ordered the glasses to be covered over. Difficulty number two was thus blotted out.

I sat in my bare room to survey my problem. What was it? On the one hand I had to envisage all the wide range of activity covered by the supply of munitions — the innumerable requirements of the Army in the field, and the multiplicity of different materials, processes, and coördinations necessary to produce those goods; and on the other I had to inform myself as to the available resources of material, machinery and labour, here and abroad, for supplying those requirements. I had to ascertain the existing state and organisation of production of munitions under War Office direction. The whole field had to be plotted out and suitable men selected to take charge of each section of it.

First came the creation of a staff. The Ministry of Munitions was from first to last a business-man organisation. Its most distinctive feature was the appointment I made of successful business men to the chief executive posts. On June 14th, 1915, I announced in the House of Commons my intention of utilising, as far as possible, the "business brains of the community . . . some of them at my elbow in London, to advise, to counsel, to guide, to inform, to instruct, and to direct," others "in the localities, to organise for us, to undertake the business in each particular locality on our behalf." The first position in every department was entrusted by me to one of these distinguished captains of industry, to whom I gave authority and personal support that enabled them to break through much of the routine and aloofness which characterised the normal administration of Government contracts. I had no office staff except my own two able private secretaries, Mr. J. T. Davies (now Sir John T. Davies) and Miss F. L. Stevenson, both of whom accompanied me from the Treasury. Miss Stevenson was the first woman secretary appointed by a Minister. The precedent, I see, has since been followed by most Ministers and heads of departments. Later on Mr. (now Sir) William Sutherland volunteered to assist when the correspondence and the interviews overwhelmed my small staff. He was an experienced Civil Servant, and a man of outstanding abilities. During the troublous times which were in store for me his shrewdness and vision served to help me to avoid many a hidden political trap. The Labour Department of the Board of Trade offered to assist in supervising and directing my arrangements with Labour. For this I was profoundly grateful. The Ordnance Department had little to spare me in the way of staff. For this also I was equally grateful. The War Office placed Sir Percy Girouard at my disposal. Of him I shall have something to say later on. But the men who were to organise and drive the production of guns, rifles, machine-guns, shell, and trench mortars were still to be found. What kind should I look for? I received hundreds of letters from "push-and-goes" and their admiring friends. I had a large number of genuine offers from Company Directors, who offered to place at my service the temporary assistance of managers in whose capacity they had acquired confidence. I had first of all to decide in my own mind the type of man I needed for the highest posts. Sir Eric Geddes told me recently that when he came to visit me at my new department it seemed to him that I was pulling names out of a hat and distributing them to the different jobs that waited to be done; but I am afraid the task of putting suitable men to departments could not be carried out quite so simply as that.

I knew that upon my success or failure in attracting the right sort of man and placing him in the right sort of place depended the efficiency of the new department and its chances of achieving its purpose. It was not sufficient to peruse testimonials or letters of recommendation — not even honest ones — testifying to the efficiency shown by men in the perfectly organised branches where they had served, and which they were prepared temporarily to quit in order to serve the State. Here each man would be called upon to build up a business of which he knew nothing, and do it better than experts who had been trained and spent their professional lives in that line of activity. The most difficult task was to choose wisely between two types of successful business men. The failures were easily spotted and eliminated. The knowledgeable men who knew all about the subject, but did not possess the essential gift of translating their knowledge into effective action, constituted the most dangerous trap, but it was discernible by judicious inquiry as to antecedents, and could then be evaded. But those who have made a success in their business careers can be divided into two classes. There is the careful and cautious man who has a complete mastery of all the details of his trade and attends to them steadily and assiduously. By this means he gradually builds up a business, or if he has acquired control of an already established concern keeps it going and slowly extends it. He does not command those gifts of intuition, rapid decision, and force which enable an improviser to create and hustle along a gigantic new enterprise, and certainly not with material of which he has no previous experience. He is useful in a secondary position, but as an initiator he would be a disappointment if not a disaster. The great improvisers who constitute the second class are rare men anywhere, but in an emergency their value to a country is beyond price, and these were the men I needed for first place. In any great crisis, time is a determining factor, and these men save the days, weeks and months which make the difference between victory and defeat. In selecting the leading hustlers I had to bear all these considerations in mind.

I cannot claim that my first choices were always the best. They were, I think, the best available at the time. I found that some were admirable workers provided they were under the control and direction of others, but not equal to the responsibility of a supreme position. It was then that I realised thoroughly for the first time that men ought to be marked like army lorries with their carrying capacity: "Not to carry more than three tons." The three-tonners are perfect so long as you do not overload them with burdens for which they are not constructed by Providence. I have seen that happen in Law and Politics. The barrister who acquired a great practice as a junior and failed completely when he took silk; the politician who showed great promise as an Under-Secretary and achieved nothing when promoted to the headship of a department. As I went along I discovered that one or two first-rate men were better suited for duties inside the department other than those for which I had originally chosen them.

During the War the neglect of this maxim was a fruitful source of our disasters; the excellent Brigadier who was promoted to a corps and the successful Corps Commander who was given an army, neither of them being equal to the higher responsibility cast upon them. In the Navy also there are many such illustrations of dashing captains who were lifted above their capabilities. However, with all able misfits, I shifted them about and found substitutes. But in the quality of the men themselves I was never disappointed, for when they found the post that suited them best they proved themselves to be first-rate. Men who did not seem to fit into the functions originally designated for them became quite indispensable in equally responsible positions where they were finally placed. And some of them were promoted from tasks where they were rendering conspicuous service to other more important positions where their compelling powers were more urgently needed.

No more remarkable collection of men was ever gathered together under the same roof. Between them they had touched the industrial life of the country and of the Empire at every point. To use a current phrase, "all the means of production, distribution, and exchange" were aggregately at their command.

One of the first to tender his services was Sir Eric Geddes.

He came from the North-Eastern Railway, and he had the make of one of their powerful locomotives. That is the impression he gave me when one morning he rolled into my room. He struck me immediately as a man of exceptional force and capacity. I knew that he was a find, and I was grateful to Lord Knaresborough, the chairman of the company, for offering to release him during the period of the War. He turned out to be one of the most remarkable men which the State called to its aid in this anxious hour for Britain and her Empire. He will appear again and again in my story of the War.

There was also Sir Ernest Moir, who had constructed some of our finest docks and harbours, a man of exceptional ability and tact. Sir Frederick T. Hopkinson, a man of similar experience, came to our aid. There was Sir Hubert Llewellyn Smith. When I first met him at the Board of Trade in 1906 I considered him to be the most resourceful and suggestive mind in the whole of our Civil Service at that time — and withal a man whose long service at the Board of Trade had brought him intelligently into direct contact with every branch of commerce and industry throughout the world. There was Sir John Hunter, who had directed the construction of our largest and most famous bridge. There were Sir Hardman Lever and Sir John Mann, two of the ablest accountants in this country. There were expert financiers like Sir Alexander Roger, who turned out to be an energetic and efficient organiser. The iron and steel industry lent us of the very best. The armament firms placed at our disposal not only Sir Percy Girouard, but Sir Glyn West, who had a much longer practical experience of the actual processes of gun making. We also had Sir Charles Ellis, whose suave and attractive personality served us so well in the handling of this collection of men of clashing temperaments. There was James Stevenson (afterwards

Lord Stevenson), whose experience in organising throughout the country business dealings in a famous brand of Scotch whisky was voluntarily transferred to the business of organising in the provinces the activities of an even more potent spirit — that of patriotism. With Sir Hubert Llewellyn Smith there was Mr. Beveridge (now Sir William Beveridge), a man who was credited with an unrivalled knowledge of labour problems. In the organisation of the welfare branch of our new factories we had the valuable direction of Mr. Seebohm Rowntree, who is not only a highly successful man of business, but a student of social conditions of world-wide fame. Coal gave us the dynamic personality of Sir L. W. Llewellyn. The railways lent us not only Sir Eric Geddes, but Sir Henry Fowler and Sir Ralph Wedgwood. There was Sir Arthur Duckham, one of the ablest engineers in the land — a man of unusual capacity and attainments. The publishing world gave us Sir Edward Iliffe, who carried out with remarkable success the vital task of organising machine tool production. Shipping was represented by Sir George Booth, a member of the well-known firm of Booth Brothers. Though known, as I have said, as the man of "push-and-go," he was neither, but he had other invaluable qualities. He was rather a conciliator than a compeller. I found his tact and geniality invaluable in a Ministry of energetic talents. And through the portals of the Board of Trade there wafted into this Ministry of solid and material industrialism a breeze from the foothills of Parnassus in the person of Mr. Umberto Wolff. The statistician of the Ministry of Munitions is now one of the most eminent economists in the world — Sir Walter Layton. The Parliamentary Under-Secretary, Dr. Addison, was a man with a high order of intellectual capacity, full of ideas, resourcefulness and courage. My military secretary, whom I designed as liaison officer with the War Office, was Sir Ivor Philipps, an experienced soldier and a good business man. The Explosives Department gave me that eminent judge, Lord Fletcher Moulton. He was one of the subtlest brains in England. As usually happens his subtlety caused distrust and misunderstanding amongst blunter minds. He was not only one of the greatest lawyers of his day, he was also a man of distinguished scientific attainments. When he placed his great gifts at the disposal of the War Office for the solution of the new problems created by the unprecedented demand for explosives, he rendered service of incalculable value to the country.

Of such were the personal components of this strange Ministry. If not a Ministry of all the talents it was undoubtedly a Ministry of all the industries — war and peace, production, transport, law, medicine, science, the Civil Service, politics, and poetry — and all at their best. It was a wonderful array of talent. It was a formidable battery of dynamic energy. But I saw that unless firmly controlled and carefully watched there would be constant explosions which would make the whole machine unworkable. At first I placed Sir Percy Girouard in charge as chief engineer of the concern. He was an out-and-out Kitchener man. He had worked with and for him in Egypt. When the War broke out and Lord Kitchener took charge, Sir Percy was taken out of Armstrong's and put in charge of part of the munition organisation at the War Office. He was delivered over to me with the Munitions problem.

Sir Percy Girouard had a great reputation, honourably won by distinguished engineering achievements in our Colonial Empire. He was a man of great natural gifts and accomplishments, and he was credited with possessing a resourcefulness which approximated to the genius of purposeful action. In addition to that he was a man of considerable charm, with a pleasant sense of humour fortified by much interesting and entertaining reminiscence. I discovered that he had a gift of persuasive speech which was invaluable at the meetings we held in London and in the provinces to stimulate coöperation. Although he was primarily a railway man and his success had been achieved in that sphere, his association with Armstrong's had furnished him with experience in the manufacture of every kind of munition of war. But I soon discovered that he suffered from the same drawback as his old chief, Lord Kitchener. They had both spent their exceptional physical reserves in hard work under climatic conditions which are not congenial to men born and bred in a temperate clime. His stock of vitality had been burnt out in great tasks driven through under tropical suns — the vivid spirit was still there and the habits and movements of an old energy were also visible, but these took the form of an unsettling restlessness rather than that of a steady activity. He dashed about from the War Office to the Ministry and back from the Ministry to the War Office, where he spent most of his time, to and from one department after another attending to no detail of any kind in any of them. When he came to see me he was always in such a hurry that he never sat down. He rushed into my room like a man who was chased by a problem and could not stay too long lest it caught him up.

He had one curious mannerism. I observed that when I pressed him with inconvenient questions of detail as to the progress made, he seemed to hide behind his eyeglass, and I could get no farther. From him I learnt less than nothing of what the various departments of the Ministry were doing, for such information as he acquired he gleaned from the War Office, and it was, therefore, misleading. All this feverish bustle gave the impression of a propelling eagerness to urge everybody along, but I soon discovered that it was the symptom of a spent nervous system. Reluctantly I felt he had no longer the steady nerve and the calm industry which are essential in the chief organiser of a new department where there were so many men quite new to the tasks entrusted to their charge, and I felt that a man of a totally different calibre would be more useful. So we parted company.

His place was not filled. I soon realised that all the hustling that was necessary would have to be done by myself, with the aid of the energetic departmental chiefs whom I had chosen.

Describing these appointments in a speech in the House of Commons on July 29th, 1915, when I was reporting progress on the arrangements of the new Ministry, I said:

"We have had practically to create a new staff. That is a very difficult undertaking if you have to do it immediately, because, obviously, everything depends upon the staff and the men you select. And under ordinary conditions you would take a very long time to choose your instruments. You cannot do that when you are engaged in emergency work. Fortunately we have had placed at our disposal the services of very considerable men in the business world — men of wide experience, men, some of them, who are in charge of very considerable undertakings. They have placed their services voluntarily at the disposal of the Minister of Munitions, and are rendering excellent services each in his own department. I think I can say that there are at least 90 men of first-class business experience who have placed their services voluntarily at the disposal of the Ministry of Munitions, the vast majority of them without any remuneration at all. [Cheers.] Some of them were managers of very great concerns, and the firms with which they were connected are in most, if not in all, cases paying them salaries which the State could not afford to pay. These men are exceedingly helpful; in fact, without their help it would have been quite impossible to have improvised a great department on the scale on which this department necessarily had to be organised and arranged."

After going as thoroughly into the actual munition position as the time and information at my disposal would permit, there were visible a few outstanding and dominant facts:

(1) The War Office had not made any thorough survey of its needs on the assumption that the British Army was to develop into a gigantic force of at least 70 divisions, that its task would necessitate breaking through formidable double and often multiple lines of entrenchments, defended by masses of artillery, heavy as well as light, and thousands of machine-guns, and that this operation would be a prolonged one. It had not, for instance, come to any final decision as to the number and calibre of the guns which would be required for this purpose. The quantity and type of the guns ordered were both obviously inadequate to the undertaking in front of it. Nor had it calculated the number of machine-guns required for so great a force.

(2) Until the number and especially the size of the guns had been decided no one could be expected to compute the numbers and sizes of the shells required.

(3) There had been no computation made of the number of machine-guns required for an army fighting under modern conditions.

(4) There had been no survey of the capacity of this country or America to produce the number of guns, shells, machine-guns, and rifles needed. It was found later on, when the programme was settled, that we did not possess in Britain and could not purchase in the States the necessary machine tools to execute the agreed programme. We had to make a start with manufacture of those tools before we began on the extra guns, etc.

(5) The War Office had instituted no inquiry into our capacity for filling shells with explosives. Investigation by the new Ministry revealed the facts (*a*) that our capacity in this respect was not more than one-tenth of the need; and (*b*) that even if we had the necessary filling appliances, we possessed only a small proportion of the explosive hitherto used. We therefore had to encourage experiments to be made in order to find other

equally effective explosives, and to provide a different set of appliances to suit the result of these experiments.

It horrifies me to imagine what would have happened if this state of things had been allowed to go on for a few more months without any perception of its existence, and therefore without any attempt at amendment. What if all Ministers had retained complete confidence in the military directors of the War? The sensitiveness of the War Office to any suggestion that established methods were not the best and the repression of civilian inquisitiveness as to these methods or their results might have postponed discovery of this fatal neglect until it was too late to set them right. Even with all the strenuous endeavour put by some of the ablest business and scientific heads in the country into survey, investigation, consultation and construction, with a view to ascertain needs, defects and remedies, and then to drive through to production, we were only just able to fulfil the requirements of the Army for the summer campaign of 1916. It is such an incredible story of lack of forethought and intelligent inquiry that it is necessary to give more detailed and documented information on these vital points. That I propose to do later on in the course of my narrative. The tale has its lessons for every form of bureaucratic enterprise. It also contains its warning to those who heedlessly lead nations towards war. They should understand something of the risk they incur and the precarious character of the gamble into which they are plunging.

The work which fell upon me was by no means wholly of a kind which could be done sitting at a desk. One very urgent problem was to secure the hearty coöperation of employers in converting their factories and workshops to the production of arms. Another was equally vital: the securing of the good will of the workers and their agreement to the further speeding-up of production and the dilution of labour which it would involve. Labour, I knew, would be one of my chief difficulties. So during the first week of June I made a tour of the districts which were the centres of the engineering industry, in order to harness local enthusiasm to munition production in the service of the new Ministry.

At Manchester, Liverpool, Birmingham, Cardiff and Bristol, I met representatives of the chief engineering firms and of the trade unions affected, and urged them to organise local committees to assist in producing munitions of war and to arrange the allocation of contracts between them in such a way as to ensure the maximum output from the engineering works of the district. I stressed the importance of local responsibility and of systematic decentralisation as a means of saving time and red tape, and I appealed to both business men and trade unionists to work together with one will.

I will quote a passage from a speech I delivered at Manchester in order to show the nature of the appeal I made to employers and workers alike:

"I have only held this office for a few days, it is true. I had some insight before then into the position of things, but what I have seen has convinced me from overwhelming testimony that the nation has not yet concentrated one half of its industrial strength on the problem of carrying this great conflict through successfully. It is a war of munitions. We are fighting against the best-organised community in the world; the best-organised whether for war or peace, and we have been employing too much the haphazard, leisurely, go-as-you-please methods, which, believe me, would not have enabled us to maintain our place as a nation, even in peace, very much longer. The nation now needs all the machinery that is capable of being used for turning out munitions or equipment, all the skill that is available for that purpose, all the industry, all the labour, and all the strength, power, and resource of everyone to the utmost, everything that would help us to overcome our difficulty and supply our shortages. We want to mobilise in such a way as to produce in the shortest space of time the greatest quantity of the best and most efficient war material. That means victory; it means a great saving of national strength and resources, for it shortens the War; it means an enormous saving of life. . . ."

I pointed out why the Government had taken powers under the Defence of the Realm Act to control the workshops of the country, and to insist that Government work — the work of the country — must take precedence over all civil work. I then discussed the relations of the Government with labour. Two things were essential to the efficiency of the new organisation for munitions of war — to increase the mobility of labour and to secure greater subordination in labour to the direction and control of the State. The State must be able to say where and under what conditions it required a man's service. "When the house is on fire, questions of procedure and precedence, of etiquette and time and division of labour must disappear." I added:

". . . I can only say this, that to introduce compulsion as an important element in organising the nation's resources of skilled industry and trade does not necessarily mean conscription in the ordinary sense of the term. Conscription means raising by compulsory methods armies to fight Britain's battles abroad. Even that is a question not of principle but of necessity. If the necessity arose I am certain no man of any party would protest. But pray do not talk about it as if it were anti-democratic. We won and saved our liberties in this land on more than one occasion by compulsory service. France saved the liberty she had won in the great Revolution from the fangs of tyrannical military empires purely by compulsory service. The great Republic of the West won its independence, saved its national existence, by compulsory service. And two of the greatest countries of Europe to-day, France and Italy, are defending their national existence and liberties by means of compulsory service. It has been the greatest weapon in the hands of democracy many a time for the winning and preservation of freedom. . . ."

I appealed to the workmen to give up, for the period of the War, the unwritten rules by which output was limited, and I gave an undertaking that piece rates should not be reduced. In the same way I urged suspension of trade union rules forbidding dilution in order that unskilled men and women might be brought in to make up for the shortage of skilled men. I pointed out that the refusal of unenlisted labour to submit to discipline contrasted strangely with the position of the voluntary army at the front:

"The enlisted workman cannot choose his locality of action. He cannot say, 'I am quite prepared to fight at Neuve-Chapelle, but I won't fight at Festubert, and I am not going near the place they call "Wipers."' He cannot say, 'I have been in the trenches eight hours and a half, and my trades union won't allow me to work more than eight hours.'"

With special reference to what I expected from Lancashire, I added in my Manchester speech:

"Lancashire's private works, when they are fully engaged, and after you have mobilised them, can turn out a quarter of a million of high-explosive shells a month. A gentleman near me tells me that you can turn out a lot more. Well, the more the merrier; but we want you to start from that and then work up in the direction of a million."

I quote a Press report of this meeting, because it gives a fair idea of the spirit which commanded all classes to whom I appealed:

"Manchester, Thursday (June 3).

"Lord Derby and the Lancashire men gave a hearty reception to Mr. Lloyd George's speech. . . . Separate munition committees were appointed for three divisions of Lancashire, embracing the whole county. . . . A satisfactory preliminary discussion took place as to the best means of mapping out the work. Mr. Lloyd George had said that he aimed at an output of a quarter of a million shells per month from Lancashire alone, and the reply was a promise of a million a month within a short time.

"All this is excellent, but the bitter tragedy is that the organisation was not accomplished six months ago. Manchester masters tell me that, in the past, they have asked the War Office again and again for a statement of what was wanted, only to be put off with a polite acknowledgment or a reference to the Labour Bureau."

On the following day I spoke in similar terms at Liverpool. I repeated my reassurance to the workers about the temporary nature of the relaxations of ordinary rules and practices which they were being asked to accept.

A resolution was carried, pledging those present to do all they could to increase the output of munitions. This resolution was seconded in a significant speech delivered by one of the workmen's representatives. It is worth quoting:

"Mr. Clarke, a representative of the Amalgamated Society of Engineers, seconded the resolution. He said: 'We have learned now that things are not going so well at the front as we thought they were. Certain newspapers have hidden the truth from us, and have presented too rosy a picture. It was only yesterday when they heard Mr. Lloyd George's speech [1] that the workmen realised the terrible urgency of the matter. Now that we know, I am sure that there will be no difficulty.' "

Press comment on this speech stated:

"The general feeling in representing trade union circles in London with regard to Mr. Lloyd George's speech is one of unanimous agreement. One prominent trade unionist said: 'We

[1] My speech at Manchester.

are delighted with the definiteness of the speech, and only wish it had been given eight months ago. We have been annoyed at the campaign in favour of conscription, because we knew there were hundreds of thousands of men for whom no equipment could be immediately obtained. . . ."

While I was thus engaged in stimulating the organisation of the country for munition production, the Ministry of Munitions Bill was carried through Parliament. This measure set up the new Ministry and gave it its powers. They were laid down as follows in Clause 2 (1) of the Act. I quote that section as it is a good example of the comprehensiveness and elasticity required in legislation for coping with an emergency.

"The Minister of Munitions shall have such administrative powers and duties in relation to the supply of munitions for the present War as may be conferred on him by his Majesty in Council, and his Majesty may also, if he considers it expedient that, in connection with the supply of munitions, any powers or duties of a Government Department or authority, whether conferred by statute or otherwise, should be transferred to, or exercised or performed concurrently by, the Minister of Munitions, by Order in Council make the necessary provision for the purpose, and any Order made in pursuance of this section may include any supplemental provisions which appear necessary for the purpose of giving full effect to the Order."

In other words, the job of the new Ministry — the responsibilities hitherto held by the War Office or Admiralty which it was to take over and the new tasks it was to undertake, were not defined by Act of Parliament, but left to be fixed by Orders in Council, which, without the waste of valuable time involved in Parliamentary procedure, could adapt the power to the need as it arose.

At the outset it was broadly laid down that the new

department should be guided by the "general requirements and specific requisitions" of the Army Council. This might have been taken to mean — and indeed, the Army Council did its best to impose such an interpretation — that the Ministry was no more than a Supply Department unable to exercise any initiative and only empowered to act on programmes and orders transmitted to it from the military authorities. Fortunately, however, the Order in Council defining my functions was more explicit. It set out that my duty was:

". . . to ensure such supply of munitions for the present War as may be required by the Army Council or the Admiralty, *or may otherwise be found necessary*."

This final saving clause which I have italicised, gave me authority, of which I made full and industrious use, to acquaint myself directly with the needs present and future of the Army and make plans to meet them. Had I been limited by the shortsighted vision of the Army Council we should have continued to be in arrears with supplies to the end of the War.

On this matter I am tempted to quote an extract from the official history of the Ministry of Munitions. This book was written years after I had left the Ministry. I had no responsibility for its preparation, and as a matter of fact was not consulted as to any part of its contents. Referring to the interpretation I placed upon my functions at the Ministry, it says:

"This wide view of his position and responsibilities is reflected throughout his career as Minister of Munitions, and his vision of the character and probable length of the conflict that lay ahead not only had a profound effect on the munitions programmes actually adopted in his period, but enabled the Ministry to meet much larger programmes later on. He laid the foundations of the Ministry's productive capacity on a scale so vast that it was almost sufficient — as far as guns, gun ammunition, rifles, machine-guns, and trench warfare supplies were concerned — to carry the country to the end of the War. The great developments undertaken under his successors were principally directed to meet new demands for aircraft, for chemical warfare, and for increased quantities of steel for shipbuilding, motor transport, tanks and railways."

A good deal of play has been made in some quarters with the fact that the new factories organised by the Ministry of Munitions, and the fresh orders for shells which it issued, only began to bear fruit on a large scale by the spring of 1916, and that until that time the bulk of the supplies reaching our armies in the field were in respect of orders given by the War Office before the new Ministry was created.

I have not the slightest desire to claim any unmerited approbation for the Ministry of Munitions, or to rob the War Office of the smallest of its true titles of praise. But in loyalty to the many splendid colleagues who coöperated with me for munitions production, and to the magnificent work they performed, I am bound to point out that this suggestion is ill-founded.

It is true that, partly under pressure from the Cabinet Committee on Munitions, and the Munitions of War Committee, appointed in the spring of 1915, to the activities of both of which I have already referred, the War Office had by the beginning of June, 1915, placed extensive orders at home and abroad for shells. But it was one thing to order, and quite another to ensure delivery. By the 29th of May, 1915, out of 5,797,274 shell bodies ordered by the War Office for delivery by or before that date, only 1,968,252 had actually been delivered — this after ten months of war. A more important consideration is the fact that of the shells actually manufactured a comparatively large number were not fitted with fuses and filled with explosive. They were just a collection of harmless steel mugs. The steps taken by the Ministry to reorganise the munitions industry throughout the country and to speed up production during these first seven months of its existence were successful in bringing up the total of deliveries on War Office orders from the two millions at which it stood on June 1st to 14 millions by the end of December, 1915, and for the first time adequate measures were taken to complete these with fuse and explosive.

The failure of the War Office orders to materialise was largely due to its stubborn and stupid adherence to the policy of dealing only with the recognised armament firms, and leaving these firms themselves to organise — or leave unorganised — the rest of the engineering industry in the country. The Ordnance Department could have exercised complete control over the manufacturing resources of the country; powers for that purpose had indeed been thrust upon them by the Defence of the Realm Act which I brought in on March 9th, 1915, but no great use had been made of them. The Ordnance Department was still convinced that it was too risky to entrust the manufacture of munitions to inexperienced firms, and that the only safe course was to give the order to the well-established armament manufacturers, leaving it to them to peddle out the simplest components. As far as American orders were concerned, a departure from this principle was enforced by the Cabinet Committee, although control was impossible and supervision difficult over production in the States. At home, where both supervision and control were practicable, War Office stubbornness was invincible. One of the attributes of small minds is that they resent a change in their accustomed methods merely because it implies a censure on their past record.

So far as the yield of War Office orders was concerned,

the difference between the deliveries from August, 1914, to June, 1915, and those from June, 1915, to April, 1916, was due largely to the fact that during the latter period the Ministry of Munitions had taken on the direct organisation of the outside firms and of the labour for munition production, and after August, 1915, had also taken charge of the Government ordnance factories, including the Royal Laboratory at Woolwich, which at that time was still responsible for nearly the whole of the shell filling and completion, and was doing the job by tedious and antiquated pre-war methods. M. Albert Thomas, the French Munition Minister, who visited Woolwich at this date, called it *"une vieille boîte."*

As I have already indicated, the lack of foresight on the part of the War Office was further shown by its failure to set up a programme authority to study the necessities, possibilities and probabilities of the future — as distinct from the mere tabulation of quantities due on contracts placed. It is necessary that I should develop the full effect of this oversight.

When certain munitions or components had to be manufactured, the Ordnance Department never undertook a careful survey of the reserves of manufacturing capacity available in this country for that purpose and how that capacity could be best utilised for the provision of an adequate supply. Had they done so they would have discovered that in order to exploit these reserves to their full capacity it was necessary to secure certain machine tools, gauges and gadgets, the manufacture of which would occupy several months. The fact that this had not been seen to at the very beginning of the War had not merely wasted the period of ten months which had already elapsed, but the delays involved a further wait of several anxious and fateful months before the process of manufacturing guns, rifles, machine-guns and even shells on an adequate scale could be even commenced. A third and in some respects a more disastrous failure was their complete neglect to investigate the explosives problem. They had taken no steps to enlarge their capacity for filling shells even to the limit of the orders which they themselves had already given for shell bodies. In fact, they had not even considered the question of whether there was a sufficient supply available of the explosive material with which these shells were charged to meet even the requirements of their own limited programmes. As I shall point out later on, the War Office had been already warned by Lord Moulton that the available supplies would not be forthcoming in sufficient quantities and that the nature of the explosive would therefore have to be changed. Had this deplorable blunder not been remedied in time, the British Army could not have been equipped in 1916 with a third of the material needful for the operations.

The Ordnance Department administered a prescribed system, and it was passive, if not hostile, where new expedients were concerned. This passivity was shown in the matter of Lord Moulton's request for executive powers in regard to the high explosives in December, 1914; in the proposed extension of his sphere to propellants in the spring of 1915; in the delay in the adoption of newer forms of high explosives, and in the reluctance to approve the Stokes gun. Perhaps the most striking illustration of the limited horizon of the War Office authorities can be found in their refusal (backed, it may be observed, by the Secretary of State) to admit the necessity for the guns which in August, 1915, I ordered in excess of War Office demand. This is an incident with which I deal more fully elsewhere.

Most of the special steps that were taken after the formation of the Ministry of Munitions to stimulate production could equally well have been taken in 1914. It was to those special steps that the greatly accelerated yield on account of outstanding War Office orders in the latter part of 1915, as well as the immense augmentation of output in 1916 on direct orders of the Ministry, was mainly due.

In the month of July the Ministry of Munitions took over from the War Office responsibility for the administration of outstanding contracts. Its work therefore had a dual character. It had, on the one hand, to speed up these existing contracts, consulting closely and coöperating actively with the existing armament firms in order to relieve their difficulties in regard to materials and labour, while on the other hand it was at the same time opening up fresh sources of supply, both by organising outside firms for munition production, and by establishing new Government factories, and securing equipment, labour and materials for their use.

It requires some effort to envisage the wide range of our task. Few people would at the outset imagine how much is covered by the phrase: "Munitions of war," or dream of the colossal ramifications of the industries concerned in their production.

The making of a gun or a shell-case, for instance, involves the metal trades, blast-furnaces, steel works, iron and steel foundries, forges, stamps, drops and dies, rolling-mills, drawn rod and wire works — and behind them, the colliery and the iron-ore quarry.

It requires factories, and these in turn require machinery, covered electrical plant, factory equipment and machine tools; engines, pumps, turbines, road and rail transport; boiler-making and constructional engineering work.

The explosives for filling and propelling the shell from the gun involve the output of chemical works, dye works, gas works, and a great deal of very careful laboratory experiment, investigation and testing.

Small arms and ammunition, and all the miscellaneous

stores used in trench warfare, involve numerous components all requiring ferrous and non-ferrous metals in manufactured forms, woodwork, textile products, optical glass, vulcanite.

Shells loomed so large in the public eye at the time when the Ministry was formed, that there is a danger of the fact being overlooked that the department became responsible for the production and supply, not only of ammunition and guns, of rifles and machine-guns, but also of mechanical transport, trench warfare stores, optical munitions and glassware, metals and materials, tanks, bombs, poison gas, railway material, machine tools, timber, electrical power, agricultural machinery, mineral oils and building materials.

In place of the War Office method of contracting with a few experienced firms for supplies of finished articles — a method which had worked satisfactorily in peace-time, but had proved quite inadequate to this war — the Ministry of Munitions had to concern itself directly with the production of every raw material and intermediate stage of manufacture of each component in its munitions supplies; and this in regard to a range and variety of armaments hitherto undreamed of.

## 2. Central and Area Organisation

Pre-existing bodies for munition production — Original departments of the new Ministry — Area organization: district committees — Encouragement of local efforts — Mr. Stevenson's scheme for area organisation — My speech of June 23rd — Stevenson's account of his task — Area offices and Boards of Management — Summary of their achievements — Driving methods adopted — Weekly reports — Specimens of my notes and comments — Weekly meetings — Growth of team spirit — Consultations with manufacturers — My daily programme of work.

When the Ministry of Munitions Act was laid before Parliament at the beginning of June, 1915, the existing bodies for the providing of munitions were three in number, *viz.:*

(*a*) The Munitions Supply Organisation under the War Office, presided over by the Master-General of Ordnance, run almost exclusively by Army officers, with the addition of one important civilian intruder in the person of Lord Moulton, who had been given a position as chairman of the Committee of High Explosives supply;

(*b*) The Armaments Output Committee, which Lord Kitchener had set up with Sir Percy Girouard and Mr. G. M. Booth at its head, originally to take up the problem of labour supply, though it had actually made an extremely useful but limited start on the question of area organisation;

(*c*) The Munitions of War Committee — now virtually defunct, as its Chairman had become Minister of Munitions (designate).

In the course of the month of June most of the supply functions for which General von Donop's department had been responsible were transferred to the Ministry, which also amalgamated with itself the work of the Armaments Output Committee; so that by July 1st, in place of the three bodies I have mentioned, there was now the one Ministry in charge of output and supply. Woolwich Arsenal remained under the Ordnance Department until August, 1915, and responsibility for design and invention until the end of the year.

Four departments were at first set up: Sir Percy Girouard undertook munitions supply; Lord Moulton explosives supply; Brigadier-General L. C. Jackson the Engineers' Munitions Department, and Mr. Beveridge took charge of the Secretariat and the organisation of labour.

Supporting them was an array of the experienced business men I have mentioned. I will not detail the whole of this original organisation, but illustrate its structure along one branch. Sir Percy Girouard, the Director-General of Munitions Supply, had immediately under him nine men, each in charge of a particular job or group of jobs. One of these, Sir Eric Geddes, held the position of a Deputy Director-General of Munitions Supply. He was set to supervise a group of sub-departments, each in charge of an experienced man; Mr. Moir was responsible to Geddes for machine guns; Mr. Hopkinson for small arms ammunition; Mr. Brown for rifles; Major Symon for guns and equipment, ammunition wagons and optical munitions; and Mr. D. Bain for horse-drawn transport vehicles. As the War progressed, several of these sub-departments grew in importance, and required the undivided attention of a Deputy Director-General. Before I left the Ministry, munitions supply was one of three supply departments (the others being explosives supply and trench warfare supply), and was divided into ten main sub-departments, half of which were again sub-divided into four or five sections; and these various departments, sub-departments and sections were being run by experienced business men on business lines.

It was in such fashion that we modelled our headquarters. In the same spirit we approached the organisation of the country into areas for munition production.

I have already mentioned how the Armaments Output Committee, acting under the direction of the Munitions of War Committee and with my active support, had in April and May made a beginning with this task of area organisation.

In a number of areas district committees were set up to coördinate munition production, and they undertook the establishment of national shell factories in their centres. The first of such schemes was the one adopted at Leeds, which received Government sanction on May 13th, on the recommendation of the Munitions of War Committee. A description of this Leeds experiment was published in leaflet form, entitled "National Munitions Factories: Working Model," with a view to stimulating similar movements in other districts.

The tour which I undertook during the first week of June had as one of its objects the encouragement of this system. At all meetings I urged that no time should be lost in setting up committees, and recommended that as far as possible districts should coördinate their efforts so as to form one organisation rather than several.

Very widespread zeal and activity was aroused by this appeal, and the effect was greatly to accelerate local organisation in the districts I had visited. This spirit of energetic devotion to the task of making good the munition shortage became general during June. Deputations from local committees called daily at the new Ministry. Many of these I saw and did my best to stimulate, direct, and assist. A copious correspondence poured in from business men offering their services and asking for information in regard to requirements, specifications, contracts, labour. Business men were encouraged to offer their services and they responded to the more sympathetic treatment accorded to them. It was imperative that anything in the nature of delay and confusion at this stage should be avoided, and I quickly saw that the branch of the Ministry dealing with local matters would have to be strengthened.

Early in June Mr. Stevenson, who had joined Mr. Booth's "District Department" almost immediately after the formation of the new Ministry and had taken up work in connection with the organisation of local committees, was asked by me to submit a scheme of area organisation.

I give the outline of the plan adopted for area organisation as it may be of value to those who will be called upon to organise the national energy for other tasks.

The scheme adopted was generally described by me in a speech in the House of Commons on June 23rd as follows:

"No staff, however able, could adequately cope from the centre with the gigantic and novel character of the operations which must be put through during the next few weeks if the country is to be saved. We have, therefore, decided to organise the country in districts. I am relying very considerably upon the decentralisation which I have outlined. There is no time to organise a Central Department which would be sufficiently strong and which would be sufficiently well equipped to make the most of the resources of each district. . . . There is only one way of organising the resources of the country efficiently within the time at our disposal. That is that each district should undertake to do the work for itself, and that we should place at their disposal everything that a Government can in the way of expert advice and in the way of material, because we have ourselves offered to supply the material wherever it is required. Anything in the way of expert advice, specifications, samples, inspection and material — that we can supply; but we must rely upon the great business men of each locality to do the organisation in those districts for themselves; and they are doing it."

Here is Stevenson's description of his methods:

"The first thing I did was to call for a map. I might as well have called for the moon. But, nothing daunted, I went out and bought one, for the price of which the Government still owe me. I divided the map into ten areas, the limits of which (with a few exceptions) followed county boundaries, and proceeded on the ordinary commercial lines of decentralisation. This scheme was approved by Mr. Lloyd George, and an Area Office was established in each (*viz.*, Newcastle, Manchester, Leeds, Birmingham, Cardiff, Bristol, London, Edinburgh, Glasgow, Dublin, and Belfast) with the object of relieving the pressure at headquarters, securing local information and disposing of sectional difficulties. Curiously enough, one county was left out — Hereford — with the remark: 'We will leave that to the Board of Agriculture!' But in that neglected county the greatest Shell Filling Factory in the Kingdom was later built. . . ."

Within the main Areas nearly fifty Boards of Management were appointed. The procedure was somewhat as follows: The Boards of Management would undertake orders for specified quantities, say of shell, to be delivered within specified dates at a specified price. These orders were distributed amongst various engineering firms in the district, or entrusted to National Factories managed by the Board, and the Boards were responsible to the Government for the shells manufactured.

The Area Offices exercised a general supervision over the local Boards of Management within their areas, and were provided with an Organising Secretary, a Superintending Engineer, and a Labour Officer. The Secretary combined with secretarial duties the work of Establishment Officer and of sub-accountant for the district; was responsible for dealing with applications for petrol by firms engaged on munition work and a variety of other tasks. The Engineer was charged to develop the resources of the Area as fully as possible along the lines laid down from time to time by the Minister of Munitions, to ascertain details of and report on available machinery, to inspect National Shell Factories, advise on the capabilities of firms, and report on the progress of contracts. The Labour Officer had, of course, to supervise the supply and distribution of labour; and the great expansion of the work in connection with dilution, and the investigation of general conditions of labour led later on, in November, 1916, to the splitting-up of this work between two independent officers, dealing respectively with dilution and investigation.

It would be a mistake to suppose that all this harnessing of local energy and creation of district organisation went through easily and smoothly. Particularly in the early stages it required constant attention and very careful handling to ensure that the machinery worked.

Frictions and hitches had constantly to be overcome, and an agreed method of working settled. I had constantly to settle local and general questions — some important, many trivial — which delayed action. On August 26th, 1915, I issued a memorandum entitled: "Decisions for the Guidance of Boards of Management," which summarised the conclusions I had come to with them on the basis of our conferences, and this served thenceforward as their charter. Summarising briefly some of the results obtained by these Boards of Management in the recruiting of hitherto inexperienced firms for munition production, I may say that in the course of the War they secured an output of 65 million empty shell, and over 606 million components; nearly 10 million trench warfare articles and over four million items in connection with aëronautical supplies. Nor was this great work done regardless of cost to the State, for it is estimated that the National Factories managed by these Boards saved the country £1¾ million based on the standard prices hitherto charged by contractors for the various articles produced.

There are many things which were done in the War that experience has taught should be done differently another time — though Heaven forbid there should be another time! But the ultimate opinion of everybody acquainted with the Area Organisation and the Boards of Management, as wartime organisations, is that exactly the same policy should be again adopted, were it ever to become necessary once more to harness the outside resources of the country to armaments supply.

Such was the machine we constructed. My next concern was to devise methods which would ensure that every department got ahead with its job at full speed, and that breakdown or failure in any quarter should be promptly remedied instead of being allowed to drift on unnoticed till disaster occurred.

The Ministry had set things moving in the country as a result of my tour of some of the industrial districts and of the communications with industrial leaders, employers and workmen throughout the country. I had gathered a very able staff of first-class men at headquarters to do the work. It remained now to drive the machine at full speed as soon as it was put together.

So I proceeded to institute a system under which, as each department of the Ministry was organised — guns, explosives, shells, machine-guns, bombs, factory construction, labour supply, and so on — its head should make a weekly report of the progress of the branch to Mr. W. T. Layton (now Sir Walter Layton), who had been appointed Director of Statistics, and that he should collect these reports and furnish me with a weekly summary. As soon as each branch definitely got into working order and was in a position to start production it was asked to submit a statement showing its anticipated output week by week. The weekly reports of results actually achieved were constantly checked against the figures of anticipation, and we were thus able to see just how far each single section was keeping abreast of its task.

The weekly budget prepared by Mr. Layton, showing the promises and performances of each department, would be handed over to me at the week-end, and I would take it down with me to my cottage at Walton Heath; for whenever I could, I would escape from London on Saturday. There I would take this weekly budget, and go carefully through it, scribbling notes to be subsequently dictated and sent to the departmental heads on points which struck me in regard to the progress of the work. A few specimens taken at random will serve to illustrate these minutings:

DR. ADDISON.

*Weekly Report.*
*Trench Warfare.*

The discrepancy between promise and deliveries is discouraging. What steps have been taken to speed it up?

*Bomb deliveries* are also disappointing.

D. LL. G.
30/9/15.

SIR FREDERICK BLACK.

*Notes on Weekly Report for Week Ending Sept. 18th.*

The contrast between shells promised and shells delivered is most discouraging, and the discrepancy is bad enough for contractors; but when you come to the national shell factories it is grotesque. Is there no means of improving the situation? Whose duty is it to call for explanations from individual contractors and from Boards of Management, and whose duty is it to keep them both up to the mark?

I am afraid that the department dealing with this phase of our work is considerably overtaxed. The men in charge are exceptionally able men, but they have too much to do.

*Filling Factories.*

Having regard to the urgent importance of increasing our filling capacity, this report is not as encouraging as I would wish it to be. The interviews at the conferences we have had the last two or three days will improve matters, but I hope special attention will be directed to this all-important branch. Both in the matter of national projectile factories and filling factories I urge that the great builders should be called into conference and invited to assist us by placing at our disposal men who can speed up erection of these buildings. Please see that this is done.

D. LL. G.
30/9/15.

GENERAL DU CANE.

I understand that the lag in the delivery of six-inch Howitzer shell is partly attributable to the delay in delivery of certain cartridges for N.T.C. charges. Could this be hurried up?

D. LL. G.
14/3/16.

GENERAL DU CANE.

As there has been a good deal of trouble about ineffective fuses and gaines, I am very anxious there should be no further failures. You spoke very highly of the latest designs, but I should like to feel that the test has been of such a character that nothing is left to chance. So much depends upon these latest designs; if they fail, the ammunition at a very critical time would not achieve the necessary results. I should be very glad if you would, therefore, take the necessary steps for proving on a considerable scale the efficiency of the new designs.

D. LL. G.
10/5/16.

In addition to firing this bombardment of notes and queries at the departmental heads of the Ministry, I was, of course, in constant personal touch with them through the week, providing them as far as possible with stimulation, correction and counsel. I was at the office from 9 A.M. until 8 P.M. and often later, and available for consultation with the officials of the Ministry when any difficulty arose.

Very early in the working of the Ministry I began the system of calling a weekly meeting of the heads of departments, at which I could discuss verbally with them the features in their weekly reports, and any matters arising in my minutes to them which required further consultation.

It was a great advantage and saving of time to have them all together for these meetings. For when one of them was asked why his output was failing to keep up to the level estimated for it he might give the explanation that he had not been supplied with some raw material, semi-manufactured product, or other component which was essential for the output of his particular section. In such a case, as the officer responsible for the supply of that missing component would also be present, the matter could be thrashed out without delay and a great deal of time and paper saved which would otherwise have been used in following a conventional routine of noting one man's complaint, sending it to another for comments, and thereafter having a docket flying about like a shuttlecock from department to department, while excuses instead of output were being multiplied.

My aim throughout was to tone up this staff to a pitch of high endeavour by every appeal that moves men to do their best — by praise; by emulation; by fear of exposure to criticism; and, above all, by the urge of a genuine spirit of patriotism. I think all those who were familiar with the working of the Ministry will agree that this aim was very successfully realised.

These meetings also stimulated healthy competition. No departmental head cared to have attention drawn to deficiencies in adapting performance to promise at meetings attended by his colleagues. There was no time to consider susceptibilities. The nation was in grave jeopardy and time counted. We had already lost months, we could not now afford to lose even a day.

The work of the whole Ministry was very closely interlocked. Failure to keep abreast of shell-filling might be the result of a failure to supply fuses or high explosives. This might proceed from a labour shortage in a particular district. In the weekly conference the trouble could be tracked down immediately to its root, and the responsible officer charged to rectify it. Meantime some arrangement might be improvised to get temporarily round the difficulty.

One immense advantage of these meetings was that in course of time they built up a very strong team-spirit among the men I had gathered round me. They were a diverse crowd — each an experienced leader accustomed to run his own business and to give orders rather than to receive them. It was essential for the success of the Ministry that they should learn to curb their independence, and to coöperate with each other. They began the process at these weekly meetings, even if at first it was occasionally in the rôle of mutual accusers. By degrees they grew to be really friendly, and with one or two possible exceptions they ended by becoming a close-knit band of fellow-workers, with a healthy *esprit de corps.*

My efforts to stimulate progress could not, of course, be confined to the staff of the Ministry. I had to be in continuous touch with industry all over the country. Frequently I would send for the manufacturers in some particular line — guns, rifles, machine tools — to consult with them about their output and stir them up to greater activity. I travelled round the country, visiting works and speaking to the workers, smoothing over labour difficulties, composing quarrels, urging increased output. The honour of the nation at home was pledged to our men at the front, that they should be furnished as fully and as speedily as was humanly possible with the weapons and defences that they needed in their struggle; and I held myself responsible that no effort should be spared and no reasonable expedient neglected to secure the fulfilment of that pledge.

I have been a pretty hard worker all my life, from boyhood right up to the present day. But I have never worked harder than during the period when I was carrying through the organisation of our munition supplies — not even during my Premiership, strenuous and arduous as those years were. I generally worked an hour or two before breakfast, perusing essential papers and annotating them. It was my custom to invite to breakfast people who wished to see me, or whom I wished to see on munition business; sometimes important and influential American visitors wanted to discuss matters of moment with me, not necessarily connected with the Ministry of Munitions, and breakfast was a convenient opportunity for meeting them.

But my day would have started much earlier than this. As I have already mentioned, I would from the moment of waking have been at work upon papers and reports which I had taken overnight to my bedside.

By nine o'clock I was at work in my office at the Ministry of Munitions. The pressure of the task made it inevitable that many ancient traditions should be broken. After dealing with any important letters or documents which had come to hand, there would be some matter which I had already decided to tackle that morning — maybe guns or shell-filling or rifles — and there would be departmental heads to see and their problems to settle; arrangements to make about division of raw material, perhaps, between rival claimants for its use, and so on. Often, too, there would be Cabinet Meetings to attend in the morning, although for the first few weeks of my tenure of the Ministry, imperative business prevented my attending. I was told that at one meeting Mr. Balfour asked: "What has become of the Minister of Munitions? I have not seen him for some time."

Lunch would probably be used, like breakfast, as an opportunity to meet someone with whom I had urgent munition business to discuss. In the afternoon the House of Commons claimed me, though as soon as I had replied to the numerous questions affecting my department which were habitually on the Paper, I would escape, if the nature of the succeeding business made it possible, to get on with my job.

Constant difficulties arose with the War Office, which

necessitated consultations with Lord Kitchener, and frequently with the Prime Minister. These were often lengthy matters. The War Office was at that period a perpetual source of obstruction.

Labour difficulties involved me in frequent visits to industrial centres, and consultation with deputations of workers or shop stewards. Especially in the earlier days, before the control of profits had become general, there was a bad spirit stirring among the men, and syndicalist agitators caused a good deal of trouble. In this respect the Glasgow district gave us the most trouble, although there was considerable agitation of an obstructive character in the Newcastle, Sheffield, and other areas.

I need not refer to the various public meetings I had to address from time to time round the country, in order to rouse the nation to the vital issues confronting us, and keep up enthusiasm for munition output. My recollection of those days is one of an unceasing drive. Although I was urging on the Ministry and all my staff there as hard as I could, I think I can claim that I asked from none of them an effort greater than I was myself making.

### 3. The Problem of Labour

Early fears of unemployment — Rise of demand for armament workers — Causes of labour shortage: Enlistment — Bargaining power of the workers — War Office policy of few contractors — Steps needed to remove labour shortage — Lord Kitchener objects to release of munition workers — War Office badging scheme introduced — Introduction of women workers — Women's War Pageant — Development of women's work for munitions — Failure of scheme for transfer of workers — Compulsory powers needed: the new D.O.R.A. — Problem of securing good will of workers to dilution — Conference with trade unionists at the Treasury — Mr. Balfour bewildered — My statement to Conference — Profits to be limited — Trade union rules must be relaxed — Treasury Agreement — Agreement with A.S.E. — Difficulty of limiting profits — Sir H. Llewellyn Smith's memorandum — Mr. Mitchell's review — Labour position when Ministry was formed — Munitions of War Bill — Statement on profit limitation — Release from the Colours — Difficulties of recovering skilled men — "Barred Units": Kitchener's objections — Census of enlisted workers — Craft unions and dilution — Machine tool problem — Unions recalcitrant — Visit to Bristol T.U.

Congress — Central Munitions Labour Supply Committee — Shop steward agitation — Visit to Glasgow, Christmas, 1915 — Meeting with Kirkwood — The morning conference — A.S.E. attitude to Munitions of War (Amendment) Bill — Mr. Asquith indignant — Agreement reached.

Looking back to-day upon the problem which from the outset of the War confronted the nation in regard to the arming and equipping of our troops, it seems a little curious that at the beginning of the hostilities there was in some quarters expectation and fear of acute unemployment. Within the first week, the Cabinet Committee on the Prevention and Relief of Distress, of which the President of the Local Government Board, Mr. (now Sir) Herbert Samuel, was chairman, invited the Mayors and Provosts throughout the country to form local committees to provide against unemployment. Local authorities were urged to expedite public works and to frame schemes which might be put in hand if serious distress should arise. Acting on this impulse, employers and workers in the engineering industry held a meeting on August 19th, 1914, "to discuss ways and means whereby the unemployment contingent upon the national distress may be minimised." The Director of Army contracts issued in the same month from the War Office a circular entitled: "Memorandum as to minimising of unemployment during the War," in which he recommended the abandonment of overtime work as a means of spreading the available employment among as many hands as possible.

By mid-September, however, the Board of Trade discovered that the feared unemployment was not materialising; by November there was an unsatisfied demand for 6000 armament workers, and the shortage of labour grew as the need for munitions increased until the deficiency of workers became one of our greatest problems.

The Cabinet Committee on munitions, the appointment of which in October, 1914, I have already described, was not called together from October 23rd until December 23rd;

and at this latter meeting the supply of labour was found to have become a matter of acute difficulty.

There were three main causes operating to accentuate the labour difficulty. The first was the fact that enlistment had been particularly heavy in the big industrial districts, especially those associated with engineering. Between August 4th and November 4th, 1914, the enlistment per 10,000 of the population had been only 80 in the East of England and 88 in the Southwest, while it was 150 in Yorkshire, Durham and Northumberland, 196 in Warwickshire, and Midland Counties and 237 in Southern Scotland, in all of which areas the population was mainly industrial. The same high percentage of recruitment obtained also in South Wales and other industrial centres. By October, 1914, 12.2 per cent. of the male workers in the engineering trades had enlisted — a proportion which rose by July, 1915, to 19.5 per cent. In far too many cases it was the most energetic and competent skilled workers who rushed to the colours and the less efficient who were left behind.

The second cause was the fact that as labour grew less plentiful and the demands on it increased, workers found themselves in a stronger bargaining position than they had ever experienced. Employers were unwilling to quarrel with and dismiss a worker whom they would find hard to replace, and there was a growing competition to secure the services of the skilled artisan. If dismissed from one post he could get another job immediately, often at higher pay. This led to a tendency among some workers to bad timekeeping, slackness at their work and in certain cases to excessive drinking. The number against whom such charges would be brought was no doubt a relatively small percentage of the whole body of workers. None the less, the failure of a few men in a factory to keep their own process up to time had often the effect of holding back all the other workers engaged on the job. As a result, we were getting nothing like the full possible output even from the staff of workers which the nation still retained in its factories.

A third cause of the shortage of labour for munition production was the fact that the War Office policy was, as I have said, to deal only with a limited number of firms. In consequence, most of the engineering shops in the country were doing little or no work for munition production, but were carrying on with private contracts, on the principle of "business as usual." This meant that a considerable proportion of the engineering labour in the country was not being mobilised for munition production.

For solving the labour problem, therefore, it was obvious that the steps needed were:

(*a*) To check the enlistment of skilled men; if possible to recover from the Army those who had already joined up; and ultimately to dilute the available supply by bringing in as much additional unskilled labour as could be safely utilised in the processes of manufacture.

(*b*) To induce workers to keep better time and abstain from slacking at their work and continually changing their employer.

(*c*) To ensure a more rigid control of drinking facilities in munition areas.

(*d*) To train and employ women for the class of work for which they were suitable.

(*e*) To bring the needed munition work and the available labour in the kingdom together, either by transferring all workers to the established armament firms, or by spreading our production among all the shops in the kingdom.

Prior to the setting up of the Ministry of Munitions, the handling of the labour problem was primarily the duty of the Board of Trade, working in consultation with the War Office. The Board of Trade gave a great deal of time and effort to this task and worked out various schemes for dealing with it. A number of causes, however, combined to hinder these schemes from having the desired effect.

At the Committee of Imperial Defence on the 27th of January, 1915, Lord Kitchener expressed fears that any attempt to conserve to British manufacturers their pivotal men might directly or indirectly prejudice recruiting more than seemed likely at first sight. He objected to any system which entailed the rejection of any willing recruit. In consequence of Lord Kitchener's attitude, the only conclusion reached by the Committee was a recommendation that when a valuable man in industry was recruited the firm should fill his place with some man or woman ineligible for the Army.

In the course of January, 1915, arrangements were made whereby valuable skilled men serving with the colours could be released and sent back to the munition firms from which they had gone out. But no considerable numbers were actually released under this system until the late summer. A War Office scheme for "badging" was brought into existence in March, 1915, but during the first seven or eight months of the War, when enthusiasm for enlistment had been at its height, the most vital industries suffered losses which no subsequent efforts could altogether repair. When once a man had joined the colours no power could make him return to civil work against his will, and the influence of all his military superiors, from the General Officer to the youngest corporal, was exerted to keep him in the Army if he looked like becoming a useful soldier.

Broadly, therefore, it may be said that the activity of the recruiting officer in denuding the country of its best skilled workers was subject to no effective check during the first year of the War. Every outside influence was against the retention of the artisan at home — especially the patriotism of the worker, who often could not be persuaded that his work was necessary to the equipment of the Army. Moreover, during the period of voluntary recruitment the man who remained at his home post was liable to be taunted as a coward and insulted in the streets with white feathers.

Arising out of the discussion in the Cabinet Committee on munitions on December 23rd, 1914, various efforts were made to bring about the expansion and dilution of the available labour. Belgian workmen were taken on as fully as possible, and a certain number of women were brought into armament work. The first systematic attempt to enrol women for replacement of male labour was made by the Board of Trade on March 16th, 1915. In 2½ months, to June 4th, 1915, some 78,946 women were enrolled on the Special War Register for women for work connected with munitions, but only 1816 of these were actually given jobs.

The subsequent history of women's work in the production of munitions is one of the brightest chapters in the story. I give elsewhere some account of their efficiency and of their fine devotion and courage in connection with shell-filling. It was one of the many curious revolutions effected by the War that the lead in organising women and girls for national service was taken by the very people who, prior to the War had been, in the cause of women's suffrage, the thorniest opponents of the Government. Mrs. Pankhurst and her daughter Christabel, Miss Annie Kenney, Mrs. Drummond and other prominent suffragettes were prime movers in this new crusade.

On July 18th, 1915, they headed a great Women's War Pageant, in which thousands of women demonstrators marched for miles along London streets through rain and mud, escorting a deputation that waited on me, as Minister of Munitions, to express their welcome of the National Register and to offer their services to help the country. While voicing the demand of the women to be permitted to take part in war work, Mrs. Pankhurst also put in a plea for wage conditions which would safeguard their standard of living and prevent them from being sweated or exploited by manufacturers. In reply I gave a guarantee that they should have a fair minimum wage for time work and should receive for piece work the same rates as were paid to men. These conditions, sedulously enforced by the Ministry throughout the duration of the War, had a permanent effect upon the status of women workers in this country. For although the emergency work upon which they were engaged was only temporary, and the regulations in which the agreement was embodied applied only to women engaging on what previously had been regarded as men's work, yet a standard was set up which could not easily be set aside afterwards; and it may confidently be claimed that the low and variable wages which were paid to women in the metal trades before the War are gone never to return.

In the War Office establishments, and the metal and chemical industries, which by mid-1916 were engaged in munition production to the extent of at least 75 per cent. of their total output, the women and girls employed rose from 82,589 in July, 1914, to 340,844 by July, 1916. By November, 1918, the grand total of women employed on work directly or indirectly to Government order was 1,587,300. These figures give some indication of the immense growth of the effort made by women on behalf of their country during the War.

The difficulties which had to be overcome to secure the admission of women workers on this scale into branches of industry which had previously been a male preserve were, of course, immense. But I will not further digress here to deal with them, as they were a part of the general problem of dilution of labour which I discuss in the following pages.

During the opening months of 1915 the Board of Trade

made a series of efforts to draw supplies of labour to the established armament firms from other engineering concerns. This was in accordance with the War Office policy of giving its contracts only to the recognised munition firms, and was based on the assumption that outside firms were doing only civilian work. The results achieved were very meagre, partly because it transpired that many of these firms were devoting a part at least of their energy to sub-contracts for munition production, partly because they resented most intensely the proposal to filch away from them their best workmen and demanded as an alternative that they should themselves be given War Office contracts to execute. A further difficulty was that the workmen themselves were unwilling to leave their homes and take up work in some distant part of the country for a strange concern. It soon became clear that the transference of labour from commercial to Government work could only be achieved by compulsory measures.

In one respect, indeed, many outside firms intimated that they would welcome compulsion. They were tied up by contracts they had entered into for civilian commercial work, and although they were anxious to assist the Government they could not break these contracts without incurring penalties. If, however, the Government would either give them statutory release from their obligations, or would take over their works under the system of Government control laid down in the Defence of the Realm Act, this difficulty would be surmounted.

On legal advice being taken, it was found that the existing powers were not adequate for this matter, and the outcome was the new Defence of the Realm Act which I laid before the House of Commons on March 9th. That measure authorised the Government "to require any work in any factory or workshop to be done in accordance with the directions of the Admiralty or Army Council given with the object of making the factory or workshop, or the plant or labour therein, as useful as possible for the production of war material." And it further provided that "where the fulfillment by any person of any contract is interfered with by the necessity on the part of himself or any other person of complying with any requirement, regulation or restriction of the Admiralty or the Army Council that necessity is a good defence to any action or proceeding taken against that person in respect of the non-fulfillment of the contract in so far as it is due to that interference."

Owing, however, to the persistence of the War Office in clinging affectionately to its traditional policy of dealing only with the established munition firms, comparatively little use was made of these powers prior to the establishment of the Ministry of Munitions.

Quite the most difficult problem in regard to labour was that of securing their wholehearted coöperation in the urgent task of munition production — by sticking in the same workshop, keeping good time, working steadily and avoiding strikes; and in particular by consenting to those relaxations of their trade union rules which would make possible an extensive dilution of skilled by unskilled workers, and a considerable use of overtime in cases of emergency.

When the first drafts for the new D.O.R.A. were under consideration, as submitted on February 26th, it was at first proposed to insert clauses which would have made illegal under penalty any strike or lock-out in any firm engaged on the construction of war material, and which would have provided compulsory arbitration in the case of all disputes. I decided, however, to see what could be done to achieve the same end by a voluntary agreement with the trade unions.

Accordingly, on March 17th, 1915, a representative

meeting of Trade Unionists was summoned "to consult with the Chancellor of the Exchequer and the President of the Board of Trade on certain matters of importance to labour arising out of the recent decision of the Government, embodied in the Defence of the Realm (Amendment) Act, to take further steps to organise the resources of the country to meet naval and military requirements."

The Conference was held in the gloomy board room of the Treasury, with the gilt throne of Queen Anne at one end of the room. There was a tradition that once upon a time it had been occupied by kings and queens who came to discuss their finances with the Lords of the Treasury. The last sovereign who sat upon it was the first Hanoverian George. Since he understood no English and the Lords of the Treasury understood no German, our sovereigns ceased to go through the formality of attending these meetings at the Treasury to arrange their finance, and the once glistening and plushed throne has now a sad look of tarnished and torn neglect. The room was so crowded with the representatives of workers in many trades that some of them had to lean against this rickety throne of the last of the Stuarts. I had invited Mr. Balfour to be present. He had addressed many an assembly largely composed of workmen, but this was his first experience of sitting down to confer with them on a basis of equality. So far he had only talked to them; now he was talked to by them. The expression on his face was one of quizzical and embarrassed wonder.

He was surprised to find the workmen's representatives talked so well. They put their points clearly and succinctly, wasting neither time nor words. On the other hand, there was just a note of aggressiveness in manner and tone to which he was not quite accustomed from such quarters. For the moment it almost quelled him, and he was silent throughout. He did not quite recover his ease even after they left.

He liked new experiences, but not of this sort. This was a portent which had for the first time appeared in the quarter of the sky where he had shone for a generation, and it came uncomfortably near. His ideas of Government were inherited from the days when Queen Anne sat on that throne. They were only changed to the extent that the fact of her being the last occupant constituted a triumph for the subject and thus modified the Constitution in a popular direction. But this scene was fundamentally different. He saw those stalwart artisans leaning against and sitting on the steps of the throne of the dead queen, and on equal terms negotiating conditions with the Government of the day upon a question vitally affecting the conduct of a great war. Queen Anne was indeed dead. I had watched his mood for years from an opposing bench. In looking at him now I felt that his detached and enquiring mind was bewildered by this sudden revelation of a new power and that he must take time to assimilate the experience.

The Conference met on the 17-19th of March, 1915.

Opening the proceedings, I said that those present were being invited to consider the need for a larger output of munitions, and the steps which the Government proposed to take to organise industry to that end. Every belligerent country had found the expenditure of war material exceeded all anticipation. I referred to the very drastic powers which the Government had now assumed to control or take over any works in the country which were either turning out munitions of war or were capable of being adapted for that purpose, and told them that this was the matter on which I wanted to consult with them.

The "taking-over" of these works would not mean that their present owners and managers would be turned out adrift, and some admiral or general put in charge. The works would be run as formerly, except that they would be entirely turned over to munition production, and, of course, under such control there would have to be a limitation of private profits.

But if the Board of Trade were going in this manner to interfere with the rights and interests of the capital, the owner and managements of these concerns, it was only just that they should similarly ask the workers to consent to such limitations as might be found vitally necessary in the national interest of their ordinary privileges. In particular, I wanted to ensure that certain trade union regulations which might be more than justified in peace-time should be modified in such a way as to avoid hampering the nation's munition supplies in the existing emergency, and particularly that if any disputes arose, either about such relaxation of normal trade union rules, or about hours or rates of pay, the matter should be settled by peaceful arbitration, and pending a settlement the workers should carry on with their job. The Government did not say that workmen ought never to complain, or to ask for an increase in wages. "Our point is that during the time the questions at issue are being adjudicated upon, the work shall go on. . . . We want to get some kind of understanding with you about that before we undertake the control of these works."

I then laid before the representatives of the trade unions a series of propositions which had the object of providing that there should be no stoppage of work for Government purposes by strike or lock-out, pending a settlement of any disputes that might arise between employers and workpeople, but that all such disputes should be referred to arbitration; and that for the duration of the War, all trade union restrictions tending to limit output or the employment of semi-skilled or female labour should be suspended.

The workers' representatives were then left together to prepare their own draft of the undertaking they were prepared to give on these points. This draft was discussed and amended, and finally on the 19th of March a memorandum was presented by Mr. Arthur Henderson which had been accepted with only two dissensions. It was accordingly signed on behalf of the Government by myself and by Mr. Runciman, and on behalf of the workmen's representatives by Mr. Henderson and Mr. Mosses. I undertook to provide enough copies for every union to send one to each of its members.

This document was known as the "Treasury Agreement." It occupied an important place throughout the War in the negotiations with labour, because it set out clearly, in terms which the trade union leaders recognised to be fair and just, the conditions under which munition labour was thereafter progressively organised. It stipulated for the admission of unskilled and semi-skilled workers to dilute the existing body of skilled labour, provided that they were paid the same wages as had customarily been paid for the work; it furnished a scheme of arbitration to take the place of strikes; and it laid down that the private profits of the manufacturers were to be subject to limitation.

In the following week an agreement on similar lines was specially negotiated by me with the Amalgamated Society of Engineers, whose representatives, though present at the previous conference, had attended without power to sign.

These two agreements, though important because of the solutions they reached, failed to become immediately operative. There was one difficulty remaining. The workers, quite naturally, declined to confirm the suggested proposals limiting their own freedom until the Government implemented its undertaking to restrict private profit. Mr. Runciman was at the time busily engaged in negotiation with the heads of the armament firms in an effort to arrive at an agreed basis of limitation of profits, but in the end these negotiations came to nothing. The matter was ultimately dealt with by the Munitions of War Act in June, 1915, which provided that the establishments engaged in munitions work could be brought under the control of the Ministry, that their profits should be limited, and that in such controlled establishments trade union rules restricting output should be suspended.

This question of controlling private profits was in fact vital to the whole issue of labour supply. It was useless to ask the workers on the plea of a grave emergency to put their whole effort into manufacture and to stop striking or agitating for higher wages or to accept modifications of rules and restrictions designed for their protection, which they had won from employers through years of struggle, when they saw those same employers busily amassing colossal fortunes out of the emergency. In a "Memorandum on Labour for Armaments," by Sir H. Llewellyn Smith, dated June 9th, 1915, this situation is expressed as follows:

> "The difficulty, as it has been expressed, both by workmen's representatives at the two Treasury Conferences and by employers themselves (as in the shipbuilding employers' deputation received to-day) is that the workmen, though engaged on armament work, still feel themselves to be working essentially for private employers, with whom they have only a 'cash nexus,' and that in the present circumstances a 'cash nexus' is quite inadequate to secure control. . . .
>
> "So long as contractors' profits are not brought under control, the workmen feel that any sacrifice they may make of their rules and restrictions will directly increase the profits of private persons, and their unwillingness to make the sacrifice is made almost insuperable by this suspicion."

It is true that during this period there had been a steady tendency for wages to rise, and that in addition, on account of the regular full work available in this country, combined with overtime, the workers were earning considerably more than they had previously done. But on the other hand, prices of food and other necessities had also been rising at a pace which in some cases almost outstripped any advance in wages. Strikes were in consequence occurring with ever-increasing frequency. Mr. I. H. Mitchell, of the Industrial Commissioners Department, when reviewing the tendencies of the last six months in June, 1915, wrote:

> "I am quite satisfied that the labour difficulty has been largely caused by the men being of opinion that, while they were being called upon to be patriotic and refrain from using the strong economic position they occupied, employers, merchants and traders were being allowed perfect freedom to exploit to the fullest the Nation's need. This view was frankly submitted to me by the leaders of the Clyde engineers' strike in February last. As soon as Labour realised that nothing was being done to curtail and prevent this exploitation by employers, it let loose the pent-up desire to make the most they could in the general scramble. This has grown until now many unions are openly exploiting the needs of the Nation. If the work is Government work, it is the signal for a demand for more money. Trade union leaders who, from August last year until February this year, loyally held their members back from making demands, are now with them in the rush to make the most of the opportunity."

I may sum up as follows the labour situation as it presented itself when the Ministry of Munitions was formed in June, 1915:

Recruiting had taken away from industry a considerable number of its most essential workers and was still being pushed forward without any limitation other than that resulting from the belated badging of key men in the more important armament firms. Arrangements had been made by Lord Kitchener to permit the release from the colours of skilled workers badly needed by firms engaged on war work, but of a quarter of a million men employed in the metal trades who had joined the forces, only about 5000 had actually been brought back.

The principle of dilution of skilled labour, though adopted in the Treasury agreement, had not yet been confirmed by the trade unions and put into force.

Profits of the firms engaged in war work were still unlimited, and were attaining unprecedented dimensions. Industrial unrest, stimulated by this spectacle, was growing rapidly. Whereas the number of disputes involving stoppage of work known to the Board of Trade at the beginning of 1915 was 10, 47 fresh disputes arose in February, 74 in March, 44 in April, and 63 in May. As regards labour this was the general situation with which the Ministry of Munitions was at the outset of its existence called upon to deal.

My first step for coping with this situation was to lay before Parliament, on June 23rd, 1915, the Munitions of War Bill. This was a measure designed to implement by statute the various proposals which had already been discussed with the employers and workers in the munition industry. It dealt with the settlement of labour differences, the prohibition of lock-outs and strikes, the controlling of establishments engaged in production of munitions and the limitation of their profits, the control of munition workers and the issue to them of badges; and it also provided for voluntary enrolment of a body of munition workers to be at the disposal of the Ministry and work where the need for their services was the greatest. Introducing this Bill, I reminded the House of the tremendous task which production of munitions for modern war had turned out to be, and outlined the steps I was taking to organise the available national resources for this end. I mentioned some of the difficulties, such as the question of supply of raw material.

I hinted that the Government might find it necessary to take complete control of the metal market. It might have to deal firmly with people who attempted to hold up necessary supplies in order to exploit higher prices. It might have to take steps to prevent a coal shortage. Existing machinery was often idle because there were no skilled men to use it. Many such men had enlisted in the Army, and must be found and brought back from the firing line to the workshop. The holding up of work through the slackness of a minority had to be remedied, and the restriction of output because of yard regulations, written and unwritten, must be avoided. The question of compulsory service in the production of munitions of war, I said, had been the subject of a very frank discussion between the leaders of the trade unions and myself, and I was bound to point out that if there were an inadequate supply of labour for the purpose of turning out the munitions of war which were necessary for the safety of the country, compulsion would be inevitable. The trade union leaders put forward as an alternative the proposal that the Government should give them an opportunity of securing the men required. They said: "Give us seven days, and if in seven days we cannot get the men, we will admit that our case is considerably weakened." To this I had agreed. But even if the required workers were forthcoming voluntarily, I explained that it would still be necessary to take powers in the Bill to enforce contracts with them and to secure discipline in the workshops. Here again an agreed solution had been reached for the setting up of a Munitions Court.

I then came to the very important provisions in the Bill with regard to limitation of profits from munition work:

"The trade unions insisted, and I think properly insisted, on their share of the bargain. They said, workmen are quite willing to work for the State, to put their whole strength and to suspend their trade union regulations, as long as they know that the work is of advantage to the country. But the objection in their minds always is that they are suspending trade union regulations important to them in order to increase the profits of individual employers. That they will not assent to, and they say, as a condition of all the other provisions to which they have given their assent, there must be a clause in the Bill which will limit the profits of those establishments which are working for the State, and that the provisions which I have enumerated only apply to establishments where the profits are limited. That is why we propose to set up controlled establishments, so that where the State assumes control of a workshop all the conditions which I have referred to shall apply to that workshop. That means the workshops where the munitions of war are being supplied at the present moment. It means practically that the State assumes control of the profits of these establishments, that whatever suspension of regulations takes place it will be entirely for the benefit of the State and not of the individual employer, and upon those conditions the trade union leaders are prepared to accept those suggestions which I have already made."

The Munitions of War Bill quickly passed through its Parliamentary stages and received the Royal Assent on July 2nd. No time was lost in bringing to the solution of the labour problem the aid which its powers afforded.

I made a systematic effort to get back skilled men serving with the colours to resume their work in the munition firms. On June 9th I sent a circular letter to engineering and shipbuilding firms to get lists of the skilled men in their employ who had enlisted, and telegrams were sent by the Adjutant-General to certain Commanding Officers to ascertain what skilled men were in their units. But Lord Kitchener stipulated that, for the time being, only those men should be released who were not yet overseas or in units ready to be sent out.

The recovery of skilled mechanics from the ranks, however, under this strict limitation was not very successful. From July to the end of October, 1915, the total number thus brought back, either under the "bulk scheme" for release of those known to be skilled mechanics, or the individual release of men specially asked for by their own firms, barely exceeded 5000. The flower of the skilled mechanics who had joined the Army was either already abroad or in the "barred" units at home. Speaking on December 20th, 1915, in the House of Commons, I said:

"We are trying to get men from the Colours. . . . It is like getting through barbed-wire entanglements without heavy guns. There are entrenchments behind entrenchments. You have not merely the Army, the Corps, the Division, the Brigade, the Battalion, and the Company, but the Platoon, and even the Squad — everybody fighting to prevent men from coming away. I am not surprised. I am not blaming them. Skilled men at any trade are skilled men at every trade. Your intelligent skilled man is a good man in the trenches, and nobody wants to lose him. Therefore, every corporal fights against parting with a good, intelligent, skilled workman. As my honourable friend points out, the men themselves feel that they are running away from danger in order to go back to comfort and high wages and emoluments, and they don't like it. It is a very creditable story. . . ."

By August I had discovered that the bulk of the men we wanted were in the "barred" units, and I wrote to Lord Kitchener making a very urgent plea for the release of at least the most valuable of these.

Throughout August and September, 1915, a correspondence was in progress between the Ministry and the War Office, and eventually arrangements were made in September for a census of skilled munition workers in all units not yet sent out of the country, and of those offering themselves some forty thousand were passed by investigators as suitable. By the end of October steps were being taken to allocate these men to munition works.

Great as were the difficulties of carrying out the schemes for return of skilled workers from the colours, the difficulties in the way of introducing dilution of labour were far greater, though the ultimate results of this policy were more fruitful.

The fundamental opposition to dilution came from the craft unions. Through long years they had built up as a protection against the dangers of cut wages, unemployment, and blackleg labour an elaborate system of rules and customs which were designed to control the rate of output and narrow the doorway into the industry. The rules were highly artificial in many cases; men appertaining to certain crafts alone were permitted to touch certain work, even though it might be of a kind which any handy man could do with little or no special training; and a man doing one job might not carry out the simplest task ancillary to it which ought by these rules to be allocated to another class of craftsman, but must stand by and wait till the other type of craftsman was called in, and executed that limited operation. Experience of a restricted market for their labour had made the unions develop every means of restricting its supply, and they were afraid, not without reason, that if the door were thrown open they would after the War suffer from a congested labour market, and that if sharp demarcations between the crafts were once broken down they would be difficult to reëstablish. It was not a fear of falling wages during the War which troubled them. I had guaranteed that this would not occur. It was rather a dread of losing the tradition of mystery and technical difficulty which they had built up to protect their craft, and the apprehension of an overcrowded supply of workmen in their particular trade, leading to unemployment, lower wage rates, and a reduced standard of craftsmanship and of living in years to come. The patriotic appeal of our national necessity made difficult headway against these quite natural and — as the event proved in some cases — justifiable fears. Clemenceau once said that there was no difficulty in inducing Frenchmen to give their lives for their country, but they would not give their money. This is not to be wondered at when we remember that in actual fact the fires of patriotism are too often quenched when they come up against the cool waters of "business." Trades Unionists flocked to the standard of their country when volunteers were called for to face death, but I was told that men at the front, daily confronted with death and needing shells to protect and defend themselves, wrote home to their fellow Trades Unionists entreating them not to surrender any of the privileges of their craft, although strict adhesion to these privileges was impeding the supply of the munitions they so sadly needed. The war-time profiteers were not infrequently brothers or fathers of those who suffered and died at the front, and with altered circumstances might have shown equal self-sacrifice. But unhappily for sentiment, when you come to business matters you discover that business is business, and admits of no divided loyalties. Our statesmen more recently have rediscovered this truism at Ottawa.

It was perhaps unfortunate that the first branch of the engineering industry where it was found necessary to raise the issue of dilution was the machine tool trade, since this was regarded as the very special preserve of the skilled worker, and was one the output of which, unlike that of shells or machine-guns, would continue its importance after the War. When we attempted to increase munitions manufacture in this country we found that our first need was machine tools, which did not as yet exist in quantities sufficient even to permit the carrying out of the orders already placed by the War Office, far less the greatly augmented production at which the Ministry aimed. At a conference I summoned of machine tool makers on July 15th, an agreement with the Trades Unions was reached for a programme of night shifts and labour dilution. But when the officers of the Ministry tried to carry through this arrangement they came up against bitter opposition from shop stewards and local trade union committees. At Woolwich Arsenal the local committee resolved: "That we refuse to entertain the proposal to allow the introduction of semi-skilled men on work now done by fully qualified mechanics, as it is not proved there is the shortage claimed." And at the works of Messrs. J. Lang and Sons, Johnstone, the workers' committee declared: "That no woman shall be put to work a lathe, and if this is done the men will know how to protect their rights." This was in August, 1915, and I had to weigh carefully the alternatives of taking drastic action or trying conciliation. Had stern action proved successful without rousing wide antagonism, it would greatly have expedited the process of dilution. If it had failed against a massed opposition on the part of the skilled workers — for it would obviously have been impossible to punish them all — the campaign for dilution might have been permanently lost. As yet the Ministry was in its early stages, and a realisation of the immense and urgent need for greater munition output had not fully captured the minds and imaginations of the whole body of workers. I decided to try persuasion first.

On September 9th, 1915, I visited the Trades Union Congress at Bristol, and addressed it on the subject. I told them how the German trades unions had organised and expanded their services for munition production. The War, I declared, had become a conflict between the mechanics of Germany and Austria and the mechanics of Great Britain and France. But as yet this country was not doing its best in the struggle. Only 15 per cent. of the machinery which could be used for turning out rifles, cannon and shells (in all of which there was a shortage) was working night shifts. The problem, I pointed out, was largely one of labour. If every skilled man were working his utmost there would still not be nearly enough. The issue of dilution was not one of turning off a skilled man to make room for an unskilled, but one of concentrating the skilled men on the work which only they could do. At present, highly skilled workmen with years of training were doing work which could as easily be done by those who had only had a few weeks' or a few days' training, and we could not equip our armies unless organised labour was prepared to assist by suspending during the War all restrictions which made it difficult to use skilled labour in the best way by employing unskilled under skilled direction wherever possible.

I then proceeded to explain the bargain which had been made with the trades unions leaders at the Treasury Conference. "Has the State kept the bargain? [A voice: 'No.'] I am going to tell you. Profits, restrictions of profits. Does anybody say we have not kept the bargain? [A voice: 'Nobody knows!'] Nobody knows? We have declared 715 establishments producing munitions of war to be 'controlled establishments'; we have put them under control of the State . . . and do not forget this, we have not asked any trade union to suspend any regulations except in an establishment where we control the profits. What have we done about controlling the profits? We have controlled them by an Act of Parliament. . . . We are restricting them on the basis of what they earned before the War. . . . They are only going to get the standard which is based upon the profit made before the War, with any allowance which is made by us in respect of increased capital which they have put in. What do we do with the balance? We put it into the Treasury to carry on the War. [Cheers.] It is the first time it has ever been done in the history of any country. You have practically taken over the whole of the engineering works of this country and controlled them by the State. I have seen resolutions passed from time to time at Trade Union Congresses [laughter] about nationalising the industries of this country. We have done it. [Cheers and laughter.] . . ."

I told the Congress about the undertaking, embodied in an Act of Parliament, that conditions would be restored at the end of the War, and, further, I gave them a guarantee that piece rates should nowhere be cut down in munition works as a result of any increase in output; and that unskilled men and women should be paid the same rate as had been given to skilled men for the jobs transferred to them. Having dealt with the way in which the Government was keeping its side of the bargain, I indulged in some plain speaking on the failure of the Trade Unionists to do their share. I referred to the refusal of men to admit semi-skilled workers, the squabbles between coppersmiths and plumbers as to the dividing line between their jobs, and the penalising of men who worked faster than the average. "A complaint came to me from Woolwich that there was a deliberate attempt to keep down the output. The Labour Advisory Committee investigated it, and a Trade Unionist defended the men in this particular case. The significance of his testimony was this — and I am quoting now from the report of the investigators: 'The trade unionist witness regretted having to acknowledge that the workmen in several departments restricted output in order to maintain the prices obtained before the War, and this was continued up to the present time.' Well, that is not carrying out the bargain. [A voice: 'It is not playing the game.'] I agree."

It is fair that I should record the fact that a crowded

assembly of trade union delegates listened to this plain speaking not only without resentment but with a swelling appreciation. A week later there was held a conference of trade union executives to discuss dilution, and a series of resolutions favourable to the plan was adopted. Following on this expression of approval, I set up a Central Munitions Labour Supply Committee, containing representatives of the Ministry, of the Employers and the Employed, presided over by Mr. Arthur Henderson, which proceeded to coöperate with the Ministry in organising labour dilution and dealing with the multitudinous problems of wage rates and local conditions of employment, transfer of labour, etc., which arose in this connection.

By the end of 1915 labour troubles were interfering seriously in some areas with the output of munitions. I suspected that in some cases the failure of a firm to deliver up to schedule was due to a certain degree of slackness and inefficiency on the part of the management, but in a great many cases it was traceable to the activities of men inside the works who deliberately fostered discontent. The trouble did not come from the Trade Unions or their officials. They honourably adhered to their agreement with the State. But an agitation known as the "shop steward" movement arose in the greatest of the munition works. These "stewards" were chosen by the workers in a given factory or workshop to present grievances to the management. They felt they must justify their existence by searching out wrongs which had escaped the notice of the local trade union secretary. It gradually became a formidable element of disturbance in the largest munition areas. Glasgow was one of the worst districts, and the agitation amongst the workers seriously interfered with the output, especially with the delivery of big guns. I decided to visit the works to see for myself what the position was, and put before the men and their leaders the exact facts with regard to the military position, and the peril in which their fellow-workmen at the front were placed by the absence of adequate artillery of the heavier kinds to enable them to contend with their foes on equal terms.

Accompanied by Mr. Arthur Henderson I arrived at Glasgow on Christmas Eve, and we both went to Beardmore's works, where the delivery of heavy artillery was being seriously retarded by labour difficulties. At my request, the shop stewards were brought together and I then told them why I had come, and made my appeal for their assistance in stimulating greater activity in production. A man who seemed to be their leader stepped to the front and started haranguing me on the servitude of labour in private establishments. He was a strong man, with a fine open face, the natural pleasantness of which was overlaid by a theatrical frown which he had succeeded in implanting upon a kindly countenance. He struck an attitude, and in a loud, challenging voice he said, "I am as much a slave of Sir William Beardmore as if I had the letter 'B' branded on my brow," his hand passing across the wrinkled forehead. This was my first acquaintance with Mr. David Kirkwood. I discovered that he was fundamentally a reasonable man to deal with. He promised that if Mr. Henderson put our case before a free assembly of workers, he would do his best to secure a fair hearing.

There was another spokesman who seemed to me to be a natural savage. He came right up to me with threatening mien and locked fists, talking in an ill-tempered and angry voice. I must say the rest of his comrades were not too pleased with his attitude. Later on I met Mr. Gallagher, a Communist, whose manners were quite perfect, and whose tones were soft, but he left no doubt in my mind that his was the most sinister influence.

The following morning (that is, Christmas morning) we

addressed a great gathering of workmen at the St. Andrew's Hall. Mr. Henderson took the chair; four-fifths of the workmen were anxious to hear all that was being said, but a minority were determined to disturb the proceedings and deprive us of a hearing. They were specially annoyed with Mr. Henderson, and he had by far the worst time. On the whole I was heard quite well, with a few surmountable interruptions. Mr. Kirkwood played the game and got up in the middle of the most turbulent elements, and put in a plea for a fair hearing. The visit, for a time at least, had a quieting effect and a quickening influence upon production. Some weeks later we had further trouble, and then strong action had to be taken in the way of deportation of some of the leaders, and the prosecution of others.

We were as yet, however, far from having reached full victory; there were still some entrenched obstructions and restrictions to break through. Even the greatest convulsion fails to tear out of the soil a well-grounded suspicion.

In this case its roots were so deep that they resisted the shattering bombardment of a year of horror. Throughout the autumn of 1915 discussion and disagreements continued as to the application of the principle of dilution, and in December I brought forward the Munitions of War (Amendment) Bill in order to give statutory force to the various points on which agreement had been reached. Even at this stage the Amalgamated Society of Engineers was still holding out, and when the Bill had reached its Committee stage, they sent a deputation to wait on Mr. Asquith and myself, armed with a resolution declaring that a series of amendments which they proposed —

". . . are essential as an element of justice in the administration of the Munitions of War Act, 1915, and should be incorporated in the Amended Act if we are to maintain our influence with our members in securing the high standard of production required.

Further, that a Committee representative of the conference be instructed to wait upon the Prime Minister and the Minister of Munitions and intimate the decision of this conference *as the basis of our continued coöperation.*"

The veiled threat in the last line of this resolution naturally stirred Mr. Asquith to anger. When challenged the deputation protested that they had not meant it in that way, and that all they wanted was to secure that the various provisions of the protection of wage levels and conditions of employment which had been set out in two circulars issued by the Ministry (Circulars L.2 and L.3) as conditions under which dilution was to be carried out should be given the force of statute. To my challenge whether they could cite a single instance in which an unskilled man, introduced into a controlled establishment, had been refused these rates, Mr. Brownlie, the engineers' secretary, had to admit they could not, and Mr. Asquith and I pointed out to them that some of their people had persistently tried to block dilution, and were at present making objections with little real substance as an excuse for their attitude. I would be willing to meet them in regard to incorporating the provisions of the two circulars in the Bill, if they on their side would guarantee that henceforward they would really coöperate in the dilution scheme, and not merely fall back upon some new demand as a pretext for doing nothing.

The deputation accepted this offer, and signed a document pledging the Conference and membership of the Society to accept the scheme of dilution and coöperating actively therein if the Government incorporated in the Bill the rates of pay and conditions of labour in controlled establishments set out in the Ministry's two circulars.

The Bill was re-committed and amended in accordance with this agreement, and thereafter dilution made rapid headway.

### 4. Royal Encouragement of Munition Workers

Problem of maintaining patriotic spirit among munition workers — The King visits the ordnance factories — Among shipbuilding workers on Clyde and Tyne — A bold speech — Personal encouragement to me on formation of Ministry — Tour of Midland munition areas — Visit to Yorkshire munition works.

The story of the steps taken to organise labour for the munition factories, and to induce them to put forward their best efforts and submit to control and the suspension of cherished trade union regulations and practices, would not be complete without a tribute to the vitally important help rendered by the King to the nation by heartening and encouraging the munition workers and those who were creating the district organisations.

It would be hard to over-estimate the value of the national service rendered by the Sovereign's visits to munitions areas and the personal relations he established with the workers there. I have shown in my narrative how dangerous a gulf had threatened to open between the outlook of the men in the trenches and that of the men at home in the workshops. While those who joined the Army felt they were serving King and Country, and put on with their khaki a spirit of loyal comradeship and unquestioning service, those who remained in the familiar civilian environment of the workshop found it hard to escape from the old traditional atmosphere of jealous care for their rights as against their employers, the fear of exploitation, the readiness to "down tools" at any threat of encroachment upon their hard-won privileges. It was no easy task to persuade them that they too were in the service of the State for the defence of the nation; and to this end nothing could have been happier than the spontaneous resolve of the King to go about among them, to shake them by the hand, talk with them, and make a direct appeal to their patriotism and citizenship.

In the spring of 1915, when labour troubles were beginning to make themselves felt, King George began this practice of visiting the places where munitions were being produced. On March 17th he went to Woolwich Arsenal, and inspected the royal gun and carriage factories there, and the royal laboratory where explosives were made and tested. At the end of April he similarly visited the other royal factories, the small arms factory at Enfield and the gunpowder factory at Waltham Abbey. He followed up this visit by sending a special royal message to the workers at these factories, expressing his keen interest in their work, and his conviction that all engaged in the workshops would do their utmost, individually and collectively, to support their comrades at the front. On May 12th the King paid a two days' visit to Portsmouth, and went through the dockyards there, and again sent them a message on his return expressing "appreciation of the part which, by their devotion to duty, they are taking in maintaining the strength and efficiency of the Fleet."

Hardly had he got back to Buckingham Palace before he was off again on a week's tour of the shipyards and armament factories of the north. He spent May 17th and 18th on the Clyde, touring round from early morning to visit shipbuilding yards. At one of the largest, that of the Fairfield Shipbuilding and Engineering Company, the workmen presented him with a resolution expressing their loyalty and determination to press forward as efficiently and rapidly as possible with the Government work on which they were engaged. Replying, he said this resolution "will be universally welcomed, and will strengthen the confidence of the Nation in ultimate victory. It will indeed be a happy outcome if my visit to the Clyde has in any way conduced to this expression of patriotic resolve on the part of the men of one of the most important shipyards in this renowned industrial centre."

From the Clyde the King went to the Tyne, where he also spent two days, and spoke personally with a number of foremen and workers in the armament works and shipyards. He met the members of the North-East Coast Armaments Committee, and encouraged them in their task. He thanked the workmen in a speech for what had been done, but urged that more was still required. He voiced the hope "that all restrictive rules and regulations would be removed, and that all would work to one common end and purpose." This was a courageous gesture on the King's part to help forward the solution of the very difficult problem of suspending the trade union restrictions, which at that time were seriously hampering output. He followed it up a fortnight later by sending a message to the Armaments Committee urging "workers to do all they can." King George concluded this tour by visiting Barrow-in-Furness on May 21st. Whilst there he received a message from the Wallsend workers declaring their resolve to get ahead with the Government work, and replied expressing his appreciation. On June 10th he sent a message to the Barrow workers, appreciating "their assurances of loyalty and of resolution to do their utmost to assist in bringing to a victorious conclusion the great war which has now been raging for ten months."

The formation of the Ministry of Munitions called forth the King's keen and sympathetic interest. I have the most grateful recollections of the good will he showed to me in my anxious task, and of his readiness to give that personal help and encouragement which was so valuable a means of maintaining and improving the spirit of the munition workers. On July 22nd he started off and toured the munition areas of the Midlands. At Coventry he went round the works, and spoke personally to the foremen in all the shops. The members of the Coventry Armaments Output Committee were presented to him. Then he went on to Birmingham, where he spent the next day. So much interested did he show himself to be in the process of munition manufacture that it was difficult for the members of his suite to draw him away and enable him to keep to his time-table. Here again he insisted on having the members of the Munitions Committee and of the District Board of Management presented to him, and spoke warmly to them of the "zeal and cheerfulness" he had noted amongst the workers. This he followed up ten days later with a special message of encouragement.

Towards the end of September the King made another munitions tour, this time in Yorkshire, where he spent three days at Leeds and Sheffield. He moved among the munition workers, chatting freely with them. He picked out one worker at Sheffield, whom he recognised as having served with him when he was a midshipman in H.M.S. *Bacchante.* He watched another making shells, and remarked to him: "I am glad you realise the importance of the work in hand. Without an adequate supply of shells we cannot expect to win."

Words like these, uttered "man to man" by the Head of State to the artisan, naturally ran like wildfire through the works. It was this directness of personal contact, free from pomp or any trace of arrogance and aloofness, which made the King's visits to the munition areas such a valuable aid in the task of rousing the workers' enthusiasm and breaking through their reluctance to accept new methods and regulations. It was a real service to the men fighting our battles at the front who were in such peril of being overwhelmed by the superior equipment of the enemy.

The stimulation of the munition workers was of course only one among the myriad tasks imposed upon the Sovereign by the War — tasks to which he applied himself with indefatigable zeal, after a fashion which established him more firmly than ever in the affection of his people. His was the only throne in all the combatant countries which did not rock throughout all those critical years. Most of them, indeed, were overthrown. As one who was privileged to hold high and responsible office under the Crown all through the War I had special opportunities of witnessing how thoroughly the King discharged his duty to the country. Nowhere was the part he played more fruitful and valuable than in the encouragement of our munition workers.

### 5. The Drink Trouble

Improved national habits since pre-war days — Dangers of alcohol in early war months — Growth of drinking — Bad effect on munition output — My warning speech at Bangor — Deputation of shipbuilders: demand for prohibition — Reply to deputation — The King's interest in the problem — "The King's Pledge" — Not followed by Parliament — The question of State Purchase — Liquor Trade Finance Committee report — Opposition of teetotal extremists — Montagu's memorandum — Control of liquor trade: the new D.O.R.A. — Time lost through drinking in armament works — Control of areas — The "No Treating" Order — Defeat of proposals to impose higher liquor taxation — "Pot *versus* Patent" — Liquor control through Food Controller — Reduced consumption of alcohol — Carlisle experiment in State management — Development of canteens — Work of voluntary organisations — Subsidising canteen development — Standard permanently improved.

One of the most serious obstacles encountered in the way of increasing the output of munitions was the heavy drinking in certain areas. France had dealt drastically with the problem by prohibiting absinthe; Russia by forbidding vodka. The question of drinking facilities has always been a dangerous topic for Governments to tackle, and the War Government, being naturally anxious to avoid controversial subjects, shrank from tackling it for many precious months. We consequently lost substantially in production. It is difficult for us to-day to realise how seriously excessive drinking contributed to diminish the output. Britain to-day is a much more sober country than it has ever been in my memory. There is still a good deal of heavy drinking, drunkenness still occurs, and the national health suffers from it, but the sight of a drunken man or woman reeling down the street has grown a rare spectacle, and the consumption of alcohol has fallen off very heavily. The discipline and restriction compelled by the exigencies of the War is largely responsible for this salutary change. This must ever be counted as one of the good things occasionally garnered from things evil. The memory of pre-war conditions is growing fainter, and it is becoming quite hard to remind oneself of the very different state of affairs which too often prevailed then. Cases of drunkenness appearing before the courts were three times as numerous in pre-war years as they are now. The quantity of spirits (alcoholic content) drunk in 1913 was two and a half times what it is to-day. That may give the rising generation, growing up to the new and better tradition of to-day, some idea how commonplace and widespread insobriety must have been in some areas of this country up to the Great War. During the first five months of the War it became a serious element in the struggle to avert defeat. On the home front alcoholic indulgence shared with professional rigidity the dishonour of being our most dangerous foe. It is one of the themes of my book to tell how both of them were beaten off, though not without heavy casualties. The first effect of the War was rather to increase the habit of excessive drinking, and, indeed, to raise it into a real menace to the nation. It is easy to understand that this would be so. The sudden onset of unaccustomed danger drove many who were out of the danger zone to the vicarious philosophy of "Let us eat and drink — especially drink — for to-morrow our comrades may die!"

The disorganization of social habit through the War, the reckless excitement that thrilled the air, the feeling that the tables of the law had once more been smashed amid the thunders of a grimmer Sinai, led some of both sexes to excesses in all directions, and as war work increased the earnings of multitudes, those who drank, drank deeply, for they could afford the indulgence as they never could before. The evil was not confined to men — it spread to women. My attention was specially directed to this problem through the reports that excessive drinking among the workers in the firms engaged on armament production was gravely hindering the output of munitions. The reports of eye-witnesses were very grave and alarming, especially when taken in conjunction with the fact — of which I was already aware — that deliveries of munitions of war were in arrears, and that there were persistent rumours of serious shortage in France. Liquor consumption had certainly gone up rapidly. Drunkenness was greatly on the increase, particularly in the industrial areas which we relied on for munitions. A considerable percentage of the workers failed to turn up on a Monday morning, and when they appeared on Tuesday they were much the worse for their week-end debauch. Some of them took to extending their leisure at both ends of the week. One bank holiday a great number of men failed to turn up for a whole week. No wonder output was unsatisfactory. I passed on such reports as I received to the War Office and Admiralty. They replied that they were only too painfully aware of the facts and that their official reports showed an even worse state of affairs than anything revealed in mine. I decided that the time demanded that this peril to our armies ought to be instantly and firmly tackled, and on February 28th, 1915, I began to stir up public opinion on the subject of this increasing and menacing evil, with a view to making strong action possible. Speaking at Bangor on that day I said:

"I hear of workmen in armament works who refuse to work a full week's work for the nation's need. What is the reason? They are a minority. The vast majority belong to a class we can depend upon. The others are a minority. But, you must remember, a small minority of workmen can throw a whole works out of gear. What is the reason? Sometimes it is one thing, sometimes it is another, but let us be perfectly candid. It is mostly the lure of the drink. They refuse to work full time, and when they return their strength and efficiency are impaired by the way in which they have spent their leisure. Drink is doing more damage in the War than all the German submarines put together. . . . We have got great powers to deal with drink, and we mean to use them. We shall use them in a spirit of moderation, we shall use them discreetly, we shall use them wisely, but we shall use them quite fearlessly, and I have no doubt that, as the country's needs demand it, the country will support our action, and will allow no indulgence of that kind to interfere with its prospects in this terrible war which has been thrust upon us."

A month later, on March 29th, 1915, I received a deputation from the Shipbuilding Employers' Federation, who were unanimous in urging that the sale of excisable liquors should be totally prohibited during the period of the War. In particular, they asked for the closing of public-houses and clubs in the areas where war munitions were being produced. They pointed out that in spite of Sunday labour and all overtime the total period worked on the average in almost all shipyards was below the normal number of hours per week, and though work was in progress night and day for seven days a week, less productiveness was being secured from the men than before the War. The deputation was of the opinion that this was principally due to drink. The figures of weekly takings in public-houses near the yards were convincing evidence of the increased sale of liquor. Allowing for the enhanced price of intoxicants and for the greater number of men now employed in shipbuilding, the takings had in one case under observation risen 20 per cent., in another 40 per cent.

The damage done by the drink habit was sufficiently

illustrated by the case of a battleship coming in for immediate repairs and having those repairs delayed a whole day by the absence of the riveters through drink and conviviality. This case, they said, was one of hundreds. Nor was this the only reason in favour of prohibition as against curtailment. As long as public-houses were open there would be found men to break the rules of the yard and come late to work in order to secure drink beforehand and the indisposition to work after the consumption of excessive alcohol was too obvious to need elaboration. They urged total prohibition during the War. It was certainly not a teetotal deputation. Neither in figure nor physiognomy did they give any indication of having spent their leisure hours in the service of the Band of Hope. When prohibition came in in America this incident explained to me why the majority of employers were stout prohibitionists. It also explained the rumours that they drew a definite line between national prohibition and personal abstinence.

The evidence was not to be lightly disregarded. Replying to the deputation, I said:

"Success in the War is now purely a question of munitions. I say that, not on my own authority, but on the authority of our great General, Sir John French. He has made it quite clear what his conviction is on the subject. I think I can venture to say that that is also the conviction of the Secretary of State for War, and it is the conviction of all those who know anything about the military problem — that in order to enable us to win, all we require is an increase, and an enormous increase, in the shells, rifles, and all the other munitions and equipment which are necessary to carry through a great war. You have proved to us to-day quite clearly that the excessive drinking in the works connected with these operations is interfering seriously with that output. I can only promise you this at the present moment, that the words you have addressed to my colleagues and myself will be taken into the most careful consideration. . . . I had the privilege of an audience with his Majesty this morning, and I am permitted by him to say that he is very deeply concerned on this question — very deeply concerned — and the concern which is felt by him is, I am certain, shared by all his subjects in this country."

His Majesty had indeed shown the most anxious interest in the problem of drink, and had talked over with me the various possible methods of combating it. Reports had been coming in to him from many quarters as to the damaging effect of drink on production. He was himself prepared to go to any length of personal self-sacrifice for this end, and on March 30th, the day after I had received this deputation, he sent me, through his secretary, Lord Stamfordham, a remarkable letter, which, after saying that "nothing but the most vigorous measures will successfully cope with the grave situation now existing in our armament factories," proceeded:

"We have before us the statements, not merely of the employers, but of the Admiralty and War Office officials responsible for the supply of munitions of war, for the transport of troops, their food, and ammunition. From this evidence it is without doubt largely due to drink that we are unable to secure the output of war material indispensable to meet the requirements of our Army in the field, and that there has been such serious delay in the conveyance of the necessary reinforcements and supplies to aid our gallant troops at the front.

"The continuance of such a state of things must inevitably result in the prolongation of the horrors and burdens of this terrible war.

"I am to add that if it be deemed advisable, the King will be prepared to set the example by giving up all alcoholic liquor himself, and issuing orders against its consumption in the Royal Household, so that no difference shall be made, so far as his

Majesty is concerned, between the treatment of rich and poor in this question."

This royal gesture became known as "The King's Pledge," which the nation at large was urged to adopt in conformity with the King's example. There was sound wisdom in the scheme, for the workers habitually complained, and with all-too-good reason, that while their employers and the members of the so-called upper classes were eternally lecturing and rebuking them for drinking, they were themselves freely and often excessively enjoying the alcohol which they sought to deny to their employees. "The King's Pledge," and the fact that a number of distinguished persons and prominent men in every branch of industry followed His Majesty in subscribing to it, very greatly strengthened the hands of the Government in the measures which it subsequently took to limit and control the supplies of intoxicants. Lord Kitchener was amongst those who gave practical support to the King's initiative and adhered to it to the end. It was always a subject of general debate at Ministerial and Military tables whether total abstinence had increased or diminished the vision and efficiency of the Secretary of State for War, or whether it had left it *in statu quo,* and there were three distinct views on this point, each emphatically held and controverted.

Unfortunately, despite its considerable moral value, the King's example was not adopted widely enough to make any deep impression on the problem itself. The House of Commons flatly declined to pass any such self-denying ordinance for its own observance, and this attitude on the part of the nation's legislators helped to prevent "The King's Pledge" from becoming the starting-point which King George and his advisers had hoped it might prove for a big voluntary movement of national sobriety. It remained, therefore, to reinforce this initial impulse by statutory powers.

I was at this time giving very serious consideration to the idea of dealing with the drink traffic by buying out on behalf of the State all the private interests, and thus enabling the Government to obtain a perfectly free hand to carry through whatever measures were felt to be in the national interest, unhindered by the immensely powerful influence which the trade has always been able to exert on politics in this country. To this end I caused an investigation to be made by Sir William Plender as to the probable total value of the interests it would be necessary to acquire. On March 30th, he furnished me with a preliminary memorandum which showed that the market value of the shares in Breweries was approximately £68,786,000, while the value of the property owned by Breweries in Great Britain, including all tied houses, together with the value of all free public-houses and other on-licences would be £225,000,000 to £250,000,000.

It will be observed that this rough estimate did not include the value of distilleries.

I then secured the appointment of a "Liquor Trade Finance Committee" to advise the Government on the financial arrangements that would have to be made if it should be decided by the State to purchase the properties of the Breweries in England and Wales, to control the branches of the Retail Liquor Trade not so purchased, and to prohibit temporarily the retail trade in spirits, while permitting the continuance of the sale of beer below a certain alcoholic strength. The Committee reported on April 15th, 1915, submitting a series of recommendations as to the extent and manner of effecting the State acquisition of liquor interests, should such a step be decided on. This Committee estimated the total cost of transfer to the State of the properties of

Breweries and the interests of the licensees of free houses in England and Wales at £250 million, excluding allowances in respect of certain off-licences for compensation to the holders of grocers' licences, compensation to officials and employees and any other expenditure involved in the carrying through of such acquisition.

To politicians bred in pre-war traditions of national expenditure, the sum involved in this purchase seemed prodigious. It was held by some that in view of the heavy burdens we were already bearing to finance our war effort, it would be folly to choose this moment to incur this further heavy outlay. The sum required was barely one-fortieth of the ultimate cost of the War. In return the nation would have secured an asset which, on the basis of present profits, would have given a return of 8 per cent.

The real statesmanship of the temperance cause was on my side. But a powerful section of temperance advocates were up in arms against the abhorrent suggestion that the State should sully its soul by becoming the manufacturer and distributor of alcoholic poison. They had no objection to share by taxation in the profits made by selling this poison to their fellow citizens. But the conscience of a devotee is an eccentric thing and argument never converts but only exasperates a true believer. The resistance of this section grew. On the practical side I was faced with the difficulty that the interests which would have to be dealt with by way of purchase or compensation were so numerous and varied in character that the negotiations threatened to take many months. I secured the adhesion of some of the leading brewers to my scheme. I did not despair of securing the adhesion of the rest. The Conservative leaders were consulted as to their attitude and they intimated that they would offer no opposition to the deal if the Government came to the conclusion that it was essential as a war measure. But a number of influential local optionists brought such pressure to bear on the Prime Minister that he feared serious trouble inside the Party, and in view of the urgency of the problem of reducing excessive drinking in the interests of munition output I decided for the time being to proceed with a more limited reform.

During the course of the negotiations I received from Mr. Edwin Montagu the following contribution to the discussions in a letter which he wrote me. As it puts the case against restriction forcibly and wittily, I think it worth reproducing:

"(1) I believe and believe firmly that almost without exception, except in the cases of apoplexy, a shot in the stomach, or a congested liver, a man with a moderate amount of alcohol is a better citizen, a better man, a more vigorous individual, than he would be without it. Medical evidence shows that alcohol is a poison; like so many other poisons in moderation, it is beneficial, and total abstinence seems to me to be morally as great a weakness as insobriety.

"(2) I cannot find myself in agreement with you that there is any evidence that drink has hampered us in this War on any substantial scale which calls for heroic remedies. Evil exists — there is broken time, there is disinclination to work; it is true that, even with Sunday labour and overtime, the average hours worked are less per week in many important trades than before the War. I believe this to be largely due to overtime itself. If a man is called upon to work substantially longer one day than he is accustomed to work, the next day he is disinclined to work, and if he is a free agent may refuse to work. Our party anyhow, believes that trade unions are good institutions. They fixed the working day and its length probably empirically because experience showed them that, let us say, eight hours was the maximum which a member of their union could work regularly to produce the full economical output of which he was capable. They insisted that overtime should be treated as overtime because they found that it was economically bad, and it seems to me that the War has proved that insistence upon overtime leads to irregular work and a smaller output, and it should be avoided as much as possible.

"(3) It is true that receipts from the sale of drink are large, but this is due mainly to your own taxation, which has increased the price of beer, and to the increase in the price of raw material and of labour, which has increased the price of whisky.

"(4) It is true that employers and officials alike attribute everything that is wrong not to drunkenness, but to drink; but you must remember that although the Tory habit of mind is to be found on both sides of the House of Commons you are now for the first time coming into contact with the Tory mind, naked and unashamed, in bulk, and I cannot help feeling alarmed that you regard it as honest, as unprejudiced as the habit of mind to which you are accustomed. I regard it as being a worse habit of mind. It is a habit of mind which treats the working man as a machine with no vested interest in his habits and with no right to humane consideration. Just as if an engine can do 500 revolutions a minute it can do 30,000 in an hour and 300,000 in 10 hours, so they think a man who can drill 6 holes in an hour ought to drill 60 in 10 hours and 600 in 100 hours. Anything wrong with their system they are accustomed to put down to the unpatriotism, to the want of a sense of duty, the gross habits of these animals whom they regard as their inferiors. When you say to me that it is not only the evidence of the employers but also the evidence of the War Office and the Admiralty I am more emphatic in regarding the source of information as tainted. Likely it was these gentlemen, who would like to work on paper according to theory, dismissing from their minds all human factors, found the British workingman an intolerable nuisance. They would like to regulate him in all his actions, to measure his food like sailors on a ship or prisoners in a gaol, to dictate to him what time he went to bed and what time he arose, where he should live and even what he should think, to drill and perhaps to flog him to approximate him to the ideal nigger working for an average mine-owner in a Rand mine.

"(5) It is said that holidays would not be so attractive to the labourers if the public-houses were closed. But you are not going to close the public-houses; you are, I think, driven by a belief that you cannot with fairness deny a stimulant to a man in the Black Squad who works under horrible climatic conditions in the open air and you are going to allow him to have light beer. He will go to the public-house to get his light beer just as he goes now to get his strong beer. His holidays will be just as attractive, and if your object is to make it unattractive you will have to close picture palaces and deprive him of all opportunity for amusement.

"(6) Every one of the deputation which waited on you the other day drinks moderately — they told you so — but they would be insulted if you told them that they were unfitted for work because of this habit, and I really believe that you run grave danger by insulting or being understood to insult the people of this country of all classes by interfering with their liberty. The agricultural labourer, the honest, self-controlled artisan, the small tradesman, inspired by patriotic motives and doing his duty, may feel that those who are running the War do not trust them, and you may impair the fighting enthusiasm of your country. I hear rumours from all sources, from the Opposition, from the Labour Party, from total abstainers and excessive drinkers, from political 'wire-pullers' that you will be met with opposition. But you will, of course, succeed in overcoming all this and I would only urge in conclusion two important things:

"(1) You must consult Labour so that you may find your difficulties lessened by their acquiescence. You may have to persuade employers to give them something else whilst you are doing this.

"(2) You ought, I think, to consult some financial expert on the finance. You will, of course, not be misled by the desire of the brewers and the distillers to get out of the trade which is continually having to fight hostility on the part of the community.

"But I think the Governor of the Bank would be able to give us information as to the best way of carrying out your project. If you issue £200,000,000 of 4 per cent. stock you must, I fear, create a disastrous effect upon our credit. The Irish Land Stock is an example of the effects of a particular stock in a particular interest. I do not see how you can expect your brewer friends to hold your stock; they will run to the market and unload it, and when it approximates to a price of 50, it will bring down with it the price of all other Government stock, not to the same level, but down, and I would urge that at once you ought to get the Stock Exchange Committee to fix a minimum price for it in order to make it unsaleable, at any rate, for the present.

"You will notice that I make two suggestions at the end, after letting myself go in the earlier part of what I have written. I am now going to assume that I am wrong in all my objections, and that you are going full steam ahead."

This pungent letter will give an idea of the division inside the Government on the drink issue. With regard to Mr. Montagu's suggestion that diminished production was due to fatigue arising from long hours, the figures I give later on as to the average hours actually worked in the yards and factories at that time supply a complete answer.

Having decided for the time being to abandon the attempt to purchase the whole of the liquor trade, I prepared a measure to secure its more effective control — a measure which further enabled the experiment to be made of State purchase and management of the liquor traffic on a small scale in particular areas. With this programme in view I laid before the House of Commons on April 29th a further instalment of D.O.R.A. — the Defence of the Realm (Amendment) (No. 3) Bill — designed to deal with the evil of drink in those munition-making areas where it was proving especially disastrous to the nation, and at the same time I outlined other plans for a nation-wide limitation of the peril.

In commending this Bill to the House I drew attention to the very alarming evidence which had come to hand of the effects of excessive drinking. A selection of this was published a couple of days later as a Government White Paper. This gave statistics of time lost in the shipyards and engineering shops of the Clyde and Tyne, and reports by officers of the Admiralty and the Home Office.

The reports were almost unanimous in making the same assertions as to lost time and energy due to alcohol. Statistics compiled from 15 firms in the Clyde district, for example, showed that of the ironworkers, 27.6 per cent. were working more than 53 hours per week, 39.4 per cent. between 40 and 53 hours, while 33 per cent. were working less than 40 hours per week. It was a minority that slacked, but a minority large and important enough to be disastrous to our national output.

The measure I proposed was to the effect that any area of importance for the production and transport of war materials might be placed under special control as regards the sale and supply of alcohol. The areas were to be defined by Orders in Council, and regulations applied to them which might empower the Government to close down the private liquor industry in the area, and become itself the sole supplier of intoxicants; to acquire, either temporarily or permanently, all licensed premises and businesses; to open, without licence, places of refreshment in which liquor could be sold; and generally to control the licensing and sale of intoxicants within the area. The Bill was duly carried, and a Central Control Board was set up to deal with Liquor Traffic. This Board issued on June 12th a set of regulations by which it took power, in any area placed under its control, to close any licensed premises or clubs, to regulate their hours of opening, to prohibit the sale or supply of any specified class of intoxicant, to impose conditions and restrictions upon licensed premises or take them under its supervision and to regulate the amount of liquor that could be brought into an area or transported within it. It further took power to prohibit in an area all sale of liquor except by the Board of Control, to prohibit "treating," etc.

In July a series of Orders in Council was issued, defining the chief munition areas in the country and placing them under the Board of Liquor Control. During the following months the Board began to make effective use of its powers issuing the "No Treating" Order in October, 1915, and drastically restricting the hours of sale of intoxicants. For the London area the hours of opening were in November narrowed down to what had previously been the "Sunday" hours.

It will be noted that I avoided total prohibition, despite the earnestness with which this policy was urged on me, in all good faith, by many who had not previously been associated with the "blue ribbon" movement. I realised clearly enough, what has since then been demonstrated in the United States, that it is futile to legislate far in advance of popular opinion or the public conscience. Restriction and limitation the nation would accept, and a considerable degree of reform could be achieved under State control, where the element of private profit and exploitation was eliminated. I confined my objective to this practical programme.

Even this reasonable scheme encountered very bitter opposition, and in my further proposals for a general discouragement of drinking I was at first compelled to swallow an almost complete defeat. In my speech on the 29th of April I had said that I intended in my Budget to impose a graded surtax on the heavier beers, to quadruple the tax on wines, to double the taxes on spirits, and to raise the maximum permissible dilution of spirits from 25 per cent. to 36 per cent. under proof. These proposals roused considerable opposition both in and out of the House of Commons. The Irish Party was particularly angry in view of the big brewing and distilling interests in that country. One by one I was compelled to abandon, for the time being, these proposed taxes, and could only retain one insignificant but quite useful little restriction in the shape of a prohibition on the sale of spirits less than three years old, the object being to prohibit the newer and more fiery spirit. Even round this a fierce controversy arose between the rival distilling interests — the "Pot versus Patent" fight — for manufacturers of pot-still whisky made a practice of keeping their product several years to mature, whereas the output of the patent still was marketed straight away.

But although I lost this opening round I succeeded in subsequent years in carrying through the policy of high taxation of alcoholic beverages, dilution of spirits and encouragement of lighter beers. In this campaign I was able to utilise the aid of the Food Controller, under whose care the supplies of grain required for brewing and distilling had been placed. Not only was the total amount brewed and distilled restricted, but the release of such grain as was allowed was made conditional upon a proportion of the beer being of a light character, and the spirits being considerably diluted. The nation sang music-hall ditties bewailing "Lloyd George's Be-e-e-er," but the statistics of insobriety showed a rapid decline. The compulsory dilution of spirits and the elimination of the heavier beers had an especially beneficial effect, for they reduced the quantity of alcohol content of the beverages imbibed by a high percentage. The weekly average of convictions for drunkenness in England and Wales, which in 1913 were 3482, had by the first part of 1917 fallen to 929.

The following are the figures for the total consumption of absolute alcohol in Great Britain during the War years:

| | |
|---|---|
| 1914 | 89 million gallons |
| 1915 | 81 " " |
| 1916 | 73 " " |
| 1917 | 45 " " |
| 1918 | 37 " " |

These figures represent the amount of alcohol estimated to have been consumed in all forms of alcoholic beverages — spirits, wines and beers — and the rapid decline in the last two years is only partly due to the fact that millions of men had left our shores. It is mainly attributable to the effectiveness of the drink restriction policy which was instituted and enforced.

While by means of progressive measures of taxation, dilution and limitation of the intoxicating beverages in the country, we were able to reduce very considerably the effective supplies of them obtained by the people, and especially the quantity of proof spirit and alcohol consumed, we were pressing forward in the industrial areas devoted to munition production the limitation of hours and drinking facilities. But I was by no means satisfied to adopt a purely negative policy. The Liquor Control Board had been given powers to take over the whole business of liquor supply within an area, and in four of the areas it experimentally adopted these powers, the first area so treated being that of Gretna Green — from which was developed the Carlisle experiment in State management of the liquor trade, an experiment which is still with us, and on which I will forbear comment beyond the unchallengeable statement that in the opinion of many highly competent observers it has more than justified the faith of those who authorised the venture, and has demonstrated that State management is capable of giving an orderly and adequate provision of alcoholic refreshment under conditions which promote sobriety and social amenity. The positive policy of the Control Board was shown in another very important direction — that of finding a satisfactory substitute in the scheduled areas for the drinking-dens whose opportunity of catering for the leisure of the workers was being curtailed. This led it to the appointment of a Canteens Committee. In its first report, dated October 12th, 1915, the Control Board stated:

> ". . . The Board incline to the view that excessive drinking may often be traced to the want of adequate facilities for food, refreshment, and recreation, particularly in conjunction with long hours and overtime. The improvement of public-houses and the provision of canteens may therefore do much to render less necessary the imposition of purely restrictive measures. . . ."

The board pointed out that drink was often resorted to when food was inadequate or improper; and that it was important "to supply for large numbers of persons at specified times a suitable dietary . . . at a reasonable cost."

> "In endeavouring to meet this requirement, the Board have proceeded on two collateral lines of action:
>
> "(*a*) The increase of facilities for obtaining suitable meals at public houses, and
>
> "(*b*) The establishment wherever necessary of industrial canteens inside or within easy access of the works, supplying both substantial meals and light refreshment at reasonable prices."

A number of voluntary organisations rendered great help in the promotion of these canteens, such as the Y.M.C.A. and Y.W.C.A., Lady Lawrence's Munition Makers' Canteen Committee, the Salvation Army, and the Church Army. As to the actual provision of canteen premises and equipment, however, there was a question whether the Board or the employers should finance this; and it seemed much more desirable that the employers should undertake this responsibility, as it ensured their interest and gave a better prospect of permanence to the canteens. Accordingly, I secured Treasury sanction for an arrangement whereby the cost of building and equipping canteens might be charged by controlled establishments against their current profits under Part III of the Munitions of War Act, 1915, on condition that such buildings were maintained thereafter permanently as canteens, save by permission of the Ministry of the Government Department which should inherit its duties.

This concession operated from November, 1915, until November, 1918, during which period 867 schemes of canteens at controlled establishments were approved, the total cost of them which was recommended for writing off gross profits being £1,909,135. About a million workpeople were employed in the establishments to which these canteens were attached.

The habit of regular and wholesome meals which these canteens encouraged, combined with the limitation and dilution of alcoholic beverages, helped to establish the post-war tradition of moderation in drinking and an improved standard of healthy living with which we are now familiar.

The progress which was made amply warranted me in stating to a temperance deputation which waited on me in 1917 to urge total prohibition, that by confining our objectives to practical and attainable limits we had been able in the last year or two to achieve a far bigger advance toward national sobriety than had hitherto been effected in a far longer period by all persuasive and legislative efforts in combination.

### 6. Welfare Conditions in the Workshops

Natural growth of the welfare movement — The State as employer of labour — Expansion of female labour — Inspection of conditions of women workers — Health of Munition Workers Committee — Mr. Seebohm Rowntree appointed Director of Welfare — Bad conditions in the factories — A policy of education adopted — Efforts for women workers — Scope of welfare provision — Success of the policy — Welfare achievements — Housing of Munition workers — Evidence of success of work — Further welfare legislation — My speech in February, 1916.

One of the most welcome features of my post as Minister of Munitions was the opportunity it placed within my reach of doing something to better the social and industrial conditions in the manufacturing establishments which came under my direct or indirect control. Legislation reflected the growing desire in industry among both workers and employers for better standards in the workshops. In matters of this kind the law cannot move very far in advance of public opinion save at the risk of becoming a dead letter. Various measures were sanctioned to a greater or less extent by the demands of workers, the successful experiment of enlightened employers, the zeal of practical reformers, and the growth of a progressive public opinion.

They represented, of course, only the minimum demand enforceable by law upon industry. Their incidence was limited and partial, and they did not go very far to ensure the highest attainable measure of amenity, health or comfort for the worker. Some employers were doing good pioneer work in the voluntary creation of improved conditions for their staffs, but they were in those days the exception rather than the rule.

The establishment of the Ministry of Munitions and the new industrial development which it organised gave an impulse to important changes in the general situation.

In the first place, the State as represented by the Ministry became a large-scale direct employer of industrial labour, and on an even larger scale an indirect employer of labour in the establishments engaged in munition work which were brought under its control. It was thus in a position to exercise persuasion, pressure, and, if necessary, compulsion, upon employers throughout the country to adopt higher standards for ensuring the welfare of their workers during the hours of employment.

In the second place, the withdrawal of a large part of the male population from industry into our fighting forces brought about the introduction of female labour on a scale never previously contemplated, and into industrial occupations which had formerly been staffed exclusively by men. There had, of course, before the War been a considerable body of female labour employed in certain types of factory — particularly in textiles — but it now invaded unusual fields of the heavy industries, the shell-filling factories, and even shipbuilding. In most of these establishments rough and unseemly conditions prevailed and had hitherto been put up with by the men workers, but it was recognised as impossible to ask women to submit to them.

A singularly favourable opportunity thus presented itself for introducing into industry a great forward movement for improving the general conditions of the welfare of the workers — an opportunity of which as Minister of Munitions I proceeded forthwith to take full advantage.

One of the first tasks of the Ministry of Munitions was the creation of national filling and explosive factories; and from August, 1915, a woman staff inspector of the Ministry was at work visiting these as fast as they were opened up and keeping in touch with the Boards of Management regarding the very important and varied questions of the welfare of women in this often dangerous work. Her duties included advice and help in the selection of women supervisors, in the training of the special types of labour required, and in the provision of doctors and nurses for its care. In

September, 1915, I appointed a Health of Munition Workers Committee to advise on questions concerning "industrial fatigue, hours of labour, and other matters affecting the personal health and physical efficiency" of the munition worker. It was a strong Committee representing the concentrated experience of the Home Office, of employers, labour, and medical experts. The Chairman was Sir George Newman and the members included Sir Thomas Barlow, Dr. Leonard E. Hill, three leading officers of the Home Office factory department, Sir W. M. Fletcher, Secretary of the Medical Research Committee, Mr. Clynes, Professor Boycott, Mr. Samuel Osborne, and Mrs. H. J. Tennant. It rendered invaluable service throughout the War by recommendations which supplied us with a practical programme for welfare work, and became a forerunner of the Industrial Fatigue Research Committee which has since the War carried out such important investigations into the conditions of industrial efficiency. Throughout the autumn of 1915 the supply departments of the Ministry of Munitions, working in consultation with this Committee, were organising measures to promote the welfare of munition workers in the national factories. In December, 1915, I took the further step of appointing Mr. B. Seebohm Rowntree Director of the Welfare Section of the Ministry, which I invited him to organise. Mr. Rowntree is well known, not only as a great employer of labour, but as one of the foremost and most successful pioneers in the development of improved conditions in his works. I should like to pay tribute here to the skill, energy, sympathy, and address with which he organised this new department. The work he did helped to transform the conditions for munition labour during the War, and has left a permanent mark upon conditions in our industries.

It was a difficult problem which confronted the new Welfare Section. In a large number of the existing factories conditions were very rough and primitive, and there was no tradition of care for the health or comfort of the employee beyond the minimum that was already compulsory under the Factory Acts. The pressure of work had, of course, been greatly intensified by the necessities of the War. Hours were long, and premises often crowded. New factories and extensions of existing factories were being rapidly run up, and these temporary erections were often occupied and buzzing with activity before any thought had been given to the provision of accessories in the shape of lavatories, cloakrooms, mess-rooms, or canteens. And, in addition, they were being increasingly staffed by women and girls, for whose supervision no appropriate arrangements had been made.

The Health of Munition Workers Committee, in a memorandum issued in January, 1916, urged the need for attention to this side of the problem of production:

> "If the present long hours, the lack of healthful and sympathetic oversight, the inability to obtain good wholesome food, and the great difficulties of travelling are allowed to continue, it will be impracticable to secure or maintain for an extended period the high maximum output of which women are undoubtedly capable."

Under the Munitions of War (Amendment) Act of January, 1916, I had taken powers to control not only the wages but the conditions of employment of women workers on munitions, and also of semi-skilled and unskilled men and boys taking the work of skilled men in controlled firms. The Welfare Section of the Ministry, however, while holding these powers in reserve, adopted the deliberate policy of educating rather than compelling the firms engaged on munition work to put in hand arrangements for the welfare of their employees. Mr. Rowntree held that this was the only way of ensuring that the improved conditions so created would continue permanently after the War.

In the first instance the Welfare Section naturally devoted its principal effort to securing proper conditions for the women workers. At the outset they were often worse off than the existing male staffs, for no special accommodation or provision had in most cases been furnished for them, and they had no person of their own sex in authority to whom to appeal. In April, 1916, I ruled that women supervisors should be appointed in all national factories where women or young persons were employed, and that they should be approved by the Welfare Section. Their introduction into these national factories served as a precedent for their introduction into controlled establishments. In the same month a start was made by the Section with the development of welfare supervision for boys.

The welfare arrangements which were initiated included the provision of staffs and proper accommodation. The staffs comprised supervisors and assistant supervisors of welfare, and in the larger works, matrons, nurses, women doctors, cloakroom attendants, etc.

The provision of welfare accommodation included such matters as washing facilities, sanitary conveniences, cloakrooms, canteens, seats in work-rooms, supplies of overalls and caps, and recreation facilities. It was necessary to persuade some employers that one broken basin and a jug of cold water was insufficient washing provision for a staff of 300 workers; that workers engaged in hot, heavy and exhausting work should be able to have convenient access to clean drinking water and not to be reduced to running the risk of typhoid by drinking water intended only for manufacturing purposes; that the efficiency of workers would be increased if they were not required to work all day in clothes drenched in the morning on the way to the factory, and if they could take their meals in comfort in a mess-room, or — better still — get cheap and wholesome food in the canteen, instead of gobbling scrappy meals beside their machines.

The policy of persuasion was, however, justified by its results. The demand for welfare supervisors grew to such an extent that special training courses were arranged by the department — a function later on taken over by the London School of Economics and by most of the provincial universities. Over 1000 supervisors of varying grades were working in munitions factories at the date of the Armistice. Allowing for the fact that their appointment had been made compulsory in T.N.T. factories and practically compulsory in national factories, probably some 700 had been appointed voluntarily by the heads of firms or boards of management.

The welfare policy of the department ensured the standard of physical comfort for nearly 350,000 workers in the national factories and Government establishments, much above the minimum required under the Factory and Workshop Acts, and it stimulated a similar provision of canteens, rest rooms, ambulance rooms, and other material comforts, to a greater or less degree in a large proportion of the other controlled establishments, in which at least 400,000 women munition workers were employed. This increased comfort was extended in some measure at least among a million and a quarter men and nearly a quarter of a million boys similarly employed by controlled firms and in national factories.

The department built, or promoted the building of, 11,738 flats and houses for munition workers. It provided hostels for more than 23,500 workers and secured further accommodation in a large number of other cases, together with lodgings and billets in private houses for munition workers. It provided directly for canteens and mess-rooms in the great majority of the 150 national and Government factories, while the Central Liquor Control Board approved on behalf of the Department the canteens of some 740 controlled establishments.

Its work in promoting intelligent care for the health and comfort of employees, the convenience of their hours, the hygienic conditions of their work, is perhaps less susceptible to statistical statement, but was at least as important in the permanent impression it made on our national industrial conditions.

As early as 1917–18 the "Factory Inspectors' Annual Report" bore witness to the effect of the welfare movement stimulated by the Ministry of Munitions in permeating the standards of non-munition trades, such as:

". . . cotton and woollen and worsted textiles, in laundries, in potteries, in biscuit factories . . . where conditions, with honourable individual exceptions, have long been stationary, but here too . . . the new movement has begun to take effect. . . . In these and many other developments moving towards social welfare in non-munition factories in 1917, there is really less sudden a growth than it is apt to be considered. Enlightened workers have been asking for these things, and enlightened manufacturers have been demonstrating for many years that these improving conditions are both rightly demanded and practicable. Now common sense awakened sees that the pace must be greatly quickened. . . . It is not only in controlled and national factories that material advance has been made. The whole spirit of management has quickly changed in many factories and industries where no new welfare order runs, and where State control of profits has not entered."

Legislative provision for the extension of the welfare movement was in full operation when the work of the department ceased. The principles established by the Ministry through persuasion were being gradually followed up by the Home Office with definite legislation. As early as August,

1916, the Police, Factories, etc., Miscellaneous Provision Acts gave definite powers of enforcing welfare provision. The Trade Boards Act of 1918 authorised trade boards "to make representations" to Government departments with regard to working conditions in their trade, while in the organised industries an increasing number of Joint Industrial Councils were beginning to consider questions of hours, conditions, and training. The prospect of legislative provision for a 48-hour week for all factory workers had appeared on the horizon.

In the light of these and other subsequent developments, there seems to have been a certain note of prophecy in a speech made by me as Minister of Munitions in February, 1916, when I remarked:

"It is a strange irony, but no small compensation, that the making of weapons of destruction should afford the occasion to humanise industry. Yet such is the case. Old prejudices have vanished, new ideas are abroad; employers and workers, the public and the State, are favourable to new methods. This opportunity must not be allowed to slip. It may well be that, when the tumult of war is a distant echo, and the making of munitions a nightmare of the past, the effort now being made to soften asperities, to secure the welfare of the workers, and to build a bridge of sympathy and understanding between employer and employed, will have left behind results of permanent and enduring value to the workers, to the nation and to mankind at large."

## CHAPTER X

# THE STRATEGY OF THE WAR

### EASTERN *versus* WESTERN FRONTS

A "no great hurry" atmosphere — My letter to the Prime Minister 31/12/14 — Collapse of plans of all the combatants — The German plan — Need for new plans — Military failure to grapple with strategical problem — Responsibility of statesmen — Quality of the new recruits — Obvious facts of the situation — Weakness of the Austrian Front — Potentialities in the Balkans — Gun superiority of enemy in the west — General Staffs have no monopoly of judgment — My memorandum on war strategy 1/1/15 — Kitchener's approval of my memorandum — Kitchener's letter to French — Sir John French's view — Opinion of General Gallieni — Misconception of a contemporary historian — Sir William Robertson's dictum.

IN the foregoing pages I have told something of the way in which the Ministry of Munitions was inaugurated, and of the human side of the problems with which it was faced. Before proceeding further to describe its practical achievements in the sphere of munition production, I must turn back to give some account of the battlefields for which these supplies were required, and the strategy they were designed to support.

For if it had involved tedious and incessant effort to break down the barriers of routine and military inertia which hampered the equipment of our forces, the parallel task of ensuring that our resources of man-power and munitions should be used in the most effective manner was still harder, and in fact was never carried out satisfactorily until the closing period of the War. I will now give a brief sketch of this problem, and of the efforts made to secure what I conceived at the time to be a wise solution.

There was during the early months of the War practically no effective War Council in the country keeping the position in constant review by directing and coördinating our efforts. There was a sense of leisureliness, if not of casualness in our exertions.

After the great battles of the Marne and Ypres the War seemed to be settling down to normality. It was becoming accepted as if it were an ordinary part of the daily existence of nations. The people everywhere were adapting themselves to war conditions. The population of Whitehall, high and low, were no exception. That may account for the fact that there was a "no great hurry" atmosphere about our movements. The Germans had failed to capture Paris. It is true their armies were clamped firmly in Belgium and some of the richest departments of France, but they were kept within the limits of these autumnal conquests and could get no farther. The safety of the Channel ports had been assured by the battle of Ypres. There was some fighting in Poland and the Russian steam-roller had been pushed back by the Germans, but it had made up for that by rolling forward in Galicia. The Central Powers had been checked. We could now take our time to enrol and equip. That was the official temper — I am not sure that it did not represent the national attitude towards the end of 1914.

The fact that we were lavishing life and treasure away every day the War was prolonged; that Russia had revealed a dangerous weakness in the matter of equipment of her great armies, and that another campaign might therefore lead to her collapse and leave all the fighting to France and ourselves; that the position of Serbia was precarious and that the Central Powers might any day sweep her out of the way and open the road to the East; that unless we stirred ourselves up immediately we might not be able to put a well-equipped army in the field until the third year of the

War: all these possibilities never seemed to come into the reckoning to disturb the general equanimity.

As far as the people at large were concerned, this composure was attributable to their unshaken confidence in our military chiefs and naval captains. What I had already seen of the official military attitude towards the equipment of our armies and their failure to grasp the new conditions of war as they had developed in France, convinced me that there was no justification for this remarkable complacency.

This induced me to write the following letter to the Prime Minister:

"11, Downing Street, W.
December 31st, 1914.

"My dear Prime Minister,

"I am uneasy about the prospects of the War unless the Government take some decisive measures to grip the situation. I can see no signs anywhere that our military leaders and guides are considering any plans for extricating us from our present unsatisfactory position. Had I not been a witness of their deplorable lack of prevision I should not have thought it possible that men so responsibly placed could have so little forethought. You remember the guns and ammunition incident. When I raised the question in the Cabinet, the War Office had only ordered 600 guns in all. These were to be delivered before next September. The immense manufacturing resources of the country had not been organised for cannon, rifles, or ammunition, and America was not even explored. As a result of the activities and suggestions of the Cabinet Committee, 4000 guns are now promised before that date. Ammunition has also been provided for those guns. Rifles not yet satisfactory . . .

"No real effort has been made until this week to ascertain the Russian position. Now K. has invited a Russian officer to come over to confer with a view of helping Russia with ammunition. Two months ago I pressed it on the War Office. Had it been done then we could have helped Russia, whilst Archangel was still open, and saved her from the peril of exhausted caissons.

"Could we not have a series of meetings of the War Committee of the C.I.D. at an early date? Occasional meetings at intervals of a week or a fortnight will end in nothing.

"Forgive me for intruding on your well-earned rest, but I feel that a continuation of the present deadlock is full of danger.

Sincerely yours,
D. LLOYD GEORGE."

This letter led to the calling of a War Committee at an early date to review the position. In order to form an opinion on the discussions and decisions of this Committee it is necessary to recall the military position at that date.

When the campaign of 1914 on all fronts came to an end owing to weather conditions, the Supreme Command, political, military and naval in the belligerent countries, had time to review the position and to decide upon their future course of action. Every army found its first plans baffled and broken by the fighting that had taken place. Not one of the elaborate schemes so carefully prepared and perfected for years by experts and lying in their bureaus ready to put into resistless operation on "the day" — for they all had their eagerly expected "day" — survived the actual clash of battle. Something went wrong with them all.

There was the long-prepared and pigeon-holed German plan for crushing France in a few weeks by an outflanking march of overwhelming forces through Belgium, followed by an immediate turning to the East with the victorious troops to roll up the armies of Russia. It had been worked out to the last detail. Nothing had been overlooked except the extent and effect of Britain's military intervention, and also perhaps the equally important fact that the execution of the plan would be in the hands of different men from those who originated it. That scheme had now failed utterly and its fragments were scattered along the banks of the Marne and the Yser. The pigeon hole at Berlin was empty. The thwarting of the invincible plan had not been anticipated. A new plan must therefore be worked out.

The French plan of attacking with the first and second armies south of Metz, and with the fourth and fifth north of it, never had a chance of success. It was based on an assumption that never materialised. The British idea of holding the Germans on the Belgian Front whilst the French dealt with them lower down was based on the same complete miscalculation of the German strategy as that which misled the French generals. This was merely conforming to the French strategy. Had Sir John French's idea of the occupation of Antwerp been adopted there would have been a different situation to deal with.

The Austrian dream of an easy march from Belgrade to Nish had a rude awakening, for the Serbian peasants inflicted two disastrous defeats on their jaunty invaders. The Russians had some successes against Austria. Against Germany, if they ever had a plan, it never came off. The invasion of East Prussia was little more than a chivalrous improvisation to save France from the blunders of her generals. It came to a bad end at Tannenberg.

The great struggles of 1914, therefore, had shattered every military dream and wrecked every military hope on both sides. The military leaders were bereft of any clear idea how ultimate victory could be attained. Every army had its failures. Every army had its successes. At the end of the 1914 campaign they all rejoiced in the victories and forgot the defeats. That was the general state of mind in and behind all lines. But no one had any clear notion what to attempt next. New plans must therefore be thought of for the 1915 campaign.

I was bold enough to form an opinion as to the general situation and rash enough to express it. As I have been severely criticised in certain professional quarters for my impertinent activities in this direction, I feel bound to state the considerations that led me to challenge the policy or lack of policy which in the event was responsible for prolonging the War, added enormously to its sacrifices in human life, increased its burdens and brought the cause of the Allies to the very brink of irretrievable disaster.

Why should a civilian who had made no study of the science of war have concerned himself at all with strategical questions? Why not leave that phase of the war problem to men who had devoted their lives to such a study? My answer to those who charge me with meddling in a business of which I knew nothing except what I had learned by a reading of past wars, and conversations with soldiers whom I had met here and in France, is that as events developed it became increasingly evident to the rawest amateur mind that the military were fumbling badly with their job. The Allied strategy in France had been a sanguinary mistake which nearly brought us to irretrievable defeat. When it failed the High Commands had no rational alternative to propose. The Allied generals were completely baffled by the decision of the Germans to dig in. They could think of nothing better than the sacrifice of millions of men in a hopeless effort to break through. Even then they had not worked out what mechanical aid was necessary to carry out such an operation, nor had they given any real systematic thought to the methods of providing their armies with the requisite machinery for putting into effect their hazy and crazy plans.

How crazy were their ideas at this stage can be ascertained by reading the painful story of a succession of foolish offensives which for years were to mow down the flower of British and French youth by the million in vain efforts to rush machine-guns, skilfully concealed and effectively protected.

The primary responsibility for success or failure rested with Governments, and they could not shuffle off any part of that responsibility by pleading that they had placed their trust in experts who were obviously unequal to their task.

By the end of the year over a million young men had volunteered and had been duly enrolled either in the Kitchener armies or in the Territorials, and thousands were still streaming in. Amongst them were the pick of the youth of the country in physique, brain and character. In every sphere of life all that was best amongst the young men of the land joined the Army. It cannot be said as yet that they had donned the King's uniform, for in the best-equipped of all countries for the manufacture of men's apparel, the War Office had not yet succeeded in procuring the necessary supply of uniforms for all their recruits. But it was already evident that the human material which was everywhere being trained into soldiers was of a higher quality than anything to which drill sergeants had hitherto been accustomed. The Universities were drained of all the physically fit — so were all the professions. Artisans, miners, labourers — all contributed of their choicest.

In some quarters the prejudice against leaving home to join the Army still lingered. Recruiting agencies had still in some areas a difficulty in overcoming the tradition about the youth who for some unsatisfactory reason "ran away to become a soldier." And it took some time and much appeal to break it down. I had taken my part in these recruiting appeals especially amongst Nonconformists, who had always been inclined to hold aloof from the Army, and also amongst my Welsh fellow-countrymen of all creeds. For these reasons, apart altogether from my responsibility as a Member of the Cabinet that declared war, I felt a special obligation to see that the men who volunteered to face death for their country's honour, should be equipped with the best their country could provide them in order to fight its battles, and that the most effective use should be made of their valour in the battlefield. The events of the last few months had shaken any confidence I ever had in the wisdom of military leadership and I was full of apprehension lest the flower of Britain's youth should be mown down through professional rigidity, narrowness and lack of vision.

I had no pretence to any knowledge of strategy, but there were certain obvious facts which were apparent even to the uninitiated in the mysteries of war.

The first was that if the resources of the belligerents on both sides were assessed — in men, material and money — the Allied Powers possessed an overwhelming advantage over their foes provided their resources were effectively utilised and wisely directed.

This Allied superiority was, however, completely neutralised by the fact that two out of the three Great Powers (Britain and Russia) that constituted the Alliance against Germany and Austria were inferior in equipment to their foes. As far as heavy artillery went France was also inferior. Equipment was therefore the most urgent problem for the Allies. Unless they exerted themselves to the utmost to make up their deficiencies in this respect, victory was unattainable. Two out of the three (Britain and France) had great manufacturing capacity, and America with its infinite resources was also at their call for that purpose. The third, Russia, was very deficient in manufacturing capacity and had no credit for purchase abroad, but had an inexhaustible reserve of the best human material. As to equipment, therefore, the problem was first to utilise all our available resources at home and across the seas to increase the numbers and power of our machinery of war and to do so without loss of time, and secondly to pool the output fairly and distribute it where it could be most effectively used for the Allied cause.

The second and outstanding fact was that the Germans had largely neutralised the Allied superiority in man-power on the Western Front not only by better equipment but by constructing the most extensive and formidable line of entrenchments ever known in the history of war.

There was no way of outflanking the German lines in France and Flanders, and any attempt to force them by frontal attacks would involve losses so colossal that no sane man would contemplate such a sacrifice of human life as a possibility, if there were any other means available of breaking through on a more vulnerable front. At any rate the Allies had not the necessary gun-power to make any effort to break through on the West a feasible operation, and it would take years to equip them with an artillery numerous and heavy enough for such an attempt.

The third was that, whilst the Central Powers had an entire front of 600 miles on the West which presented no great physical difficulties for them in the way of entrenchment in length or in the character of the soil, on the Eastern and Southeastern Fronts they had a line of thousands of miles to defend, much of it swamp which was too soft in summer and too hard in winter for any entrenching tools to handle. Moreover, their man-power would not suffice to garrison effectively so extensive a fortress.

The fourth was that on that front, Germans and Austrians were confronted with a foe who could turn out millions of brave men traditionally fearless and skilful in war, who only needed efficient equipment to make their numbers and their valour irresistible.

On the southeastern and southern sections of that front the Central Powers had to defend their positions with an army drawn from a population, three-fifths of which belonged to races hostile to the governing races in the two Empires and entirely sympathetic to the Allied population on their frontiers. The Slavs, Roumanians, and Italians who constituted the majority of the people ruled by Franz Joseph had been straining for freedom from the dominion of a privileged racial caste, and their prospect of gaining it would be accelerated by the defeat of the German régime, whilst it might be indefinitely postponed by a Teutonic victory.

Out of a total population of over 50 millions in Austria-Hungary, only 12 millions were Germans and 10 millions Magyars. Almost 30 millions belonged to populations which were kith and kin to the nations with which Austria was either at war, or was about to wage war. Even the Magyars were not too eager to follow the rash lead of Vienna. It was known that Count Tisza, the ablest and calmest of all the Hungarian statesmen, was rootedly opposed to the mad plunge into war with the Serbian Slavs. What made Austria specially vulnerable was that the provinces contiguous to her actual or contingent foes were populated by the races who by blood were closely related to the enemies of the Empire. This proved to be a source of weakness to the Austrian armies during the whole course of the War, and a danger against which they found it impossible to guard. Whenever the Russians gained an appreciable advantage in their attacks, Slavonic regiments surrendered with ease and even with ill-concealed satisfaction, to the onslaught of ill-equipped Russian armies. One Czech regiment marched through into predestined captivity in Russia with the band playing.

It was also quite obvious to anyone who surveyed the possibilities of the Balkans with some knowledge of the disposition and quality of its peoples, that if the Allied Powers had taken strong and timely action they could have organised out of the warlike races that inhabit this turbulent peninsula from the Danube down to the Chersonese and thence southward to the Peloponnesus, a formidable confederation with an army of trained men already tempered in the fires of war. The Serbians had at that time an available force of 300,000 men. The Roumanians could put at least half a million men in the field. The number of fighting men available in Roumania was placed by the War Office at 900,000. The Greeks had 400,000 trained men. The Bulgarians owed a deep debt of gratitude to Russia for the part she had played in their liberation, and their memories of Gladstone's fiery crusade on their behalf against Turkish oppression turned their hearts towards Britain. If attached to the Allied side they could have placed another 400,000 men at the disposal of the Alliance. All the contingents were of the doughtiest fighting material with recent war experience. The organisation of such a confederacy would have involved loans which in the aggregate would not have amounted to one week's cost of the War to the British and the French taxpayer. There would also have been some difficulty in the way of a preliminary arrangement of the spoils. But this was by no means an insuperable obstacle to agreement. There was plenty of honest loot awaiting the plunderers without transgressing any principle of racial liberty or self-determination. The Slavonic provinces of Southern Austria would have satisfied Serbia. Roumania would have been only too pleased at the prospect of annexing Transylvania with its three millions of men of Roumanian blood. The Bulgarians could have been brought in by the prospect of the re-annexation of Adrianople and a port on the Ægean; and the Greeks had an eye on the littoral of Asia Minor, where their own people had built up prosperous towns and brought the valleys into fruitful cultivation. It would have been necessary to take in hand immediately the equipment of the various armies that composed the confederation. That would have been a gradual process. At first an addition of light artillery and ammunition, with a few machine guns, would have sufficed in these mountain fastnesses. The presence of 100,000 British troops, or a composite army of British and French, equal to half the forces subsequently sent to the Dardanelles or one-third of the numbers sacrificed in the spring and summer of 1915 in vain attacks on infrangible German redoubts in France and Flanders, would have given that moral strength to the Balkan Armies imparted by the physical presence of the banners and soldiers of the great Western Powers. Such a contingent would have had an incalculable effect in welding, inspiring, sustaining and restraining all the other elements in this formidable combination.

The Central Powers were much better equipped in the matter of heavy artillery than were the Allies. A break through in France demanded superiority in guns of the heaviest calibre and an overwhelming supply of ammunition. The Allies could not hope to achieve supremacy in this respect for two years. The question of inferior equipment in the heavier calibres did not present so formidable a difficulty in a great operation on the Eastern and Southeastern Fronts as it did in the west. The Eastern Front not being so well fortified, the Allies could then, with lighter guns and less ammunition, make more effective use of their superiority in numbers. The Russians repeatedly demonstrated this fact in their attacks on the Austrians. They only failed to exploit their victories because of the shortage of gun ammunition for their field artillery and of the lack of rifles. These deficiencies could have been supplied by their western allies, had they consented to forego their unpractical and costly offensives.

Apart from the heterogeneity of the Austrian Armies their organisation, training, munitionment and direction were not comparable to that of their great military neighbour. For these reasons Austria was often a source of weakness, and constantly a source of anxiety, to the German Supreme Headquarters, and more than once they had to detach troops which they could ill dispense from their own special tasks and their own frontiers, in order either to save Austria from collapse or to clear some impending menace from her frontiers. This weakness, which was so painfully apparent to the German Staff, was completely overlooked by both the French and British military direction. The French and British commands were therefore implored by statesmen and soldiers of position and experience in both countries not to commit their armies to repeated and wasteful attacks delivered against an impregnable front defended by an invincible armament, whilst completely neglecting a vulnerable front which could have been penetrated with a third of the troops wasted so prodigally in the ghastly carnage of the western battlefield.

Before coming to these conclusions I had made a careful study of the main facts of the military position with such information as was available to me. I never missed an opportunity of seeking the opinions of such military experts as were accessible to a civilian minister on every aspect of the situation.

It is a mistake to assume that a competent opinion can only be formed by general officers who have taken no part in the actual fighting, and who have never had any personal acquaintance with the physical conditions under which modern warfare is conducted. Men who have passed months of vigilance, anxiety and horror in the fighting line have also their contribution to make to the facts upon which strategy must be based. It is a curious reflection on the methods of promotion in the British Army during the Great War that scarcely one of these men ever reached the topmost ranks — except amongst the Dominion troops. I saw many of these fighting officers right through the War and learned much from them.

As to equipment, I have already given an idea of the efforts I made up to the end of 1914 to quicken manufacture at home and in America. I had also drawn attention to the pressing need for helping Russia. As to the general strategy of the War, at the end of December, 1914, I wrote the following memorandum, which I circulated to the War Council.

2, Whitehall Gardens, S.W.
January 1, 1915.

Suggestions as to the Military Position

Now that the new armies are in course of training and will, with the Territorials, be ready by the end of March to the extent of at least half a million men, I suggest that it is time the Government should take counsel with the military experts as to the use which shall be made of this magnificent force. It is a force of a totally different character from any which has hitherto left these shores. It has been drawn almost exclusively from the better class of artisan, the upper and the lower middle classes. In intelligence, education and character it is vastly superior to any army ever raised in this country, and as it has been drawn not from the ranks of those who have generally cut themselves off from home ties and about whose fate there is therefore not the same anxiety at home, the people of this country will take an intimate personal interest in its fate of a kind which they have never displayed before in our military expeditions. So that if this superb army is thrown away upon futile enterprises such as those we have witnessed during the last few weeks, the country will be uncontrollably indignant at the lack of prevision and intelligence shown in our plans. I may add that operations such as those we have witnessed during the past few months will inevitably destroy the *morale* of the best of troops. Good soldiers will face any dangers and endure any hardships which promise ultimate progress, but this intermittent flinging themselves against impregnable positions breaks the stoutest hearts in the end.

There are therefore three or four considerations I wish to urge on the military situation.

### 1. Stalemate on the Western Front

I cannot pretend to have any military knowledge, but the little I saw and gathered in France as to the military position, coupled with such reading on the subjects as I have been able to indulge in, convinced me that any attempt to force the carefully prepared German lines in the west would end in failure and in appalling loss of life, and I then expressed this view to my colleagues. General Foch told me that there would be no more retreats on the French side, and I could well appreciate his confidence after I had driven past trench behind trench from Paris all the way to the Aisne. The French generals are confident that even if the whole of the German Army now occupied in Poland were thrown on the Western Front, the French and British troops would still be able to hold their own. The same observation, of course, must apply to the German military position. We were told the other day that the Germans had, during the last few months, prepared a series of trenches of the same kind on their side right up to the Rhine. After three or four months of the most tenacious fighting, involving very heavy losses, the French have not at any one point on the line gained a couple of miles. Would the throwing of an additional half-million men on this front make any real difference? To force the line you would require at least three to one; our reinforcements would not guarantee two to one, or anything approaching such a predominance. Is it not therefore better that we should recognise the impossibility of this particular tack, and try and think out some way by which the distinct numerical advantage which the Allies will have attained a few months hence can be rendered effective?

### 2. Extension, and Consequent Attenuation, of Enemy's Front

Another consideration which ought to weigh with us is the importance of attenuating the enemy's line by forcing him largely to extend it. The Germans now defend a front of 600 miles. No wastage in sight will so reduce their forces to such numbers as would make any part of this line untenable. The French returns of wounded prove that 79 per cent. of the wounded return to the line: 54 per cent. of the French wounded have already returned; 25 per cent. are convalescent and will soon be back. It is a fundamental mistake always committed by the press to exaggerate the enemy's losses; the slight and curable character of most wounds is always overlooked. But if the length of the German line is doubled, even at the present rate of attrition, it might become at an early date so thin as to be easily penetrable.

### 3. Forcing the Enemy to Fight on Unfavourable Ground

The enemy is now fighting in country which is admirably adapted to his present entrenching tactics. He would be at a disadvantage if he were forced to fight in the open.

### 4. Necessity of Winning a Definite Victory Somewhere

There is another consideration which is political as well as military, but which nevertheless cannot be overlooked in an exhausting war like this, where we have to secure continuous exertion and sacrifice on the part of our people, and where we have also to think of hesitating neutrals with large armies who are still in doubt as to their action. There is a real danger that the people of Great Britain and of France will sooner or later get tired of long casualty lists explained by monotonous and rather banal telegrams from headquarters about "heavy cannonades," "making a little progress" at certain points, "recovering trenches," the loss of which has never been reported, etc., with the net result that we have not advanced a yard after weeks of heavy fighting. Britishers have ceased to be taken in by reports which exaggerate slight successes and suppress reverses; neutral states have never been deceived by these reports. The public will soon realise that the Germans are now in effective occupation of a larger proportion of Allied territory than they were in possession of at the date of the Battle of the Aisne. This is true of Belgium, of France, and of Poland. These occupied territories contain some of the richest coalfields and industrial centres in Europe, and the most sanguinary attacks have not succeeded in moving the Germans (on an average) a single yard out of these territories. A clear, definite victory which has visibly materialised in guns and prisoners captured, in unmistakable retreats of the enemy's armies, and in large sections of the enemy territory occupied, will alone satisfy the public that tangible results are being achieved by the great sacrifices they are making, and decide neutrals that it is at last safe for them to throw in their lot with us.

### 5. An Alternative Suggestion

Inasmuch as these objects cannot be accomplished by attacks on the Western Front, some alternative ought to be sought. I venture to make one or two suggestions. I have heard of a proposal that there should be an attack in the direction of Denmark upon the north coast of Germany. This proposal is associated with the name of Lord Fisher. For the moment I cannot venture to express any opinion upon it, as I should like to know more about the military and naval possibilities of such an enterprise. It strikes me as being very hazardous, and by no means certain to fulfil the purpose which its originators have in view. Schleswig-Holstein, with its narrow neck, could be easily defended by a comparatively small German force, strongly entrenched against a hostile army seeking to advance into Prussian territory, and there is no room for flanging operations. But at the present moment I would rather not criticise this plan. My purpose is rather to put forward another alternative, and I think more promising scheme for consideration by the Prime Minister and his advisers. It would involve *two independent operations* which would have the common purpose of bringing Germany down by the process of knocking the props under her, and the further purpose of so compelling her to attenuate her line of defence as to make it more easily penetrable. I will explain these two propositions in a little more detail.

### 6. The First Operation

I suggest that our new forces should be employed in an attack upon Austria, in conjunction with the Serbians, the Roumanians and the Greeks. The assistance of the two latter countries would be assured if they knew that a great English force would be there to support them. Roumania could put 300,000 men in the field, whilst retaining a sufficient force to keep the Bulgarians in check. As this move might decide the Bulgarians to remain honestly neutral, the Roumanians could spare another 200,000. The Greeks and Montenegrins have an army of 200,000 available. How many men could we spare? By the beginning of April we shall have in this country 700,000 men who will have undergone a six months' training. Of these, 400,000 would be Territorials, 200,000 of whom will have been in camp continuously for eight months. We shall have in France a force of 300,000 men, provided we do not waste it on barbed wire. The French can easily defend their lines against the troops which Germany can spare from defending Silesia after the Austrian armies have been withdrawn to defend their southern frontier. We should require 200,000 experienced troops to stiffen the new armies. We should thus have a force of 1,000,000 available. Four hundred thousand men might be left here as a reserve to throw into France in case of need if the French were hard pressed before the southern diversion against Austria had developed. Some of them might be sent to Boulogne so as to be at hand in case of emergency. Subsequently this force could be used to reinforce the new Expeditionary Force from time to time. This would leave 600,000 available for the Austrian expedition. Gradually this force could be increased as the new armies were equipped.

This would mean an army of between 1,400,000 and 1,600,000 men to attack Austria on her most vulnerable frontier. Here the population is almost entirely friendly, consisting as it does of Slavonic races who hate both the Germans and the Magyars. We could send our troops up either through Salonika or, I believe, by landing them on the Dalmatian coast. We could seize islands there which might make an admirable base for supplies not far removed from the railway through Bosnia into Austria. This operation would force the Austrians to detach a considerable army from the defence of Cracow, and thus leave Silesia undefended. The Austrians could not withdraw the whole of their army to face this new attack, because in that case the Russians could pour through the Carpathians and capture either Vienna or Budapest. The front which would be developed would be much too lengthy for the Austrian forces to entrench and hold. The Germans would be compelled either to send large forces to support their Austrian allies or to abandon them. In the first case the Germans would have to hold an enormous length of extended front, in the aggregate 1200 miles, and the Allies would, for the first time, enjoy the full advantage of the superior numbers which by that time they can put into the field.[1] On the other hand, if the Germans decline to quit their own frontiers, and leave the Austrians to their fate, that empire would be rapidly disposed of as a military entity, and about 2,500,000 men (including Russians), engaged in the task of attacking it would be free to assail the Germans.

### 7. Two Incidental Advantages of this Course

1. Something which could be called a victory would be thus within our reach, and the public would be satisfied to support with all their resources the conduct of the War for a much longer period without grumbling or stint.

2. Italy would not only be encouraged by this formidable demonstration, she would be forced to come in in her own interest, because the operations would be conducted largely along the coast which she is looking forward to annexing to her kingdom, as the population is predominantly Italian. She must view

[1] The Germans would also render themselves liable to a dangerous attack in the rear from the immense forces which by that date Russia will have placed in the field.

with very great jealousy any occupation of this territory by Serbian troops, and Italian public opinion would not countenance any proposal on the part of the Italian Ministry to come to the aid of Austria if we made it clear that the whole of this littoral would become Italian territory if Italy helped to conquer it.

### 8. The Second Operation

This involves an attack upon Turkey. There are four conditions which an attack on Turkey ought, in my judgment, to fulfil:

1. That it should not involve the absorption of such a large force as to weaken our offensive in the main field of operations;
2. That we should operate at a distance which would not be far from the sea, so as not to waste too many of our troops in maintaining long lines of communication and so as also to have the support of the Fleet in any eventualities;
3. That it should have the effect of forcing Turkey to fight at a long distance from her base of supplies and in country which would be disadvantageous to her;
4. That it should give us the chance of winning a dramatic victory, which would encourage our people at home, whilst it would be a corresponding discouragement to our enemies.

Perhaps I ought to add a fifth: it would be a great advantage from this point of view if it were in territory which appeals to the imagination of the people as a whole.

What operations would meet these conditions? It is supposed that the Turks are gathering together a great army for the invasion of Egypt. The sections show that they have collected something like 80,000 troops in Syria, and that they are slowly moving them along towards the Egyptian frontier. I would let them entangle themselves in this venture, and whilst they were engaged in attacking our forces on the Suez Canal, I would suggest that a force of 100,000 should be landed in Syria to cut them off. They could not maintain themselves in that country very long once their railway communications were cut. They would therefore be forced either to fight or to surrender. The distance from Constantinople to Syria would not permit them to bring up reinforcements in time to produce any impression upon the situation. A force of 80,000 Turks would be wiped out and the whole of Syria would fall into our hands. The pressure upon Russia in the Caucasus would be relieved; the Turkish Army in Europe could not effectively attack our lines of communication as they would be bound to take steps to redeem the situation in Syria, and, if possible, recover the country.

Unless we are prepared for some project of this character I frankly despair of our achieving any success in this war. I can see nothing but an eternal stalemate on any other lines. The process of economic exhaustion alone will not bring us a triumphant peace as long as Germany is in possession of these rich allied territories. No country has ever given in under such pressure, apart from defeat in the field. Burke was always indulging in prophecies of victory as a result of France's exhaustion. The war with France went on for twenty years after he indulged in his futile predictions. Germany and Austria between them have 3,000,000 young men quite as well trained as the men of the Kitchener Armies, ready to take the place of the men now in the trenches when these fall. At that rate the process of exhaustion will take at least ten years. In soil, in minerals, in scientific equipment, Germany is a country of enormous resources. In the number of men who have a scientific training it is infinitely the richest country in the world. That must not be left out of account when we talk about the process of exhaustion. No doubt they will suffer a good deal from lack of copper. We must not depend too much on this. German industries dependent on copper will suffer, but one way or another copper will be found for ammunition. Copper in small quantities will get in through neutral countries; neutrals cannot resist the prices offered by Germany for their copper supplies. Moreover, they have some copper mines in Germany. Some of them were working at a profit at the date of the War. There must be many more lower grade copper mines which would not have paid under ordinary conditions, just like the copper mines of North Wales, but which would become immediately profitable when the price of copper is doubled or trebled. Moreover, they have inexhaustible supplies of coal and iron, and as long as they have the Hungarian plains they can frugally feed themselves. There is an enthusiasm and a spirit, according to every testimony, which cannot be worn down by a two or three years' siege of German armies entrenched in enemy territory. The German spirit will not be broken by the bombardment of Dixmude or Roulers.

We cannot allow things to drift. We ought to look well ahead and discuss every possible project for bringing the War to a successful conclusion. Supply and ammunition difficulties, severe economic pressure, financial embarrassments, even privation and distress — nations will face them cheerfully as long as their armies in the field are in unbeaten possession of their enemies' land. But once defeat which is unmistakable comes their way, moderate economic troubles make a deep impression on their judgment. Such defeats are not to be compassed along our present lines of attack, and we ought to seek others.

If a decision were come to in favour of some such plan of campaign as I have outlined, it will take weeks to make the necessary preparations for it. I cannot recollect that in our discussions at the C.I.D. such an operation was ever contemplated. The ground therefore has not been surveyed. It would take some time to collect the necessary intelligence as to the country, so as to decide where to land the Army and what shall be the line of attack. Transport would have to be carefully and secretly gathered. Large forces might have to be accumulated in the Mediterranean, ostensibly for Egypt. It might be desirable to send an advance force through Salonika, to assist Serbia. Military arrangements would have to be made with Roumania, Serbia, Greece and, perhaps, Italy. All this must take time. Expeditions decided upon and organised with insufficient care and preparation generally end disastrously. And as similar considerations will probably apply to any alternative campaign, I urge the importance of our taking counsel and pressing to a decision without delay.

D. Ll. G.

When I wrote this memorandum I had five months' experience of what war under modern conditions meant. After four and a half years of the closest acquaintance with its problems I stand by the main thesis of this document.

Both the rival armies had attempted to break through the defences of their opponents in the west and had failed after the most sanguinary battles. The Germans recognised the impracticability of attempting to force the western barrier and decided to go for the east. By strengthening their entrenchments in the west they reckoned on being able to hold the Allied forces with two men to the combined French and British three. When in 1916 they changed their strategy and attacked the strongly fortified French positions at Verdun, their effort failed and they wasted irrecoverable time and opportunity. On the Allied side there was considerable division of opinion on the issue of the "way round" by the eastern flank.

The controversy that arose on this subject has been represented as a struggle between the amateur and the professional soldier — between the ignorant politician and the trained warrior. This is a wanton and rather silly misrepresentation of the origin of that conflict of ideas which divided those who were responsible for war direction in the Allied countries from 1915 up to the end. There were highly placed politicians on both sides of the controversy. But there were also military men of outstanding ability who took different sides. I had a conversation with Lord Kitchener on my memorandum. His attitude towards it was certainly not that of the professional who resents the intrusion of amateurs. Quite the contrary. He expressed a considerable measure of agreement with my general theme. He was emphatic about the impossibility of penetrating the German lines on the Western Front, and driving the German Armies out of France and Flanders, without incurring sacrifices which he rightly considered prohibitive if another way could be found of defeating the Central Powers involving the payment of a smaller toll in human life.

The day after I circulated my memorandum, Lord Kitchener, in one of his periodic flashes of insight, wrote this remarkable letter to Sir John French to the headquarters in France: [1]

"January 2nd, 1915.

"There does not appear to be much sign of the contemplated push through on the part of the French Army. Probably they find themselves up against the same problem all along the line as you do in your part, *viz.*, trenches that render attack only a waste of men for a few yards gained of quite worthless ground. The feeling is gaining ground that, although it is essential to defend the lines we hold, troops over and above what are necessary for that service could be better employed elsewhere.

"I suppose we must now recognise that the French Army cannot make a sufficient break through the German lines of defence to cause a complete change of the situation and bring about the retreat of the German forces from Northern Belgium. If that is so, then the German lines in France may be looked upon as a fortress that cannot be carried by assault, and also cannot be completely invested — with the result that the lines can only be held by an investing force, while operations proceed elsewhere.

"The question of *where* anything effective can be accomplished opens a large field, and requires a good deal of study. What are the views of your staff? Russia is hard pressed in the Caucasus, and can only just hold her own in Poland. Fresh forces are necessary to change the deadlock; Italy and Roumania seem the most likely providers; therefore some action that would help to bring these out seems attractive, though full of difficulties."

[1] Sir George Arthur's "Life of Lord Kitchener," Vol. II, p. 35.

At that moment Kitchener was definitely opposed to the Western Front superstition and had turned his mind to the "way round."

In coming to this conclusion I do not suggest that Lord Kitchener had been influenced by the arguments submitted to him in my memorandum the day before he wrote this letter, but in giving expression to views he had no doubt already formed as to the unwisdom of wasting his new armies on impossible frontal attacks in France, and as to the desirability of forcing the issue on some other front, he was sustained by the fact that he discovered he had political support inside the Cabinet for his ideas. At the same time Mr. Winston Churchill's mind was moving in the same direction. Lord Kitchener, Mr. Churchill and I arrived at similar conclusions independently of each other.

A few days later Sir John French, when brought over from France to attend a Committee that was examining the strategical position, expressed his opinion that "complete success against the Germans in the western theatre of war, though possible, was not probable. If we found it impossible to break through, he agreed that it would be desirable to seek new spheres of activity in Austria, for example."

It is a rather significant coincidence that a proposal almost identical with mine was submitted on January 1st, 1915, by General Gallieni to M. Briand and to the French Premier, M. Viviani. Gallieni was a man of tried genius, and was recognised as being one of the most resourceful of the Allied generals. M. Poincaré in his "Memoirs" refers sympathetically to the Gallieni plan and he goes on to say that General Franchet d'Esperey, one of the soundest and most successful of the French generals, had already suggested it to him when he saw him at his Army Headquarters at the French Front. General Gallieni's views on the subject are recorded by his secretaries in their highly interesting book "Gallieni Parle. . . ."

"The participation of France in the War in the East, the intervention of one of our armies in the Balkan theatre, is perhaps the question which interested him most deeply from the time he became Minister! He saw in it consequences such as no one then anticipated.

"From 1914 on a French Expedition to the Balkans could and should be for us the happy solution; in fact the only one which would permit a prompt ending of the War in victory. *One cannot break through on the Western Front,* he complained. The German offensive on the Yser, made under excellent conditions and which nevertheless failed, proves that to us. Therefore we must find another way. Towards the East! Take Constantinople. How? We need a harbour, quays, in order to disembark troops, and a railway, in order to transport them. Therefore Salonika. Therefore through Salonika march on Constantinople. From there go up the Danube with the Balkans people who will have joined us. *And would have solved the important question of corn:* The Roumanians, even the Russians whose ports we would have opened up, would not be obliged to sell at a miserable price to Germany and so supply her.

"Such was my plan. I had been to see Briand. He, Briand, went to consult Joffre, who said: 'That is a personal ambition of Gallieni who wants to get a command. I won't give a man. Why search elsewhere and far off for what I shall get here in March (1915)? I feel sure I shall break through and drive the Germans back home.'

"We had spoken about this plan with the English who agreed. The matter had been studied very closely here and with the Allies. It was in view of Joffre's opposition that the English decided — an idea from their Navy — to take Constantinople from the sea; to force the Dardanelles. And the French followed them."

I have been informed on unimpeachable authority that General Castelnau was also of the same opinion.

A contemporary historian, who had obviously drawn his inspiration from the War Office, rather contemptuously refers to the Salonika idea as "Mr. Lloyd George's fancy." The fact that some of the ablest statesmen and soldiers in France had conceived the same "fancy" reconciles me to this flippant and ill-informed comment.

I have quoted sufficient military authority of unchallenged distinction to make it clear that my idea of an attack on the Central Powers through the Balkans was not the wild phantasy of an inexpert civilian mind, wandering recklessly into regions which he was not qualified to explore.

When these great soldiers expressed a doubt as to the feasibility of battering a way through the barriers erected by the Germans in the west, they did not mean it could never be done at any time and at any cost. They meant that it could not be achieved without an expenditure of time, treasure and life which no normal person would be prepared to contemplate. The "Westerners" never visualised a massacre of millions of the best young men of France and Britain. At first they deluded themselves with the assurance of speedy victory. Later on, the Western Front became the shrine of Moloch, demanding and justifying such sacrifice as even its most infatuated priest would not have dreamt of offering had he known in 1915 what this worship meant.

The policy of western holocausts was only tolerated by British, French and Italian public opinion owing to an elaborate system of concealing repulses and suppressing casualties.

We did not "break through" until the autumn of 1918, although we made several attempts in 1915, 1916 and 1917, all ending in terrible slaughter. In every case the losses we actually sustained were appreciably greater than those we inflicted, although officially they were less. Until the Germans had been weakened by poor and scanty food, and were confronted with the overwhelming Allied reinforcements pouring in from America, our offensives on the Western Front invariably failed to accomplish the object we sought to attain. Even then we had not succeeded in driving them out of France and Belgium at the date of the Armistice, and they only gave up their resistance when the Turks and Bulgarians had been broken in the southeast and Austria had consequently decided to relinquish the fight. The French and ourselves lost over 5,000,000 men in killed and wounded in attack after attack upon the scientific frontiers erected by the Germans in the west. Sir William Robertson, in one of the several memoranda he submitted to the Cabinet for its enlightenment on the true principles of sound strategy, once stated that "Every fool knows that you cannot be too strong at the decisive point." This is an observation none the less sensible because it is a platitude. But every wise man also knows that the decisive point is the one at which you have the best chance of beating your enemy with the least risk and at the lowest cost, and that only "every fool" would deliberately choose to fight him at the point which presents the greatest difficulty in overcoming him and offers him the best opportunity for beating off your attacks and inflicting the heaviest losses on your troops. "Every fool" would also know that the attack at the decisive point must be made at the decisive moment. In 1915 the moment had certainly not arrived which made the Western Front the decisive point. The poor fools to whose judgment Sir William Robertson referred in his memorandum know now what the strategy of attacking the foe at his strongest point has cost the world. But unfortunately they could not foresee it then — except for a few "meddlers," military and amateur.

There was, at least, some excuse for French reluctance to detach their troops from their own country. As M. Clemenceau almost daily reminded the French public: "The Germans are at Noyon" — that is, they were within forty miles of the cherished capital, which at one moment they had within their clutch, had they but closed their fingers before withdrawing their hands. Some of the fairest provinces of France were in German occupation: and only a leader who commanded the unchallenged confidence of his countrymen could possess the influence necessary under those conditions to induce them to acquiesce in the withdrawal of French men and French guns from the defence of the *patrie,* and ship them hundreds of miles away to the east to fight alongside and on behalf of races, and to liberate provinces, in which they had no particular interest.

But the British military direction had no such excuse. Wellington was not sent to Spain because Castlereagh preferred Spaniards to Prussians, but because someone in authority had the sense to perceive that the Spanish Peninsula was the flank where British troops could direct the most dangerous blow against the might of their great foe. Sherman in the famous march through Georgia acted upon the same principle.

It was these considerations that prompted Lord Kitchener, Mr. Winston Churchill and myself simultaneously, but without previous consultation, to come to the conclusion that the greatest help that Britain with her command of the sea could afford to the Allies, was to organise, equip and strengthen an attack upon the weakest point of the great fortress in which the Central Powers were entrenched.

CHAPTER XI

# THE WAR COUNCIL AND THE BALKANS

Appointment of a War Council — Pros and cons of the Dardanelles venture — Kitchener refuses military support — His contempt for the Territorials — Calamity of failure to make early use of Territorials — Possibilities at Salonika — Churchill wins Kitchener for the Dardanelles plan — Plan adopted — Decision to improve railway in the Balkans — War Office failure to implement decision — Mr. George Trevelyan's letter — Appeal for British troops to aid Serbia — Doubts of Bulgaria's attitude — Exchange of letters with Kitchener — British troops available — Kitchener advocates central control of strategy — Paris consulted — M. Millerand's visit to London — My trip to Paris — French claim primacy for their own staff — First meeting with Sir William Robertson — My letter to Grey — French support for Salonika expedition — Doubts as to Russia — Robertson's view — Need for joint Note to Greece and Roumania — Suggestion for Conference in the Ægean — Sir Edward Grey wrecks proposal — A blow to Czar Ferdinand's pride — Discussion in the War Council — Russian weakness — More men needed in the Dardanelles — Stalemate on the Western Front — My opposition to military venture in Dardanelles.

DURING the first two months of the War there was no established War Council. There were sporadic and irregular consultations from time to time between the Secretary of State for War and the First Lord, between each of them individually and the Prime Minister and, now and again, between the two War Lords and the Prime Minister sitting together. The Foreign Secretary was occasionally brought in. I was not summoned to these conferences except when there were matters to be decided that directly affected finance. At the end of November the Prime Minister decided to establish a War Council and early in January he assembled it to examine the various proposals put forward by Mr. Winston Churchill, Sir Maurice Hankey, and myself. Mr. Churchill urged with all the inexorable force and pertinacity, together with the mastery of detail which he always commands when he is really interested in a subject, the merits of his Dardanelles scheme. I gave my reasons for preferring a landing at Salonika. The plan of forcing the Dardanelles by naval action had been examined more than once in the past by naval authorities when the possibility of bringing pressure to bear upon the Turkish rulers of Constantinople had been contemplated. Each time it had been condemned as being too risky an operation without the occupation not merely of Gallipoli but of the Asiatic shores as well. Every time the project was explored the dangers were foreseen which were actually experienced when it was tried later on by the Allies. The difficulty was obvious — that of forcing by marine action a passage through narrow straits commanded on both sides by defensible heights. It was always apprehended that even if the Narrows could be forced in spite of mines and fortifications, they might be closed against the return of the Fleet as long as either of the two shores remained in the hands of the enemy. When the Greeks offered to join the Allies earlier on in the War they were prepared to send an adequate contingent to occupy the Gallipoli Peninsula. Had they done so the whole story of the Dardanelles would have been different. The story of the whole War would also have differed fundamentally from that which was told by the event. But for some inscrutable reason Sir Edward Grey rejected Greek overtures of help. His tiresome hesitancies helped us into the War, but they hindered us when we were well into it. A more virile and understanding treatment of the Balkan situation would have brought Greece and also Bulgaria into the War. Italy could also have been brought in sooner.

If Lord Kitchener had had at his disposal an adequate force to subdue the Gallipoli garrison, and also to occupy the Asiatic side of the Straits and to hold their own there against the attacks of the Turkish Army on the mainland, then there was a great deal to be said for the Dardanelles plan. But he stoutly insisted that he could not spare more than a brigade at that time. That, I was convinced at the time, was an underestimate of the reserves of men at his disposal, and I know it now. It was due primarily to apprehension that the Russian Army might collapse, enabling Germany to concentrate great forces on the Western Front. In addition, Lord Kitchener was from time to time afflicted by incomprehensible fear of denuding this country of regular troops and thus leaving it open to all the peril of an impossible invasion from an enemy that dare not sail his ships in any part of the German ocean, except for a few hours' dash half-way across and back at full speed.

There was another factor which played a great part in Lord Kitchener's estimate of our available military strength at this stage of the War. He had the old regular general's contempt for the quality of our Territorial army. He had always in his mind the volunteers of his younger days — imperfectly organised, deficient in equipment, with inadequate fire practice and hardly drilled at all. The Volunteer Force was the bedraggled starveling of the War Office, eking out its meagre finances by local concerts, entertainments and subscriptions. I recall its financial straits. The lawyer to whom I was articled was the local captain in his little town. Such training for war as I ever acquired was given me by a sergeant major in that company of Volunteers to which I belonged. He drilled the men, played the cornet in the band, and sold tickets for the concerts. When Kitchener returned to England to take over the direction of the War and found a great force of 270,000 men called the Territorial Army, he thought of it in the terms of the Volunteers who were the joke of the Regulars — a few hundred thousand young men officered by middle-aged professional men who were allowed to put on uniform and play at soldiers. He did not realise the revolution which had been effected in this force by Haldane's genius. On the first occasion on which I had any lengthy and intimate conversation with Kitchener on the War, one evening after the declaration, he spent nearly the whole of the time in deriding the Territorial Army. He was full of jest and merriment at its expense. This miscalculation had quite an important effect upon the course of the War during the first few months. There are competent soldiers who maintain that Lord Kitchener could easily have thrown at least ten more divisions of excellent troops into the battle line during the decisive days of the Battle of Ypres had he placed greater trust in the Territorials that were available. And there is no doubt that if he had known their full value he could by the spring of 1915 have sent several divisions to Salonika. They were excellent material and by that time they had received six months of constant training in camps. The Balkan Expeditionary Force need not have been made up exclusively of Territorials. Some of the Territorial divisions might have been sent to France to relieve Regular divisions who were garrisoning sloppy trenches, and these highly trained soldiers could have been spared for the Balkans as a stiffening for the Expeditionary Force. The weather was not propitious for fighting in Flanders. There was also a substantial force of Australians and New Zealanders mustered in Egypt. These might have been sent to Salonika. We all know what first-class fighters they were.

But unless one takes the Territorials and Dominion troops into account, even if there had been a division or two of Regulars available and these had been doubled by the accession of an equivalent French contingent, Lord Kitchener was clearly not in a position at that time to send a sufficient number of troops for the double operation of driving the Turks out of Gallipoli and of holding Chanak against the main Turkish Army. On the other hand, the occupation of Salonika was not a big military operation. The Greeks would have offered no real protest against the landing and there was no enemy within striking reach to prevent it. The first two or three months of the year would have been occupied in improving the railway communications — a very necessary operation. Parts of the line could have been doubled. Locomotives, carriages and wagons for the conveyance of troops and material could have been landed, sidings could have been erected and roads could have been improved.[1] By the time the winter snows had melted in the Balkans and the river floods from the Danube to the Vardar had subsided, Lord Kitchener could have accumulated a considerable force on the spot, and with the aid of the French troops which by that time could have been spared, the Salonika Army would have been so formidable that the Bulgarians would have hesitated to intervene on the side of our foes. The Official War History is emphatically of that opinion.[2] Long before Germany disentangled herself from her great drive in Russia, the combined Allied forces in that area drawn from Serbia, Britain and France with a probable accession of over half a million men from Greece and Roumania would have been so powerful that it would have been a hopeless enterprise for Austria, even with German assistance, to launch an attack in so difficult a terrain. The bastion of the Balkans would have been behind us as an impregnable fortress, and not in front of us, impenetrable

[1] The Official Military History of the Military Operations in Macedonia discussing the suitability of Salonika for a landing says: "The carrying-power of the railways was low, but, according to the estimate of the British General Staff, it could have been greatly increased under British, or French control — it was indeed considered that the six trains a day in each direction on the Belgrade line could have been at least doubled if an understanding had been reached with Greece at an early stage. The road communication with and in New Serbia was very much worse than that of the railways, but that again could have been bettered. . . ."

[2] Page 48, Military Operations: Macedonia.

and unscaleable when defended by resolute troops as we found it to be from 1916 to 1918.

Even the equipment at our disposal at that date would have been sufficient to enable us to defend such a position against any enemy.

Shrapnel, of which we had a fair supply, would have been effective against troops advancing in the open across slopes visible from the high ground which the Allied forces would have occupied. We could then at our leisure have perfected the equipment and organisation of our Balkan allies, and when all was ready launched an attack on Austria in combination with Russia and Italy. Italy came in on the Allied side in May and would have come in sooner had there been resolute action on an effective scale in the Balkans.

We had several discussions at the War Committee on the various and rival proposals that were put forward. These lasted several days. Sir John French was brought over from France to take part in one of the discussions. His opinions, which I have already quoted, were favourable to an attack on the southeastern flank.

I presented the case for a Salonika landing to the War Council, but I was at a disadvantage in converting my colleagues. Mr. Winston Churchill had been in constant touch with Lord Kitchener, and when the former has a scheme agitating his powerful mind, as everyone who is acquainted with his method knows quite well, he is indefatigable in pressing it upon the acceptance of everyone who matters in the decision. On the other hand, I saw Lord Kitchener only on very rare occasions. At that date the War Lords were very exclusive and kept very much to themselves. They were both naturally very busy and had no time to spare for civilian amateurs.

The First Lord of the Admiralty had another advantage in urging his proposal, and that was decisive. He was prepared to act without waiting for an immediate dispatch of troops. His proposal was a purely naval operation in its initial stages. Troops would only be called for after the Narrows had been forced, and therefore after all the forts had been demolished. Even then their rôle was to be a modest one. Lord Kitchener knew that the completion of such a task by the Navy would take some time. Meanwhile, there would be no call for troops or ammunition from the Army. On the other hand, the Salonika plan did involve the immediate landing of a certain number of troops, with guns, ammunition, stores, sea and land transport. This idea of a purely naval operation was a welcome relief to an embarrassed Secretary of State who was always being pressed to send more troops and munitions to every theatre. His worries in this quarter would be shouldered for two or three months by the Admirals. So Lord Kitchener swung round to the Dardanelles plan, and that settled it. Every Minister at that Council, including the Prime Minister, Sir Edward Grey, Mr. Balfour and Lord Crewe, followed Lord Kitchener's lead as to the Dardanelles attack. I stood alone in expressing a different and doubting view. Lord Fisher was dumb. I was not aware at the time that he and other Admirals were opposed to the venture as a purely naval operation unsupported by troops.

The Dardanelles scheme was, therefore, resolved upon and preparations were immediately made to carry it through. Mr. Churchill threw into the execution of his scheme all his impulse and ardent energy. I pressed at a later meeting of the Committee that some action should be taken to make the Salonika expedition more practicable in the event of the attack on the Dardanelles failing. Accordingly, after the Dardanelles decision had been taken I secured the unanimous consent of the Committee to a proposal that Lord Kitchener should take steps immediately to improve the transport arrangements from Salonika to Nish by doubling the line where feasible, and by increasing the number of locomotives, sidings, carriage wagons, and other transport facilities on the Salonika railway. Lord Kitchener undertook to take the matter in hand. But nothing was done to carry out the order of the War Committee, and no further notice was taken of it. When we were compelled to send an expeditionary force at the end of the year to prevent the victorious Central Powers and Bulgaria from marching through to the Mediterranean, not a single additional rail had been placed, not an additional siding had been constructed, not an additional wagon had been landed. Not a road had been widened or mended. Not even a survey had been made of the transport facilities available on rail or road and the means by which they could be improved. The result was that when Serbia was attacked in the autumn by the Central Powers the General Staff gave it as one of their reasons against sending an expeditionary force at that date to the aid of the hard-pressed Serbians, that there were no means of transporting such a force up the line. Even at the end of 1916, when General Joffre had been thoroughly converted to the importance of Salonika, and the Allies had been in occupation of that port for twelve months, the number of troops that could be despatched and effectively used in that area was limited by the fact that up to that date no steps had been taken to improve the transport accommodation. A force adequate to the need could not be sent there for that reason.

As soon as the Cabinet Committee had come to a final decision that the attack on the Dardanelles was to proceed, I ceased to challenge the wisdom of the enterprise, feeling that it was better to press forward energetically with one or other of these outflanking operations than to abandon all idea of taking action in that direction. I continued to urge the despatch of troops to Gallipoli in time and sufficient numbers, and especially with an adequate equipment of guns and ammunition. Whilst discussions and preparations were proceeding, reports came in from the Balkans that emphasised the peril of delay. A very striking letter from Mr. George Trevelyan, the eminent historian, written to Mr. (now Sir Francis) Acland, was passed on to me amongst other members of the Cabinet including the Foreign Secretary. He was at the time travelling in the Balkans with Mr. Seton Watson, the great authority on Balkan politics, and his letter is a very calm and informative view of the position and the attitude of the various Balkan States at that time.

"Sofia,
January 15th, 1915.

"Dear Francis Acland,

"We[1] came here from Nish yesterday and are going on to Bucharest to-morrow. We had a long conversation with Sir Henry Bax Ironside, who is as much impressed as Mr. Des Graz by the danger Serbia will be in if a big Austrian army with German corps to stiffen it comes to the attack. As everything we have seen and heard in Serbia leads us to suppose that Serbia cannot resist such an attack successfully if unaided, we have to-day telegraphed to Grey urging that every diplomatic and military effort should be made to save Serbia and prevent the annihilation of our influence in the Near East which will certainly result from a disaster to Serbia.

"I wrote to you in much the same sense from Nish — you may even get this letter and that one together — urging that British troops should be sent from Egypt or anywhere else, if the Germans come against Serbia or a fresh and overwhelming number of Austrians. The moral effect would be very great on a mercurial people like the Serbians, just as the moral effect of the arrival of the ammunition was very great in December. On the Austrians also the moral effect would be great — they were

[1] Mr. Seton Watson and himself.

much disconcerted in December by a false report that the Russians had joined the Serbians at the time of the Serbian *retour* offensive — because ten Russian N.C.O.'s were seen. Even the presence of our Blue-jackets at Belgrade has done the Austrians intellectual damage.

"We did not wire from Nish, not because Mr. Des Graz [1] was opposed to this view, but I talked the matter over with him and he was most deeply impressed with the danger of Serbia and the need for military help if the expected invasion in force took place, especially with German aid. I deferred wiring till I came here, because I wanted to know whether there was any danger of Bulgaria marching against Greece, if Greece came up the Vardar valley to help Serbia. Bax Ironside is confident there is no longer such a danger, that Bulgaria has now decided on neutrality at least unless and until Serbia is crushed and the whole Entente game lost in these parts. If this is so we could use the Vardar valley to convey British troops to aid Serbia and Greece herself ought to march. Watson points out that British troops might also or alternatively be sent via Antivari or Dalmatia — but there we trench on military questions where I am out of my depth. The *principle* is that we must save Serbia or lose the whole Near East with results on the whole War imaginable to you.

"We have not yet been to Bucharest and may not be much wiser when we have been. But though all have hopes, none we have yet seen, Serbian or English, has any confidence that Roumania will march till after the battle is lost and won. Other measures must, therefore, be taken to save Serbia if she is attacked in force, besides efforts to bring Roumania in.

"You may wonder why we have wired and written so little about the Macedonian question. I have told you what the general Serbian attitude is about it — I did so in my last letter. But as we don't know what Prince Trubetskoi has been and is doing about it, we don't know enough to proffer advice or to judge whether any special treatment of the Macedonian question now can help to save Serbia *now* — for the crisis of the invasion, if it

[1] The British representative in Serbia.

comes, may be on her any week. In general, however, we can say from numerous conversations with Serbians from the Crown Prince downwards that the more Yugo-Slavia and Adriatic expansion are dwelt upon, the more Serbians will be willing to concede to Macedonia. And that Serbia will only concede at the friendly dictation of the Great Powers her Allies.

"It should be borne in mind that the Serbians are a mercurial people, though they have such stout stuff in them. They may begin retiring, even in disorder and despair, and then if something is done, or something turns up to put fresh heart in them, they may do wonders.

"Diplomatically everything seems uncertain and fluctuating from hour to hour with regard to the action or inaction of Roumania and Bulgaria — perhaps of Greece. It is no very wild guess to suppose that the ultimate choice of Roumania and Bulgaria respectively or jointly, will depend on the result of the coming attempt to conquer Serbia if such attempt is made. Of course, the Roumanians ought to help to save her during that invasion, and they *may*, and every effort should be made to make Roumania do so. But other plans should be prepared to save Serbia, on the assumption that Roumania will not march till she sees who is the victor, for that is the only safe assumption. We do not wish to give the impression that Serbia is at the last gasp. Her spirit is splendid and her Army, if halved by losses, is in good estate. But if, as at present expected, Germany and Austria can mobilise against her numbers that are beyond her power to resist, the result of the whole War may be affected by an abnormal effort to help her.

George Trevelyan."

We were to discover too soon how accurate were Mr. Trevelyan's and Mr. Seton Watson's prognostications about Bulgaria and Serbia. We had other communications which confirmed the impression given by Mr. Trevelyan's letter. The Balkans were a frightful mix-up, and it was clear that they might be consolidated on the side that took the boldest action in that quarter ere it was too late.

At the end of January a report was received from our Minister at Sofia referring to a message from the Russian Foreign Minister, which expressed great apprehension as to the possible attitude of Bulgaria. The Minister thought these fears well founded, that there was a growing feeling at Sofia that Russia was not succeeding in her military operations, and that when the weather improved sufficiently to enable the Germans to advance, Warsaw would fall into their hands. That was the opinion of the Bulgarian generals, and the Minister warned us that unless Bulgaria was persuaded we were on the winning side no territorial bribe would bring her into the Alliance. They were not as much concerned about territorial extensions as with the drift of the War, which they were watching with anxious eyes before deciding which side to join. I called Lord Kitchener's attention to this telegram, and the following correspondence ensued:

"January 29th, 1915.

"Dear Lord Kitchener,

"You will I am sure have seen Telegram Number 14 in last night's sections from Sofia. It is so obviously the German interest to crush Serbia in order to detach Bulgaria from the Triple Entente and to free a way to Constantinople that it is risky to doubt the accuracy of the telegram. The French delayed assistance to Antwerp until it was too late. This time the responsibility is ours and we shall not be held blameless if a catastrophe occurs.

Ever sincerely,

D. Lloyd George."

"War Office,
Whitehall.
29th January, 1915.

"My dear Lloyd George,

"I think we all see the danger. The difficulty is that our forces are tied up in France and that the situation requires a fighting force in Serbia. To go there with a small force such as a Brigade would be useless unless followed by others, as we should be laughed at as soon as it was discovered that we were only an Army *pour rire*. We might force Greece in as a belligerent, but very few Greek troops would reach Serbia while Bulgaria maintained the attitude she has adopted.

"I cannot help thinking Bulgaria wishes to see Serbia perish and with that object stops all assistance being given her by Roumania and Greece. See enclosed which please return.

Yours very truly,

KITCHENER."

As to Lord Kitchener's plea that he could spare only a brigade for the occupation of Salonika, he had at home at that time a fine division of regular troops not yet sent to any front. This would have provided the necessary nucleus and stiffening for the 14 Territorial divisions available at that date at home. Two or three divisions of these gallant Territorial troops he soon after sent to Flanders and found fit enough to take their place in the first-line trenches to defend the British position against Germany's best soldiers. There were also 39,000 Australians and New Zealanders in Egypt. They were all equal, to say the least, to anything the Bulgarians or Austrians could have brought against them. On the Western Front the French and ourselves already considerably outnumbered the Germans, and, although we lacked the heavy artillery necessary for attack, we had shown ourselves, even when we were much weaker, strong enough to resist a German attack. Had we sent a few of these available divisions the French could and would also have sent an equal number of troops. Their pride would not have permitted them to go unrepresented in equal strength in so important a theatre. On that point they always displayed a certain useful touchiness, if not jealousy. If the French and ourselves had, in consequence of this expedition to the East, been compelled to economise our men on the Western Front, the foolish offensives which cost the Allies over 100,000 men during the first four months of 1915 would have been avoided. There were plenty of men for rash and ill-considered ventures on the Western Front, but only a brigade could be spared for an enterprise which, as events proved before the end of the year, was essential to save the Allied cause from a great disaster.

As the enclosure of Lord Kitchener's letter was concerned with the attitude of Roumania, which was also represented as waiting and watching, but not yet willing to take the risk of joining the Allies, I replied to Lord Kitchener:

"Treasury Chambers,
Whitehall, S.W.
January 29th, 1915.

"Dear Lord Kitchener,

"I return the Sofia despatch. Thanks.

"I am fairly confident you will not get these Balkan States to decide until they see Khaki!

Ever sincerely,
D. Lloyd George."

At a meeting of the War Council on January 28th Lord Kitchener had one more of those flashes which now and again cast their rays deep into the gloom of the stormy problems which were raging around us. He said that he was impressed by the advantages which Germany derived from her central position. This enabled the enemy to coordinate their efforts. The Allies, on the other hand, were all acting independently. In his opinion there should be some central authority where all the Allies were represented and full information was available. Attacks should be arranged to take place simultaneously. This would cause appeals for assistance to be made to the German Great General Staff from all parts of the War simultaneously. These attacks might be continued for ten days or so, after which there would be a period of rest. During these offensive operations he would suspend all communication between the Allied countries and Germany.

I was entirely in favour of Lord Kitchener's suggestion, and I said that I was going to Paris shortly to meet the Finance Ministers of the Allies. Possibly an opportunity might occur to make the suggestion informally and to get one or other of the Allies to put forward a more formal proposal. Mr. Balfour agreed. The conclusion arrived at was that I was to avail myself of any favourable opportunity which might present itself in Paris to start the idea of a central body to provide the Allies with facilities for consultation with a view to greater coördination of effort.

Somewhere about the end of January and the beginning of February, the French Secretary for War, M. Millerand, had visited London to discuss the position. He was a sturdy and aggressive exponent of the views of the French Commander-in-Chief. He held a brief for General Joffre and fought his case with all the tenacity and forensic skill of a tenacious advocate. General Joffre did not want to part with a single battalion from his French command. He was convinced that he could break through the German lines that year. Later on this confidence received a horrible interpretation in a succession of sanguinary and futile offensives which culminated in that climax of stubborn folly — the Champagne attack, which was repelled with a loss of 200,000 men. However, all the decisions of the War Cabinet were unfolded to him, including the preparations that were to be made for a landing at Salonika when troops were available. When I visited Paris I found that M. Millerand had never repeated these conversations to his colleagues.

I visited France in company with the Governor of the Bank of England (the late Lord Cunliffe) and we met M. Ribot, the French Finance Minister, and M. Bark, the Russian Foreign Minister, to discuss the terms on which advances should be made to Russia with a view to enabling that country to make necessary purchases in America. As suggested, I took occasion to discuss the whole military position with the leading members of the French Cabinet.

Nothing came of the discussions at the time, the French military authorities being obsessed by the notion that their Great Headquarters had, and ought to have, the supreme control of the land war. The naval direction they were prepared to leave to us. But their view was that as far as the Continent was concerned we had neither the forces nor the experience that entitled us to equality of authority in the strategy of the War. Joffre was at that time the unchallenged dictator as far as the War direction was concerned.

I also visited Sir John French's Headquarters and there met Sir William Robertson for the first time. He had hitherto taken no part in the fighting, either directly or indirectly. For the first part of the War he was Quartermaster-General, and as such was reported to have organised supplies in the confusion of the hurried retreat from Mons, to the general satisfaction of the Army. He was then promoted from stores to strategy, and was now chief of Sir John French's staff. So far he had not been responsible for planning any of the battles. Later on he was the Commander-in-Chief's principal adviser in deciding the strategy and planning the tactics of Neuve-Chapelle and Loos. He was an impressive personality, with that slowness of speech and positiveness of statement which gives confidence to the uninitiated in the mysteries of a profession. He also possessed a blunt humour which pleased the Army, especially when it was expressed in ranker language and when exercised at the expense of someone other than the person who repeated the scornful witticisms.

On my return there was a further discussion on the Serbian intentions. I greatly regretted our delays in taking action in the Balkans. I pointed out that the War Council had approved this Serbian project in principle some weeks ago. When I was in Paris I had discussed it with members of the French Government, with the result that they had brought it to the attention of their Cabinet Meeting, and the French Government had now expressed approval in principle.

I thought it certain that if we made it clear that we intended to send a division the French would do the same. They were very anxious to coöperate in any military enterprise in the Near East.

I subsequently embodied in a letter to Sir Edward Grey the result of my conversations in Paris and at the British Headquarters:

"February 7th, 1915.

"My dear Grey,

"During my visit to Paris I had several opportunities of discussing with Ministers the question of the Balkans. When I first mentioned it to the Minister of Finance I found that Millerand had never repeated to his colleagues that the suggestion of an expeditionary force to Salonika had been made to him when he was in England. I found subsequently, in conversations with the Prime Minister, Delcassé, and with Briand, that they had also been kept in the dark as to the conversations which took place in England between Millerand and British Ministers. They were astonished, and not a little annoyed, that the matter had not been reported to them. I found that their attitude was much more friendly to the idea than was that of Millerand. Briand, who is much the ablest man in the Ministry, was strongly for it — in fact, he told me that he had been for some time urging some diversion of this kind upon General Joffre. I met Briand at Sir Francis Bertie's and the three of us had a prolonged talk on the position. Briand told us that the Cabinet had considered the suggestion on Thursday; that Millerand stood absolutely alone in his opposition to it, Delcassé hesitating a little, not knowing what the attitude of Russia would be towards it: the rest of the Cabinet being perfectly unanimously in favour of the principle of an expeditionary force of two divisions being sent to Salonika at the earliest practicable moment, preparations to be made at once, and the troops to be sent as soon as Generals Joffre and French could be persuaded to spare them. The French wished for an expeditionary force in which the French Army should be represented. They therefore suggested that one British and one French division should be sent. The President of the Republic was present at the Council; he also approved of this course.

"It is now a question of persuading Joffre. Briand was of opinion, and so was the President, that if a joint note were addressed to Roumania and Greece, asking them whether they would be prepared to declare war immediately if an expeditionary force of two divisions were sent to Salonika, and if they replied in the affirmative, then no doubt General Joffre would gladly spare the necessary force. Briand said it was too preposterous to imagine that if 40,000 men from the west brought in 800,000 from the east, thus withdrawing German pressure on the west, any General could possibly object to such a plan.

"Briand told Bertie and myself that he would propose at yesterday's meeting of the French Cabinet that a joint note should be sent in those terms to Roumania and to Greece. Bark, the Russian Finance Minister, who was present, strongly supported the proposal and thought Russia would gladly send a small force to occupy Serbian Macedonia, so as to make an attack by Bulgaria impossible. Isvolsky, whom Bark consulted on the subject, was also emphatically of the same opinion.

"The French are very anxious to be represented in the expeditionary force. Briand thinks it desirable from the point of view of a final settlement that France and England should establish a right to a voice in the settlement of the Balkans by having a force there. He does not want Russia to feel that she alone is the arbiter of the fate of the Balkan peoples.

"I found the President, Briand and the Prime Minister very sceptical as to what Russia would or could do in the immediate future. They were very doubtful as to whether Russia was in a position, owing to her lack of rifles and ammunition, to bring in anything like an overwhelming force on the eastern frontier for some months; in fact, they were very inclined to take our War Office view as to the effective number of the Russian troops in the coming spring and summer.

"I have no idea what Delcassé's view is after yesterday's Cabinet Council, but I hope you will bear in mind in discussing the question with him that with the exception of Millerand he was the only man amongst the French Ministers who expressed any doubt at all as to the feasibility of this plan. Briand is in favour of an operation on a much larger scale, *and he told me that he had had the idea examined by experts in the War Office, and that they reported favourably on the proposal, provided troops could be spared by General Joffre and Lord Kitchener.*

"Bertie was present and heard the whole of the conversation, and he may have reported to you its purport separately. When he and I first saw the President he examined all the objections, but I could see that even then he was quite friendly to the idea and at the Council on the following day, as I have already pointed out, he spoke in favour of its adoption.

"Yesterday I saw Sir John French and General Robertson, the new Chief of Staff. Every soldier I have met since the beginning of the War has placed Robertson in the forefront as the most conspicuous success amongst our generals, and he made a deep impression on the Governor of the Bank, Montagu, and myself yesterday. He is a shrewd, clear-headed, strong man. No general except Kitchener made quite the same impression on my mind as Robertson did yesterday. French introduced the idea of an expedition, and at first he was hostile, not in principle, but on the ground that he could not spare the troops. *However, he called Robertson in, and when I explained to him exactly what the proposal was, he had no hesitation in saying that it was 'good strategy.' He maintained that view throughout the discussion.* This influenced French's attitude very considerably. I told him we were very anxious to carry his judgment along with ours in any scheme which affected the military operations for which he was responsible. Ultimately he agreed that if the Roumanians and the Greeks promised to march on our undertaking to send an expeditionary force to Salonika, he would spare at least a Division for the purpose. He is willing, and, I think, anxious, to come over to discuss the project with the War Council. He suggested that he should be invited, and I hope that the Prime Minister and Kitchener can see their way to asking him to attend an early meeting of the War Council.

*"Robertson would have gone further than French: he would send not merely one but two Divisions at once if Greece came in, and even on the offchance of forcing a decision in the Balkans. He thinks it will compel Bulgaria to at least neutrality.* If Briand is as successful in the mission which he promised to undertake to General Joffre, then there is no reason why the expeditionary force should not start within a week or ten days at the outside.

"I am sure you will agree that there is every reason why the joint note should be sent without delay. It is quite clear from the telegrams which have appeared in the sections during the last few days that anything in the nature of an arrangement between the Balkan States is impossible. I think the attitude of the Serbian Prime Minister as revealed in our telegrams from Nish is unalterable. I doubt whether it would be possible for him to give up a substantial part of his territory in advance until he actually gets something in return. It would produce such a feeling of discouragement in his army as to paralyse their efforts. They have done so brilliantly that it would be a misfortune if this were to happen.

*"There are several ominous telegrams which indicate clearly that Bulgaria is hardening into opposition to the Triple Entente.* There is the telegram about the success of their borrowing mission to Berlin. The Germans are not such fools as to advance money without receiving some assurance as to Bulgaria's action in certain contingencies. There are the telegrams from Dedeagatch

about the laying of mines. Those mines can only be used against the Entente Powers. There are the rumours about bands being organised to attack the railways: and there are one or two others, all pointing in the same direction. Then the Roumanian news is for the moment discouraging — the trouble they have taken to explain away the loan raised in England, amongst other items of news. I am afraid that they have a better appreciation of the Russian position than we have, and that they are losing confidence in the Russian strength. *Unless, therefore, we mean to allow the great possibilities of the Balkans to slip out of our hands, we ought not to dilly-dally any longer. If we fail to take timely action here, our condemnation will be a terrible one.* As I read the sections I feel that even days count now. My experience yesterday shows that the generals, if properly taken in hand, can be persuaded. No general likes to have his troops taken away to another sphere of action. His mind is naturally concentrated on the trenches in front of him, unless he is a very big man indeed, and a man, moreover, who has the responsibility, not merely for the success of the operations under his immediate control: and neither Joffre nor French are quite in this position.

"I should like to see you to-morrow to give you a fuller account of my interviews, but I thought it well to send you a summarised report before you see Delcassé.

Yours sincerely,

D. LLOYD GEORGE."

In the conversations which I had subsequently with the Prime Minister and the Foreign Secretary, I strongly urged that a conference should immediately be summoned either at Salonika or one of the Greek islands which the Foreign Ministers of France, Russia, Serbia, Greece and Roumania should be invited to attend, in order to deliberate on the whole of the position in the Balkans, and endeavour to establish the basis of an understanding for effective cooperation between all these States against the Central Powers. I was strongly of the opinion that the Bulgarian

Government should also be asked to send a representative to this conference. Sir Edward Grey objected to such a gathering on the ground that it would be quite impossible for him to leave the Foreign Office at so critical a moment for the length of time it would take to attend a meeting at such a distance. I pointed out that proceeding by way of Brindisi it would take him less than a week to get there, and that he need not be absent for a longer period than a fortnight or three weeks in all. There would be no difficulty in getting M. Sazonow there as far as travelling was concerned, for from Petrograd to Salonika would be a matter of three or four days' journey at the outside. The Foreign Secretary was, however, so unwilling to entertain this proposal that it fell through.

Had this suggestion been adopted a Balkan Confederation on the Allied side could have been negotiated. It would have been necessary to give our plenipotentiary full powers not only to arrange geographical terms, but also to dispense liberal financial aid. The Balkan kingdoms — never rich — had been impoverished by a succession of wars with Turkey and amongst themselves. Loans from Britain and France would have encouraged them to take the risks of war. It was not a question of bribery but of sheer necessity, if they were to equip themselves adequately to encounter the hazards of alliance. The Germans realised that. They therefore did not trust their interests to the ordinary diplomatic representation, but sent to Sofia a special emissary of high standing and great ability. He knew the importance of giving financial help to Bulgaria and accordingly promised a handsome advance. It was not the decisive factor in her choice, but it was one of the inducements. Grey might not have been the best man to manipulate and persuade the fractious elements that had to be brought together. In fact, he was not. But he might have found a suitable colleague or a substitute. The Czar Ferdinand was not at that date as pro-German as was generally assumed. On the contrary he was definitely anti-Kaiser. He was a man who possessed an inordinate pride of pedigree. He was a Bourbon. And Wilhelm in one of his fits of boyish recklessness had offended his vanity when they were visiting at the same Schloss. He had been tempted to greet the self-important Bulgarian Emperor rather rudely as he was leaning over a parapet in deep contemplation of the view. The Bourbon blood never forgave the insult. Ferdinand would have been personally better pleased to coöperate with the Czar of Russia and the Kings of England and Italy. But as the issue of the War was very much in doubt he waited for some clear indication of the way things were going on the battlefield. By September the chances of Bulgarian expansion seemed more likely to be realised by throwing in his lot with the Central Powers than by joining the Allies, so he declared finally, but after considerable hesitation, for the former. A meeting with him in the spring would have produced different results. We were then about to attack the Dardanelles. By September our attacks had been beaten off. It is true that in the early spring Russia was not doing too well, but her position was by no means irretrievable. By the autumn her armies had been driven helter-skelter out of Poland and beyond. Ferdinand then came to the conclusion that the Bulgarian opportunity was with the victorious Germans. We missed our chance of organising a confederation that would have decided the War by 1916, and all through lack of enterprise and gumption.

If special diplomatic methods were not to be tried in the Balkans I begged the War Council to send more troops to that theatre so as to secure a favourable military decision there.

On February 19th the War Council met and the discussion is very illuminating because of the light it throws upon the views taken at the time of the prospects of the War.

Lord Kitchener said that the War Committee ought to consider very seriously before advising the removal of the Twenty-Ninth Division to the East. The situation in Russia had greatly deteriorated during the last week or two. The Russians had lost very heavily in men and, what was more serious, they had lost very heavily in rifles, of which they were short. If the Germans could inflict a sufficiently decisive defeat on the Russians they would be in a position to bring back great masses of troops very rapidly to France, and there would be a great demand for reinforcements in the western theatre of war.

Mr. Lloyd George agreed that the position was very serious. Russia might receive a knockout blow. Had we to admit that we were impotent in view of such a contingency? *In his opinion the Germans would not send their forces west, but would endeavour to smash Serbia and settle the Balkan question. The view appeared now to prevail that Germany would aim at the conquest of the north-east corner of Serbia with a view to establishing through communication and direct access to Bulgaria and thence to Constantinople.* (My italics.)

The Prime Minister agreed, but considered that the most effective way would be to strike a big blow at the Dardanelles.

Lord Kitchener agreed with the Prime Minister. If the fact of not sending the Twenty-Ninth Division would in any way jeopardise the success of the attack on the Dardanelles he would dispatch it. *He doubted whether the Germans would attack Serbia as suggested by Mr. Lloyd George.*

Mr. Lloyd George suggested that we ought to send more than three divisions. It was worth while to take some risks in order to achieve a decisive operation which might win the War. From the discussion he gathered that the maximum force available for operations in the East was as follows:

| | |
|---|---|
| The Australians and New Zealanders (including mounted troops) | 39,000 |
| The Twenty-Ninth Division | 19,000 |
| Naval Division | 10,000 |
| Marines | 4,000 |
| French Division | 15,000 |
| Russians | 10,000 |
| Total | 97,000 |

LORD KITCHENER said he had every intention of supporting the Dardanelles operation, but considered two divisions on the spot to be sufficient at first. There was no object in sending out troops from here which he might require.

SIR EDWARD GREY asked if we were safe in the West.

MR. LLOYD GEORGE said he had spoken on this subject with a great many officers who had been at the Front. There was a general agreement that our army could not carry out a successful attack without a very heavy loss of life, and the same was true of the French Army. No doubt it was also true of the Germans; for the Germans to attack, therefore, would be the best thing that could happen. It was just as costly for them to try and break us as for us to try and break them. . . .

On February 24th there was a further discussion which constitutes a very useful addendum to the report of the last meeting.

. . . MR. LLOYD GEORGE agreed that a force ought to be sent to the Levant, which could, if necessary, be used after the Navy had cleared the Dardanelles to occupy the Gallipoli Peninsula or Constantinople. He wished to know, however, whether in the event of a naval attack failing (and it was something of an experiment) it was proposed that the Army should be used to undertake an operation in which the Navy had failed.

MR. CHURCHILL said that this was not the intention. He could, however, conceive a case where the Navy had almost succeeded, but where a military force would just make the difference between failure and success.

Mr. Lloyd George hoped that the Army would not be required or expected to pull the chestnuts out of the fire for the Navy. If we failed at the Dardanelles we ought to be ready immediately to try something else. In his opinion we were committed by this operation to some action in the Near East, but not necessarily to a siege of the Dardanelles.

## CHAPTER XII

# ALLIED PROCRASTINATION

Cabinet ignorance of the war situation — My uneasiness at our lack of drive — My memorandum of February 22nd — Serious outlook — Suppression of the truth — Facts of the situation — Weakness of Russia — Need for Allied reinforcements — Reliable estimate of our resources wanted — Man-power problem — Munitions problem — Our untapped resources of men — Aid from the Dominions — A long war must be assumed — Bring in the Balkan States — Effect of success in the Dardanelles — Counter-measures in case of failure — Expedition to Salonika urged — Proposed diplomatic mission to Greece and Roumania — Importance of Paget's report — Fisher's comment — Substance of Paget's report — Roumania waits too long — Kitchener's reply to my memorandum — Praise of Russian effort — Alternative roads to success: victory or attrition? — Need to organise munition effort — Labour shortage — Trade union restrictions — Drink — Slow progress in equipping new armies — Too late at the Dardanelles — Futility of western campaign.

SUCH meagre and cautious reports as were vouchsafed to Cabinet Ministers as to the progress of the War did not enlighten us as to what was really happening on or behind the battlefields. There was an impression left on our minds that the military authorities thought it better we should not be told too much. Secrecy was essential to success. The Prime Minister and Mr. Churchill knew a good deal more about the situation than we did. But they were not fully apprised of the facts. Casualties were scrupulously withheld. In fact, there was no considered statement submitted to the War Council on the military position, showing the relative strength of the Allies and of the Central Powers in men or machinery. I often doubt whether anyone inside the War Office had taken the trouble to make a careful survey. We therefore knew nothing of the numbers on the various fronts, either our own or those of our Allies or our foes; what reserves were available; what was the equipment in guns, machine guns, rifles or ammunition on both sides; or when our new armies would be ready. Lord Kitchener told us he had no troops to send to the Dardanelles. We had to accept it on his authority for he never condescended to details. We had to decide every issue without being informed as to the most relevant facts. Those of us who were members of the so-called Council of War were not much better off in that respect than other Ministers who had to be satisfied with a perfunctory statement from Lord Kitchener at the beginning of a Cabinet sitting. We had to forage here and there on our own initiative for information essential to our utility as war councillors. Sometimes we scrounged an important fact, more often we picked a snub.

I was a diligent seeker after truth. In spite of travestied and medicated reports I was convinced we were not doing well. I was equally convinced we were not doing our best. We had decided to launch a serious adventure in the Dardanelles. We had also resolved to prepare the ground for an alternative in Salonika if the Dardanelles failed. I saw clearly that we were tackling neither of these plans with the whole of our available military strength. We just dawdled and put off. In the Dardanelles both Lord Kitchener and the Prime Minister were hopeful that the Navy would do the trick, in which case very few troops would be needed. If the Navy failed altogether then no soldiers would be required for that enterprise. Elsewhere there was nothing in particular happening in France. Germany had abandoned any idea of attempting a further advance in the west. We were building up an army to turn her out altogether. We were raising great new armies but not taking adequate steps to equip them. We were very dependent for ultimate success on Russia. But we knew nothing about her plans, and very little about the resources in men or munitions with which these plans had to be carried out. All we knew about Russia was that she was being beaten, that she was short of rifles and getting shorter because she was losing more in retreat than she gained in manufacture. But we were not at pains to ascertain the truth. There was no co-ordination of effort. There was no connected plan of action. There was no sense of the importance of time. We were still much too leisurely and casual for a matter of life and death. It was not an absence of fussing but a lack of clear vision and resolute drive. I began to realise that it was not composure but confusion. In spite of official reticence, disquieting scraps of news and rumours percolated through. They made me uneasy as to the course of events, still uneasier as to the way events were directed on the Allied side.

On the 22nd of February I circulated to my colleagues the following memorandum:

"I am anxious to put before my colleagues a few considerations on the general situation. It must be acknowledged to be one of the utmost gravity, and one which, if it is not taken in hand at once firmly and boldly, may end in irretrievable disaster for the cause of the Allies and for the future of the British Empire. This may very well appear to some of my colleagues to be the language of morbid pessimism, but I hope, before they come to that conclusion, they will do me the honour of perusing the reasons set forth here which have led me to this conclusion.

"The Press and the Country have up to the present treated the progress of the War as one of almost unbroken success. Their method is a simple one. Every trivial military incident which turns to our advantage is magnified and elaborated in headlines which occupy half a column and descriptions which take a page. On the other hand, grave misfortunes such as those which have befallen the armies of our Russian Allies in the course of the last few days are relegated to a few lines of type, whilst they are explained away in a column of leaded matter. I am afraid that many who have a more intimate acquaintance with the facts are pursuing the same mental process. They concentrate their gaze upon those incidents and aspects of the military situation which suit their hopes, whilst they deliberately shut their eyes to the developments which might conduce to the awakening of their fears. The only pathway to ultimate success is paved by reality. Unless we look facts, however unpleasant, in the face, we shall never grapple with them.

"What are the salient facts of the situation? Not a yard of German territory is now in the occupation of the Allies. Practically the whole of Belgium is in German occupation. Some of the richest departments of France and Russia are now firmly held by the enemy. The Germans are now in possession of larger tracts of allied territory than they have ever held before. A still more serious fact: whilst they maintain possession of the country occupied by them in the west with comparative ease, they have at last established a complete military predominance in the east. It is true that they drove the Russians out of East Prussia some months ago, and the Russians came back afterwards; but as Lord Kitchener pointed out, there is a serious difference between what happened then and what is occurring now. Then the Russians were in a position to bring up considerable reserves to overpower the enemy, and the German reserves were not ready to take the field. Now the position is entirely reversed. Large German reserves have taken the field. The remarkable report circulated by Lord Kitchener from the pen of a Dutch officer points out that after sending huge reinforcements to East Prussia and North Poland to overwhelm the Russians, they have still numbers behind them they could throw in, but which have not been sent to the frontiers because there is no room for them.

"That is the German position now. What about the Russian position?"

I then proceeded to examine in detail the seriousness of the Russian position in reference to rifles and the present situation and the future prospects of the Allies and the Central Powers in respect of man-power. I dwelt on the fact that it was useless to reckon the enormous reserves of men available in Russia without taking into account the possibility of arming them. And I drew the inference that unless and until we took steps to equip the Russians, the Central Powers had more fighting men than the Allies at their disposal. I then proceeded:

"Having regard to the superior equipment of the German-Austrian forces and to the fact that when we came to attack them they will be found to have entrenched their positions in allied soil, it is idle to hope for victory unless we secure a great numerical superiority over these forces. Where can we hope to find it? Russia cannot now, according to the War Office report, put and maintain 2,000,000 of fully armed and equipped men on all her assailed frontiers. Even if she could, that leaves us with a deficiency of 2,000,000. It will be observed that in the figures which I have given I have credited Great Britain with 2,000,000. When can she put 2,000,000 into the field? When can she put 1,000,000 into the fighting line? Is it quite certain that by the time 1,000,000 are ready Germany will not have added at least another 1,000,000 to her reserves?

"I am sorry to draw so menacing a picture, but I should, indeed, be happy if I thought the appearance of the landscape did not justify the gloomy colours with which I have attempted to paint it. The Dutch report circulated by Lord Kitchener gives still more alarming figures. If these be even approximately accurate we could not hope to bring the War to a successful termination for years to come. But even with my more moderate figures, the problem is the most serious with which British statesmen have ever been faced.

"The first thing to do is to find out exactly where we stand. Who can present a reliable estimate of the military resources of the Allies? We ought to have a conference between the military authorities of the three countries, at which a candid exposure of the position of each country is made and some military convention agreed to as to our future action. General Paget is a good soldier, but his qualities are not altogether fitted for a detailed investigation into questions of equipment. We know approximately, at any rate, how France is situated. We have not the slightest notion of what the position of Russia is. I strongly urged as far back as October that we should take drastic measures to ascertain accurately the Russian position as to equipment and munitions. We are entitled not merely to ask but to demand frankness from our Russian Allies. Russia is not in this war to help France and Belgium and ourselves. France came in to assist Russia when she was menaced; Belgium came in on account of France; we came in to protect Belgium; so that indirectly we are in because Russia was attacked. Germany was not merely at peace with us but was extremely anxious to maintain the peace not merely with us, but with France as well. She engaged in this war to try conclusions with Russia before Russia was prepared to attack her. We are helping Russia with men, with material, with money. France and ourselves have already advanced £50,000,000 or £60,000,000 of money to Russia and we have promised another £100,000,000. We are, therefore, justified in demanding candour from Russia. Germany knows all about the Russian forces, their numbers, disposition and equipment. All we want is that our great ally should supply us with information which her enemies already possess.

"What next? Every effort must be made to increase the number of men whom we can put into the field and to shorten the period in which they could be put into the fighting lines. How is that to be done? If France could put 3,000,000 of men under arms and Germany 5,000,000, then the whole of the Allied countries ought to be able, on the basis of population, sooner or later to count on 20,000,000. That may be an impossibility, but it is an indication of the enormous reserves of men fit to bear arms that the Allies have to draw upon. The problem resolves itself into one of:

1. The training and equipping of these men in the shortest space of time.
2. The maintaining of the *status quo* without any appreciable aggravation until the Allied countries are prepared to throw overwhelming forces into the battlefield.

How are these two objects to be attained?"

Here followed a passage on the urgent need for developing our potential resources for munition production which I have already quoted on page 151 in telling the story of the fight for munitions. After dealing with the issue of materials, I proceeded as follows:

"Now with regard to the raising of men. France has probably brought every available man she can spare into line. That is far from being the case with either the British Empire or with Russia. Great Britain, on the French basis, ought to have 3,500,000 now under arms, instead of 2,000,000. The Dominions of the Colonies ought to have, on the same basis, 1,200,000 men instead of 100,000. I believe we could with a special effort raise our 3,500,000, or, if that be found inconsistent with the turning out of the necessary equipment, we could certainly raise 3,000,000. I still think it is unnecessary to obtain compulsory powers. The young men of this country will enlist in our armies if it is brought home to them that their services are needed. I ventured to suggest some time ago that the best method of doing so would be by determining the quota each county and town ought to contribute in proportion to its population, and leaving it to local pressure and local patriotism to do the rest. If we officially announce that a particular county is expected to contribute, say, 10,000 men; that up to the present 6000 have been enrolled in that country, and that 4000 more ought to enlist in order to make up the quota, local pride will fill up the ranks for us.

"Some means ought also to be taken to induce our self-governing colonies to take upon themselves a larger share of responsibility in the matter of levies. They are under the impression now that they are doing all that is expected of them. The peril ought to be brought home to them. The optimistic telegrams which we publish have deluded them into the belief that all is going well, and that all they need to do is to send a few thousand to the Mother Country as a token of their sympathy and esteem for her. When they realise that she is in real peril, I do not doubt their response.

"Russia, on the French basis,[1] ought to have 12,000,000 men under arms. That is probably more than she could equip for some years, but having regard to her primary responsibility as far as the Allies are concerned for the struggle, the numbers of her men ought to bear some relation to her enormous resources in vigorous manhood.

"All this must necessarily take time. We have hitherto proceeded as if the War could not possibly last beyond next autumn. We should now take exactly the other line — assume that it will last not merely through the year, but conceivably through next year as well. Capital, therefore, ought to be spent on laying down machinery which will enormously expedite the output of rifles, cannon and all other machinery and munitions of war towards the latter end of the year and the beginning of the next. If it turns out that my estimate errs on the side of pessimism the worst that happens will be that we shall have spent a considerable amount of money, we shall have caused a considerable amount of inconvenience to the population. But all that is nothing compared with the disaster of having to face another year of war with inadequate preparation. This the public will never forgive after the warning we have received, nor ought they to be expected to forgive.

"But what is to be done in the meantime? It looks as if during the best part of the present year the Allies must content themselves to be in a position of military inferiority to Germany. During this period the best we can hope for is that we shall be able to hold our own. Can we even accomplish this without summoning some fresh forces to our aid? Having regard to the overwhelming forces at the disposal of Germany there is at least an element of doubt. There are only two directions in which we can turn for any prospect of assistance — the Balkan States and Italy. The Balkans we might conceivably have brought in some months ago, but the Allies have been unfortunate in this quarter. We have only succeeded in bringing in the Turks against us without engaging any other Balkan Power on our behalf. Is it

[1] Of the proportion of recruits to population.

too late to do anything now? Lord Kitchener pointed out the other day at the Council that the Germans had taken risks by attacking the Russians with their full forces before they were quite ready, in order to be prepared to meet the attack of our reinforcements in April. With the one exception of our initial action against Turkey, where our promptitude was unmistakable, our risks have all been in the contrary direction; we have generally taken them too late. The momentous step we have taken in attempting to force the Dardanelles must have a decisive effect one way or the other on the Balkans. Are we prepared for either or for any event?

"If this great movement succeeds — then, if we are prepared to take immediate advantage of it — its influence may be decisive as far as the Balkan States are concerned. This means that if we have a large force ready, not merely to occupy Gallipoli, but to take any other military action which may be necessary in order to establish our supremacy in that quarter, Roumania, Greece, and, I think, very probably, Bulgaria will declare for us. If, on the other hand, we have no force on the spot adequate to cope with the Turkish army, it may be that most of the effect of such a brilliant *coup* might be lost. To bring Bulgaria, Roumania and Greece in with Serbia means throwing an aggregate army of 1,500,000 onto the Austrian flank. This will not only relieve the pressure on Russia, but indirectly on France. It will tend to equalise things, and thus give time to reëquip the Russian army.

"Now let us take the other contingency — the failure of the Dardanelles effort. Unless it is at once countered, such a failure will be disastrous in the Balkans, and might very well be disastrous throughout the East. The Bulgarian general pointed out that not merely Bulgaria but Roumania and Italy have a good deal to gain in the way of territory by throwing in their lot with Germany. There is only one guarantee against a catastrophe being precipitated in that quarter as a result of a repulse in the Dardanelles. There must be a strong British force there available to support our friends. Is it quite out of the question that we should anticipate our April preparations by three or four weeks and thus follow the German example of taking risks so as to arrive in time?

"The sending of a large expeditionary force undoubtedly involves large preparations — ships, transports to carry troops and their equipment to Salonika or Lemnos, also preparations for transporting them up country; and the Committee of Imperial Defence decided some weeks ago that these preparations should be immediately undertaken, so that if an expedition were at any time determined upon, no delay need ensue owing to lack of sea or land transport. I understand that the Admiralty have done all that was entrusted to them in this respect; I know nothing of the steps taken by the War Office respecting the railways and the roads.

"My final suggestion is that a special diplomatic mission, based on our readiness to despatch and maintain a large expeditionary force in the Balkans, should immediately be sent to Greece and Roumania to negotiate a military convention. Germany has not depended upon her ordinary diplomatic representatives where the situation presented any greater possibilities friendly or hostile to her welfare. She has sent Von der Goltz to Constantinople, Sofia, and Bucharest; Von Bülow to Italy; Dernberg to America. She has not yet depended upon her X——s in critical situations. No doubt they are very good men in their way, but the mere fact that they have remained so long in inferior diplomatic berths proves that, in the opinion of the Foreign Office, their qualities are not of the first order.

D. Ll. G.

"P.S. — Since writing the above I have read a remarkable report from General Paget, which confirms in essentials the view I have repeatedly expressed as to the Balkan situation. I was privileged to see this document through the courtesy of the Prime Minister. I respectfully suggest that every member of the War Council should have an opportunity of perusing reports which bear so intimately on decisions they are asked to come to. To consult them without trusting them with the only information which makes their judgment worth having is worse than futile.

D. Ll. G."

February 22, 1915.

On receipt of this memorandum Lord Fisher sent me a letter which is worth reproducing as a characteristic comment from a very remarkable man.

"Admiralty.

"Dear Mr. Lloyd George,

"I am in complete accord with your phenomenal paper! Yesterday I had to write these following words to a most influential personage:

*"'Rashness in War is Prudence, and Prudence in War is Criminal.*

*"The Dardanelles futile without soldiers!*

Yours,

FISHER."

23/2/15.

Lord Kitchener had sent General Paget to the Balkans to report on the position there. That report confirmed all the information I had previously gathered as to the prospects and probabilities in that quarter. According to him, the Serbian Army, after a series of brilliant victories against overwhelming Austrian forces, had succeeded in clearing their country of all enemy troops, and were now in a strong position behind their Danubian frontier. They had neither the numbers nor the transport and equipment which would enable them to take the offensive, but the very able generals which they were fortunate enough to possess were satisfied that if Roumania could be persuaded to join the Entente and advance against the Austrian with a force of 300,000 men, the Serbian Army would conform and take up the offensive. The Report urged that one or two Divisions of British, French or Russian troops should coöperate with the Serbian Army and that the presence of British troops would most certainly tend to induce Bulgaria to maintain neutrality, if indeed she would not seize the opportunity of attacking the Turks. Such action on our part, or even the definite proposal of such action, would in his opinion cause Roumania to enter into the War, at such a time when her aid would be most invaluable. During the passage of the Russian Army across the Carpathians, the Roumanian Army of even 200,000 men operating against the southern flank of the already somewhat demoralised Austrian Army, would assist the Russians to an almost invaluable extent. Roumania was hesitating, but her action would be most prompt if British troops were to coöperate in a campaign on the Danube. There were no fortifications of modern standard between Belgrade and Vienna. That was the substance of the Paget report. It was a soldier's opinion confirming that which had already been formed by other soldiers as well as civilians.

Eighteen months later Roumania came in with an army of four or five hundred thousand men, but by that time Russia was beaten and broken. Her armies had been driven hundreds of miles nearer Petrograd. They could no longer hold their own when attacked, even in their own country. The Balkans were in the hands of the Central Powers; communication between the west and Roumania was completely cut off; we could afford no aid in either men or material, and fighting alone she fell without rendering any service to the Allies by her sacrifice. The poor aid Russia was able to give to the last remnant of her beaten army could not avail, and the very effort to afford that aid finally exhausted the Russian strength.

Two or three days after my memo. was circulated, Lord Kitchener circulated a reply to it. The document recalled the curious mixture of sagacity and opacity which constituted the make-up of this extraordinary man:

"REMARKS BY THE SECRETARY OF STATE FOR WAR ON THE CHANCELLOR OF THE EXCHEQUER'S MEMORANDUM ON THE CONDUCT OF THE WAR.

"I would like to make the following observations on the Chancellor of the Exchequer's very interesting paper on the state of the War.

"I will not now refer to the figures quoted by the Chancellor, as the seriousness of our position can be realised and considered quite apart from the question of the numbers of the combatants on either side. The Chancellor rightly points out that the Russian Colossus, as some people described our Russian ally, has not produced that effect on the progress of the War which those who took an optimistic view anticipated. Nevertheless, in my opinion Russia has done remarkably well, and, according to my view of the situation, she will be found to have saved us six months out of the three years which, as my colleagues will remember, I estimated, in the House of Lords, might be the duration of the War. We must remember that at the outset our chief requirement was time, and though the Germans have strained every effort they have not succeeded in giving a knock-out blow at any time during the seven months of hostilities. It is true that they occupy a large expanse of territory outside their country, but the War is not on that account more likely to end in their favour.

"If we are victorious the end of the War must come through one of the two following causes: (1) by a decisive victory, or a succession of decisive victories, of the Allies, which may take place just as well outside German territory as within it; or (2) by attrition, for when Germany is no longer able to support her armies in sufficient strength in the field she must sue for peace. I think it would be interesting to obtain, and I am arranging with Lord Moulton to furnish, a mathematical calculation of approximate dates when attrition might force our enemies to sue for peace. *As far as I can judge now, I think that about the beginning of 1917 this state of affairs may be reached.* [My italics.]

"I leave out of calculation the possibility of the starving of Germany and Austria, where 105 millions of civilian population have to be fed.

"With regard to the Chancellor of the Exchequer's practical suggestions, I am glad to think that there are more factories available for the output of war material in this country, but the real crux of the situation is, in my opinion, the organisation of the skilled labour required to work the machinery, and, if the Chancellor of the Exchequer could help us in this and in the many labour difficulties with which we are confronted, I have little doubt that in time an increased number of men, up to a total of 3,000,000, may be recruited and trained fit to take the field.

"In the efforts we are now making to raise, arm and equip 2,000,000 men we are faced with grave difficulties, not the least of which is that, constantly, our manufacturers find themselves unable, owing to shortage of skilled labour, to keep their promises of delivery of arms, ammunition, etc. This shortage could be very much lessened by the employment of unskilled together with skilled labour on the same machines, but trade union rules do not admit of this. One of the first essentials, therefore, is to secure the requisite modifications of those rules.

"A committee is sitting, on which Sir George Gibb represents the War Office, for the purpose of organising labour. I understand that they have been more or less successful in some of their efforts to induce trade unions to agree to modify the restrictive regulations which they now impose on labour; but if the Chancellor of the Exchequer could use his great powers to persuade the trade unions to deal with this matter at once, he would be doing a great deal to help us in preparing an army of the dimensions he regards as necessary. I quite agree with him that the closing of public houses in areas occupied by our labouring classes would have a very good effect, but such a measure would no doubt have to be carried out with care, as the men might resent any interference with their present habits. I would suggest, in this connection, that by keeping the public-houses closed up to 11 A.M. it would be possible to get the men into the works before they had had an opportunity of obtaining intoxicants.

"We are making a great effort to increase our armies in the theatre of the War up to 2,000,000 men, including those required to maintain the force in the field. We are just beginning to see the results that have been achieved, and the difficulties that we have to face in the creation of these new armies. Until we can actually put into the field a considerable number of our new forces I doubt whether it would be advisable to attempt further increases, except as regards the placing of orders for the necessary armament. Our present output will, of course, be continuous, and will not cease when any specific quantities of articles are delivered: every effort is continually being made to increase production, but the great difficulty I foresee is that to which I have referred, *viz.*, the labour question.

"When our new armies are prepared to take the field, it will be undoubtedly a matter of vital importance that they should be employed in the most effective manner, so as to secure decisive results, and that they should not be scattered on subsidiary enterprises.

"Much depends upon the success of the Navy in forcing the Dardanelles, but we have not sufficient men available at present to attack the Turkish troops on the Gallipoli Peninsula. As the situation develops in the Near East, we shall be better able to judge how our troops could be best employed when ready.

**K.**

"February 25, 1915."

This document is the first in which our Generals committed themselves to the idea of a "War of Attrition." Their avowed aim was to "break through" and drive the Germans back across the Rhine, a routed and broken mob, chased by cavalry.

It is no part of my task to describe military operations and I shall therefore not attempt even to summarise the story of the Dardanelles Campaign with its incomprehensible blunders and its tragic failure. The poignant tale has been told by a master hand in Mr. Winston Churchill's volumes of the "World Crisis." A small force of a few thousands landed in time would easily have overwhelmed the wretched garrison to whom the defence of Gallipoli had been entrusted by the careless Turks. When we sent an army numbering tens of thousands to attack in April, Turkish reinforcements had arrived which were strong enough to prevent us from capturing one of our objectives. We were always too late. We ran race after race with the sluggish Turk and each time he invariably won, and arrived first at the winning post. He delayed and procrastinated according to his wont, but we beat him at the dawdling game. He gave us many chances and we never took one.

Whilst that tragedy was visibly developing scene by scene and act after act, I was a helpless spectator who possessed neither the official position nor the personal influence with the War Directors which would enable me effectively to intervene.

During the whole of the summer months the Serbians remained on the defensive, whilst our strength was being muddled away on the Western Front in attack after attack upon German positions defended by much more powerful artillery than any of the Allies could command. Hundreds of thousands of British and French troops were killed and wounded, and ammunition was lavished upon fruitless and costly attacks against impregnable fortresses. The Germans soon became convinced that they need feel no anxiety as to these onslaughts. As soon as they saw how feckless our efforts were in the Dardanelles they ceased to worry about that operation and postponed dealing with it until the autumn. They were right. Scores of thousands of the Allied troops fell in belated and therefore fruitless assaults on Achi Baba and the heights above Suvla and in clinging onto the rocky slopes of Anzac. In the east, as well as in the west, the German game of attrition was a great success. So they left the southeastern flank to the Turk and in the west they left their entrenchments to be defended by numbers which were considerably inferior to those which were arrayed against them, and they turned their attention to the east with a resolve not merely to relieve the pressure upon their sorely tried allies in the Carpathians but to defeat the Russian Army along the whole front, and if possible, to destroy it.

CHAPTER XIII

# THE RUSSIAN COLLAPSE

## Poignant Appeals from the Russian Soldiers

Stagnation in the west: movement in the east — Russian artillery shortage — Examples of appeals from Russian armies — Surrenders of ill-equipped Russian troops — My alarm over the Russian situation: letter to the Prime Minister — Jews as scapegoats — Reports of British military observer in Russia — Lord Kitchener's help invoked — Rifle shortage — German preponderance in heavy artillery — Ammunition famine turns victory into defeat — Russian *morale* shattered by German guns — German infantry "pampered and spoilt" — The Russian retreat — German munitions inexhaustible — Steam-roller or threshing-machine? — War Office tries to stifle news of Russian weakness — How Russian Revolution was bred — Russia's allies blamed.

The failure of the Allied military chiefs to realise that the event of this War would ultimately be determined by equipment on land, sea and air ought to have been brought home to the most blinkered mind by the Russian defeats in 1915, and by the grave consequences that ensued.

On the Western Front we hailed a recovery of ground on a front of two or three kilometres to a depth of one kilometre as a victory. We had several triumphs of that kind during the year 1915. They were attained at a heavy cost of human life on our own side, and comparatively small losses to the Germans. In the aggregate we succeeded in tearing out of German claws a few square miles of French and Flemish soil. The balance of advantage was every time with the enemy. We captured nothing of any strategic value. We expended over 10,000,000 shells and added hundreds of thousands to the ghastly casualty lists of the War. During the same period on the Eastern Front the Germans drove the Russian armies on a front of 500 miles to a distance ranging from 90 to 300 miles from their original entrenchments. Every shell told. The price they paid in German lives for their vast conquests was not half what we sacrificed in the attainment of trivial results. They captured more great cities and provinces than we did hamlets and shell-harrowed fields.

The great retreat of 1915, in which, with unexampled carnage the Russian armies were driven pell-mell out of Poland and the Baltic provinces up to Riga, was entirely due to Russian inferiority in artillery, rifles and ammunition of all kinds. Amongst my papers there are reports written at that date by British officers who were observers of the actual fighting, and I have had the advantage of perusing some of the dispatches sent from the Russian generals at the front to their Government. They afford poignant and convincing evidence of the fact that the Russian rout was due to lack of material. Even before the end of the campaign of 1914, the Russian Army's resistance threatened to break down altogether through lack of equipment. There were some distressing appeals sent in November and December, 1914, from General Yanushkevitch, the Chief of the Staff of the Grand Duke Nicholas, Commander-in-Chief of the Russian Armies, from the fighting front to General Sukhomlinoff, the Secretary of State for War.

Here are a few specimens couched in language which might well be called hysterical had it not been fully justified by the tragic facts:

22/XI/1914

*Yanushkevitch to Sukhomlinoff.*

". . . I should be infinitely obliged to you, on behalf of the Army, if you would consider it possible to hurry up Rudsky (a well-known metallurgical works in the Baltic provinces) for the promptest output of shells. This is a nightmare to me. With the reduction in the number of guns and quantity of cartridges, 50 to 60 per cent. more casualties have started."

He went so far as to suggest that even the appearance of shells without any means of explosion might encourage the troops.

> "Would it not be possible in addition to everything else to increase the quantity of shells (fuses are not necessary, but there will be shots). At any rate the spirits of the troops will be kept up. (A drowning man always catches at a straw.) The matter of the provision of rifles has been successfully arranged: up to 50 per cent. has been secured. . . ."

General Sukhomlinoff, in reply, sent a telegram which he intended to be reassuring, but which must have had a very depressing effect upon its recipient. He was doing his best to speed up production, and ends up by saying:

> ". . . I myself visit the works and urge them, but come upon strikes, shortage of coal, non-delivery of lathes from abroad — and we have none."

Workmen, miners, railwaymen and foreigners were all to blame. The Czarist Ministers were alone blameless. How completely the equipment of the poor Russian soldiers had been neglected is revealed in a fuller message from Yanushkevitch to Sukhomlinoff dated December 6th, 1914:

> "I know that by my wailing I caused you trouble and worry, but what is to be done? You know that my hair stands on end at the thought that, owing to the shortage of cartridges and rifles, we shall have to submit to Wilhelm. . . . *The fewer the cartridges the greater the loss.* If it were possible to throw in 150,000 to 250,000 men at once, it would be possible in 1 to 1½ weeks to hurl back the enemy and secure an advantageous position immediately. . . . That is why I consider it my duty to make a humble appeal to you. Many of the men are without boots and have frost-bitten feet; they are without short fur coats or sweaters, and are beginning to catch severe colds. As a result, where officers

have been killed off, mass surrenders and captures have started, in some cases on the initiative of ensigns. They say, 'Why should we perish of hunger and cold, without boots; the artillery is silent, and we are killed like partridges. The Germans are better off. Let us go.' The Cossacks, who in an attack had recovered 500 that had been captured, were abused by the latter: 'Who asked you, fools; we do not want to hunger and freeze again.' These occurrences are truly sad — but they are threatening. That is why I am now raising my voice. The English offer to help in executing the orders in their country, in America and Japan. Be merciful and give us instructions for everything possible to be ordered (horse-shoes, cartridges, rifles). Nothing will be in excess. The Army will absorb everything like an insatiable monster. Forgive me, for God's sake. Believe me that I am not exaggerating. I am speaking from my conscience. . . ."

Here was a war that had been foreseen for years past by the Government of the Czar. For this contingency preparations had been made; at least the Russian peasants had supplied cash in plenty for such preparations. How had it been spent?

The Grand Duke Nicholas, who commanded this Army, was a fine soldier, and an honourable man. He took for granted that his colleagues and comrades at the War Office were of the same pure metal. His disappointments come out in the telegrams of the Chief of his Staff. Here is another to the egregious Sukhomlinoff:

"10/12/14.

"In order not to worry you, I have, by order of the G.D. [Grand Duke], sent an S O S by wire to General Vernander, describing to him the picture in regard to the cartridges. Both Commanders-in-Chief [at the fronts] have sent such telegrams that my hair stands on end. Cartridges are disappearing. In Germany articles have already appeared that 'we are at our last gasp, as we are almost not replying to their firing; that on the evidence of our soldiers [prisoners] our numbers are shrinking without being replaced, and the artillery has been forbidden to shoot.' The deduction to be made from this is that victory is at hand. And the reinforcements promised for the 1st December have not as yet come to hand."

*General Yanushkevitch to General Sukhomlinoff.*

"February, 1915.

". . . 2–3 times a day cartridges are asked for from the fronts, and there are none. My heart is heavy. . . ."

*General Sukhomlinoff to General Yanushkevitch.*

"24th February, 1915.

". . . The eighth month of a fierce campaign is making itself felt by an exhaustion of stocks with all armies, and with use of projectiles.

"Positively all possible measures are being taken, and the Grand Duke Serge Mikhailovitch, who is now at the head of this business, can convince himself that the constant orders abroad have not promoted the development of our private industry, and with Government factories one does not get very far, especially when, moreover, the means therefore had to be acquired by sheer force — at the bayonet point and at a risk of losing one's position in the service. . . ."

At that time such information as I was able to secure about the Russian situation, despite the reticence of the military authorities, increased my already acute uneasiness. In February I laid my views before Mr. Asquith in writing as follows:

"*Treasury Chambers,*
Whitehall, S.W.
February 18th, 1915.

"My dear Prime Minister,

"The situation revealed by Lord Kitchener's statement at this morning's Cabinet is a grave one, and I strongly urge that the

War Council should take it into consideration at once. After seven months' war we do not even now know approximately the position of the Russians. Sir John French told me that he had been assured by the Russian officers who visited him that Russia would have 3,000,000 of men fully equipped in the field next month, and that they could then sweep back the German and Austrian armies opposed to them. The War Office compute the Russian forces now at 1,200,000. If Sir John French's information be correct the Russian reinforcements available in March would come to 1,800,000. Now we learn that the Russians have no rifles to equip their new men with and that they can only turn out rifles at the rate of 40,000 per month. At that rate they can only bring 500,000 more men into the field by this time next year. The Germans are capturing more than 40,000 Russians with their rifles each month. What is the truth about their equipment? We surely ought to know. Our fate depends upon it.

"I ventured in October last to express my doubts as to the Russian equipment, and I suggested then that we should take definite steps to ascertain how they were situated. I thought then it might be possible to arrange a meeting between the three War Ministers — or responsible representatives. X is a futile person with no authority and but little intelligence. Y, for this kind of work, is no better.

"We ought to have a searching and candid survey of the whole military situation with a view to devising the best means of meeting it — otherwise we shall drift into irretrievable disaster.

"There has been a deplorable lack of coördination between East and West, and as long as it lasts the Germans will continue winning. *Mere optimistic bluff is not going to float us through this hurricane.*

Ever sincerely,

D. LLOYD GEORGE."

Nothing was done, however, to improve the position. The same kind of messages as I have already quoted continued to come from Russian generals at the front, and much the same sort of reply came from the self-complacent ministers at Petrograd.

*General Yanushkevitch to General Sukhomlinoff.*

"March, 1915.

". . . Our strategy is now dead, as we cannot undertake anything, since we are helpless materially. If we could only repel attacks; it is painful that instead of being able to throw in every month 1440 companies we must be satisfied with 350 . . ."

*Yanushkevitch to Sukhomlinoff.*

"March, 1915.

". . . You know that during the Russo-Japanese war they fought for about two weeks and vegetated for 2–3 months but now there are divisions that have already been fighting for 85 days. That is no longer fighting, but a titanic struggle to the death. . . . I feel quite heavy at heart. At night I imagine I hear someone's voice: 'You have been sold, you have missed, you have over-slept.' "

As usual in Russia when failure was due to an incompetent and corrupt system the blame was attributed to other causes. The Jews always come in handy on occasions when corrupt or incompetent Gentiles make a mess of national affairs.

*Yanushkevitch to Sukhomlinoff.*

"27th April, 1915.

". . . In some places they are already blowing up bridges, stores. This is all done for money; probably the Jews are doing it. *There is no one else to do it.*

"The question of cartridges and rifles is, I may say, a bloody one."

*Yanushkevitch to Sukhomlinoff.*

"21st May.

". . . Ivanoff, reckoning 40 shots per day per rifle, and 5000 rifles to the division, requires five million rifle cartridges per day and 40 parks of light cartridges per month. If one compares this with the colossal expenditure of the French during the last operations in Champagne (100,000 per 24 hours for 10 days, over 50,000 along the whole front daily) one's tongue clings to one's throat. . . .

"From all armies the cry goes up: Give cartridges!"

*Yanushkevitch to Sukhomlinoff.*

"27th May.

". . . Yesterday the Germans dropped on to a section of one of the regiments 3000 heavy shells. They demolished everything. And we fired barely 100 . . ."

Some hint of the difficulties which beset the Russian arrangements for munition production may be gleaned from the following extracts taken from a report sent us at the time from a British officer who was then in Russia:

"May 26th, 1915.

"It is rumoured that Manikovski is to be nominated as Chief of the Artillery Department . . . and that the Grand Duke Serge is to be asked to take sick leave . . . He [Manikovski] said that the Grand Duke Serge was a man of great ability, but he had never smelt powder, and he loved the Artillery Department and all its ways 'like a man will still love a woman, though he knows all the time that she is a bad lot.' . . . He has worked hard and has all details at his finger-tips, though he is very ill and should be in bed. His fault is that he obstinately underestimates the number of shell required per gun per month, and sees no necessity for an adequate reserve. *He has trusted too much to the promises of Vickers and Creusot, whose failure has upset all calculations. . . .*"

Yanushkevitch wrote on the same date that the Commander-in-Chief "was appointing Lord Kitchener his agent, with '*carte blanche*' to procure shells, rifles and ammunition." He added that it was against the law of Russia to give such powers to a foreign General, but "since it is a question now whether Russia should be victorious or defeated, we will spit on those laws. . . ."

A despatch on May 30th, 1915, stated:

"The powder expert in the French Mission thinks it would be impossible to form new factories, as there is already a want of trained personnel. . . . The Russian Government should be urged to give larger orders for machinery, provided Lord Kitchener really sees his way to providing fuses."

The Russians had a pathetic belief in Lord Kitchener and talked with confidence of shells provided on the guarantee of Lord Kitchener.

Here is a telegram from Yanushkevitch to the Russian War Office:

"June, 1915.

"Orders have been given to Kitchener, as the political situation and the phantom of strikes, etc., do not entitle one to ignore this not very profitable offer from abroad, *but one secured by the guarantee of Kitchener* [to give prompt assistance] . . . The III and VIII Armies have melted away. Three corps from three divisions with 5000 bayonets each. Staffs of officers are vanishing, and the supplementary units, on receipt of rifles on the fighting days vie with each other in surrendering!"

*Yanushkevitch to Sukhomlinoff.*

"June, 1915.

". . . A bilious telegram was sent to Ivanoff. The reply was 'in 12 corps there are seven divisions, representing 12,000 bayonets! There are no rifles and 150,000 are without rifles. . . . From hour to hour it is worse. We await the heavenly manna from you. The chief thing is — cannot rifles be purchased?. . . '"

A further despatch of June 8th throws a sinister light on the working of the professional mind when confronted with the consequences of its inefficiency, lack of vision and energy:

". . . The French Technical Mission regards Smislovski as the real enemy of all progress. They say he has opposed their work in every way in his power because, if they show themselves able to produce shell in Russia, it will be direct proof of inefficiency in the Artillery Department, which people will say might have increased the output months ago. . . ."

The story reads painfully like an echo in a higher key of the lethargy, the lack of vision, the conflict between patriotism and professional vanity which hampered munition supply everywhere.

In July and August we also had reports from British officers at the Russian Front as to what was happening there. They wrote within sound of the German guns:

"The First Army was hopelessly weak in heavy artillery. For instance, north of Tysekanov the 1st Turkestan Corps had to fight 42 enemy guns of big calibre with only two. As a result, the 11th Siberian Division was practically destroyed. The German preponderance in heavy artillery seems to have created something of a panic."

It was not that the Russians had not entrenched. They were driven out of territory which for thirty years had been prepared for defence by highly skilled engineers. Great fortresses, which had been devised with ingenuity and constructed with an immense amount of labour, were destroyed in a few hours by the terrible cannon brought up by the German Army. The Russians, with their inferior equipment and serious shell deficiency, were quite unable to reply. Retreat was the only expedient open to them to save their armies from complete destruction. They were short of the machine-guns which would have enabled them to fight rearguard actions to delay the enemy and inflict upon his advancing troops losses which, in course of time, would have exhausted his strength and forced him to pause. In this unequal contest between machinery and men the great losses were almost entirely amongst Russian men, and these are described as "appalling." They had no guns which would stand up for one hour against the massed cannon of their ruthless foe, and when they had a few they were either silenced by the crashing missiles that rained on and around them, or their scant supply of ammunition was soon exhausted.

From another part of the Front where the Russians had made considerable progress against the Austrians it was reported that the victorious Russians had been forced to retreat because of the lack of ammunition. Such ammunition as Headquarters could spare was urgently needed to meet the German onslaught. The vanquished Austrians then avenged their retreat in perfect security against the disarmed victors. The report further stated (June 18th, 1915):

"As we are forced to save shells the enemy can inflict loss unpunished."

Another account states:

"All the late advances have been pure murder, as we attacked against a large quantity of field and heavy artillery without adequate preparation. I think the casualties in the ordinary sense of the word must have been 1½ millions."

Here is another extract from another quarter of the 900-mile battlefield, where the Germans were still pursuing their long-range massacre of defenceless Russians:

"This Army [the Third Russian Army] is now a harmless mob. We are very short of ammunition and guns. All realise the futility of sending men against the enemy; they with their artillery and we with ours."

At this time — ten months after the outbreak of war — Britain was just beginning to set about the task of systematically organising her enormous manufacturing resources to produce suitable weapons and sufficient supplies of ammunition for herself.

Until the Germans arrived with their superior equipment and technique, the Russians had been doing very well against the Austrians, but when Mackensen came with his great guns and his efficiently trained German soldiers, the Russians were quite unable with their inferior equipment to withstand the onslaught. As one British officer said during the retreat in May: "To-day is the eighteenth day of uninterrupted battle and retreat. I fancy they have had very little to eat. This army has been thoroughly spoilt up to now [May 30th] by having only Austrians against them. They did not know what real fighting meant. . . . The Russians even now are possibly in numerical superiority, but the *morale* of the Third Army has been temporarily shattered." And by June he reported that "the Third Army is reduced to a quarter of its strength, and its *morale* has been crushed owing to losses from artillery fire to which the Russians are unable to reply in consequence of lack of shell and rifle ammunition." The Russian General Staff, in their official apology for the retirement, point out how overwhelming was the German concentration of guns, and proceed, "as a natural result all the Russians in the beaten zone who were not killed or wounded were stunned and contused." In this remarkable document there is a paragraph which is reminiscent of something I heard from the lips of an eminent British General as to the stupidity of spoiling troops by teaching them to expect that their enemies should be crushed by a preliminary bombardment before they were called upon to attack them. "It is evident that the enemy infantry which has been pampered and spoilt by such artillery support, and has been accustomed to attack only when the enemy is poisoned and overwhelmed by it, will soon be forced to fight in far more difficult conditions."

A comment written at the time (May 30th) upon that observation by Colonel Knox, the shrewdest and best informed of the British officers at the Russian Front, was: "It is a pity that the poor Russian infantry cannot get a little pampering and spoiling of the same kind."

It was not merely an inferiority in guns that contributed to this disaster. There was a shortage of rifles and of rifle ammunition. Of the units which were sent to the front to replace the enormous casualties, only 25 per cent. came with a rifle. And there were no rifles at the front to supply the deficiency. Once more to quote from one of the British observers (June 18th):

> "The Russian guns are everywhere outnumbered by the German, and we have, of course, far less shell. The Russian infantry has not only to fight without proper artillery support; many of the units are much below strength, for there are insufficient rifles to arm the drafts, and, to crown them all, there seems to be serious danger of shortage in rifle ammunition."

When the Russians held their own they could pick up and pass on to the unarmed living the rifles of the fallen, and the unexhausted bandoliers of the stricken multitude also provided a reserve for cartridges; but when the retreat began these sources of supply failed, and the shortage became more and more serious.

That was early in June, and the fighting went on until the end of September. By July the Russians had ceased to fight with any hope of victory; strategy was confined to the problem of an extrication which fell short of annihilation. The Russian strategy was reduced to an effort to frustrate the German effort to Sedanise them on a grand scale. Their highest idea of tactics was a skilful retreat.

"August 29, 1915.

"The men were tired out from retiring every night and digging trenches in the morning, only to be shelled in the afternoon by an artillery to which they could hardly reply. The casualties were appalling. They were put at one million and a half in this summer drive."

As one Russian officer said: "The munitions shortage is bleeding the Russian army to death."

At first the Russian generals were sustained by the thought that the Germans had exhausted all their reserves of ammunition in their first overwhelming attack, that they would not be able to continue to bombard on such a formidable scale, and that once they left depots which they had taken weeks to stock and store, the advantages which their superior artillery had given them would disappear. In the sequel they were sadly disillusioned, for throughout the summer and into the late autumn, the Germans renewed the attack by the same methods and with a superiority of equipment which became greater and greater through the loss of Russian guns and the depletion of Russian dumps. Weeks after the date of that characteristic military document about the danger of demoralising storm troops by too much artillery preparation, the "spoilt and pampered" Germans drove the shattered Russian armies before them across rivers, through marshes, demolishing carefully prepared defences and redoubtable fortresses until the Russian winter which had destroyed Napoleon once more came to the rescue of the hunted defenders of Holy Russia.

In Britain we were apt to compare the immense might of Russia to a steam-roller which moved slowly, but crushed surely as it moved forward. When the great retreat began we were reminded that a steam-roller always moved backwards as well as forwards. The French comment upon the steam-roller obsession was that the Russians were more of a thresh-

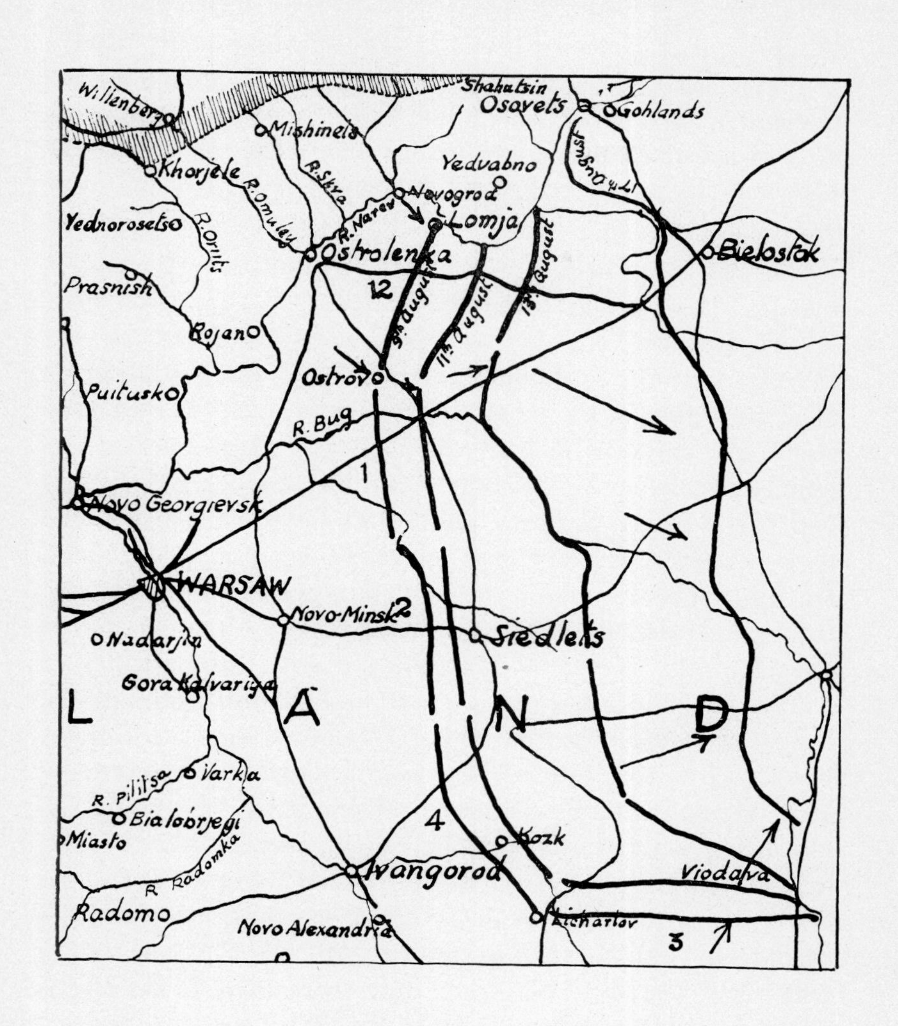


MAP SHOWING THE SUCCESSIVE RUSSIAN RETREATS IN AUGUST, 1915

ing machine which gradually absorbed the German strength and ultimately beat it all into straw. This disastrous campaign proved that the Germans possessed the machine and that the Russians provided the battered sheaves.

Whilst these disturbing reports were coming in from the Russian Front, a well-authenticated rumour reached me that the War Office were annoyed with their tenor and were taking steps to remove the man who had despatched them from Russia. These tales from the Russian Front were discouraging the soldiers who lined the trenches in Whitehall. The question of whether they were reliable or not had nothing to do with the case. The old maxim applied: The greater the truth, the worse the libel. These reports were depressing and the greater their truth, the deeper the depression which they caused; so the man who was principally responsible for sending them must be taken away from a position where he was bound to see things that were disheartening, and where he evidently felt he was in duty bound to pass them on to his chiefs with a view to procuring amendment. When I heard this on good authority I immediately went to the Prime Minister and Lord Grey, and asked them to intervene. There was far too much repression of the real facts on all fronts, and I contended that to dismiss a man because he was letting us know in time what was the actual situation in Russia was an outrage and a peril. The Prime Minister promptly interposed his authority and this distinguished officer remained at his post. But the detailed reports of defeats on the Eastern Front and their cause which came into the hands of Cabinet Ministers in 1915 were much toned down when 1916 arrived. Whether this happened at Petrograd or London I am not in a position to tell.

These resounding disasters laid the foundations of the Russian Revolution. The true state of affairs might be kept from British Cabinet Ministers, and, with the help of the

Censor, from the British public, but they could not be concealed for any length of time from the people they most concerned — the people of Russia. When mutilated soldiers returned to their homes and carried the news to the Russian villages of defeat after defeat and of the fact that these defeats were attributable to lack of preparation on the part of their rulers, and told their neighbours of the ghastly casualities which had been inflicted upon their fellow-countrymen in consequence of this neglect, the effect was, first of all, one of consternation, and gradually of smouldering resentment. In one small village, out of 26 young men who had gone to the front, 24 had been destroyed in the murderous campaign. The Russian peasant moved slowly but the town workers expressed their indignation in alarming riots which were only quelled by the rifles of the police. From the Moscow rioters came the cry: "Beasts! Beasts! You have no ammunition to fight the Germans, but you have plenty to shoot down Russians."

Inside the Army the deficiencies in equipment naturally created a sense of growing dissatisfaction and distrust. At first it was directed against the Allies: later on it turned against the Czar and his advisers, and then both Czardom and the Alliance fell together into the same pit of righteous wrath. Here is a report from the Russian Front which came into my hands just as I entered upon my duties as Minister of Munitions:

"August 29, 1915.

"Officers cannot understand why England, with her highly developed industries, is unable to help Russia with munitions. They come to me and ask why we do not send out shell and rifles. When I tried to explain that we have not sufficient for our own requirements, they simply do not believe, and go on to argue that it is in our own interest to help, for they will do the fighting if we will only give them the wherewithal to do it."

CHAPTER XIV

## WHY WERE THE RUSSIAN ARMIES ILL EQUIPPED?

**Allies to blame for Russian collapse — Foolish delay in developing munition output — Failure to utilise Russia's man-power — Quality of the Russian troops — Russia's lack of engineering resources — France short of men — Britain untrained for war — British engineering resources — Characteristics of the Russians — War research side-tracked by pure science — Incompetent management of arsenals.**

THE bitter rebuke of those bewildered Russian officers whose men had been slaughtered for lack of proper munitions is true in substance and in fact, and history will return a true bill against the military directors of France and Britain for their selfish obtuseness in abandoning their Russian comrades in arms to hopeless carnage, when they might so easily have saved them and in so doing have rendered the most effective help to their own countries. They never could be taught to appreciate the fact that a great victory over the Germans in Poland would be a greater service to France and Belgium than a slight advance into the German lines in Champagne, or even than the capture of a molehill in Flanders.

They could unquestionably have saved Russia had they taken the right action and taken it in time. For instance, had the manufacturing resources of our country been mobilised for the production of munitions of war as soon as we decided to fight in August, 1914, and had the military chiefs foreseen in time (as they ought to have realised as soon as the Germans dug themselves into the soil of France after the Marne) that the War would resolve itself into an attack and defence of formidable earthworks, impenetrable except by overwhelming artillery, then the same systematic methods for increasing the output of rifles, machine-guns and guns of heavier calibre with abundant ammunition as were inaugurated by the Ministry of Munitions in 1915, might just as easily have been taken in August or September, 1914 — in fact, more easily, for all the pivotal skilled men would have been kept at home. The result of prompt action on an adequate scale would have been that by the end of the year we could have increased our output of the lighter type of shell by hundreds of thousands, and by the summer of 1915 we should have had at our disposal a fine equipment of guns of every calibre — light, medium and heavy, with a full complement of shells. We could have added hundreds of thousands to our stocks of rifles, and what is quite as important, we should have had thousands of machine-guns, which owing to the delays, were not available until late in 1916. In 1915, this great equipment would have exceeded the needs of our armies for defence in the field at that time. The new recruits were not ready to take part in the fighting until September, 1915, and those who were then placed in the battle line were barely one-tenth of the total recruitment up to that date. That fact would have enabled us, without impinging on our own requirements, to double the Russian equipment of medium and heavy guns, and to more than treble their meagre supply of shells. Had we postponed efforts to break through in the west until we were quite ready, the Russian Armies could have been supplied with an equipment which would have enabled them to break up the Austrians whilst repelling the Germans. We could have furnished them with sufficient rifles for their fighting men, and with hundreds of machine-guns to assist them in defending their fortified posts. Had the French contributed even a moderate quota out of their more considerable supplies of guns and ammunition, the Russian armies, instead of being a mere target for Krupp's great guns, would have become a redoubtable weapon for attack and defence. That would have compelled the Germans to weaken their forces on the Western Front in men and mechanism and thus make their defensive line in France and Flanders more vulnerable.

The way the Allied War direction failed to utilise the gigantic resources of Russia in men is the best proof of the lack of vision and of ordinary business intelligence which nearly lost the War and succeeded in prolonging it for years with increasing havoc, ruin and ghastliness.

Russia had such reserves of vigorous and sturdy youth that four and a half years of devastating war, followed by many more years of ravaging disease and the wholesale massacre of revolution and counter-revolution, seem to have made no appreciable impression upon their inexhaustible numbers. By the end of 1916 over 13,000,000 had been called up, and it was estimated then that there were still left several millions of fit men of military age never yet summoned to the colours. As to the 13,000,000 that joined the army, the first contingent of these millions were highly trained and well officered. Most of the number who were waiting their turn at the gates of the slaughter-house had received quite as thorough a training for military service as that which either Britain, France, or America could afford to give to their recruits the last year or two of the War. As one Russian general was reported to have said when the Duma complained of the horrible casualties: "Don't worry yourself. Thank God, of men at all events we have enough." In courage and endurance they had no superior on either side on any battlefield. But their equipment in guns, rifles, machine-guns, ammunition, and transport was the poorest in the field (except later on, when our Salonika Army was deliberately kept on quarter rations of shot and shell), and for that reason they were beaten in action by troops inferior in numbers and sometimes in quality, and slaughtered by the million without the means of defence or retaliation. Their country was a half-primitive peasant land, unskilled in industrial arts and therefore unable to provide her gallant young defenders with adequate weapons. In spite of the infinite natural resources of the country, it had none of the developed or accumulated wealth which commanded the credit that would have enabled it to purchase essential equipment or supplies in the only available neutral market in the world that could furnish it with its needs — the United States of America. When that credit was partially forthcoming it was frittered away by corrupt incompetence. On the other hand, France with a population less than a third that of Russia soon came to the end of her man-power, and for filling up the terrible gaps made by war in her armies had to depend upon successive combings from her workshops and farms, upon the patch-ups turned out from the hospitals, and upon the young boys who became of military age during the years of the War. She supplemented these by coloured men from French Colonies in Africa and Asia. Any and every material for soldiering she could lay her hands on was thrown into the fiery furnace. Her divisions at the commencement of the War each numbered 20,000 men. By 1918 many of them had been reduced to less than half this strength, and even at that were kept up with difficulty. But France has some of the finest arsenals in the world for the production of weapons, especially for land warfare, and her engineers in other departments were highly skilled craftsmen. Her resources for turning out every machine and device for waging a mechanical war were capable of an expansion which seemed to be limited only by the demand. France was also a country rich in wealth accumulated by generations of toil and frugality. Her credit thus stood high in the world.

As for Great Britain, when the War broke out she had

millions of young men of military age, but not four per cent. of them had received any military training. As soon as war was proclaimed hundred thousand after hundred thousand flocked to the colours. But only gradually were they absorbed, drilled and fashioned into an army. It was the end of the second year of the War before a million of them could be placed in the battle line. By that time France had lost over 2,000,000 and the Russian casualties were 5,000,000. We did not possess the officers, the training sergeants, and all that constitutes a cadre capable without loss of valuable time of making out of the best raw material soldiers fit to encounter the finest army in the world. But we were the greatest manufacturing country in Europe. There are no finer craftsmen in the world than those employed in our metal trades of all kinds. Their resourcefulness and adaptability were amply demonstrated as soon as they were put to the test. We were also the richest nation in Europe. Britain was the greatest creditor nation in the world. She had lent £4,000,000,000 to the nations of the earth and in the main the security was good. So British credit in America was good enough to guarantee any order for equipment which that country had any reasonable hope of executing. Britain and France jointly arranged a substantial credit for Russia in America, but when I entered the Ministry of Munitions I found that the more powerful financial countries had managed to hustle and trample down Russia's best chances of utilising her foreign credits. M. Albert Thomas and I did our best to secure a fair distribution and coördination of the Allied orders in America. It was then almost too late.

Had Britain explored her unsuspected resources and then organised them for war as soon as she risked her own greatness and the lives of her own children in the demoniac venture she could, in the late summer of 1915, have equipped 2,000,000 Russians with almost as powerful an armoury of machines and missiles as that with which she sent 1,500,000 Britons into action in the summer and autumn of 1916. With some help from France, which her armies could, as I shall point out later on, easily spare and spare to their own advantage, and with the further aid of the American factories which our credit could purchase, Russia would easily, in the campaign of 1915, have held Germany in check and overthrown the inferior armies of Austria. Instead of which, what happened? I have endeavoured to summarise the pitiful story of the disaster that befell a great country and the mutilation and death that came to millions of her brave sons through the incompetency of her rulers and the blind and selfish folly of her friends.

The Russian failure to make the best of the resources at their command, natural and acquired, was not due to any lack of mental quality in the race. They are an exceptionally gifted nation. But they have the leisurely and casual habits of a peasant people. With them time does not count and organisation has no meaning. They wait for the seasons, and for months of the year there is nothing they can do to help fruition but keep warm until the sun comes round to call them to their labours. When their first spell of toil is over they have another period of loitering about, doing little until the fructifying rays have completed their task. The industrialism of the West, which demands incessant, well-directed, wasteless toil, has never entered the lives or fashioned the habits of 90 per cent. of the Russian people. One or two illustrations of the way this ingrained and hereditary tendency of mind affected all their work came to my notice during the War. A Russian officer whom I met at a Conference during the War told me that the real Russian was essentially an unpractical dreamer, and he challenged me to name one who had ever displayed any aptitude for business in trade, finance or politics. I named several. He annotated each name by saying: "He is not a Russian, he is a German," or again, "He is an Armenian." "He is a Georgian." "He is a Scandinavian." "He is a Jew." Then I said: "What about yourself?" He replied: "I am a Greek." That is much too wholesale an indictment of a race that numbers well over a hundred millions and has accomplished great things. But my experience of doing business with them taught me that there was an unwelcome ingredient of truth in this cynicism.

Here is a fair illustration of their strange combination of genius and ineptitude. Their chemists were men of exceptional knowledge, ingenuity and imagination. Early in 1915 the Russian munitionment encountered the same class of difficulty as arrested our activities at one point. There was an inadequate supply of the kind of explosive which had hitherto been used for the purpose of filling their cartridges and shells, and it was essential that another source of supply should be discovered without loss of time. In their case as in ours the matter was referred to chemists for investigation. After weeks spent by these scientists apparently without any practical issue, enquiry was made at the laboratory to ascertain what progress had been made with the solution of the difficulty. It was discovered that the chemists had forgotten all about the urgent task which they had been specifically invited to solve. They had in the course of their experiments got on the track of a new chemical discovery which was infinitely more important to them than the explosive ingredients of a shell, and they were pursuing this trail with an eagerness and an enthusiasm which made them quite oblivious of the fact that their country was engaged in a life and death struggle with a foreign foe, and that they had been called upon to use their scientific skill to save it from an impending catastrophe. Here is another illustration of the same kind of practical defect in the Russian temperament. When the Germans let loose their first gas attack in Russia there were at first the same crude improvisations to protect the troops as we were forced to attempt. These proving ineffective, British and French aid was invoked. We were asked to send immediately a supply of the masks which had been invented for the protection of the Allied troops in the west from these chemical horrors. We instantly sent to Petrograd hundreds of thousands of our latest pattern. Before they were forwarded to the front they were submitted to a preliminary examination by a Russian chemist, who had no hesitation in coming to the conclusion that they were by no means perfect. The consignment was, therefore, detained at Petrograd, whilst Russian professors were devoting their time to devising something better. The perfect mask was never invented. The English masks were ultimately transmitted to their destination, but meanwhile thousands of gallant Russian soldiers had been choked by the agonising fumes.

Had we not known something of the inefficiency of Russia under its autocracy we might have pointed to the great arsenals of Perm and Petrograd and many another finely equipped workshop planted here and there in their vast country. For our neglect we could have put in the plea that we honestly thought Russia was quite able to furnish the needs of her own armies without much outside aid. M. Albert Thomas told me on his return from a visit to Russia in 1916 that he was filled with envy when he went through the Purtiloff works near Petrograd. They were equipped with the most modern machinery. In that respect they surpassed the finest of the French arsenals. But the management was incompetent, indolent and muddled. The incompetence of Russian management, however, was not a new discovery, and it needed no special journey to reveal it to Western eyes. At any rate, it was known by 1915, and Britain and France in coöperation ought to have averted its calamitous results to the Allied cause by supplying the equipment which Russian management had failed to provide. When the Teutonic hurricane burst on the doomed armies of the Muscovites in May, 1915, their fine arsenals had succeeded in turning out the first four heavy guns manufactured there since the War began. But not a gun above the calibre of three inches reached Russia from abroad in 1914, and in 1915 Russia had to face the calamities of that year without any adequate help in heavy artillery and ammunition, for lack of which her valiant army was perishing.

## CHAPTER XV

# WHAT WOULD HAVE HAPPENED HAD THE ALLIES POOLED THEIR RESOURCES

Miserly attitude of army chiefs to munition supplies — Western generals refuse to realise possibilities in the East — German artillery superiority at Verdun — Strong German entrenchments in the West — Mobility of Eastern Front — High potential value of Russian Armies — Man-power wasted through munition shortage — What a well-equipped Russian Army could have accomplished — Futility of the Western offensives — Balkan possibilities — My growing dissatisfaction with our strategy — My memorandum of September, 1915 — Need to suppress German militarism — Victory possible — Central powers overwhelmingly superior at present — Need for Allies to do more — Britain's task — Munitions problem the crucial issue.

WHILST the Russian armies were being shattered and pounded by the overwhelming artillery of Germany, and were unable to put up any defence owing to the lack of rifles and ammunition, the French were hoarding their shells as if they were golden francs, and were pointing with pride to the enormous accumulation of reserve dumps behind the lines. I recollect a munition conference in Paris where French generals flourished their statistics of accumulated millions with all the pride of possession and of achievement. What about Britain? When Britain began to manufacture in earnest, and turned out her hundreds of guns, great and small, and her hundreds of thousands of shells of all calibres, the British generals treated the production as if we were preparing to enter for some great race or contest where it was essential that the British equipment should be equal to and if achievable better than that which had been provided for any other competitor in the field. The military leaders in both these countries never seemed to have grasped what ought to have been their dominant thought — that they were engaged with Russia in a common enterprise where it was vital to the attainment of a common end that they should pool their resources, and each of them be put in the best position to contribute his share to the speedy accomplishment of that aim. The team spirit was conspicuously absent during the first years of the War. Each player was thinking too much of his own scoring and too little of victory for his side. The recognition by the French generals of the towering fact that Russia had an overwhelming superiority in men never had any effective practical outcome, except a constantly expressed demand that Russia should send a large contingent of these men to France to aid the French army in its defence of French territory, and to save French manhood from an undue share of the sacrifice which such defence involved. Quantities of guns, rifles and ammunition were sent from Britain and France to Russia before her final collapse, but they were dispatched reluctantly; they were quite inadequate to the need, and when they reached the hard-pressed armies of Russia, they came too late to avert the final collapse.

The answer of the French and British generals to every suggestion for the remunitionment of Russia was that they had nothing to spare in 1914, 1915 or 1916, and that when they gave anything away to Russia it was out of their own dire need. That was a complete answer if fatuous and wasteful efforts to crash through the formidable German entrenchment were the best strategy for either of those years. Allied generalship on the Western Front never gave any weight to the fact that up to the third quarter of 1916, the Germans had a definite superiority in heavy guns in the west as well as in the east. I am not sure that they even realised it. They could see their own guns; they could not visualise those of the enemy. And yet their own Intelligence Officers supplied them with abundant evidence of the Allied inferiority in artillery. In 1916 I was shown a French memorandum which gave the comparative strength of the German and French artillery in the greatest battle of the War — the Battle of Verdun — three months after it had commenced, when both sides had brought up every gun they could spare in the west.

The following is a translation of this memorandum, in which I have, for the convenience of the reader, rendered the French measurements of calibres into their equivalents in inches:

SUB-SECRETARIAT OF STATE
for Artillery and Munitions.
CABINET.
Technical Service.

9th July, 1916.

**COMPARATIVE TABLE OF FRENCH AND GERMAN ARTILLERY IN LINE ON THE VERDUN FRONT.**

| Subdivisions. | On the German side on 26th May, 1916. | | On the French side. Average between 21st February and 20th May, 1916 | |
|---|---|---|---|---|
| | % | Description of calibres. | % | Description of calibres. |
| Very heavy | 2 | 16½ in., 15 in., 12 in. | 1 | A.L.G.P. (very powerful heavy guns*) |
| Heavy | 35 | 8.3 in., 5.9 in. | 13 | 6.1 in., 8.7 in., 10.6 in. |
| Medium | 43 | 4.1 in. | 19 | 3¾ in., 4.1 in., 4.7 in. |
| Light | 20 | 3 in. | 67 | 2.95 in., 3.1 in., 3½ in. |
| TOTAL OF PIECES IN THE LINE | | 2000 | | 1600 |

* 5½ in., 7½ in., 7.9 in., 9½ in., 11 in., 12 in., 14.6 in.

This table shows that the Germans not only possessed a total numerical superiority of guns on the Verdun Front, but that they had approximately 740 heavy and very heavy guns against the French 224 — or more than three times their equipment of these powerful weapons. They had more guns and heavier guns than the French in the west, although they were engaged in massing all the artillery they could spare for their campaign in the east against Russia.

The western generals will point to these figures as a proof that they could not send a single gun or shell away from their front to help at any other. What it does demonstrate is the folly of attempting with inferior artillery to attack a highly trained army skilfully entrenched and armed with superior weapons. Anyone who has seen the German entrenchments will realise how formidable an enterprise it was to capture them. The fortresses of Beaumont Hamel, Posières and Thiepval will serve as specimens. They were excavated deep down under the surface. These dug-out fortresses were strengthened by iron girders and concrete so that no shell could hope to pentrate their well-equipped depths. To shell them was like bombarding the Catacombs. On the other hand, the German task in attacking the French lines was equally hopeless. The Allies had considerable numerical superiority on the Western Front. They also could entrench, and they had a sufficient equipment of guns, machine-guns, rifles and grenades to repel every advance by German troops. That was the lesson of Verdun.

On the Russian Front there was not the same need for heavy artillery as on the west. Neither Austrians nor Germans could dig such a tremendous line of triplex entrenchments along so vast a front. It was more of a war of movement. There the *soixante-quinze* would have come by its own, provided there were plenty of ammunition. The millions blazed away in stubborn and stupid offensives in the west would have served. Had there been enough heavy artillery to effect a break in the Austrian lines the lighter and more mobile guns would have done the rest. And a few hundred machine-guns with adequate ammunition would have completely held up the German advance.

To anyone who had the advantage of perusing the

despatches from our able military representative on the Eastern Front, or any reliable history of the 1915 campaign, it must be evident that the overwhelming defeats sustained by the Russian armies were not due to any inferiority in numbers (the Russians outnumbered the Germans along the whole line) or to any lack of courage, endurance or discipline on the part of Russian soldiers — their undaunted valour under dismaying conditions must always remain a marvel. Neither were these disasters attributable to lack of skill on the part of the Russian generals in the field. By common consent their conduct of the retreat was at least competent. The enveloping tactics of the German marshals were thwarted at every turn and the Russian armies escaped without any wholesale loss of equipment. This was due to a combination of skilful generalship on the part of the leaders and fine fighting qualities in the men they led. It is easy to lead into action a well-equipped army hopeful of victory. It is not so easy to lead broken and discouraged troops out of a succession of fields where they have been stricken and stricken again by a foe whom they know to be much better equipped than they are. Let us give the Grand Duke Nicholas and his generals the credit of having achieved this feat. But why was so gallant an army, so competently led, driven like a herd of cattle across the plains and marshes of Poland? The answer is to be found in the extracts I have given from the reports of impartial British officers, who witnessed this agony of brave men who had been deprived by official stupidity of the means of defending themselves and the country for which they were prepared to die. They were not vanquished by better troops — they never had a chance of measuring their quality as fighting-men with the soldiers who were arrayed against them. They saw millions of German shells hurtling through the air in their direction and bursting into destructive fury amongst them, they heard the deadly rattle of the machine-guns carried forward by the advancing Germans, but they rarely came up against the foe that pelted them at a safe distance with bullet and shell. Their defences were shattered by the monster guns of Germany. The survivors of this bombardment were left among the débris without a shelter to protect them from such a rain of fire and brimstone as has not fallen on mankind since the days of Gomorrah. Had they advanced, machine-guns would have mowed them down. Orderly retreat was their only chance of saving themselves and their country. Even in retreat hundreds of thousands were destroyed in the open by the terrible blizzard of shrapnel and high explosive.

Had the Russian artillery been doubled, especially in the medium and heavy calibres; had there been an abundant supply of shell for light as well as heavy; had the Russian posts been defended by an adequate quota of machine-guns, the German troops would have encountered the same resistance on the Eastern Front as they experienced whenever they attacked in the west, and they could not have afforded the cumulative losses inflicted upon them in a series of attacks. On the Austrian Front, where the quality of the enemy troops was distinctly inferior for a variety of reasons which I have already given — reasons which do not in the least reflect on Austrian valour — the impetuous onslaught of the Russians following a sufficient preliminary attack would not only have successfully broken the Austrian lines, but that success could have been exploited and pushed perhaps to the gates of Vienna. The Austrian armies were a different proposition from the German. The German armies were homogeneous and bore an equal intensity of hatred against Slav and Gaul. In a struggle between Teuton and Slav three-fifths of the Austrian troops had a deeper detestation of their Teutonic comrades than of their Slavonic foes. The Russians partly for that reason won comparatively easy victories against the Austrians, and they were only unable to take advantage of the victories owing to lack of ammunition. A well-equipped Russian army could have crossed the Carpathians, penetrated through the Hungarian and Austrian plains up to their Slavonic kinsmen in Croatia or Czecho-Slovakia and then imperilled the capital of the Empire. Roumania would, under those conditions, have felt safe in throwing her 500,000 on the Austrian flank, and Bulgaria would have known it was better to fight on the Allied side or to keep out of it altogether.

It may be said that the Germans would then have come to the rescue of their chief ally. Of course they would. They would have been bound to do so for their own preservation. But they could not have afforded Austria effective assistance without dangerously weakening their own Western Front. They could not have withdrawn any part of their troops from the Polish Front, as that would have placed in jeopardy the roads that led to the heart of Prussia. The battles of Loos, Artois and Champagne, if they had been fought at all, would have been fought under conditions twice as favourable to the French and British Armies as those which turned them into a futile massacre of myriads of brave young men. These gallant fellows were sacrificed on the altar of misguided and antiquated theories which had already been discredited by repeated exposure. The sacrifice was in vain. It did not liberate France and it failed to save Russia. The excuse they put forward after their failure, for fighting these profligate battles, was that hard-pressed Russia demanded these attacks in order to prevent the Germans from increasing their forces on the Eastern Front. The Germans never arrested their victorious march for a single hour, because hundreds of miles to the west the French and British generals were piling up shell dumps behind the front and making other elaborate preparations to send their infantry to be shot down by German machine-guns in fruitless efforts to break through impregnable German defences. Each time French and British generals were sure of victory. Previous experience ought to have taught them to know better. The best help we could have given Russia would have been to send her artillery a portion of the ammunition we wasted in battles that achieved nothing but the building up still higher of the ghastly pyramid of casualties amongst our own troops.

To sum up: Had we sent to Russia half the shells subsequently wasted in these ill-conceived battles and one-fifth of the guns that fired them, not only would the Russian defeat have been averted, but the Germans would have sustained a repulse by the side of which the capture of a few blood-stained kilometres in France would have seemed a mockery. What more? Austria would have been crumpled up. Only prompt transference to the Austrian Front of several divisions of German infantry and several batteries of German guns from France could have saved the Dual Monarchy from utter collapse. Had Russia been victorious, then Bulgaria would have entered the War on the Allied side. A Balkan Federation — including Serbia, Roumania and Greece, and perhaps Bulgaria — on the south, and an Italian army on the west, with a victorious Russia on the east marching against a routed and divided Austria, might have ended the War in 1915. That may be a sanguine estimate of possibilities. The certainty is that if the Russian equipment had been strengthened Austria would, by the end of the 1915 campaign, have been tottering towards her fall. Germany would have been hard put to it to keep her troublesome ally from collapsing. By the spring of 1916 Britain, Russia, Italy and the Balkan Confederation, all now fully equipped (certainly if we had started manufacturing in time), could have directed a convergent attack on Austria which would have completed her disintegration. An isolated and weakened

Germany would then have had to face the full strength of France and Britain and would gladly have made the peace of a foe outmanœuvred and overwhelmed.

Instead of this we left Russia to her fate and we thereby precipitated the Balkan tragedy, which had such an influence on the prolongation of the War.

Surveying the position twelve months after we had entered into the War, I felt that things were going badly for the Allies in the east and in the west. All our attacks in France had turned out to be costly failures, and I had a conviction, shared to a certain extent by Lord Kitchener, that the one in which we were then engaged would turn out to be a sanguinary defeat for the Allied cause. The armies of our greatest Ally were in a position where they hailed a mere escape from complete destruction as a triumph of strategy. The bumper harvest of a conquered Poland was pouring into the depleted granaries of Germany (whose harvest had failed), thus neutralising our blockade. In the East we were making no progress in Mesopotamia, and we were not only held up in Egypt but we lived in daily dread of an invasion of the Delta by the Turkish forces across the Canal. In Gallipoli we had suffered defeat after defeat and there were rumours, which proved to be only too true, that Serbia was soon to be trampled down under the ruthless heel of the advancing legions of the Teuton. My ten weeks at the Ministry of Munitions had driven home to my consciousness the painful truth that most of this could have been avoided, had we organised our resources in time and distributed them wisely. This prompted me to write the following statement in September, 1915, as a preface to a collection of my War appeals. I was anxious to rouse public opinion from a complacency created by official reports concocted out of spurious victories. I felt it was the only way to enforce a change. Reading it now, seventeen years after it was written, when one is able to peruse the story of 1914–1915 and to ruminate upon it in the quiet of one's study, I cannot find any essential inaccuracy or exaggeration in the survey which I then gave of the Allied position.

"After twelve months of war my conviction is stronger than ever that this country could not have kept out of it without imperilling its security and impairing its honour. We could not have looked on cynically with folded arms whilst the country we had given our word to protect was being ravaged and trodden by one of our co-trustees. If British women and children were being brutally destroyed on the high seas by German submarines this nation would have insisted on calling the infanticide Empire to a stern reckoning. Everything that has happened since the declaration of war has demonstrated clearly that a military system so regardless of good faith, of honourable obligations, and of the elementary impulses of humanity, constituted a menace to civilisation of the most sinister character; and despite the cost of suppressing it, the well-being of humanity demands that such a system should be challenged and destroyed. The fact that events have also shown that the might of this military clique has exceeded the gloomiest prognostications provides an additional argument for its destruction. The greater the might the darker the menace.

"Nor have the untoward incidents of the War weakened my faith in ultimate victory — always provided that the Allied nations put forth the whole of their strength ere it is too late. Anything less must lead to defeat. The Allied countries have an overwhelming preponderance in the raw material that goes to the making and equipment of armies, whether in men, money, or accessible metals and machinery. But this material has to be mobilised and utilised. It would be idle to pretend that the first twelve months of the War have seen this task accomplished satisfactorily. Had the Allies realised in time the full strength of their redoubtable and resourceful foes — nay, what is more, had they realised their own strength and resources, and taken prompt action to organise them, to-day we should have witnessed the triumphant spectacle of their guns pouring out a stream of shot and shell which would have deluged the German trenches with fire and scorched the German legions back across their own frontiers.

"What is the actual position? It is thoroughly well known to the Germans, and anyone in any land, belligerent or neutral, who reads intelligently the military news must by now have a comprehension of it. With the resources of Great Britain, France, Russia — yea, of the whole industrial world — at the disposal of the Allies, it is obvious that the Central Powers have still an overwhelming superiority in all the material and equipment of war. The result of this deplorable fact is exactly what might have been foreseen. The iron heel of Germany has sunk deeper than ever into French and Belgian soil. Poland is entirely German. Lithuania is rapidly following. Russian fortresses, deemed impregnable, are falling like sand castles before the resistless tide of Teutonic invasion. When will that tide recede? When will it be stemmed? As soon as the Allies are supplied with abundance of war material.

"That is why I am recalling these unpleasant facts, because I wish to stir my countrymen to put forth their strength to amend the situation. To dwell on such events is the most disagreeable task which can fall to the lot of a public man. For all that, the public man who either shirks these facts himself, or does not do his best to force others to face them until they are redressed, is guilty of high treason to the State which he has sworn to serve.

"There has been a great awakening in all the Allied countries, and prodigious efforts are being put forth to equip the armies in the field. I know what we are doing, our exertions are undoubtedly immense. But can we do more, either in men or material? Nothing but our best and utmost can pull us through. Are we now straining every nerve to make up for lost time? Are we getting all the men we shall want to put into the fighting line next year to enable us even to hold our own? Does every man who can help, whether by fighting or by providing material, understand clearly that ruin awaits remissness? How many people in this country fully apprehend the full significance of the Russian retreat? For over twelve months Russia has, in spite of deficiencies in equipment, absorbed the energies of half the German and four-fifths of the Austrian forces. Is it realised that Russia has for the time being made her contribution — and what an heroic contribution it is! — to the struggle for European freedom, and that we cannot for many months to come expect the same active help from the Russian Armies that we have hitherto received? Who is to take the Russian place in the fight while those armies are reëquipping? Who is to bear the weight which has hitherto fallen on Russian shoulders? France cannot be expected to sustain much heavier burdens than those which she now bears with a quiet courage that has astonished and moved the world. Italy is putting her strength into the fight. What could she do more? There is only Britain left. Is Britain prepared to fill up the great gap that will be created when Russia has retired to re-arm? Is she fully prepared to cope with all the possibilities of the next few months — in the west, without forgetting the east? Upon the answer which Government, employers, workmen, financiers, young men who can bear arms, women who can work in factories — in fact, the whole people of this great land — give to this question will depend the liberties of Europe for many a generation.

"A shrewd and sagacious observer told me the other day that in his judgment the course pursued by this country during the next three months would decide the fate of the War. If we are not allowed to equip our factories and workshops with adequate labour to supply our armies, because we must not transgress regulations applicable to normal conditions; if practices are maintained which restrict the output of essential war material; if the nation hesitates, when the need is clear, to take the necessary steps to call forth its manhood to defend honour and existence; if vital decisions are postponed until too late; if we neglect to make ready for all probable eventualities; if, in fact, we give ground for the accusation that we are slouching into disaster as if we were walking along the ordinary paths of peace without an enemy in sight; then I can see no hope; but if we sacrifice all we own, and all we like for our native land; if our preparations are characterised by grip, resolution, and a prompt readiness in every sphere, then victory is assured."

CHAPTER XVI

# THE FUTILE ALLIED OFFENSIVES ON THE WESTERN FRONT

Playing the enemy's game — Feebleness in the East — Doubts about the autumn offensive — View of the British military authorities — Cabinet not informed till too late — Failure of Lord Kitchener's mission to postpone offensive — Long drawn-out carnage.

WHILST the Germans were engaged in these tremendous operations to rout and wreck the great armies of Russia, the military authorities in France, Britain and Italy could think of no more effective means of coming to their aid than to hurl great masses of their troops against impregnable positions in France, Flanders, and the Austrian Alps. No decision on the part of their enemies could have suited the Central Powers better than this course, pursued with an obstinate and senseless determination which sacrificed the flower of the Allied armies in vain efforts to break through defences bristling with cannon and machine-guns, and with two or three equally powerful positions to fall back upon in the event of the first being carried. The Allies at the same time pursued in listless and ineffective fashion, with inadequate troops, inefficiently equipped, and always timed to arrive too late, their efforts to capture Gallipoli. Had they spared in time one-fifth of the soldiers sacrificed in these futile attempts in France to reinforce the Dardanelles Expedition, Gallipoli could have been captured with comparative ease. We encountered defeat after defeat in that quarter, each defeat being a telling blow which resounded throughout the Balkans where Bulgaria and Roumania were watching the turn of events. As the collapse of Russia became more and more complete, as our failure to force the Dardanelles was becoming more and more evident, the fight of our friends in Bulgaria became fainter and feebler, the pro-German party in military circles at Sofia became more buoyant and insistent, the wily Bulgarian monarch thought he saw more clearly on which side his bread was buttered, and the brave Serbian Army behind the Danube became more and more despondent. They saw now the approaching doom of their isolated country.

The infatuation of a break-through which haunted the western generals like a disease of the mind still prompted them to organise another and, as they thought, overwhelming attack on the German entrenchments. This was timed to take place in September, 1915. After the decision had been taken, a lingering doubt seems to have entered Lord Kitchener's mind as to the wisdom of such a proceeding.

According to the "Official History of the War," published under the auspices of the War Office, the British Military Authorities, after the Boulogne Munitions Conference in June, seem to have undertaken for the first time a careful survey of the equipment of the armies on the Western Front — French, British and German — more especially in heavy guns and ammunition. They discovered what they ought to have ascertained and provided against in September, 1914, — that the German proportion of heavy artillery was twice that of the Allies and that the German shell production per day was also double that of France and Britain together and that:

"Taking these several important factors into consideration, the British Military Authorities arrived at the conclusion that an offensive on the Western Front, if it was to have a reasonable chance of success, would have to be delivered on a continuous front of twenty-five miles, by a force of not less than thirty-six divisions, supported by 1150 heavy guns and howitzers and the normal complement of field artillery. They maintained that this quantity of guns and the necessary ammunition could not be provided before the spring of 1916, and that until then it was preferable, whatever the general situation, to remain on the active defensive in the western theatre of war."

This sensible conclusion was not conveyed by the generals to their respective Governments in time to influence a decision. I have no recollection that Lord Kitchener ever communicated to the Cabinet or the War Council the resolution now revealed by the Official History.

It was not good for civilians to be told that events had proved them to be right and the military wrong. But Lord Kitchener did at last inform the Cabinet that he was opposed to the autumn offensive which General Joffre contemplated launching in September, and in which the latter was anxious that the British Army should participate by an attack on the German right. Sir John French was fully alive to the drawbacks and dangers of the proposed operation, and I believe that at first Sir Douglas Haig shared his opinion. These risks of the proposed operation were pointed out with great force by members of the Cabinet, including the Prime Minister. Nevertheless, the Cabinet as a whole (there were at least two exceptions) adopted Lord Kitchener's view that we had no option in the matter but to fall in with the plan to which the French Commander-in-Chief so stubbornly and stupidly adhered. In consequence of this weak decision the great autumn offensive was undertaken. The Allied armies were badly beaten with terrible casualties. Our new armies entered into action for the first time and fought with conspicuous valour, and tens of thousands of them fell in the futile carnage of the Loos offensive.

On the eve of this offensive Lord Kitchener was authorised to visit France in order to persuade General Joffre to postpone the attack, but his mission was a failure. He reported that "General Joffre was quite determined both on political and military grounds (the main element in the former being the situation in Russia) to take the offensive without delay and on a considerable scale. Sir John French agreed with the French Commander-in-Chief as to the urgency of the step from the military point of view. Lord Kitchener, though far from sanguine that any substantial military advantage would be achieved, was strongly of opinion that we could not without serious and perhaps fatal injury to the Alliance refuse the coöperation which Joffre expected.

Even after the failure of this last ill-judged offensive of the 1915 campaign had become quite evident to any sane observer, General Joffre persisted for weeks in attack after attack. When he became convinced that further efforts were fruitless except to add to the already appalling casualty list, he intimated to his Government that he had no intention of persevering with his plan that year. Accordingly he said he would be prepared to assist in carrying out the project which had been urged upon him by the ablest members of the French Government for sending a force to Salonika to help Serbia. Before General Joffre was convinced by lacerating facts that his offensive had failed, the losses in the Champagne attack were three times those in the Dardanelles. Millions of shells were also wasted — 10,000,000 in all, including French and British. Half of the men who fell in these criminal attacks would either have stormed Gallipoli or, had they been sent to Salonika, would have enabled Serbia to throw the invading army into the Danube. One-third of the shells would have averted the Russian retreat.

CHAPTER XVII

# THE SERBIAN TRAGEDY

Rumours of danger to Serbia — Effect of fall of Kovno on Bulgarian attitude — Sir Edward Grey's pledge to Serbia — Sir Edward Carson's subsequent comment — Germans welcome our Western offensive — Sir William Robertson's thesis — Attack launched on Serbia — General Joffre's notes — Troops for the Balkans refused — More ineffectual slaughter needed around Loos — French distrust of Dardanelles venture — No improvement made in transport facilities in Balkans — A chaos of divided counsels — Conclusion of Dardanelles Committee — Lord Kitchener goes east — Decline of Kitchener's prestige — My memorandum of 12/10/15 — Advantages to Germany of a Balkan success — Reasons compelling prompt German action — Incomprehensible blindness of the military authorities — How are we to set it right? — Reasons for rescuing Serbia — Man-power issue in the Balkans — Need to mobilise Roumania and Greece — Postpone the Western offensive — Send men to Salonika — Provide Russia with rifles — Folly of pursuing the Dardanelles venture — Lord Grey's reply to my memorandum — Military support needed for Balkan diplomacy — Delay in dispatch of troops to Salonika — Joint memorandum by M. Millerand and myself — Appeal to Greece made too late — Resignation of Sir Edward Carson — Mr. Asquith's proposal for a War Committee — My reply: the Committee useless unless it overrules the War Office — War Office neglect of munition production — Neglected resources in the Balkans — Capacity of War Lords for blundering — Signs of uneasiness in the Press — Lord Kitchener's ignorance of attack on Serbia — Asquith's letter: Kitchener to go east — General Monro's visit to Mediterranean — Letter from Lord Charles Beresford — Gallipoli must be evacuated — Reinforcements needed at Salonika — Lord Kitchener's blunders — Recommendations for our policy — Withdrawal from Salonika proposed — Angry complaints from France — Withdrawal from Salonika agreed upon — My opposition to Balkan evacuation — Decision to evacuate Salonika reversed.

WHILST the billy-goat tactics of western generals in butting away the strength of their armies against unbreakable walls was proceeding in a succession of sickening thuds, what was happening to the Allies on the Eastern and Southeastern Fronts? I have told the story of how the might of Russia was broken through lack of equipment. What about Serbia? Ominous warnings came from Sofia, Bucharest, Athens and Nish in the summer of 1915 that Austria was gathering a great force in the valleys that pointed towards the Danube.

Later on we heard that German troops were arriving in great numbers. It was known that Bulgaria had practically decided to throw in her lot with the Central Powers and join them in the attack on her neighbour.

The sinister effect of the Russian disaster was soon felt in the changed attitude of Bulgaria. About the third week in August, 1915, when what was supposed to be the impregnable fortress of Kovno fell before the German guns and the Russian armies were still being driven daily league after league towards Petrograd, a message reached the British Foreign Office from its representative at Sofia warning us that "the capture of Kovno had made a deep impression on the governing and military circles at the Bulgarian capital and had given rise to anticipation of a crushing disaster to Russian arms." He further warned us that the elements most favourable to us had, during the last few days, become so impressed with Germany's military strength that they would hesitate to take the course which would expose Bulgaria to a German attack. A few weeks later the crafty Ferdinand, who had been crouching behind a complacent Ministry until he found which belligerent alliance was the highest bidder and the likeliest winner, thought the time had come to throw in his lot openly with Germany and Austria. If the blow fell upon Serbia it was not for lack of timely information as to what fate was being prepared for her by the Central Powers. Late in September news percolated through that the Austrians were massing troops in the valleys which ran towards the Danube and that several German divisions had already arrived to reinforce them. There would be no doubt as to the intention and imminence of their movements.

The probability of a German-Austrian attack on Serbia was alluded to in the Press, and was even discussed in the House of Commons about the end of September, 1915. When the matter was raised, in Parliament Sir Edward Grey made a statement to the House in the following terms:

> "If, on the other hand, the Bulgarian mobilisation were to result in Bulgaria assuming an aggressive attitude on the side of our enemies, *we are prepared to give to our friends in the Balkans all the support in our power, in the manner that would be the most welcome to them, in concert with our Allies, without reserve and without qualification. We are, of course, in consultation with our Allies on the situation, and I believe the view that I express is theirs also.*"

As Sir Edward Carson subsequently said, after the blow had fallen:

> "That was one of the most important declarations that could be made in this House. I believed it, when I was a party to it, to be the policy of His Majesty's Government, but I believed more. I believed that our military advisers never would have allowed us to make that declaration unless we had actual preparations and plans which were ready when the moment came to enable us to strike and assist our gallant little Ally in the field of battle."

The Grey declaration satisfied an anxious House of Commons. It was hailed with delight throughout Serbia as a promise that her powerful friends in the west would come to her rescue if any evil befell her, and, of course, come in time to save her. The Germans had a better understanding of the value of Allied pledges than either Parliament or the Serbian people. They never faltered or halted in their march. The German military leaders had come to the conclusion that there was nothing to apprehend from the attack which was being carefully engineered on the Western Front. In fact, they welcomed it. They knew their General Joffre, and they felt that whilst his mind was concentrated on his plans in Champagne he had none left for any other theatre of war. The Allied generals were preparing a smoke screen, not to conceal their own designs — those were visible from any aëroplane — but to hide from their own vision those of the Central Powers lest the spectacle should induce the Allied statesmen to divert their forces from the pursuit of the impracticable. The western offensive began on September 25th. In two days it was obvious to any intelligent observer that the French had failed in their main purpose of breaking through the German lines and that the British attack had equally failed at Loos. The Germans knew it, and continued to pour division after division into the Danubian basin. General Joffre, however, persisted in hurling troops against German entrenchments only to discover after he had captured them what he knew before, that there was an equally formidable position a few hundred yards behind. Still he persevered week after week, making no perceptible indent in this succession of entrenchments. There was nothing new in this. Every soldier in France could have told him in advance what he had rediscovered with a loss of scores of thousands of precious lives. Sir William Robertson, in a memorandum he issued about that time, said: "We know perfectly well there is no insuperable difficulty in breaking through the first-line defence. It has been done several times in this theatre during the summer. It is the second and third lines which give the trouble." These lines were never reached, or at least, were not retained. Whilst this was going on, the western generals, heedless of the pitiful appeals of the Serbian people watching the fall of the avalanche towards their home, continued to waste valuable time on a hopeless task in France. Once engaged on it, the French and British generals found it difficult to extricate their armies without further hard struggling. They threw all their reserves into the cruel German trap with its teeth of steel that pierced and crushed flesh and blood with a relentless grip.

On October 7th, the Germans and Austrians crossed the

Danube at five different points. A telegram announcing that fact reached here the same day. As I shall point out later on, Lord Kitchener did not see that telegram until the following day, and when a War Council met to discuss the military position on the 8th he was not aware that the armies of the Central Powers had already invaded Serbia. When at last he heard of it and communicated the news to the Cabinet, it was decided that he should go over to France to confer with General Joffre on the new situation which had arisen in the East. They discussed the sending of French and British troops to help the hard-pressed Serbs. On October 9th, General Joffre submitted to Lord Kitchener a memorandum which is summarised as follows:

"The reasons for the intervention of the Allies in the Balkans are:

"The necessity to check German projects in the new theatre of operations which they have now commenced, and the moral obligation not to leave our Ally Serbia alone to bear the brunt of our common enemies.

"The initiative of the operations in the Balkans belongs to our adversaries and they are capable of keeping a numerical superiority whatever we do. There can, therefore, be no question of our engaging in a general action which would offer no chances of success.

"Our rôle should be to prevent the crushing of the Serbs, to ensure their communication with the sea, and eventually to secure a zone of retreat. Also we should thus bar the way to the Germans from access to Salonika."

He considers therefore:

"1. That the mission of the troops should be to hold Salonika strongly as a base for the French, English and Serbian Armies.

"2. To cover and hold the railway line between Salonika and Uskub in order to ensure our communication with the Serbian Army and the supplies of that army.

"3. To cover the right of the Serbian Army, preventing any attempt of the enemy on Central Serbia.

"To attain these objects a force of 150,000 men, which is more than the Bulgarians can put in the field on this side, appears sufficient.

"In case events such as, for example, a new distribution of Greek and Roumanian forces, lead the Allies to take a different attitude, and to increase later the amount of their effort, General Joffre states that France, having a limited number of men at her disposal, cannot take part in such an effort, the responsibility for which would fall entirely on the British Government.

"General Joffre strongly advocates that the Italian Government should be urged at first to send forces to Salonika and eventually to open the road to Serbia via Durazzo."

This document contains proposals so like those I had repeatedly pressed on the Cabinet that I feel entitled to call attention to the similarity. The only difference is one of date — a fatal divergence.

If the document had been penned three — even two — months earlier and acted upon immediately, the Balkans would not have fallen into German hands and Lord Kitchener's prediction of victory in 1917 would have been realised. It was now too late to avert disaster, and this was obvious to anyone who could see beyond the trenches in front of him. General Joffre was not gifted with such vision.

This report was discussed at a full meeting of what was still known as the Dardanelles Committee on October 11th. The military advice given to that Committee was that no troops should be sent to the Mediterranean, either to the Dardanelles or to Salonika, until the offensive in France had been brought to a conclusion. Both Sir Douglas Haig and General Joffre had stated "that their object was to gain further ground in order to consolidate what we had already won." In their judgment "our position was such that in certain sections we had either to go forward or to go back." Sir William Robertson thought that "to do this would entail a considerable amount of fighting generally in the neighbourhood of Loos." When asked whether, if the result of this contemplated action were favourable, it would lead to any modification of the strategic position, he admitted "it would not, unless General Joffre was also able to supply pressure and make progress in Champagne." We were given to understand that General Joffre had practically come to the conclusion already that the general offensive must be postponed for three months. The great offensive was an admitted failure. All the same, the French Commander-in-Chief declared he could not send any troops away from France until he knew definitely whether the Germans contemplated a counter-offensive. Of that he could not be certain for another fortnight. That meant, according to Sir William Robertson, that no troops could be moved, either British or French, from the battle area for another two or three weeks. Whilst this discussion was taking place the Germans and Austrians were advancing in Serbian territory (they had already marched onward for four days) and the Bulgarians on that very day were hurling 300,000 men across the lines of communication between Serbia and Salonika. What strategy! What generals! What statesmen to tolerate either!

The military experts were pressed for information as to the date when they could be in a position to spare troops from France. There was a good deal of desultory and confusing talk on this point as to what ought to be the destination of these troops, assuming they could be spared. Some suggested that they should be dispatched to the Dardanelles to reinforce the army in Gallipoli, to enable it to make another attack on the Turkish positions in that Peninsula. The French were opposed to this plan unless at the same time an army was landed to occupy the Asiatic shore. They were strongly of opinion that the mere capture of Gallipoli, and the forcing of the Narrows would only entice the Allied fleets into a trap, which would be closed as soon as they entered the Marmora. The Allied fleets would there have no means of replenishing their fuel supplies, and would soon be reduced to impotence. They ought to have thought of that before agreeing to the Gallipoli Expedition. Others, notably Mr. Bonar Law and Sir Edward Carson, were for landing the troops at Salonika and pushing along immediately to the help of Serbia. The Chief of the Staff objected that the Salonika railway was not equipped with the necessary means of transport to enable the Allies to carry any considerable body of troops even as far as Uskub. That revealed the fact that although the War Committee had decided in January last to take immediate steps to double the line where feasible, to construct sidings, and to increase the rolling stock, nothing had been done to carry out that order. I supported the view urged so strongly by Mr. Bonar Law and Sir Edward Carson. I supplemented this with a suggestion that we should immediately communicate with the Greeks and the Roumanians, pledging the Allies to send 250,000 troops without delay to Salonika, if they on their part were prepared to join in a combined effort to rescue Serbia. I pointed out that the Roumanians could put 400,000 men in the field, and the Greeks at least 200,000, which with our 250,000 would make an aggregate of 850,000; that with such a force Bulgaria could be neutralised, or if she intervened could be crushed; and that at any rate it would enable the Serbians to hold their own against the attack which was being made upon them. Lord Curzon and others thought it was too late to send any support, and that we had better utilise our troops as reinforcements for the Gallipoli expeditionary force with a view to making a fresh attack on the Turks.

Others suggested a landing at Alexandretta, and others that we should dispatch our forces to Egypt without prejudice to their ultimate destination or action, and for this purpose neither Alexandretta nor Salonika, nor the Adriatic side of the Straits would be ruled out. Meanwhile some distinguished general officer should be sent out to the Mediterranean to survey the situation, report upon it, and advise as to the best course to be adopted.

A "too-late" council is necessarily desperate and distracted. The conclusions of this distracted council were an embodiment of its despair. They were as follows:

"1. Immediate instructions to be given for the dispatch, *so soon as the present operations are over,* of an adequate substantial force from France to Egypt without prejudice to its ultimate destination, transport for which is to be prepared by the Admiralty.

"2. A specially selected general to proceed without delay to the Near East and to consider and report as to which particular sphere, and with what particular objective, we should direct our attention.

"3. The General Staff, War Office, to state in what way their views given in their Appreciation of the 9th October would be modified if both Greece and Roumania were to act with the Allies."

These conclusions meant the practical abandonment of Serbia to her doom. The combined armies of Germany, Austria and Bulgaria had no difficulty in sweeping the depleted, outnumbered and ill-equipped army of Serbia out of the way, capturing the Balkans and clearing the road to Constantinople.

In the meantime it was decided to send General Monro to the Mediterranean. On October 31st he recommended the evacuation of the Gallipoli Peninsula. At the first meeting of the new War Committee on November 3rd (to which I

A SLIGHT DISCREPANCY SOMEWHERE

HASQUITH *(to his pal Jawge).*

"'Ere!! Not s'much o' your 'Too Late'!!! Wot's the blinkin' good o' me a-'ollerin' aht what I'm a-'ollerin' aht if you go a-'ollerin' aht wot you're a-'ollerin' aht?!!!"

*Cartoon by the late E. T. Reed, reproduced by courtesy of* The Bystander

shall refer later on) it was decided to send Lord Kitchener to view the situation for himself. Their decision was not dictated solely by military considerations. Lord Kitchener's influence in the Cabinet was not what it had been in the first year of the War. It had waned very rapidly in recent months. In 1914 he was practically military dictator and his decisions upon any questions affecting the War were final. The Members of the Cabinet were frankly intimidated by his presence because of his repute and his enormous influence amongst all classes of the people outside. A word from him was decisive and no one dared to challenge it at a Cabinet meeting. I think I may say I was the first to do so on munitions and on subsidiary questions like the Welsh Division and the appointment of Nonconformist chaplains. But my colleagues regarded my intervention on these questions with a certain amount of uneasiness approaching dismay. Gradually one mistake after another committed by the military, for which he was held responsible as the Supreme War Lord, lowered his prestige and weakened his influence; and there was a very general feeling that his usefulness had been exhausted. This feeling subsequently found practical expression in the appointment of Sir William Robertson as Chief of the Imperial General Staff, with exceptional powers all carved out of Lord Kitchener's authority. On this occasion there was a mute hope that once Lord Kitchener went to the Mediterranean, and especially if he returned to Egypt, the sphere of his greatest triumphs, he might find it worth while to remain there to direct the great forces accumulated in the western Mediterranean, in Egypt, Gallipoli, and either Salonika or Alexandretta. When the appointment was made, a member of the Cabinet pushed a note to me on which was written: *"Malbrouck s'en va t'en guerre*. But will he return?"

I was much disturbed about the abandonment of Serbia

and the gross neglect to take the most obvious precautions to avert it. On October 12th I circulated the following memorandum on the position to my colleagues:

"The helplessness of four great Powers to save from destruction one little country after another that relied on their protection is one of the most pitiable spectacles of this War.

"The appreciation of the existing situation in the Balkans circulated by the General Staff is a distressing document! It might all be compressed into two words: Too late! It might easily have been foreseen that a march through Serbia into Bulgaria would be one of the most obvious and profitable of moves for the German General Staff to contemplate, by connecting up their railway system with Turkey:

"1. They could aim a most direct and effective blow — in fact, the only direct and effective blow they could possibly aim — at the British Empire.

"2. They could have at their disposal a reserve of two or three millions of men of the best fighting quality added to their own reserves, and thus more than redress in their favour the balance in the war of attrition which is now proceeding.

"3. They could have a fair chance of destroying a great British force which is holding on by tooth and claw to a rim of the Gallipoli Peninsula.

"4. They could strike a ringing blow at our prestige in the east.

"5. They could render perfectly nugatory our sea-power in so far as South-Eastern Europe and a large part of Asia are concerned.

"6. By the process of equipping the Turks and ultimately perhaps the Persians and Afghans, they could force us in 1916 to divert large masses of troops from the main theatre of operations in France to defend our own possessions in Egypt and in the Far East.

"7. They could, by the same means, divert a large number of Russians to defend their frontiers in the Caucasus and their interests in Persia.

"8. All this they could achieve by overcoming the resistance of an ill-equipped army of 300,000 Serbians, a considerable portion of these having their attention engaged by the prospect of a hostile Bulgarian army attacking them from behind. Not a very formidable proposition for the military power that has rolled up the great armies of Russia, whilst, at the same time, holding in check the combined forces of France and Britain! It was therefore obvious even to the civilian mind that it was too tempting a project for the Germans not to seize upon.

"There were two or three reasons why it was clear that they could not postpone putting this project into execution:

"1. The Turkish ammunition was gradually being exhausted, and Turkey could not have sustained a series of attacks such as those we had been making on the Gallipoli Peninsula much longer without having her store of ammunition replenished.

"2. The winter was coming on, when Serbian roads and passes would be very difficult to negotiate.

"3. This year the Germans have an undoubted superiority over the Allies in:

(*a*) Material of war;

(*b*) Equipped and trained men.

"Next year the position will be equalised in both respects. It would not be like the Germans if they did not take full advantage of their temporary superiority.

"It is, of course, easy to be wise after the event, but these are considerations which have been repeatedly urged during the past few months at the War Council and Cabinet meetings. I have often braved my colleagues by the frequency with which I have called attention to them. I circulated two papers calling attention to the possibilities in the Near East as far back as December and February last. It perplexes the mere civilian to find any explanation for the neglect of the military authorities to provide against so disastrous a blow to our Empire, when it was so clear to any careful observer that it was impending. It is incredible that the fifth day after the blow had actually fallen finds us without a plan — unless the sending of some general — not yet fixed upon — to the eastern Mediterranean to scout for a scheme of operations can be called a plan. The Cabinet may depend upon it that when it becomes clear to the British public that we have been taken by surprise and that we have not made the slightest preparation to counter the German thrust, confidence will vanish in our capacity to conduct the War, and rightly so.

"It may be asked: What would you do now? The question is not, Who is to blame, but How are we to set it right? I am not at all sure that they are not more or less the same questions. This is a matter which I propose to return to later on, because I think it is essential. We have been let down so often that it is criminal folly on our part to depend any longer for the safety of the Empire on our present military organisation. But dealing merely with the Balkan tangle, I think even now we ought to make one great effort to save Serbia. There are two reasons for doing so. The first is that the abandonment of Serbia to her fate would be fatal to the prestige of Great Britain among the Allies and throughout the world. The hostility of Bulgaria and the neutrality of Greece and Roumania are attributable to the conviction which has permeated all neutral countries that Germany is irresistible and that we are impotent to protect nations which have incurred her wrath. Our complete failure to protect Belgium started this idea. Our inability to give effective support to Russia has confirmed it: and the abandonment of Serbia to her doom will root it deeper than ever in the mind of the world. The effect in the east will be incalculable.

"The second reason is that Serbia now provides the only barrier between us and the military reconstruction of a great hostile Moslem Power, which would be a menace to Egypt, Tripoli, Tunis, Algiers and Morocco, and also to our hold on India. Surely the averting of such a catastrophe is worth one great final effort? Is such an effort beyond our compass?

"The General Staff reckon that the German and Austrian armies engaged in the operations aggregate 200,000 men; that the Bulgarians number 300,000. We have, therefore, a total force of 500,000 to cope with in the Balkans. It is also, I understand, the reckoning of the General Staff that unless the Germans withdraw troops either from Russia or from France they cannot materially increase the strength of their armies in the Balkans. Serbia has an army of 300,000 men, very brave, very ably led. Their defeat of the Austrians last year demonstrated these two facts. They are fighting in a country they thoroughly understand, and they are fighting with all the ferocity with which a small mountain race always defend their native land. In numbers, therefore, the combined Bulgarian and Teutonic forces only overtop the Serbians alone by 200,000 men. Is it quite out of the question to make up this deficiency when so much depends on it for the Allies? Could not Roumania and Greece be persuaded or pressed to come in even now? Mere appeals to their sense of honour and their treaty obligations will not affect them in the least. They are naturally thinking about the security of their own countries, and they are paralysed by the German power and our impotence. It must be shown to them that we are quite capable of giving them all the necessary military support to protect them and enable them to carry through their undertaking. Why should we not promise them support, provided they come to the aid of Serbia immediately? They have men and equipment quite adequate to the conducting of a three months' campaign. Roumania, Serbia and Greece between them could put nearly a million men into the field, as against the Germano-Bulgarian combination of half a million. We could hold the Turkish forces in Gallipoli so as to prevent Turkey from sending any considerable reinforcements to the aid of the Bulgarians. Turkey has plenty of men available, but until the Germans arrive in Constantinople she has not the necessary munitions to equip fresh armies. If we said to the Greeks and the Roumanians that if they took the field immediately we could place at their disposal straight away 30,000 men who have already landed at Salonika, and that in a month's time we would guarantee that those 30,000 would be 100,000; that in two months' time the 100,000 would become 150,000; and that by the end of the year we could undertake to have at least 250,000 men operating the Balkans; that in addition to that we could help them with ammunition — a promise which France and ourselves could afford to give if we dropped the offensive in the west — their whole attitude would be changed. In addition to this we could undertake, with the aid of Italy, to furnish the Russians with 500,000 rifles, thus enabling Russia to place another three-quarters of a million men in the line. If this were done, Roumania would feel herself secure from any Austro-German attack as the Austro-German armies would have as much as they could possibly do to hold their own against the increased pressure of the Russian armies. Russia might, under these circumstances, even promise definitely to detach 100,000 men to assist the Roumanians against any attack which might be made upon them.

"The situation is desperate, and nothing but prompt, courageous, and even daring action can retrieve it. What risks do we run by making this promise?

"1. We should have definitely to postpone the offensive in the west. When it has failed now, after the most prolonged and careful preparation, why should it be assumed that it will succeed three months hence? The French and ourselves will not be appreciably better off in the matter of big guns — not until the late spring of next year. We have already lost — French and British — between 500,000 and 600,000 men in the two great attempts made since May last to pierce the German line. To ignore the costly lesson thus given us and to make another effort of the same kind without adequate equipment of heavy guns and ammunition would be wantonly to throw away the lives of the very fine body of men who have volunteered for the new armies.

"2. We might fail to redeem our promise to the Roumanians and Greeks. The French have promised 64,000 men when the offensive is over. I am not sure whether those 64,000 include the 15,000 French troops already landed at Salonika. But let us assume that they do. I understand that there are considerable drafts on their way to the Dardanelles. These might be safely diverted to Salonika so long as the Turks on the Gallipoli Peninsula are cut off from the fresh supplies of ammunition they are hoping to get from the Germans. That would bring our forces at Salonika up to about 100,000 men.[1] We should have to find the remaining 150,000. I understand that on the Western Front the French claim that with our army they have a superiority of very nearly 1,000,000 over the Germans. If even 400,000 men were taken away from the west our superiority would still be overwhelming. The Germans have already demonstrated clearly that a superiority of three to two does not enable the offensive to break through a well-entrenched line. Why, then, should it be supposed that when the Germans are in inferior numbers they could break through our lines? Are the French soldiers and ours so inferior in quality to the German *Landsturm?*

"If the Germans brought half a million from the east they would still be in a slight minority in the west. With the increased pressure the Russians could bring to bear by means of the reinforcements we had enabled them to equip and put into the field, the Germans, so far from being in a position to withdraw troops from the East, might have to draw heavily on their reserves in order to hold their own on that frontier.

"3. The risk that we could not furnish the 500,000 rifles for Russia. Why not? Our American rifles will be coming in shortly, and we could, for the sake of a great effort to save a desperate situation, spare 150,000 rifles to equip 200,000 Russians who are ready in every other respect for the field. The temporary risks we might have to face by parting with the rifles are not comparable with those we run if nothing effective is done to save the situation in the Balkans. The Italians must be financed to part with their 300,000 Vitalis, and the French would surely spare 50,000 rifles to help the Allied cause out of the worst plight it has yet been in.

"I earnestly press that the offer should be definitely made to Russia and Greece without loss of time. If Greece shows any re-

[1] 

| | |
|---|---|
| French | 64,000 |
| British withdrawn from Gallipoli plus drafts, about | 35,000 |
| | 99,000 |

luctance to come in, the appeal to her might take the form of a demand that she should redeem her treaty obligations to Serbia. We are in this War to enforce international treaties, and a demand of that kind could not be interpreted as the bullying of a small nationality when we are actually engaged in a war with the greatest military power in the world on the same ground. Greece is always at the mercy of a great Sea Power. Germany cannot protect her against us, and I have information from reliable Greek sources that this line would have much greater effect upon the King of Greece than an appeal to his honour to redeem his bond to Serbia.

"The notion that we are satisfying the needs of this critical situation by making another attack on the Gallipoli Peninsula is, to my mind, an insane one. We have failed repeatedly when the Turks were short of ammunition. Are we now to succeed when they are reinforced with German heavy guns and abundance of ammunition? It is by no means improbable that the Turks, thus reëquipped, might drive us into the sea before reinforcements ever reached our army on that Peninsula. This probability is indicated in clear terms in Colonel Hankey's report. If we neglect his warning our responsibility will be great. But even assuming we can hold our own, an attack on positions which have been proved to be impregnable against gallant assaults would end in the loss of another 50,000 or 60,000 men with nothing achieved. It is quite clear to anyone who reads the document prepared by the General Staff that this was no part of their original plan. It has simply been spatch-cocked into their document by strong Dardanellian influences. It has been done so badly that the simplest of us can see it. The recommendations of the General Staff were that it would confine ourselves to the offensive in France. We are now not merely to send out a general to trawl the eastern Mediterranean for a new policy, but before he reports we are to send 150,000 men away from France — from the only objective which the General Staff are prepared to stake their reputation upon recommending!

D. Ll. G."

October 12, 1915.

To this Sir Edward Grey replied:

"Foreign Office, October 13th, 1915.

"My dear Lloyd George,

"Your memorandum has come to me since the telegrams to Bucharest and Athens were sent last night, and for the moment I suppose they settle one point in your memorandum.

"I am no judge of the military consideration involved, but as Kitchener agrees and you desire it and the Prime Minister authorises it I sent the telegrams at once. From the political point of view I am as strongly in favour of the line now taken as you can be, and I am glad to be able to say anything diplomatically which is backed by action or the prospect of action.

"What I do feel to be useless is constant diplomatic effort based neither on military nor naval success, without the prospect of such success, and without any offer of action. These last telegrams are not open to that criticism.

"For the rest I wish to avoid drift in our strategy, and if I differ from the conclusions of your paper at all it is that I think our strategic decisions should be based on naval and military opinion founded on good staff work. I urged strongly and I understood you also to urge the same thing, and I hope the staff work now being done under Murray will be encouraged and continued. I do not like to discard its conclusions. But I agree that the opinion expressed by the Staff about the Gallipoli Peninsula is more provisional and tentative than final.

"It is, however, vital to come to a decision quickly either to attempt to force the Dardanelles or to evacuate — so it seems to me, and I would accept either decision rather than none.

"I was not sure whether your memorandum was addressed specially to me or not; it deals mainly with military strategy on which I am qualified to be guided rather than to guide.

Yours sincerely,

E. Grey."

The irony of his sentence about "military and naval opinion based on good staff work" is withering. But the greatest irony of all, after what had happened, was that he meant every word of it. The way he had been betrayed by the Military to give in the House of Commons pledges to Serbia they had no hope of redeeming did not seem to diminish his childish faith in their advice.

Considerable delays ensued in sending troops to the Mediterranean. On October 19th M. Millerand, the French Secretary of State for War, came over to discuss the position. He was accompanied by General Joffre. I find amongst my papers the following note made by a secretary of what took place at the discussions:

"Ll. G. saw Millerand to-day, who says that Ll. G. was right after all and that an expedition in the Balkans should have been undertaken last spring. He is now concerned that the Dardanelles operations are a failure, and though he fears it is too late to render very effective assistance in the Balkans, yet he is in favour of France and Britain sending troops there. He and Ll. G. together drew up a plan upon which France and England are to act for a campaign in the Balkans."

Our plan suggested that:

"The prevention of the German effort to get through to Constantinople should be regarded as the primary objective of the joint expeditionary force. If, by the time the new force can arrive at the eastern Mediterranean, Serbia is still blocking the way, the French and British forces should proceed to Salonika to help the Serbians to keep the railway free to Uskub.

"If by the date of the arrival of the troops the Germans have forced their way through to Constantinople, the two Governments to decide their course then on the advice of their Generals. . . . The two Governments have agreed to go on sending to the help of Serbia sufficient contingents to constitute a force of 150,000 men.

"Should the present situation become greatly altered owing to unforeseen circumstances arising, both Governments would then take steps in common as to the new directions to give to their troops."

Greece was pressed to send troops to assist in saving Russia, but the appeal to her came too late, because by that time the armies of the Central Powers and of Bulgaria had overwhelmed Serbian resistance, and the Greeks put in the plea that they were afraid of standing up against the victors when there were no Allied troops within sight to assist them. They had the fate of Serbia before their eyes. Serbia had been abandoned by the Allies in defiance of the solemn pledges of timely support. The Greeks were naturally apprehensive of a repetition of the same desertion in their own case. The sweeping victories of the Central Powers on the Eastern Front naturally impressed all the Southeastern States more than the capture by the Allies of a few kilometres in France. Russia had collapsed; Serbia had been overrun; the Dardanelles expedition had been a complete failure, and even in the west the Allies had not succeeded in breaking through, and the Germans, victorious on every front, were advancing southwards with seven-league boots. They were already in the defiles of the Balkans, soon they would be on their southern slopes. At that time there was nothing between them and the Greek frontier. Greece with her small army would be easily devoured by this terrible monster.

Sir Edward Carson, disgusted with what he conceived to be the deception practised upon Serbia, had resigned. Mr. Bonar Law and I shared his opinion about the whole transaction, but on the whole decided that we could not withdraw from the Ministry at this critical juncture. I am not sure that we were right.

There was a general feeling that there was a disastrous lack of grip in the direction of the War, and that the Cabinet ought to take upon itself a more direct responsibility in controlling its conduct. Suggestions were put forward for the setting-up of a War Committee which would exercise a more constant supervision over the direction of the War. I was amongst those who made representations to the Prime Minister upon this point. On the 29th of October I received from him the following memorandum:

### CONDUCT OF THE WAR

The proposal, as I understand it, is that there should be a small Committee of the Cabinet, not less than three or more than five in number, to deal executively with the conduct of the War.

It is understood that the Committee will from time to time call to their aid, for the purposes both of discussion and decision, other members of the Cabinet, either because their departments are concerned in the particular matter which is being dealt with or for other special reasons.

The Cabinet to remain as it is in numbers and composition.

The plenum of the Cabinet to be constantly informed of the decisions and actions of the Committee, and in all questions which involve a change or new departure in policy to be consulted before decisive action is taken.

Parliament to be informed that this method of procedure has been adopted, and to be told the names of the members of the Committee.

H. H. A.

October 28, 1915.

On October 31st I replied:

"11, Downing Street,
Whitehall, S.W.
October 31, 1915.

"My dear Prime Minister,

"I am sorry to trouble you when you must be worried with the anxieties of the situation, but I feel I must put to you my view of the position before you come to a final decision. The appointment of a small Committee with fairly full powers will undoubtedly be a great improvement on the sort of Duma which has been sitting on war problems up to the present. But unless there is a complete change in the War Office the new Council will be just as impotent as the Cabinet and old Council have proved themselves to be. Our war Administration have committed every blunder that the enemy could wish them to be guilty of. It was quite clear, even to the civilian mind, soon after the War began that this War would ultimately be decided by superiority in quality and quantity of material, and by the wearing down of the enemy in numbers. The Allies had the advantage in both respects, and the War Office have by an incredible lack of foresight and energy thrown away both these advantages.

"As to material, whilst the Germans were spending the whole of the late autumn and winter of 1914 in increasing their guns, rifles and ammunition for the summer campaign, our War Office did nothing substantial till the end of 1914 and in the spring of 1915. Then they did it under pressure from outside, and even then they were satisfied with giving orders whilst taking no steps to see that they were or even could be executed. The result has been that the campaign of 1915 has been lost to us. We could not help Russia in ammunition because we have not even now an adequate equipment, more especially in rifles and heavy guns and trench appliances, for ourselves. The full story of the neglect of the War Office in this respect has not yet been told. It is worse than I expected it would be when I first took up the work of the Ministry of Munitions — how they ordered shell without taking measures to see that there were fuses and primers, cartridge cases, gaines and the necessary arrangements for filling, so that huge stocks of empty shells were piled up at Woolwich with no means of completing them which was in the least commensurate with the demand.

"As to attrition, by prompt action in the Balkans we could have added a million and a half to our reserves of men, most of it excellent fighting material. Roumania, Greece, and, I think, Bulgaria, could have been brought in, not by words, but by prompt and strong action. On the other hand, we could have cut off the enemy from the magnificent reservoir of men in the Turkish Empire who are only awaiting equipment to become one of the most formidable fighting machines in the world. *In July the Intelligence Department of the War Office warned Kitchener that the Germans were likely to break through to Constantinople. We were constantly warned that Bulgaria was becoming more and more hostile.* One or two Cabinet Ministers, including myself, urged that steps should be taken to prepare for this probable German move. Nothing was done; even when information came in that the Germans and Austrians were accumulating forces in the valleys of Hungary and in the Bukovina, no plan of action was thought out. *Kitchener never knew that they had crossed the Danube 20 hours after the news reached the War Office that they had effected a crossing at five points.* A fortnight after the crossing his only plan was to send a general to the Mediterranean to report on the situation. Days after the road to Constantinople had been cleared through Bulgaria and weeks after the actual commencement of the struggle upon which the fate of our rule in Egypt may depend, we are forced by the French to take some action. You will recollect that the Committee of Imperial Defence as far back as February last decided that all the necessary preparations should be made for rendering a landing at Salonika effective whenever the Cabinet decided to take that course. Kitchener never took the slightest notice of that decision, and not even a mule had been bought for transport when the German blow fell on Serbia.

"The public may have delusions now about Kitchener, but the moment these facts are told in the House of Commons I have very little doubt what will be thought and said by all sections.

"If I thought the appointment of a small Committee would put an end to all these amazing series of blunders, I should be satisfied. But I have gone on for months always thinking that every mistake must surely be the last, and finding myself constantly surprised by the capacity of our great War Lords for blundering. I wrote you in December last calling your attention to the stupidity of the War Office, and telling you that, in my judgment, unless we showed greater grip as a Government in the management of the War, it must end in inevitable disaster. I have protested at each stage, sometimes in writing, sometimes by intervention in the Cabinet and at the War Council. I did so long before the Northcliffe Press began its campaign. At best the chances are against the next few weeks bringing much cheer — they might bring ruin to Serbia and for us retreat in the Balkans and disaster in Gallipoli. The nation would endure this and a good deal more if they knew everything was being done that human effort and foresight could compass to ensure final victory; but their confidence has been rudely shaken by what they can see of our unpreparedness in the Balkans. The friendly Press are showing marked symptoms of mutiny. The steadfast loyalty of our own party to your leadership has so far saved the Government, but you will forgive me for saying that I doubt whether that would save us if a catastrophe befell Serbia or our forces in the Dardanelles and all the facts on the conduct of the War were dragged out as they would be. Every mistake and omission would then be brought out with accumulative force. The row in the Commons will come last. Press and public will be moved before the party politician, but in the end he will follow public opinion, and we must have a good answer when the time comes. There is only one answer that can satisfy the public; and that is that you have already made an end of the futile régime that tumbled along from one fatuity to another. I am quite willing to face the inevitable tumult when it comes if this answer can be given, but I have very reluctantly come to the conclusion that I can no longer be responsible for the present war direction, and at the Cabinet to-morrow I propose with your permission to raise the real issue.

Ever sincerely,
D. Lloyd George."

The allusion in my letter to the fact that Lord Kitchener *never knew the Germans had crossed the Danube for 20 hours after the news had reached the War Office* is explained in the following note made after the Committee meeting by one of my secretaries:

"At a Cabinet last week, before the German advance into Serbia had begun, but when news of it was being expected at every moment, Ll. G. asked K. in the Cabinet whether there was any news of the Germans having crossed the Danube. K. said that up to the time when he came to the Cabinet he had received no news. Ll. G. suggested that the news might have come in since and said he would get the P. M.'s secretary to telephone to the War Office and ask if any news had been received, as he considered it most important to know when the Germans had begun to cross the Danube. The following is the reply which Ll. G. received and which he read out to the Cabinet. A telegram had been received in the War Office the day before. K. did not express the least surprise that he had not seen the telegram. Here is a copy of it:

" 'Late *yesterday* afternoon enemy xd. Danube with one batt. at                . Aust. troops xd. the Slava in 5 difft. places between Sabac and Belgrade. They are so far not in large force. Fight is continuing.'

"Immediately this telegram was read to the Cabinet, Sir Edward Carson passed Ll. G. the following note:

" 'K. does not read the telegrams — and we don't see them — it is intolerable.'

E. C."

On November 4th I received the following letter from Mr. Asquith:

"*Secret.*

10, Downing Street,
Whitehall, S.W.
3rd Nov. 1915.

"My dear Lloyd George,

"What I wanted you to know before to-morrow's Cabinet was that, in view of the conflicting opinions now to hand of Monro

losing 140,000 men there now, plus another 140,000 or 200,000 necessary for reinforcements, owing to casualties and the ravages of disease which has now set in. We cannot get through the Dardanelles, and we are wasting life and destroying prestige by remaining in the Gallipoli Peninsula. I believe the Fleet could secure the retreat, even to a portion of the rearguard.

"In every way fronts are changed, new military situations created, and new objectives undertaken. We have now taken a new objective and formed a new front at Salonika — an excellent reason for withdrawing from an impossible position in Gallipoli.

"We want about 200,000 men of the Allies landed at Salonika. It would be fatal to send them in driblets. If the Serbians are crushed the Germans will get to Constantinople. They will open up the whole of Asia for supplies. Roumania and Greece will out of fear probably throw in their lot with Germany. There is a spark in Islam now which would under these circumstances be fanned into a violent flame, more particularly if we remain in the Gallipoli Peninsula. Looking ahead, we should probably have to denude our Allies in France of a large portion of our army in order to fight for the defence of our Empire in the East and Egypt. Surely some dispatch should be sent or method taken to show the Greeks that they must come out on one side or the other.

"There will be a tremendous reaction in the country when the people know the truth, and I am afraid that the whole of the Cabinet will go down. Democracy are not reasonable when they are excited. If the people bring about the downfall of the Cabinet what have we got to put in its place? We should have a reign of chaos during the greatest crisis the Empire has ever faced.

"One of the great dangers consists in having Lord Kitchener in the Cabinet. The people believe in him, but they do not know he is wasting his time talking on political subjects. I have been to him several times and pointed out that he ought to leave the Cabinet on the plea that he cannot devote his time to it. His business is to take an envelope, write on it what men he wants, and what munitions he wants, and present that to the Cabinet.

The question of how they are to be got has nothing whatever to do with him. It is a political question of tremendous difficulty which must be argued out by the Cabinet. Lord Kitchener's difficulty would be well illustrated if there was a debate in the Cabinet on conscription or voluntary service. Which side would he take?

"In war, quick decisions and prompt actions are wanted. Neither are possible without a definite policy, and a clear objective for the military and naval forces, upon which depends the success or failure of the policy. The Government have no policy, and the military have no objective. It does not require that a man should be in the Cabinet to see the danger that exists to our Empire through this lamentable state of affairs. We are wasting days and weeks, when every hour, indeed, every minute, is of vital importance to us in the near future.

"In my opinion, our policy should be:

1. Evacuate the Dardanelles;
2. Send 200,000 (an allied force) men to Salonika with plenty of guns;
3. Get across the railway between Belgrade and Constantinople by some means between Nish and Sofia.

"I know the country and the difficulties attending such a proposition, but risks and difficulties must be met in war provided a substantial result is possible of attainment. Risks such as we are undertaking in Gallipoli have no excuse whatever. It was a risk courting defeat, and is certain to affect our prestige in the Balkans, with the Allies, and worse than all, with our great Eastern Empire.

Yours very sincerely,
CHARLES BERESFORD.

"The Rt. Hon. D. Lloyd George, M.P."

This letter reflects the rising and spreading sense of dubiety amongst men who were watching the course of events with some accumulated knowledge and experience. As yet the general public were still trustful if a little mystified. Their faith in Kitchener and their invincible belief in British luck had not yet been shaken.

One culminating illustration at this period of our military leaders' capacity for blundering remains to be recorded. Upon the return of Lord Kitchener, at the end of November, 1915, from his expedition to the Balkans, the antipathy of the British General Staff to any operations in that theatre crystallised into a definite recommendation that the Salonika expedition should be recalled. Rumour had it that Kitchener had somehow been talked over by the plausible and adroit King Constantine of Greece into favouring this step. The General Staff advised that we should withdraw from both the Dardanelles and Salonika and concentrate our forces on the defence of Egypt.

The French Government had vision enough to be furious at this suggestion. It urged very wisely that such an action would be naturally regarded throughout the East as a token of weakness and irresolution, and would mean the utter loss of the Balkans. Not only would it spell the final abandonment of the last shattered remnants of the army of our ally, Serbia: it would also drive both Roumania and Greece into the arms of Germany, adding something like another million men to their forces in that war theatre, imperilling the southern flank of the Russians, and turning the whole Balkan coast, including the harbours of Greece, into enemy bases for submarine activity in the Mediterranean. On Friday, December 3rd, 1915, the French sent an angry telegram, challenging the shilly-shallying attitude of the British Government, the proposal to leave Salonika and the lack of firmness we were showing in our handling of Greece. They complained bitterly that we had gone back on our decision at the Paris Council which had taken place a week previously, and that Lord Kitchener had evidently made arrangements with the King of Greece which were quite outside the intentions of the French. They requested that representatives of the British Government should meet them the following day at Calais to discuss the position.

As yet the British Cabinet had not reached a definite decision upon the issue. It had been postponed from one meeting to another. Upon receipt of the French Government's telegram, the Prime Minister went to Calais, taking Lord Kitchener and Mr. Balfour with him. He did not invite me to join the party, doubtless because my strong opposition to any abandonment of the Balkans was well known, and I did not even hear of the telegram from France till the Saturday morning when our representatives had already departed for Calais.

On their return we were informed that they had succeeded in talking the French round to their point of view and that the evacuation of Salonika had been agreed upon. But the telegrams on Monday from Paris were far from supporting this interpretation of the proceedings, and showed that the French were still much dissatisfied, and that no satisfactory arrangement had really been arrived at on the Saturday.

While everything was in this state of chaos, a telegram came to say that M. Albert Thomas was on his way over to have a talk with me on the subject of the Calais Conference, and to explain to me the real opinion of the French. Meanwhile at the War Council that morning (December 6th, 1915) the matter was discussed. Mr. Bonar Law was the only one present who agreed with my view of the matter, all the rest being for immediate evacuation. Lord Kitchener read a telegram from Greece which said that the Germans demanded the evacuation of the Balkans by the Allied troops, and were willing to allow the Greeks to cover the reëmbarkation. I am recorded as having said, "It is a good thing that the Germans and the British have found something to agree upon at last. Surely this must be the beginning of peace!"

Shortly afterwards M. Albert Thomas arrived, and explained to me the reason for his visit. I learned that when the French deputation to the Calais conference returned to Paris and admitted that they had agreed to the evacuation of the Balkans, the rest of the French Cabinet expressed the greatest dissatisfaction with this conclusion. The deputation insisted that they had been told that this was the view taken unanimously by the British Government, and that in those circumstances they had felt bound to acquiesce: whereupon M. Thomas interposed that he knew it was not the view of the whole British Cabinet, as I had told him when he was last in London that I was entirely opposed to evacuating the Balkans and was very much in favour of engaging in a Balkan campaign this year or next. The French Cabinet ultimately refused to accept the decision arrived at on the previous day at Calais. Thereupon, M. Thomas offered to come over to London and see me in an effort to obtain a reconsideration of their decision by the British Government.

Naturally I promised him all the help and backing I could furnish. He attended more than one prolonged meeting of our leaders at which he set forth very passionately the desire of the French to remain at Salonika. Perhaps the best help I afforded him was an arrangement I made for him to lunch at 10 Downing Street with the Prime Minister. I am not sure that the favourable personal impression he made on his host and hostess was not more helpful to his cause than all his eloquence in Council. However that may be, the final outcome of these discussions was that Lord Kitchener was sent over to Paris to consult with the French Cabinet, with full powers to make any arrangements on behalf of our Government. He did not much like the idea of going. "The French are not very keen on me at present for some reason," he said. However, he went, and the upshot was an agreement for the Allies to remain at Salonika and fortify it in preparation for an effective campaign in 1916. So narrowly was averted an act of incredible folly. But the effective campaign was not waged in 1916. The French and British military chiefs took care that the Salonika expedition should not be equipped with the guns and ammunition which would justify offensive operations. And in order further to deprive General Sarrail of all temptation to attack they deprived him of all the means of transport essential to an advance.

Speaking on the 20th of December, 1915, in the House of Commons, having in mind the fatal tardiness which had brought so much disaster to the Allied cause in the Dardanelles, the Balkans, Russia and Mesopotamia I used the following words:

> ". . . Too late in moving here, too late in arriving there, too late in coming to this decision, too late in starting with enterprises, too late in preparing! In this war the footsteps of the Allied forces have been dogged by the mocking spectre of 'too late,' and unless we quicken our movements damnation will fall on the sacred cause for which so much gallant blood has flowed. . . ."

That summed up my considered opinion at the time on the muddled campaign of 1915. That is my judgment to-day after a careful perusal of all the documents and histories written on the subject from every point of view.

# INDEX

# INDEX